Asparagus, Eels and Mattresses

of the

Ace of Diamonds

By

Günter Schiemann

First Published 2007
by
Gwisch Publishing

St.Anne's Grove, Dunmere, Bodmin, Cornwall, PL31 2RD
Tel 01208 72932 email <gwisch@btinternet.com>

ISBN
978 0 9556120 0 8

British Library Cataloguing in Publication Data.

A catalogue record for this book is available from the British Library.

Printed in Cornwall by T J International Ltd.

With love and thanks to my family

Particularly to Sylvia.

Preface.

History books do not always cover the whole story. A story, such as this one, may help to fill-in some of the gaps.

This story is largely based on the experiences of the writer, his family and his former comrades. As it was written purely from memory without the help of any diaries, all character names, boat-names and boat numbers are fictional.

However, the overall picture is a true reflection of life on a large German Type IXD2 U-boat from 1943 to 1945, as experienced by an ordinary teenage sailor.

Günter Schiemann (2007)

INTRODUCTION

The next twenty-four hours were going to be quite different from any other day in my long and very active working life. Not that it had started in any different way from other mornings. The alarm clock made sure I rose at 6 o'clock after what had been an unusually restless night.

However, before I have time to think about anything else, there are the considerable needs of our livestock to be met. Wrapped up warm against the easterly wind, which prevails at this time of year, I am met with friendly nickering from the inmates of our three stables as I arrive to supply them with their usual breakfast. The warmth of their breaths and the moistness of their muzzles on my face help me to shake off any remaining sleepiness. I take a deep breath to savour the pungent smell of their warm bodies as I change their padded night-rugs for equally warm weatherproof ones. Later, after they had finished their morning rations, I open the gate and let them out to spend the day rummaging around in the fields.

Yes! Horses had been part of my life in one-way or the other, lately though, thanks to my daughters' interest in anything equine.

While the rest of our household could still look forward to another hour in their warm beds, I take my time over a hearty breakfast, have a brief glance through this mornings newspapers, after which I am ready to drive myself two miles to my office, which is located on the far side of our small market town in the southwestern corner of England. Darkness still reigns as my car cruises through the narrow streets leading to the Industrial Estate and since at this time in the morning there is little or no traffic about, I can afford to let my thoughts wander a bit.

Today is the very last day of my active working life, which has spanned more than half a century.

Next week, at the start of the New Year, I will officially become a pensioner and join the large army of Senior Citizens.

But, before that happens, I must take my leave of my men and my factory, which I had founded some twentyfive years ago, not long after my family and I had settled here after moving all the way from Scotland, to help in the transfer of a small production company.

I still don't know where the idea to branch-out on my own came from, but being at an age where many people decide what they want to do with the rest of their lives, my wife and I decided, the time to go solo was now, before it was too late.

From a couple of clapped-out second-hand machines, which were acquired at an auction, taken apart for ease of transport and re-built and refurbished in my spare time in our garage at home, it had grown ever so slowly. During the first years the going was extremely tough, there was only work for three of us to be found locally. The demand, which I had forecast for the services we could provide, was only slow in materialising. But when it did come, the ex-War Department ablution/toilet block of less than 80 square metres had to be exchanged for 1,000 square metres of factory and office space.

The company had after this grown to become one of the finest and most modern precision engineering companies in this area. Young men, who after leaving school had served their apprenticeship with us, became the core of our crew. And all of this had to be achieved with only very limited help from banks, after all, who would back an engineering enterprise in a beautiful area best known for its holiday trade. The fact that I, a German ex-Prisoner of War, could foresee a growing influx of light industries into the county, for which we could provide a valuable, even essential back-up service, cut little ice with hard-headed financiers.

Their answers were predictable.

The absence of financial support held us back, but it certainly did not stop us. Working all hour God gave us became the norm. By that time, other industries had moved into the area and most of them made use of our service. At last, we were appreciated.

'A fairy-tale like story lies behind the success of a company of precision engineers, which designs and manufactures all types of tooling for industry. The head of the firm is a German ex-Prisoner of War who decided not to go home when hostilities ended...' a local newspaper quoted.

The happenings of those early days of the company occupied my mind on this last journey to work. Having parked my car, I made my way to the office. It was super modern, well equipped with electronic gadgets, telephones, fax-machines and the very latest in computer technology. This was the nerve-centre of the undertaking.

Making my way on to the factory floor, I passed through the Design- and Drawing office with its modern drawing machines and computers to aid design and manufacture. What a change those electronic toys had brought about, when one compared the new methods with those of earlier years.

But now, as the time for my retirement has arrived, I am passing the company over to a large international corporation. Previously our largest customer, they had come to rely on our expertise to design, manufacture and service specialist tools used in the production of pharmaceutical components. Having worked with them for a number of years, I know they will invest to further expand the firm and its work force.

On this morning, I am looking forward to personally thank everybody who had supported me through thick and thin. In future times we would probably meet again, especially since this town is so very small.

As far as the machines are concerned, this could be the last time I would ever see them. Every single one of them had been bought after weeks and months of deliberation and heart-searching.

Always the question has either been 'could we really afford to buy them,' or 'could we afford **NOT** to have them?

Each one of those computer-controlled giants had become part of all our lives. For the last time I watch them going through their paces, their drills, reamers, taps and other cutters moving here, there and everywhere, as if guided by invisible hands. They are attacking thick plates of steel, tearing, and cutting into them as if they were merely made of butter. Other machines, also computer-controlled, are spraying showers of sparks through the air in an effort to fashion large chunks of hard metal into the accurate shapes required by the designers. Through the whole plant runs a rhythm-like pulse, oozing vitality and purpose.

How can I possible describe my inner feelings as I cast a last lingering look at all the hustle and bustle.

Pride in achievement and gratitude for being given the opportunity to be part of all this are mixed with regret and sorrow for having to leave it all behind.

I find it impossible to keep a tremor out my voice as I take my leave from the staff, many of which have become dear friends. They appear to be equally sorry to see me depart.

Just think of it! For years it has been part of my job to boss them around, to criticise or to praise when necessary, to instruct and encourage, to listen to grievances and to give advice. This advice often had little to do with work itself, but was sought in very private capacity. I, known as the 'Old Man', was flattered to have had the confidence and trust of the men who worked with me.

In fact, the type of comradeship I experienced in this small company is very much comparable with that, I had experienced in wartime, as an ordinary member of a German **U-boat** crew. As was the case here, in those dark days each and every man of the crew had to rely implicitly on one another.

Not long after taking my leave, I clear out my desk, take down my family-photographs, and for the last time shut the door behind me. Sitting in my car I take a few moments to sort out my emotions. For weeks, I had prepared myself for this day by making sure that I would have other interests to occupy my time in the future. But now that the time has arrived, it feels terrible.

Finally, I take one last look at the old place. The building itself is stark - more practical than pretty - but it looks very businesslike.

The space above the large ground floor windows across the whole width of the building is occupied by the name the of company:

Schuler Tool Company

The company's name is preceded and followed by pictures of a certain playing card and together the words and pictures form a sort of Trademark. Nobody has ever asked me, why twenty-five years ago I chose to add those pictures to the name of my company.

It certainly was not just a whim.

There is an actual card like that tucked away in the back of my wallet - dog-eared and filthy it is - but then, I have carried it around since I was only 16 years old, when I adopted it as my 'rabbit's foot'.

Whether it is true or not, I am convinced that it has looked after me and brought me luck during all those years.

Now, as the daily pressure of making a living has been lifted from my shoulders, I should have plenty of time to reminisce about those distant days of my youth, nearly half a century ago.

CHAPTER ONE

A few metres in front of where I was patrolling, a river was flowing, moving quietly and sedately, giving no sign that it had already completed over three hundred kilometres of its twisting and often torturous journey from its source. Fed by two major rivers as well as by many other tributaries, the Weser had travelled from the mountains of central Germany to this spot. From rivulets flowing down the sides of mountains it had grown to a width of nearly 500 metres but, because of all its efforts rushing here, there and everywhere, it now seemed almost too tired to complete the remaining few kilometres to its destination, the North Sea.

Not very long ago I had watched with fascination the reflections of thousands of stars, as they seemed to dance on the surface of the nearly calm water. Now, as the new day was beginning to break, its surface had taken on a reddish glow, mirroring the rays of an early morning sun.

All around me the scene was one of serenity and peacefulness, awakening almost forgotten childhood memories, when as a family we were on holiday in the mountains of Silesia, where we spent hours on end just sitting by the side of streams, hypnotized by the sound and the sight of the flowing water. Now, at the tender age of less than 18 years, I find that this impression of 'heavenly peace and goodwill to all men on earth' was nothing more than a grand delusion.

After all, this was the end of 1943, when our country was already deeply involved in nearly four years of bloody fighting against the Allied forces. British and the US air forces were almost nightly reminding us that this was no walkover. Peace was a thing of the past, a distant memory; to regain it we would first have buckle to, in an all-out effort to win this nasty war.

And that was part of the reason why I happened to be here.

Tucked away beside the river and out of sight of prying eyes, in one of the quietest corners of a sheltered basin was our little ship bobbing up and down in the gentle swell.

As the sun was not yet strong enough to penetrate the camouflage netting above us, the gleaming new vessel sheltering underneath it appeared menacingly dark and sinister.

Until late last night this battle-grey, almost black shape, had still been high and dry in a dock in the busiest part of the dockyard. There, amid the never-ending noise of metal being hammered, shaped and riveted, the arcs of the countless electric welders sent flashes of lightning across the basin and illuminated dozens of partly finished U-boats still resting on the stocks. Up to midnight hordes of men, armed with brushes and pots of paint, had been busy applying the finishing touches to this latest addition to the German U-boat fleet.

This morning her paint was still tacky, but completion targets had to be met. Shortcuts had to be taken in times of national emergency to satisfy the increasing demand for more and more ***Unterseeboote.*** Our country's very survival depended on those U-boats, to attack the busy shipping lanes across the Atlantic, through which America and Canada supplied food and war materials to their British allies.

Type IXD2 U-boat
under camouflage netting

The boat, with the Construction Number 1092, was duly completed. In the early hours, while it was still dark, she was towed to her present position inside the naval base a couple of kilometres upstream, ready for the next chapter in her life.

By 0900 hours, seventy sailors, officers and other ranks were drawn up in immaculate straight lines of three abreast on the very narrow quarterdeck behind the boat's conning tower. Dressed in our best No.1 uniforms, we faced forward towards the flagstaff, which rose above us on the upper *Wintergarten*/gun-deck, behind the boat's bridge. Two ratings stood by in readiness to run up her spanking new battle ensign.

Between our crew and the flag staff, but standing on the slightly raised lower *Wintergarten*/gun-deck, also facing the same way, stood our new commanding officer and his quartermaster.

As it was low water, the boat floated some metres below the jetty. But the crew could still see most of the shore-party drawn up above them on the dockside.

The few civilians, whom we assumed to be top men from the dockyard, were greatly outnumbered by the uniforms of the many high-ranking officers of the German fighting forces, the Navy, the Army and the Air force. The VIPs were flanked by a small naval brass band on one side and on the other side by a small drill party.

This shore party, together with the boat's crew, had been assembled to be part of the commissioning of this latest Type IXD2 U-boat into Germany's already sizeable U-boat fleet.

As one of the dockyard's directors stepped forward to open this simple ceremony, we heard a car pulling up behind the crowd ashore. From where we stood below the pier, we couldn't see what was going on. But, judging by the body language of the shore party, somebody important must have joined them. Because over 800 U-boat commissioning ceremonies had preceded this one, they had gradually become simpler and shorter: a few words from one of the directors of the yard, followed by a high-ranking naval officer officially accepting the boat into the German navy.

On a command from our CO, our crew came to attention. The ceremonial drill party presented arms, all the officers saluted in military fashion and the civilians gave the *Heil-Hitler* salute. Our quartermaster, on his silver 'boatswain's call', piped the signal to run up our boat's new ensign. While the band played the National Anthem, the flag under which we were to sail, fight and possibly die was slowly raised to the top of the staff, where, helped by a barely noticeable breeze, it unfurled for the very first time.

As one of the tallest members of the crew I was in the front rank, immediately behind the officers, chiefs and petty officers.

Commissioning ceremony of a Type IXD2 U-boat

Standing at ease, I managed to cast a furtive look behind me at my new comrades.

We had all chosen a career in the navy and then volunteered for the *Himmelfahrtkommando* (Ascension command), as the U-boat service was popularly known.

Chests out and chins up, the entire crew appeared every bit as proud as I was to be a part of this show.

At long last, all the hanging about in training establishments and at U-boat school was coming to an end and from now on we would be able to contribute positively to our country's defence.

Next, on a request from the jetty above, the 'Old Man', as our Commanding Officer was already known to us, moved over to the steep gangplank. The quartermaster 'piped the side' in true naval tradition, as one of the naval officers, who had golden piston rings covering his sleeves up to his elbows, came aboard.

'Shit! Do you see who that is?' said someone behind me. There was no mistaking the tall, erect figure, which up to now we had seen only in newspapers or in newsreels at the cinema.

After returning our captain's salute by raising his Admiral's Staff, he shook hands with the captain and the two men made their way over to the quarterdeck, where we were still standing to attention.
The new arrival greeted us with a few simple words – words that have remained etched on my mind ever since:

'My Men!
I am glad I could manage to attend the commissioning of your boat. Welcome into the ranks of our glorious U-boat service. We have been chosen to play an important part in our country's just struggle against our sworn enemies. True to our Oath of Allegiance, we shall live up to that expectation and if necessary we shall offer our lives in the fight for our freedom from foreign domination and for the greater glory of our Führer und Vaterland.'

The entire crew, not only we young ones, were struck dumb when we realised who we had actually come face to face with - the supreme Commander-in-Chief of the German navy, *Grossadmiral* (Admiral of the Fleet) Karl Dönitz.

Even a babe in arms would have known that, as its chief, he had been responsible for the rebuilding of the present-day U-boat force. A submariner himself from the First World War, he was respected by all who served under him and fondly known as 'Papa Dönitz'.

After the crew stood down, we were ordered to our action-stations, while the Grand Admiral inspected the boat. The smell of fresh paint was everywhere. The basic colour inside the boat was plain white, but splashes of crimson, blue, green and yellow were dotted about on the colour coded pipes and cables and on the hand-wheels and handles of valves, levers and gauges.

When the *Großadmiral* followed the Old Man from the bridge to the control-room, a six-metre drop, in true submariner's fashion his feet never touched the rungs of the ladders. For a man in his fifties, who was probably tied to a desk for most of the time, this was quite a performance, but it was clear that he was thoroughly at home in the narrow confine of a U-boat and moreover that he was familiar with all the latest refinements that had been built into the boat, which the Old Man tried to show off.

Most of the latest innovations were aids to tracking and detecting enemy radio signals and acoustic listening devices. But true to his reputation, Papa was even keener to chat to all the crew- members.

It was in these circumstances that he really came to life. His ability to inspire all those around him had become legendary.

When it was my turn he asked, 'what's your name, sailor, and where do you come from?' My knees turned to jelly as I struggled to get the words out. 'Artificer Gerhard Schuler f-f-from B-B-Berlin, Sir.'
He looked me straight in the eye and put his hand on my shoulder as if he had known me all his life. 'Are your folks at home well?' he asked. He was obviously referring to the night raids by the RAF on our city. 'Yes Sir, they are.'

After this I was pleased to note that my fellow crewmembers were even more tongue-tied than I was when he spoke to them. My opposite number, Werner, went as red as a beetroot and it took him a while after the party had moved into the engine rooms before he could say anything at all. 'Gerhard,' he stuttered 'who the hell is going to believe us when we tell the folks at home that we've talked to HIM?' I couldn't agree more. 'I'm always accused of spinning yarns anyway, so I assume they'll put it down to my fertile imagination.'

It must have been pure coincidence that he was travelling through Bremen on that particular day. Now that he had assumed overall command of the *Kriegsmarine*, his present HQ was rumoured to be in Berlin.

Once the *Großadmiral* had gone back ashore, perhaps to take part in another commissioning, our Old Man marched us over to one of the classrooms at the base and started to tell us a bit more about the role we were expected to play in our country's war effort.

'I must remind you here and now that all of us, old hands as well as rookies, are professional sailors and that we are privileged to serve in our U-boat service. We are an *élite* outfit, which is respected by friend and foe, a fact that should make us proud to be associated with it.

Every one us, has an important function to perform.

To make our ship a successful one, we must all be able to rely on each other, especially in times of danger. Our crew will only be as good as its weakest member. As professionals,' he went on, 'we have sworn to fight for our country, irrespective of any political considerations. On my ship we shall do so in a honourable way, without hate or malice, but with respect for our opponents and with due regard to the laws of the seas. Our enemy will be the ships and their cargoes, not their crews, who like us have a job to do.'

This must be one of the longest speeches the Old Man had ever made. It was direct and to the point and we were aware that we better remember every word of it if we knew what was good for us. Perhaps he was unaccustomed to public speaking, but every word seemed to come straight from the heart.

Most of us, particularly the engineering crews, had been with this command since she had first slid into the water some three months before, but until now we had known little or nothing about the Old Man's background. Yet he had already won our respect as a fair, decent guy. The *Deutsche Kreuz* (German Cross) in gold and U-boat badge on his chest were proof of his experience. How he had risen through the ranks to his present position, we were to learn later.

The crew of a newly commissioned Type IXD2 U-boat

For the remainder of the day we were left to our own devices, on condition that we would be all spruced up for the evening's festivities in one of the best restaurants in town.

There was a special meal, some speeches, which we could hardly hear, and then a cabaret with all the free beer we could drink.

'God! We must be something special after all.'

That was our general feeling.

Even some of our less respected superiors didn't seem all that bad after we had downed enough beer to float a battleship.

Drunk as 'Lords' (not a cliché in this instance but the way ordinary German sailors refer to themselves) and arm in arm we staggered back to our

our quarters in the base, where we had been billeted during the building of our boat and where we would stay until we put to sea. I crawled into my bunk but found it difficult to get to sleep. Memories of my last visit to Berlin came to mind. While enjoying the attractions of the all-night bars, I had met a couple of bearded U-boat men with a king-sized thirst. They had just travelled up from their base at St Nazaire, having completed a very successful patrol in the North Atlantic.

Their Commandant had been to see the Führer, who had decorated him with the Knight's Cross. Both seamen were also sporting the spanking-new black, white and red ribbon of the Iron Cross II Class beside their U-boat badges.

Hearing that I had just completed a course at a U-boat school and was ready to join my first command on a sub, they put my wind up with their pessimistic talk. 'The talk at Lorient is that we lost almost as many front-boats in the past few months as new ones were being built and commissioned. There are rumours that Tommy is using new weapons, with which he can locate us day and night. His planes have been known to attack us in the dead of night as if he was able to actually see in the dark.'

Losses of boats or other setbacks never got a mention in the newspapers or on the radio, only the successes. But, depressed as I was after that encounter, I had been cheered by *Großadmiral's* speech, which had wiped away any doubts I had about our future contribution in this war. More than ever I was glad that I had kept my mouth shut about my meeting in Berlin.

After breakfast the next morning, it was back on board, this time carrying our kitbags containing all our worldly goods, but as I stumbled across the gangplank, which led from the quay to the boat's forecastle, I nearly dropped mine overboard.

Either I had missed it the day before, or it had only been revealed since the commissioning, but on both sides of the conning tower somebody had painted pictures of a playing card, 60 cm high.

The sight of this particular one took my breath away!

In times of peace, German U-boats usually displayed their boat numbers there. In wartime, however, I guess for reasons of secrecy, those numbers were concealed and replaced by tactical signs, which often took the form of cartoons, coats of arms, heraldic paintings, animals or whatever else took the CO's fancy and would give the boats an identity, especially during the running-in and working-up periods.

Once we were back in the stern torpedo room, which doubled as our dormitory, dining room and mess, and I was stowing away my belongings in the minuscule locker by the side of my new bunk, my mood changed. I was pinning a post-card-sized photo of a bathing beauty on my locker door and whistling to myself. My opposite number Werner looked up, 'What the hell's up with you?' he demanded. 'Yesterday evening at the club you were down in the dumps and almost cried into your beer. And listen to you now, singing and generally exuding good will to all mankind.'

Of course, he had hit the nail on the head. So I went rummaging through my kitbag to find my pay-book. Out of its back-pages I fished a bit of cardboard and held it under Werner's nose.

'See this dirty old playing card? I've been carrying it around with me for a couple of years. Whether it is actually true or not, I honestly believe it once saved my bacon!

It is my lucky mascot!'

It was an old and tattered playing card, the same as the new paintings now adorning the conning tower of our ship.

'Take it from me, Werner, this little old boat of ours is going to be the luckiest one on all the high seas.' And to myself I thought, I may be superstitious, but in the days ahead all U-boats could well do with a large chunk of luck.

Here we were, surrounded by two thousand tonnes of tough, cold steel and I just couldn't decide whether living inside this shell we should feel safer or more vulnerable. Was it meant to shield us from our enemies and the elements or was it meant to be a shroud to cover us on our journey into eternity?

I began to see what people meant when they referred to our type of vessel as 'iron coffins'.

But those silly thoughts disappeared from my mind after a few seconds as during the next day or two we were kept busy familiarising ourselves with the new love in our lives.

Now we could study her in peace and play with her without the whole dockyard labour force crawling all over every inch of her. Until she was commissioned, they were in charge and we, who were to sail in her, were only just tolerated in our quest to get to know her. Manuals and charts of pipe systems had to be studied and compared with the real thing. Colour-coded valves, cables and pipes would eventually be imprinted on our brains. While we, the engineers, had plenty of diesels, pumps, motors and batteries to keep us occupied, the seamen were attending to taking on and stowing away supplies.

It was during the very first days of actually living and working aboard our new ship, that we started to realise one or two very important facts about her. It was plain to see that in the first instance, all U-boats had been designed to be formidable fighting machines. Every inch of her had been crammed full of gadgetry, machinery and weaponry.

There was just one little fact, however, which in our opinion had escaped those clever designers: a **crew was needed to operate this wonderful machine.**

'What a nuisance,' you could just about hear them saying to themselves. 'If those boats really do need a crew, where can we stick them?

I know. How about this for a solution?

Apart from the radio and tracking shacks, there is further space above the two main batteries where we can accommodate bunks for the Commandant, the other officers, the chief petty officers and the petty officers. For the ordinary seamen we can string up a few bunks or hammocks in the bow torpedo room and do the same for the ordinary stokers and the mechanics in the stern torpedo room.

But be careful! Those bunks and hammocks must not be permanent fixtures as their space will often be required when torpedoes need to be retracted from their tubes for regular servicing.'

What also came to the designers' aid was the fact that less than half of the crew would be on watch at any given time, so they had to provide only enough bunks for the remainder.

Brilliant!

Problem solved.

When moored up in a port we would continue to use the living facilities at the base, with the exception of perhaps half a dozen men under the command of a petty officer, who would stay on board and perform round-the-clock guard duties.

As it happened, on this day it was our turn.

After working on board, most of our crew had gone back to their quarters ashore for their evening meal. Our meal had been delivered to us in mess tins. Werner and I were scheduled to do our two-hour stint at midnight, which gave us a chance to while away a little time sitting on the bridge, puffing away like chimneys on our cigarette rations and generally spinning all sorts of yarns.

From below us, on the lower gun-deck, came the soft strains of a sea shanty, sung by a few seamen to the accompaniment of an accordion, played by Hansi Gerhards, one of our radio operators. Before long we all joined in, ignoring the fact that few of us had the faintest idea what the words meant, because the refrain was in English:

'Blow boys, blow for Ca-li-for-ni-o;
There is plenty of gold, so I am told,
on the banks of Sa-cra-men-to.'

But then, we didn't understand the words of the verses either, which were a mixture of *Plattdeutsch*, a Low German dialect quite unintelligible to most of us, plus a few English phrases. Sea shanties are predominantly in English because that was the language of most sailors in days gone by.

We spent many evenings having these impromptu sing-songs and when a few U-boats happened be moored near one another, you would find them competing for applause from whoever was in the vicinity.

Eventually we made our way back to our bunks in readiness for our watch duties. I was about to have a little nap when Werner said, 'Listen, Gerhard, you were telling us about this playing card of yours. What was it that made it so special to you?'

Well, it really was a strange tale. I had asked myself a few times in the past year or so whether I hadn't dreamt the whole episode. But I took a deep breath and began.

Fifteen months ago, at the end of 1942, I was an apprentice in a factory, which was producing aircraft components. I was in the last year of my training and had already spent some months in various departments of this firm. One month was spent with the electricians, another month in the heat treatment department, a further two months with the blacksmith, and so on. It was now time to return to our training school workshop to acquire our final polish in the trade of our choice, which in my case was that of a tool-maker. In another three months we would have to take our final theoretical and practical exams. It was vital for me to pass those with good marks if I wanted to join the navy. I knew I had to get my head down and work like a beaver, especially on preparations for the practical test.

One evening, looking forward to the end of the day's work, I was listening to the music from the loudspeakers above our heads and quietly humming to myself. Each tool had its own place, either inside the cupboard or in the sliding drawer underneath the bench top, and had to be spotless before everything was packed away every evening.

It was already dark outside, the reflection of the moon in the factory-roof windows indicating that we might be in for a cold night. Bruno Altmann, my colleague, and I, had quite an eventful time that day. Sooner or later we were due to be called up for military service and the odds were we would finish up in the dirt and muck of the eastern front, if not in the Waffen-SS.

For that reason we had decided some time ago to volunteer to become professionals. His wish was to go to the *Luftwaffe* and I was equally keen to join the *Kriegsmarine*. During our lunch break we had skipped out of the factory and gone along to the nearest recruitment office a few blocks away.

Here we collected the necessary forms and a little booklet to help us filling in the applications. During the course of the afternoon we had both taken a preliminary glance through the forms, which looked pretty straightforward.

There appeared to be just one little problem though.

Being under the age of eighteen, we would have to get the permission of our legal guardians to sign up.

Bruno didn't have a problem there; he had already discussed things with his parents and received their blessing, but every time I broached the subject with mine, my dad declined to discuss it.

'There's still plenty of time. Don't be in too great a hurry to commit suicide.'

I was left with just two choices.

One was to wait until I could get him in the right frame of mind, perhaps after he had some of our home made tipple or, more realistically, start practising a harmless bit of forgery.

We'd have to wait and see!

Meanwhile, Bruno reminded me that we had an important table-tennis match after work. Because the train in our homeward direction wasn't due for over an hour, my friend and I usually killed time by having a thrash-about on the table-tennis tables in the works canteen. We were quite well matched, but only one of us was going to be apprentice champion after tonight.

But, *verdammtes Donnerwetter* and damn and blast, somebody must have forgotten to tell Tommy and Uncle Sam about our arrangement! Like gatecrashers at a party they proceeded to disrupt our plans.

Sirens screamed from the top of the building.

They were the signal to run for cover. 'Don't forget,' our chief instructor said, 'remember to switch off your machines and lock away all your tools and belongings. Then get the hell out of here.'

Proper air-raid shelters were some distance away and those inside our factory were still incomplete. In the meantime we had to shelter in the changing rooms and toilets under our workshop. Convenient if not ideal, they were certainly better than no shelter at all.

Once down in the dungeons we intended to while away the time by chatting or reading or playing cards.

A pontoon school was already in progress, by the sound of the arguments the stakes were high. High, that is, by our standards. Since we didn't get wages as such, we relied mostly on our parents to finance our travelling costs. Few of us received any pocket money. To make matters worse, the bank was made by our resident bullyboy Horst Walters. A few months older than me, he had, for reasons known only to himself, developed a real dislike for me. Could it have been because I had replaced him as top dog on the achievement graphs?

Gambling for money was the very last thing I could afford; on the other hand I would have loved to take some loot off him as he was in the habit of flashing it around. My sidekick Bruno, who knew my financial position just as well as I did, went bananas when he realised what I intended to do and tactfully put it to me.

'You should go and have your thick head examined,' he protested. 'You know very well that the banker never loses.'

Of course he was right. All I had in my pockets that evening was the money for my next weekly train ticket.

Still, the old saying there's one born every minute' was as true then as it is now. It didn't take many lost hands before I started to have visions of doing a two-hour trek each morning and evening between home and work. Riding a bike was out, in winter, with all the snow and ice about.

I honestly didn't bet more than a few *Pfennigs* at a time, but every time I lost I insisted on increasing the stakes, with some silly idea in my head of recouping my previous losses.

I just couldn't let go, even when I needed a pee so badly, that I was jumping from one leg to the other. This was definitely my last effort to get my fare back.

And it looked good!

The first card Horst dealt me was an ace!

Now it was decision time.

My brain screamed to back off - but the devil within me commanded:

'What are you waiting for? Go for it, you coward.'

What else could I do but to stake my last *Mark* on this beautiful card?

I asked for another card.

But as soon as Horst had thrown the card down in front of me, the whole damned world seemed to explode around our ears. The factory building shook and trembled, as though an earthquake had struck. Doors from the shower and toilet cubicles were blown clean out of their frames and came flying through the room. One of the doors just missed us and finished up right between us. Any thoughts of pontoon had been wiped from our minds by this time; we were all too busy counting our limbs and checking that we were all in one piece.

As soon as the dust had settled and we could see again, we did a head count. Luck was with us that day. Everyone was accounted for, although a few of our colleagues had minor cuts and bruises, probably from flying sherds from the washbasins that had been shattered by the blast. Injuries were soon patched up while we continued to assess the damage.

We had been down here once or twice during earlier raids, but never before had Tommy bothered to go for factories. I always assumed he was more interested in destroying our morale than our ability to produce war machinery such as tanks and cannon.

So what on earth had happened this time?

Was it an accident or was it deliberate? The fact was that one of those eggs Tommy had laid had fallen through the workshop above us and exploded in the toilets next door. It couldn't have been a very big one or it would have blown every one of us to kingdom come. However, the explosion was big enough to turn a whole section of our workshop into a heap of rubble. The works canteen had also taken a hit, as a result of which our table-tennis championship decider was postponed indefinitely.

As we started to clean up the mess in the washroom and pick up the metal lockers that had been thrown over, we came to the door that had nearly knocked our brains out. Under it we found our cards and all the money in the kitty, just where we had dropped them during the melee.

Nothing was further from our minds after the fright we had than to carry on gambling. But out of sheer curiosity I picked up the card I had been holding when the earth fell in. There it was, that ace, which made me ask for another card. And next to it was the card Horst had subsequently dealt me, the Queen of Hearts. This meant that together with the original ace, my 'twenty-one' would have won the game.

While I was staring at the cards, it hit me right between the eyes.

How lucky can you get?

If it had not been for the fact that I had been dealt that ace as a first card, I would have been standing in front of the urinal, and that egg would have dropped right smack on my poor head. By that time I would have been on my way up to St Peter, tuning up the old harp in the company of a few heavenly angels.

There was no doubt about it; the ***KARO-AS*** (Ace of Diamonds) had saved my life!

Without thinking, I put it in my pocket and there it stayed until the day mother went to wash my overalls. As usual, she emptied the pockets and put everything on my bedside table. But she missed the card in the hip pocket and by the time I found it again it had been washed, dried and mangled and was then truly tattered and torn. Thinking back over the whole episode, I decided to look after this silly scrap of paper, just as it had looked after me when I most needed looking after.

Anyway, that is the story of my lucky playing card, my rabbit's foot, if you like'

That was the end of my tale and, although Werner looked at me as if I had a screw loose, I was convinced that any boat that had the **Ace of Diamonds** as her tactical sign, could not fail to be protected by my lucky card.

CHAPTER TWO

A few days later, on a dark and cold evening, ***KARO-AS*** left her mooring for more engine trials. As usual, it took us down river toward the open sea, during which time the Diesel experts from the M.A.N. factory carried out further tests on our 4,000 horses. The stethoscopes and other measuring devices were working overtime. However, at the end of our usual run, when normally we would turn 180 degrees and run back up-river, unexpectedly the engines were shut off. A launch came alongside to pick-up the M.A.N. engineers and their gear. As soon they'd cast off, the orders from the bridge were, 'Both engines half ahead.'

Steaming out into the open sea, we didn't have to wait long to find out what caused the change of routine. The voice of the Old Man came over the tannoy. 'Our acceptance trials have now been completed to the entire satisfaction of the *Kriegsmarine* and we're now on our way to Kiel. As you know, it's in the Baltic Sea that we shall do all our working-up trials, hopefully in perfect peace and quiet from Allied ship or aircraft. We'll stay there until we, and our boat, come up to a standard which makes us fit to be sent on our first patrol.'

Even before the Old Man finished his little speech, I could hear behind me the high-pitched voice of my sidekick. *"Verdammte Scheisse!"* (Damned shit!) Werner commented as he realised we had waved good-bye to our haunts in Bremen for the very last time. 'Why haven't we been given the chance to bid a proper farewell to the many friends we made during our time here?' Werner carried on as if somebody had spilled his beer.

'For heaven's sake calm down,' I tried my best to console him. 'You couldn't expect the Old Man to advertise our departure or to fly the 'Blue Peter' from the top of the periscope, just to let everybody know that we're leaving.'

It was a well-known fact, 'Walls really do have ears!'

However, I had to admit to being a bit miffed as well. Not that marriage ever crossed our minds.

When we first arrived at our new command a few months ago, our boat was only half-finished and was still lying high and dry on the stocks.

Therefore, we had all the time and opportunity to find out more about this interesting city and its citizens. Werner and I had struck-up quite a friendship. We were both not quite eighteen years old and, just like me, he didn't have a need for a razor. We had met for the first time on the train, which brought us from our hometown Berlin to this base. Until then our paths hadn't crossed, he had been initiated in one U-boat school and I in another. Otherwise, our careers had followed similar lines.

'Wouldn't it be funny if we both finished up on the same tub?'

Not only were we posted to the same boat; we also became colleagues on her control room's starboard watch.

During our stay in town and whenever we were allowed shore leave, we would go out together. Our flat-mates laughingly called us *Dick und Dof* (Laurel and Hardy). Werner was barely 163 cm and I rose to a majestic 188 - the long and the short of it.

Like many other things we had in common, our liking for company, female one in particular, was an important one.

Of course, young ladies were in relatively short supply in a port with two large dockyards. More than 20 U-boats of one type or another were under construction here, most of them still on the stocks while others had been launched and were awaiting the finishing touches. With an average of 60 men on each boat there were at least 1,500 lonely, young and able sailors stationed in Bremen at any given time.

Since few 'nice girls' would have been seen dead with the likes of us, it boiled down to competition for the 'not so nice' ones. Those were usually found hanging out in the taverns in the back streets by the inner harbour.

The establishment Werner and I liked to visit was called *"La Paloma Blanca"* (The white dove). We learned later that there was at least one low dive with the same name in every other port on the North Sea and the Baltic Sea coasts. In this well attended club, the tables were tucked away into dark corners, while in the centre of the room, on a small and raised platform, a couple of elderly seafarers, were entertaining their customers by singing shanties to the accompaniment of a *Schifferklavier* (sailor's piano), an accordion. Now and again a not so young and slightly rolly-polly belly dancer would give a turn to the rapturous applause from some, and to the invitation to 'get them off' from others. She didn't look bad at all, especially after we had done justice to few strong beers.

Not long after one newly commissioned U-boat had departed for exercises in the Baltic, two quite presentable looking young ladies, had taken up our offer for a drink and joined us on our table. Having promised to be faithful and true to the Lords of one U-boat, they were already on the lookout for fresh pickings. Maxine and Giselle, if those were their given names, weren't going to get very rich from us. We didn't have a fortune, but what we did have, burned a hole in our pockets, so our new friends might as well help us to get rid of it. And to be fair, the two amateur beauties did their best to amuse us. While we were happy to drink beer, our lady-friends could only drink Champagne. However, we soon caught-on and realised, their glasses contained nothing more than coloured water, but came at Champagne prices. No doubt M and G would get a little payback at a later date.

However, Bremen was history now; soon it would be ‘Hello’ to new friends and new adventure on the Baltic.

With my cup of coffee, I proposed a toast. ‘Bless you all, girls of *La Paloma* and all other low dives in Bremen. We will love you for ever, or at least until we get to our next port of call.’

Ever so quietly, we crept out past Bremerhaven into the North Sea. I overheard the Old Man telling the *1WO* (Officer of the First Watch) that from here until we get to the Elbe estuary we will have the company of a Minesweeper. There we would pick-up the entrance to the canal, which connected the North Sea to the Baltic Sea. All ports and estuaries were well protected by mine fields to keep out unwelcome visitors, but the escort should safely lead us through those and also clear any other random mines, which might have been dropped by Tommy’s planes on their way to bomb Hamburg or Berlin. To avoid unwanted attention from those planes was the main reason for our slinking about in the dark. Tommy seemed to be able to come and go, as he liked. Which raised the question: ‘Where the hell is the *Luftwaffe*?’

It was for our aircraft’s benefit that we had painted two broad yellow lines across the boat’s decks as recognition signals, one forward, one aft and there was also a narrower one horizontally around the conning-tower.

Maybe in the comparative safety of the Baltic we would see more of our aircraft, as they were conspicuous by their absence here.

Our very first six-hour spell on watch lasted until 0200 hours in the morning and passed quite uneventfully. Every one of us, from the Old Man down to us lackeys, was trying to get acquainted with our new tasks. It would take a little time to find our feet. Werner had gone to wake our opposite numbers Philip and Karl-Heinz, so they could be ready to man our stations. I had just finished pumping out all the bilges throughout the length of the boat, a task, which from now on was to done as a matter of routine at the end of every watch. The bilges under the large batteries needed special attention, as here existed real danger. If seawater was allowed to accumulate in those, perhaps from leaks in pipes or valves, the resulting lethal cocktail of volatile chlorine gas posed perhaps the biggest danger for boat and crew. Fear of explosion was the main reason for enforcing a blanket 'No Smoking' policy inside all U-boats.

Once off duty, Werner and I were given permission to come on the bridge to breathe fresh air and to top-up our lungs with cigarette smoke, before returning to our mess to catch a few hours sleep.

As mentioned before, sleeping arrangements were a novel experience, we were able to jump into a bunk, which was still warm from its previous occupant. Philip and Werner shared our top bunk and in my case, in the bottom bunk, the human hot-water bottle was Karl-Heinz. Although each one of us were issued with our own bed sheets, blanket-covers and pillowcases, the changing of them soon proved to be too time consuming and was often abandoned. At most, we managed to turn the pillows over before crashing out in the still warm bunk. Some times we would undress and sometimes we would not. If you could tolerate the strange smell, then hot bunking was the cat's whiskers. At first, Karl-Heinz did make me feel just a little bit uncomfortable. He was a bit of a pretty-pretty boy, very dark and very handsome and tended to keep to himself, never revealing where he spent his time when going ashore. He spent a lot of time getting ready, his uniform seemed spotless and his bell-bottoms were ironed to perfection. He then spent an equal amount of time lovingly admiring himself in the mirror.

Once he left the harbour area, we never saw which way he went. All this didn't really bother me until I had to listen to sly advice: 'If I was you, I would watch my back'. Whatever did they mean?

Next morning we had breakfast at 0700 and were back on watch by 0800, just in time to learn that the pilot, who was to guide ***KARO-AS*** through the Kiel Canal to the Baltic, had come aboard. Soon afterwards the diesels slowed to a faint murmur. This waterway had been built a long time ago; at one time it was called the *Kaiser Wilhelm Kanal,* later again the *Nord-Ostsee Kanal.* At one time it had been widened to allow even the largest battleships of the German navy to sail through it instead of having to travel all the way round Denmark. Most surface ships had a shallower draft than the 5.35 metres of ***KARO-AS***, as 90 percent of her was below the waterline when running surfaced. So as not to stir up the mud at the bottom of the channel, we had to creep along at less than 5 knots, which meant it would take more than ten hours to get to the *Holtenauer Schleuse* (locks) at the entrance to the bay at Kiel. It meant ten hours pleasure-cruising in flat, calm waters and with not a lot of work to do, or so we thought.

Pilot taking Type IXD2 U-boat through Nord-Ostsee canal

Type IXD2 U-boat en route through Nord-Ostsee canal to Kiel.

Trust the Old Man, he had other ideas. He ordered the heads of all departments to use the time for intense training.

In the control-room, especially on the starboard watch, Werner and I greeted the idea with a hollow laugh.

Why?

Because after only a very short time on board, we had already formed very firm opinions of our immediate boss, Petty Officer (III) Franz Ebler, and his suitability to be in part-charge of a U-boat's nerve centre. To say that he was as thick as stonewall would be doing an injustice to said masonry. How he ever got to be a petty officer defied all reasoning.

Granted, his U-boat expertise, just like ours, was non-existent. His previous experience was gained on battleships, on which he had a lot of space to lose himself in a large number of sailors. In a small unit, such as ours, there was no place to hide and all the bluster and all the bullshit were not going to help him. Alas, he had to show that he was on top of his job.

He produced manuals and charts of the various pipe-systems running through the boat, which also pinpointed the location, shape and colour of every valve in those systems. He referred to the books and charts and then asked us to point out where they were to be found. Werner and I were no Einsteins, but we had not wasted the three months training at the U-boat schools. We did well at this little game. The fun really started when the Chief Petty Officer Georg Schulz decided to take a hand in the proceedings. He was in charge of the entire control-room personnel on the two watches. Now here we had somebody quite different. When our CPO first arrived on board he was wearing a chest-full of gongs, all of them earned in the U-boat service. He was reputed to have served under some of the most successful U-boat aces of the early war years. Apart from knowing his job blindfold from a technical point of view, he was also a super communicator.

In fact, only the Old Man had anything like his experience and it was not unexpected to see both of them with their heads together on more than one occasion. As for us, we had already decided that Georg had seawater and oil in his veins instead of blood and we were ready to do everything possible to please him.

Under some pretext or other or by pure chance, he took the manual from Ebler and started to leaf through it.

There followed a silence.

'Just carry on, *Herr Obermaat*', said Georg to the poor soul, who was now without his book of words. Ebler was like fish out of water without the manuals and could do nothing but stall for time. Luckily for him, CPO Georg didn't want to embarrass him in front of us, so he himself took a more active part in the training session, making sure we were kept on our toes until it was time for the port watch to take over at 1200 hours.

'Let's get up into the fresh air while we can' was the idea of all men not on duty, which meant just about everybody not urgently required to make the boat go forward. On the bridge and on the wintergarden we lolled about, watching the world go by.

The bridge watch, who would normally be required to scan the horizons in all directions within a 360-degree circle for ships or aircraft, had to stay at their posts. On this part of the trip, their only task was to watch out for enemy planes. It meant that the numerous cattle and sheep, which were grazing lazily on both banks of the waterway, could quite safely be ignored. Surely they were on our side!

But lots of feverish activity was taking place on the quarterdeck behind the conning tower. The seamen of the 1st division', i.e. the non-technical crew, were assembled there.

Under the watchful eye of the *1WO* they were made to brush up their semaphore, which was a system of signalling by means of two hand-held flags.

This traditional type of communication, as well as the sending Morse signals by means of a signal lamp, had to a large extent become obsolete and had been replaced by radio telegraphy. But in a ship-to-ship situation at sea it was still very useful, as it could not be easily intercepted or overheard by the enemy.

Leaning over the rails of the upper wintergarden, I watched with mild amusement the poor efforts of some of the Lords and their petty officer instructor. My sidekick wanted to know 'Can you really read all this jumble of arm waving,' to which I could honestly reply 'Yes. At the speed they're signalling I could read them in my sleep.' I told him that I had passed a few advanced exams in semaphore and Morse code and could both signal and read at a respectable rate.

Should I, a mere stoker of the 2nd division, keep my nose out of it or should I let my prowess be known?

Helmsman Friedrich, who shared our quarters in the stern mess, had undergone similar training in the Naval Hitler Youths (*Hitler Jugend, HJ* for short). He was standing at the very stern of the boat. Just for a laugh I gave him a call with imaginary flags. Just using my arms, I slowly flashed a message to him. 'Hello, Fritz! Do you mind if I interrupt, I'd like to see how good you really are?' to which he replied 'If you can't transmit a bit faster, you're wasting my time.'

Right you are, how's that for speed' and this time I really let him have it.

'Yeeees, that's much better. Why're you wasting your time in the 2nd division? Why don't you become a real sailor and learn a bit about seamanship?' 'I tell you one thing, Fritz, I would make a better seaman than any of your other mates, they're proper dummies when it comes to signalling and your PO isn't much better.'

'You're not kidding, they haven't got a clue.'

At the speed we were signalling even the *1WO* was unable to read us, or so I hoped, as we continued to malign the rest of the motley crew. Thus encouraged I continued 'I wonder to which God-forsaken port the Old Man is taking us, once we get through to the Baltic.'

Before Friedrich had a chance to reply, a voice came from behind me: 'You'll just have to wait and see, won't you, you cheeky beggar!'

I nearly fell overboard with surprise. The Old Man was standing there and had followed every word we signalled. He hasn't been at sea all his life for nothing and probably forgotten more about semaphore than anyone of us shall ever know. Trust me to put my foot in it! But he did have a smirk on his face while he was ticking me off!

However, I thought it extremely prudent to disappear down below, where stokers were supposed to be and off I went. As I was halfway down through the hatch, the Old Man asked, 'And where did you learn your flag-waving?' Red-faced, I stuttered when I told him about the few years I was a member of the Naval *HJ* and about the time I spent on *'Gorch Fock'* one of the navy's three-mast barques, which been loaned to the *HJ* during wartime. Before the war it was used for training officer-cadets.

Werner had looked on with open mouth and once we were back in our mess he asked, 'what was it you told the Old Man about you and *Gorch Fock?* Why've you kept that story under your hat? I hope you'll tell me all about it sometime.'

'I certainly will, but not now, when the meal is on the table.'

And so we tucked in like hungry wolves, although the meal was cold and almost inedible. The last thing I wanted now was to be disturbed in the process of eating; peace and quiet was all I wished for. But it was not to be; someone tried to squeeze past me while I was shovelling it in. He has been getting on my nerves in a big way ever since he came aboard. Its funny, well not really, but some people can get under your skin without really trying. In the needling department Walter Grau was a real natural.

'Why the hell do you have to go to the bog just when we're sitting down to eat?' I asked him politely 'You must be saving it up, so that you can climb all over us, you stupid torpedo-mixing bastard.' He just gave me a dirty look.

To understand my annoyance, you have to visualise bunks on both sides of the middle gangway with just enough room between the bunks for a folding table. There was no room for dining room chairs; we had to sit on the bottom bunks. Anybody wanting to squeeze past from aft to go forward to the heads, forced everybody to either get up and stand aside or lie back on the bunks with legs up in the air. Try and do that with you mouth full of grub. Either way it was a bloody nuisance, particularly since we all knew that he would want to come back in a minute or two. Others, who also had to make way for him, advised Walter in passing, 'Please make sure you wash your hands.'

Werner, who knew Berlin better than I did, had some time ago put me in the picture about Walter's background: 'As far as I can gather, he comes from the stockbroker district of Zehlendorf, by the side of the Wannsee, a large lake in the south of Berlin. Nearby, his father has his own factory, *Grau und Sohn AG,* which employs about fifty workers. Walter is the boss's only son and heir. Their mansion is right beside the water's edge with their private yacht moored nearby.'

All this fitted in with my estimate of Walter, No wonder he always has his damned nose up in the air and treats those around him like dirt.

The funny coincidence was, my own father often worked in *Zehlendorf.* He and his elder brother, my uncle Franz, worked as bin-men on a horse-drawn dustcart. All the toys children in our family ever received for Christmas or for birthdays were scavenged from the dustbins of those rich folk like the Family *Grau.*

After finishing my meal, I put my feet up and tried to get a few minutes sleep. In another hour we were due back on watch. I told myself to calm down, and not to let Walter get to me. I also told myself not to be jealous of his silver spoon; he couldn't help being a bastard.

On the whole I had been able to cope quite well with the watch-system of four hours on/four hours off, followed by six hours on/six hours off. I managed to sleep wherever or whenever I put my head down. But tonight, for some unknown reason, the old wheels were crunching away in my brain and neither the normally sleep-inducing hum of the engines nor the conventional sheep counting had the slightest effect on my wish to give my body and brain some time off.

I was wide-awake.

Staring at the shape of Werner's backside outlined in the bunk above me, I let my thoughts wandered back and forth in time.

What devilish coincidence has brought this motley collection of humanity together and deposited them inside this iron box. They came from all ends of the country and from all sorts of family backgrounds. What had moved each one of them to volunteer not only for service in the *Kriegsmarine* but also for the Kamikaze type job called the U-boat service?

Was it a desire to broaden our horizons, to experience the wide and wild oceans of the world or just the wish to visit far-off and strange lands, which we would normally never see?

Or was it simply a will to find out more about ourselves; how would we react when the chips were down in times of extreme stress and danger?

I suppose, as time goes by, I will find out what my colleagues had to say about this subject. Not that I was so sure about my own feelings, which hadn't developed all of a sudden but had taken shape over a period of years and which up till now had brought me a lot of joy and satisfaction. Joy of being a useful member of a team, which had a single purpose and the satisfaction of being a trained engineer, who was given the opportunity to work inside a mechanical wonder.

The process, of deciding that my own future lay in the navy, started a few years ago on one specific day in late summer.

Until then, I hadn't given a thought, serious or otherwise, to my future. After all, I had only just reached my fourteenth birthday and there were still seven months of school in front of me.

There I was, sound asleep in my comfortable featherbed, when suddenly the tranquillity of my bedroom was invaded by an ear-shattering blast of mind busting marching music.

Boom - Boom - Booom of drums and then the Ta Ra - Ta Ra of fanfares.

Help!

Hiding my head under the bed-covers and putting my hands over both ears didn't help in the least.

The din was unbearable.

It was my mother's usual way of making sure that I got up in good time to get ready for school every morning. She would come into the living room, which doubled as my bedroom, and switch on the big radio. With its volume at full blast, I had no choice but to throw-off my bed-covers, jump out of bed and turn the damned thing off.

But before I could reach the switch, the proverbial bombshell was dropped in our laps by way of a special announcement from the headquarters of our Führer.

'Today, the 3rd of September 1939, England has declared war on Germany!'

Those were the only words I remembered. The rest of the lengthy speech was lost on me.

Everybody knew that trouble was brewing, but the involvement of England (meaning Britain) was unexpected, especially since we had been assured that our beef was not with the West but with the East. Poland in particular was accused of mistreating the German minorities in the former German areas of West Prussia and Posen.

Until this bombshell landed, this had been one of the best summers of my life. Where we lived, in the northern suburbs of Berlin, we had the most glorious weather and it had lasted right through our long school holidays during July and August. First came a three-week summer camp in the forests and hills of Silesia with the *Jungvolk*, which was the part of the Hitler Youths that catered for boys, aged 10 to 14.

After the hyperactivity of the camp in the great outdoors, I thoroughly enjoyed three weeks of delicious inactivity with my uncle and aunt in Dresden, the most beautiful city in Germany and worthy of it's reputation as the Venice of the North. My artist cousin Helmut saw to it that I learned to appreciate the ARTS a little more, teaching me to thump-out a few classical passages on their piano. But what I enjoyed most was being dragged through numerous Picture Galleries and having him explain famous paintings and painters with their own little quirks, all as seen through the eyes of an expert. When not soaking-up culture, I could be found sitting on 10m wide steps leading from a high terrace down to the side of the wide river Elbe. Here I stayed for hours, watching the paddle steamers leaving on and returning from pleasure cruises to the Sandstone Mountains near Czechoslovakia.

As I said before, it had been a fantastic summer, until that fateful morning when Mister Chamberlain had to go and spoil it all.

At war with England!

Could you believe it! After all that was agreed between him and our Führer in Munich. According to our radio and newspapers, it was all because our troops tried to help our persecuted cousins in Poland.

But, being very naïve, I thought to myself, 'Ah well! So be it!' Perhaps we can get our own back on Tommy for the way he bled us dry after the so-called Treaty of Versailles.

However, Mother, who had come back into the room when she heard the noisy announcements, had gone as white as a sheet. But Gerhard, this means real WAR! It is not just a game! We haven't got over the last one twenty years ago. How many people will be killed this time! Our Heinz will be one of the first to be in action, seeing that he's already in the navy. And in a few years it'll be your turn to follow your brother.'

Tears ran down her cheeks as she remembered what the last war had been like. My father had been conscripted to serve as a sapper in the Army on the Western Front, where at the drawn out battles of the Somme he was wounded. I never found out for what he had earned the 'Iron Cross' 2nd Class, which could be found under the socks and underwear in the drawer of his dressing table. He tried hard to forget all about those terrible years, but when on occasions he talked about the trench warfare and the sight of his comrades being blinded and disfigured by poison gas, you could feel the horror of it all. But then, he was one of the very few lucky ones, to return with only a piece of shrapnel still lodged in his shoulder.

Mother had lost two of her brothers in this futile war.

Other young men had retuned with their bodies broken, limbs missing and what was even worst, their spirits in tatters.

All the Iron Crosses in the world couldn't compensate for that.

'We didn't bring you into this world to see you all killed' Mum said while she hugged me tightly.

I couldn't doubt the depth of her feelings, especially since she had never been very demonstrative before. That embrace shook me to the core. 'But mum, it won't come to that. We've got to stand-up for ourselves against our enemies, because if we don't, we'll be their slaves all our lives. And anyway, the trouble will be over long before I'm old enough to follow Heinz into the navy.'

What was I saying?

It had been in the back of my mind for many months; on that day I put it in words for the very first time. Not that I was really sure why I wanted to follow Heinz into the navy.

Was it the smart sailor's uniform with the wide bellbottoms and skin-tight blue shirt, or was there really some salt-water in my veins bequeathed to me by previous generations of Schulers?

By 5 o'clock that same evening, France had also declared war on Germany.

This was less of a surprise, because of the continual niggling of the two countries about the Rheinland and the former German area of Alsace-Lorraine. Our West-Wall defence was built to protect us from them and they had the Maginot-line to protect them from us.

We could also expect America to come in against us, but Uncle Sam would probably sit on the fence for some time, to see which way the hare was going to run.

But what were the Russians going to do? Nobody knew where he or she stood.

Italy, Spain and Japan might come in on our side however. Not that we would get a lot of help from any of them.

The more I thought about it, the more I realised that from that day on our lives would change - dramatically.

This was crunch time – win or die in the process.

We could succeed in making our opponents pay for the indignities of the (so-called) Treaty of Versailles, retrieve our colonies and the lost areas of Posen and West-Prussia in the east and Alsac-Lorrain in the west. We could be paid back for the hardships suffered by almost everybody by the unemployment caused by the country's industries being stripped of all means of making a living and made worst by the resulting Hyper-inflation, when 1 Mark became 5,000 Million Paper Marks in the short space of 2 years.

On the other hand, we could lose everything we had gained in the last few years and finish up in a greater mess then back at the end of WWI in 1919.

Alas, I had to go back to school for my very last term, which finished at the end of March. My original hope of going on to higher education, with a view to become a teacher, would have to be shelved. I had been offered an assisted place at a college and I would have liked to give it a try.

My dad, on the other hand, had some idea of keeping to one's station in life - we were working class people.

In any case, with the war on I had only three and a half years in which to prepare myself for being able to stand on my own two feet and earn my living in life before I was liable for military service.

I was afraid that there was too little time!

I had to think of something else before Easter.

Blast you, Tommy!

First, there were seven months of schoolwork ahead of me. It gave me enough time to look around, to decide what I would like to do. It did rankle that living in a so-called Socialist country, the ability to pay for further education was still decisive. Being bright was not enough. When friends in my class and I were 12 years old, some of them went on to High School. It mattered little that they were not among the very cleverest.

I had to watch that I didn't develop a king-sized chip on my shoulder.

However, my Mum and Dad thought it a good idea to learn a trade, get an apprenticeship, even when they knew that they would have to support me for another three or four years. They pointed out that this would have three advantages. In the first place I would be able to finish an apprenticeship before I was old enough to go to war.

Secondly I would have a better chance to dodge having to join the Infantry or, worst still, the dreaded *Waffen-SS,* as engineers were always wanted in the Navy or in the *Luftwaffe.*

Thirdly I would have the means to support myself when the damned war finished.

It had worked for my older brother Heinz as he went on to became a skilled boilermaker. After he finished his apprenticeship and before he went into the Navy, he had started to earn good money.

It didn't sound too bad to me either.

My best friend Hansi, who was one year ahead of me, had started his apprenticeship as an Engine Mechanic at a large Aircraft Engine Factory. His tales persuaded me to try and get in there as well. My school-certificates were good enough, I passed all the entrance exams, I was even a member of the Hitler Youths... which was a pre-condition, but to my utter disgrace I failed the Medical.

I had flat feet!

But as it turned out, I was lucky even then. I managed to get the offer of an apprenticeship with another company, one that laid more stress on intelligence and dexterity then on the height of your instep. I was to become a toolmaker.

So, I had good reason to look forward to leaving school and starting my working life after Easter.

Easter came and Easter went, as did my Confirmation.

Soon thereafter, at 5.30 am on a cold April morning, I could be found cycling to my place of work on the Western edge of Greater Berlin. Before the war had started, here at our factory the skeletons of the huge Airships *"Hindenburg"* and *"Graf Zeppelin"* were manufactured from aluminium.

Now, the production had been switched to equip *Hermann Göring's Luftwaffe* with aircraft parts for *Messerschmidts* and *Junkers*.

Although we, the apprentices, had a completely separate workshop to ourselves, in which to do nothing but training exercises, in our second and third year we would already be working on building moulds and dies to aid the mass-production of those parts.

The head of our department, a youngish foreman by the name of *Herr* Krüger, together with his two elderly charge-hands were overseeing some forty apprentices between the ages of 14 to 17 years old. Because of an accident or through illness he had lost the lower part of his right arm and was therefore doing his bit for our country by trying to make us into some sort of engineers. They were instructing us in the finer points of metal bashing by using encouragement or threats and sometimes even by praising us.

Being a chain-smoker, *Herr* Krüger had the habit of holding his cigarette in his left hand between thumb and forefinger, with his pinkie constantly knocking imaginary ash from the end of it. Doing that and looking at you from under his bushy eyebrows he could be saying ‘well done', or more often than not, telling me that I would make a much better cobbler than a toolmaker.

Charming!

But in spite of it, I just loved my job because I was besotted by anything mechanical. The beauty and regularity of engineered items fascinated me, especially since every item had a purpose, without which they would be nothing... less than useless. It helped, that from a very young age I had spent a lot of my time building things. It started with bits of old Meccano sets which had been discarded by others. While other kids were playing outdoors, a lot of weird and wonderful constructions, powered by an old wind-up gramophone, appeared in our attic. Eventually model-ships and model aircraft filled every corner of our house. It didn't please mother, as she had the job of dusting them, but this experience stood me in good stead in my new job.

Every day brought me some new knowledge. Apart from the usual training in the factory itself, we now had one day's theoretical instruction at a technical college nearby. Never in my wildest dreams had I expected to learn about Metallurgy in addition to the usual Geometry, Trigonometry and Algebra.

With the onset of winter it became impractical to get to work by bike. Being pitch-black in the mornings as well as in the evening and not having a decent light because of the black-out, there was no way to avoid the thousand-and-one pieces of shrapnel on the roads, deposited there by the nightly FLAK (Anti-aircraft canons) activity.

Three ripped tyres during one week had convinced me, that it was better to get-up an hour earlier, in time for a thirty-minute walk to the nearest station and there board a train into the city. Here I changed to another platform to board the train heading for the industrial West of the city. This train started to fill up very quickly. Since most able-bodied men had already been called-up, the passengers were youngsters like myself, or men, who were too old for service on the front. But the majority were foreign nationals, Eastern European guest workers. Their smell was unbearable and their chatter was unintelligible and, what was more, at this unearthly hour in the morning it tended to give me a stinking headache.

Half way along the line, at another junction, hundreds of other young men and women joined the train. By now the compartments were really crowded. Some of them alighted with me at our station, but most of them carried on to the end of the line, where they worked in munitions or armament factories. Just like us, they were well wrapped up against the cold winter air, but what made they instantly different from us was their six-pointed 'Star of David' badge, which had the inscription *Jude* (Jew).

We knew that people classified as Enemies of the State were held in internment camps. The nearest one to Berlin, the one these men and women seemed to come from, was at Oranienburg. They obviously were expected to work for their living just like everyone else. If there were guards with them, I failed to see them and where would they run to anyway?

Until troubles were reported, mainly in the inner city, about shops being attacked and daubed with the word *Jude*, questions of religion and race were not uppermost in working people's lives. In fact, I didn't realise until much later, after he had left the country, that our family doctor was Jewish. What I did remember was that on his surgery wall he had a framed certificate with the actual Iron Cross 1st Class, which he had won in WWI.

And I also remember mother taking us into Jewish shops for our school clothes, as they were the only shops in which working people could afford the prices.

After my first ten months at our training workshop, we were now given a taste of real work in various other departments of the factory. My very first department was the blacksmith's shop. No, we didn't have to shoe horses, but simple forgings were made from malleable steel, such as chisels or punches.

In charge was Herr Schultz, an elderly foreman. He as bald as a coot, no taller than 5 ft, but with muscles to put Max Schmeling's and Joe Luis' to shame. His shortness in stature was matched by an even shorter temper. He was in charge of a team of three, himself plus me, a fifteen year old boy. Six foot tall but so narrow chested as to be almost invisible when seen from side on. I was stationed on one side of the anvil, while on the opposite side stood the third member of the team, a young man by the name of "Ivan". I am not at all sure that this was his real name, but he was a Ukrainian "Guest worker". He must have been almost seven feet in height, with shoulders as wide as the proverbial barn door. Pound for pound he would make at least three of me.

Ivan and I were given a ten-pound sledge hammer each. Herr Schultz, gripping the white hot steel with tongs, placed it on the anvil. On a signal from him, Ivan and I had to start hitting the work-piece with our long-handled hammers, keeping to a rhythm set by the him tapping on the anvil with a small hammer or by nodding his pate.

Everything considered, we didn't manage too badly. Other apprentices, who had been here before me, had warned me of the consequences of missing a beat or even missing the target, I had prepared myself. If it happened that you missed, the secret was to duck as quickly as possible. With a bit of luck the hammer thrown by the boss would miss you. Ivan didn't duck... he got it squarely in the chest, where it bounced off quite harmlessly. I wasn't prepared for the next bit, however. The white-hot bit of steel was wrenched out of the foreman's hand and landed back in the fire, while Herr Schultz was hoisted into the air by the scuff of his neck and held suspended in mid-air. Once he started to get blue in the face, he was released and dumped in a heap in the corner of the smithy, the poor old sod. By then, Ivan had calmed down and in his own way started to apologise for his reaction as well as getting an apology from the boss.

Peace had returned to the shop after what could have been a nasty international incident.

After this, every time I missed the target I still ducked automatically, but I needn't have bothered. A wide, toothless grin was all the punishment we ever got after this. I didn't know for sure whether that was for the better or not!

I believe Ivan stayed in his job until the end of the war. My education was furthered by his incessant accounts of his nightly encounters with the female guest workers at his lodgings, and told in broken German. I never knew whether to believe him or not, but I felt extreme pity for his ladies, as well as a being ashamed of my own inadequacy. He thought nothing of frequently whipping out his asset and showing it off in all its glory!

Bloody hell... how lucky can you get? Talk of a howitzer, the "Big Bertha" had nothing on him.

I did find it hard to believe his story, that the girls paid him in cigarettes for his favours. He didn't smoke himself but he always had some to hand out. I managed to scrounge a few, but the main beneficiary was Herr Schultz.

Talking of cigarettes reminds me of another little incident.

One had to understand, that in those days the daily cigarette ration for civilians over the age of eighteen was two cigarettes per day. Dad smoked only his old pipe, stuffed with his own home-grown and self-cured tobacco, known by all and sundry as "Railway embankment-early crop". It was avoided by everybody like the plague, particularly if the wind was in your direction. There was nothing to smoke for a fifteen year old, who had acquired the habit behind the school’s bicycle shed.

My Mum used to collect both her and Dad’s cigarette rations and every now and again send them to my brother.

But one day, on my return from work, I saw a French prisoner of War carrying bags of coal from the coalman’s lorry to our coal bunker. On his last trip, I saw Mum slipping a packet of fags into his coat pocket.

Hell!

Once the PoW had gone, I showed my annoyance by asking Mum what had possessed her to give those precious things to one of our enemies? Our Heinz could well do with those!

‘I expect you will never be in the same position as this French boy, but if you ever are... I can only hope to God that somebody will show some kindness to you!' she told me.

In later years I was to remember those words. They stayed imprinted on my mind and made me thoroughly ashamed of myself..

The remainder of this year went by reasonably uneventful.

After my work-experience in the blacksmith shop I spent one month with the electricians attached to the maintenance department. Although electrical work had little to do with toolmaking, it did give me an appreciation of the power and flexibility of this element and taught me to respect it properly.

Next came three months with the mechanics of the same maintenance department. They had the job of keeping all and every bit of machinery in the factory in proper working order. There was absolutely no excuse for any of the presses, furnaces, lathes, milling machines or any other kind of mechanical equipment being unavailable for production as and when needed.

Oil-cans and grease-guns were our principle weapons used to achieve that objective. Needless to say, Mum was not too enamoured with the greasy overalls I brought home to be washed. But it mollified her somewhat, when she realised how much I enjoyed working with machinery and how much I learned every day.

And of course there came a lengthy spell in the toolroom.

The principle products in here were moulds for the production of aircraft parts, to be use in huge drop-forge presses. Each mould was a very accurate mirror-image of the actual part to be produced and was in two parts. The bottom half was clamped on the bottom part of the press and the upper half was attached to the ram. A hot piece of aluminium of the correct weight or size was placed on the bottom tool and after closing safety guards, the ram was released to shoot down with almost unbelievable force, battering the aluminium pellet into the recognisable shape of a component for a *Messerschmidt* or *Junkers* plane. Hundreds of moulds had to be made, either for new designs or as replacements for worn or broken moulds.

Since all the younger toolmakers were drafted to serve in the various armed forces, the workshop was manned by elderly men. In peacetime they had followed other trades, some had been engravers or silversmiths, and others had made jewellery or repaired watches. All of them were very experienced in precision work and served as very capable taskmasters for us youngsters. We owed them a great debt.

Christmas 1941 appeared on the horizon and for a short spell we went back to the training school.

The three weeks leading up to Christmas proved to be quite eventful, things were happening in the East. The Nips had a go at the Yanks in Pearl Harbour and who could blame Uncle Sam after that, when he decided it was time to take a hand in the proceedings. It has been clear for some time that sooner or later he would come in against us. For years he had been supplying hundreds of ships, planes and other materials to Mister Churchill and his cronies.

As for us apprentices, we were allowed to work on individual projects. As long as we were prepared to pay for any of the materials, we had permission to take the finished articles home with us. Our factory was mainly engaged in working with aluminium, all kinds of shapes and profiles of that material were therefore freely available. This led most of the apprentices to build things like table-lamps, standard lamps or picture and mirror frames.

After machining the individual bits, some could be polished while others were coloured by an electro/chemical process called anodizing, provided you could talk nicely to the operators of that equipment or if you were able bribe them. The contrasting effects of some highly polished and mirror-like aluminium parts with other perhaps matt-black pieces were quite spectacular. But as usual, I had to be a little different.

I had started to build a scale model of one of the Navy's School Ships, on which Naval Cadets were being trained. The hull of the model and most of the other work had already been done at home but a number of important items were still to be manufactured. Aluminium rods of various diameters were the ideal material from which to make the masts, yards, spars and other parts for the riggings. It was a real help to be able to use a small lathe for a professional job. For sewing the sails, I borrowed Mum's Singer sewing machine. The terminology of sailing ships, clippers and windjammers were already known to me, when asked about the various bits I was turning, I was able to blind everybody with science. Upper Fore Top Gallant Yard, Spanker Boom, Main Lower Top Sail Yard, Jig Boom, Main Mast, Main Top Mast, and Main Gallant Mast... those words rolled off my tongue as if I had been a Jack Tar all my life.

Mounted on a stand, I entered the all-white model in a competition at work and won a first prize.

The combination of the sea and engineering had become an obsession with me. Engineering during the day and the sea in the evenings, when I would attend *Marine HJ* meetings in one of the neighbouring suburbs. An empty shop was made available to our unit to be made into a permanent headquarter. With everybody pitching in, we soon turned it into place of worship, a shrine to the sea and seafarers. A black-out-curtain, to go across the shop window, was supplied by one of the mothers, while a local church hall donate a dozen folding tables and folding benches. Four of those tables, when they were pushed together in the middle of the room, formed the base of a nearly-to-scale tableau depicting a river estuary and port with all its facilities. It was not based on any particular harbour, but it had all the usual features of a base like Kiel or Stettin, with miniature cargo loading and unloading facilities, a fishing boat jetty as well as military installations such as dry-docks, dock yard and U-boat bunkers. The harbour opened out into a bay. All the landscape and seascape was made from paper-mache and painted realistically. Scale models of ships, such as a battleships, a couple of cruisers, some destroyers, frigates, U-boats, torpedo boats, an Ocean-liner, tanker, cargo ships trawlers, windjammer, yachts etc. were made as well as lighthouses, different types of buoys and lightships. In fact we finished with a set-up, which was so variable, as to allow many different situations to be created. We could illustrate the "highway code" of the sea, who had the right of way over other vessels. We could also show how wrecks were marked with special buoys, as well as marking deep-water channels in and out of the port. At a model shore-station we had a scale flagpole on which we could display miniature flag-signals spelling out different messages in an international flag-code. Every member of our group had contributed something to all this and whenever something else was required, somebody would volunteer to get it.

My biggest contributing was the scale model of the *Gorch Fock*, because once it was finished with all the riggings, stays, sheets and sails, as well as capstans and different types of anchors, it could be used in lectures to illustrate the history of the age of sail.

Placed around the walls were more tables and benches to accommodate as many as 50 boys. The size of our actual group stationed here, was nearer a hundred. But this was sub-divided into three sections of about thirty-five each. I always assumed that the structure of the *HJ* was in the first instance based on the Scout Movement, out of which it grown at the start of the Third Reich. Because the premises were not large enough, each one of the three sections would meet on a different evening during the winter months.

Along one of the sidewalls we had made a display of every knot or hitch known to mankind, as well as spliced joints of hemp, sisal or wire rope. Example of blocks and tackle, anchor-chains, shackles, rigging screws and lots of other devices used in the rigging of a ship. On the opposing wall, the boys had collected pictures, paintings and posters, which showed nearly every unit of the present day *Kriegsmarine* as well as silhouettes of assorted Merchant Ships to aid identification.

Bookshelves housed a collection of manuals, textbooks, almanacs, charts and other naval books. In the back was a storeroom, which we used to store all our gear. At one of the many yacht anchorages on the river Havel, in the western part of the city, we kept a 15 m long double-banked, clinker-built cutter, mostly used for rowing practice and competitions races against other units in Berlin. A total of twelve oars as well as the rudder and tiller were kept in the store. A set of masts and sails was also there, but it was seldom used, as it was too cumbersome. Other goods stored there were life jackets, ropes, signal flags, Morse-lamps and semaphore flags and a thousand and one other things. I can tell you, that we were extremely proud to have created a little bit of the *Waaterkant* ('Water's edge' as the coasts of the North Sea and the Baltic were known as) in the middle of Landlubber country.

As in many other youth organisation, exams were taken in the various skills. For instance, once you could send and read Morse signals at a certain rate, or send and read semaphore flag signals at the required speed, you could take a test and if you passed you could wear a special badge on the right sleeve of your uniform. Some of us were proud to have the whole sleeve covered with them. Best of all I enjoyed the instructions about navigation, chart reading and plotting of the course after establishing you position by using sextants to 'shoot stars'. The sextants we used could only be used at certain times of a day, when both the stars as well as the horizon were to be seen. Properly used, it established the angle between the horizon and a given star. Nominal values for each star could be found in tables or charts. Comparing those with your sextant findings would give you a line in the sea, where your position was somewhere on that line. By taking another reading, preferably at right angles to your previous one you would establish another line. At the intersection of both lines your present position would be found on the sea-chart.

On a flat calm lake around Berlin, this method of finding your position can be fun. Even to us landlubbers, however, it was quite obvious that on the bridge of a tiny U-boat, in the middle of the Atlantic in a storm force 10 or 12 this necessary job could be a proper nightmare. Since a sextant is a system of lenses and mirrors, keeping the spray off it while peering through the eyepiece would be a major miracle. Yet a system such as this had been used for hundreds of years by all the seafaring nations, as the only method of navigation available to them. In sight of land, lighthouses with their own individual light-sequences or newly developed radio beacons can be more accurate and certainly more pleasant.

'Heaving the log' to measure your speed through the water was another of the necessary aids to navigation. The old-fashioned way of slinging a block of wood overboard at the bow of the ship and with a stopwatch measure the time it takes to pass your stern, had already been superseded by a propeller type device which, when towed behind the ship, would indicate the actual speed through the water on a dial. The problem all seafarers faced was to convert that knowledge into actual speed over the seabed, when wind, tides, and drift had to be taken into account as well.

Another piece of useful information for navigation, particularly in coastal waters, was to be gained from 'swinging the lead'. It had nothing to do with being lazy or with 'dodging the column' but was the name given to the measuring of water depth below the keel of the ship or boat. All charts showed shallows, sandbanks and deep-water channels and noted their depths. If for instance you had established your position on the chart, which showed the depth of water to be 15 metres by swinging the lead you found that there were only 4 metres below the keel, then you knew for sure that you were in entirely the wrong place and that very shortly you would be left high and dry on a sandbank. The actual lead was a sort of bell shaped and in its larger bottom end it had a recess filled with tallow or thick grease. When it touched the bottom, the tallow would pick-up some debris. The depth could then be established by counting the number of knots, which had passed through your hand at that point and you could also see what the sea bottom was made of. As with most things, after using the lead for hundreds of years, they were now mostly superseded by echo sounders.

My interest in all this was rewarded with a three-week training course on board the said training ship 'Gorch Fock'. It was named after a famous writer of sea-stories, who lived in the first part of this century and who gave his life at the Battle of Jutland while serving in the Imperial Navy. I already knew this vessel fairly well (at least, as a model at the reduced scale of 100 to 1).

On the train to Stralsund, I could enlighten my fellow travellers with my superior knowledge. 'She is 90 metres long and has a total of 22 sails totalling 2,000 square metres of canvass. She has three masts, the tallest of which is 45 metres high.'

But nothing had prepared us for the vision of sheer elegance and beauty, with which we were confronted. The sleek, snowy white hull, offset by a touch of crimson at the water line and topped by a mass of masts, yards, shrouds and stays, presented a postcard picture of days gone by.

Tied-up between two mooring-buoys, she was gently moving with the swell caused by small boats plying back and forth in the harbour, on the coast of the Baltic Sea.

Our group of about one hundred Naval Hitler Youths were ferried across to the ship in small groups. To most of us landlubbers this was the first time we had seen a port of any size. It also was the first opportunity, and probably the last one, to set a foot on a square-rigger.

As we proceeded on the gangway, we were greeted with shouts of 'Get your bloody boots off'. Once on board in our stocking feet, we were allowed to rummage around in our kit bags for the crepe-soled sailing shoes, which we had been ordered to bring along. All this palaver seemed a bit like typical Navy bullshit, but we were soon given to understand the reason for all this. Wooden decks do not take kindly to hob-nailed boots.

Come to think of it, here on board a U-boat we also had to wear rubber-soled shoes, but for a much different reason. Because our deck-plates were made of metal, any other soles would be too noisy and could probably overheard by nosy people with big ears and who were set to finish us.

Lined up on deck, three abreast in military fashion, we were addressed by the ship's captain. A Commander by rank, he spoke to us from the railings on the quarterdeck, some 2 m above us. He welcomed us aboard, stressing the fact that we were privileged to be here and that it was up to us to take the fullest advantage of this opportunity presented to us.

Well! We knew all that anyway.

Sail Training Ship "Gorch Fock"

He explained that normally this ship would be crewed by about 200 cadets. Along with the instructors and Officers, this was the number of men required to sail it. But unfortunately in wartime the training of Officers had to be curtailed; there wasn't enough time to train them on school-ships any more. The Navy was keen to return to normal as soon as possible after the war and kept a skeleton staff of instructors on board. They kept their hand in by training lads like us - future officers?

He followed by telling us, 'Of course, it won't be possible to take the ship out under sail, but otherwise your training will be identical to that of cadets.'

We were screened according to our past experience in seamanship, divided into three watches and subdivided into groups of about 8-10 boys. As one of the oldest and most advanced, I joined the top group of the first watch. It was headed by a Chief Petty Officer, who wore the insignia of those wounded in action as well as the U-boat broach and the Iron Cross 2nd Class. On first sight there seemed to be nothing wrong with him, but later, when we went for a swim, we saw that he had only one leg. The other one he could sling over his shoulder.

As usual, I struck lucky. The guys in our group were just as keen as I was to use this opportunity to further their knowledge. Our instructor soon caught on and really put us through our paces, although in a good-humoured kind of way.

Issued with a set of working-kit and a hammock complete with bedding, he took us down below, to show us our quarters, where we could stow our few belongings.

We had already spent most of the day travelling and were more than ready to be fed.

But where is the dining room, somebody asked innocently?

Stupid question!

'This is it. There are folding tables and folding benches for our use, but when at sea you would probably sit anywhere on the deck.'

But where do we sleep?

Stupid question again!

'See those ringbolts above you? This is where you sling your hammock.'

'And this is also your living room and your classroom and in the old days this was the place where you worked.

Backshafters (sailors who, according to a roster, collected food in big cans from the galley and followed by clearing the decks after eating) were appointed for this day.

The food, when it did arrive, tasted magnificent. It must be the sea-air.

Afterwards, our instructor showed us the timetables for the next two weeks.

They were organised in such a fashion that none of the groups would be in each other's way. I suppose the organisers had plenty of experience in dealing with ignorant lots like us. There wouldn't be much time for ourselves, not that we had expected anything else. We hadn't come all this way for a holiday.

Our instructor showed us where to sling the hammocks. Their lanyards (ropes to the uninitiated) were tied or lashed to the ringbolts above our heads. I thought I managed extremely well. But bless me! The instructor thought otherwise. He ordered the whole group to come and look at my effort. 'Now here's an example of how not to tie a hammock!' he told them. 'This is how it should be done' he demonstrated a simple example of a slipknot. 'Can anyone tell me why it should be fastened with a slip-knot?' Well! That was an easy one for us. It's surely done this way to give the boatswain a chance to tip us out on deck, if we didn't get up quick enough on hearing the piped signal to 'show a leg.'

It sounded plausible enough and everyone nodded in agreement with that suggestion.

But we might have known that there was a much better reason for it - one based on the history of the old 'Men-of-War'.

The deck such as ours, directly below the quarterdeck, in addition to all the other functions already mentioned, was also the Gun Deck.

2, 24 or 32 pounder guns on that deck had to be made ready in double-quick time in times of emergency. Gun-ports had to be dropped and ammunition had to be moved to the guns. There was no room for hammocks hanging round gunners necks and not too much time to get rid of them.

Hence the slipknot as one tug at the loose end of the lanyards and they were clear. There was no time to undo elaborate knots and it saved the ropes being cut by a sharp knife or an officer's sabre.

Ah, well! We did come here to learn, didn't we?

As for the hammocks themselves, they were just great. Even here, in the slight swell in the harbour, there was a constant creaking to be heard, which came from the lanyards rubbing against the eyebolts or hooks on the beams. Inside the waxed sailcloth outer part of the hammock there was a thin mattress and a blanket with a washable cover. All in all, quite enough to keep a tired Jack Tar as snug as a bug in a rug. The instructor told us that our hammocks here on the school-ship were more or less identical to the ones used by seafarers all over the world in the old days of sail, with the possible exception of refinements like washable covers for the mattresses.

Before 'Lights out' out instructor warned us that first thing in the morning we would have to parade on deck with our life rafts.

What life rafts? Have I missed something? I haven't been issued with one. My mates in the hammocks beside me were just as puzzled as I was, before we all crashed-out, thoroughly exhausted.

The fresh sea air and the food, which tasted so much better aboard ship, made sure that all of us slept well, dreamless and without needing to turn over as that would have been difficult in a hammock.

And so it came about that at 6 am in the morning, when the boatswains whistle called to "show a leg", we jumped out on deck thoroughly rested and eager to get dressed for another day of adventure.

'Right, men! I am going to demonstrate how to turn your hammock into a life raft.'

Thus he showed us how fold-in the top and the bottom ends and then to roll-up the outer part, the oiled sailcloth part, tightly and tidily and finally lash it together with the little bits of thin rope which were sawn on the outside of the hammock. Our comfortable beds had now become sausage-shaped rolls of waterproof sailcloth, which in cases of shipwreck at sea were the sailors life rafts. If the hammock has been properly trussed, the trapped air inside the outer cloth will provide the buoyancy to survive in the water for at least some hours.

'I want you to practice the rolling-up and lashing for the next hour, at the end of which I want you parade up on deck, together with your hammocks, when I will inspect them.

It should now be said that this procedure did absolutely nothing for our still very delicate hands and it certainly wiped out any of our fingernails. At the end of our practice we assembled on deck and at which point we expected to be praised for our not inconsiderable efforts. Instead of which our man threw the lot overboard into the water.

Now we will see who has done the job properly and who has not. Some of you, if you find that you are sleeping on a wet mattress, will try and do a better lashing job in future.'

During the remainder of the next weeks we were made to sweat. Up and down in the riggings, scrubbing the wooden deck with a type of pumice stone to avoid men slipping in high seas, splicing hemp and wire ropes, weighing and dropping anchor with eight men on a capstan running in circles to the singing sea shanties, practicing Morse and semaphore until our arms dropped off and any other job which seafarers all over the world had to put up with.

Lucky us! We were doing it all in the calm waters of the harbour.

Those thoughts about the past few years raced through my mind a lot quicker than I am able to relate them. However, there isn't a better place in the world to relive all those memories, happy or otherwise, than the pre-warmed bunk of a U-boat such as our ***KARO-AS***.

Not long after, I manage to drop off to sleep, dreaming of the friends we left behind in Bremen.

After two hours of my next watch, at around 6 o'clock in the evening, the very comfortable trip through the canal ended. Before ***KARO-AS*** could enter the Bay of Kiel, the most westerly part of the Baltic Sea, she had to go through the Holtenauer Locks, where any differences in sea level between the North Sea and the Bay of Kiel were taken care of.

So far so good! Sooner or later every German sailor had to come to Kiel, the birthplace of the modern German *Kriegsmarine*. Today it was our turn, but to our dismay, we were only passing through and we weren't given a chance of going ashore to get to know this 'Mecca' of ours. That opportunity would probably come at the end of our working-up period, before we leave on our first enemy patrol.

Our Old Man and the *2WO* had gone ashore for a briefing, while the Chief supervised the taking-on of more fuel and a few more provisions. There appeared to be a great shortage of '*Sprit'* (fuel) and a strict rationing system was in operation. We were only given enough diesel fuel to make it to our new homeport Stettin, where we were to join the 4th U-boat Flotilla and where our boat would be kitted-out for the working-up trials ahead of us.

As our luck would have it, we didn't get much sleep on that night either.

Shortly before midnight the air raid sirens howled their tiresome message all over the Bay. Since the Old Man was still at HQ, the *1WO* took over the command. The 22 years old Sub-Lieutenant Schwarz was not the highest ranked officer on board, both the Chief Engineer and the MO were more senior but as the Officer of the First Watch he was in fact the Old Man's understudy. And didn't he let everybody it? Different from the Old Man, he had the mannerisms of the old-fashioned Prussian Officer, which didn't go down all that well with others on board. But, give him his due, he made sure that we didn't hang around and wait for Tommy's birds to drop things down our funnel.

He immediately ordered 'stations' and 'prepare to cast-off'. With all haste ***KARO-AS*** and every other U-boat moored at the base, made their way out into the bay. Scattered over a wide area and under the cover of darkness, some 20 boats stayed there most of the night until the 'all-clear' was sounded at 0400 hours. Returning to the base, we picked up our CO and finished preparations for our passage to Stettin.

On this occasion Kiel hadn't been Tommy's target and we weren't going to hang around to see whether he would return another time. A few weeks later, in a letter from my mother, I learned that Berlin had been their destination on that night.

CHAPTER THREE

After we cast-off for our onward journey, the weather had taken a turn for the worst. The Old Man set a course, which took her right over to the northeastern side of the one kilometre wide inlet. Less than 100 metres offshore, ***KARO-AS*** hugged the coastline while steaming at 'slow-ahead both engines'.

We wondered - why doesn't he stay in the centre of the channel? It soon became clear. All hands not required down below were ordered on deck, where we had to line up, seamen on the forecastle, stokers on the quarterdeck, all of us facing landward. Ahead, on a piece of land which jutted out into the water, stood a high column topped by a golden eagle.

Over the tannoy, we heard the Old Man's commentary.

U-Boat Memorial
Möltenort

'The column ahead at Möltenort is our own U-boat Memorial, erected in honour of the five thousand U-boat men who lost their lives during the 1914/1918 war. They represented 50 percent of all men who served in the Imperial U-boat fleet. Their names are remembered on tall bronze-tablets at the base of the column.'

It's funny how your mind works in those situations. I could almost imagine that one day our own names might be part of this metallic record. Trouble is, that that would mean our premature demise.

Not the most pleasant thought to have at this time!

Perhaps I should show a little more faith in that scrap of paper in my pay- book, the remnants of my lucky ***KARO-AS***?

As we drew near, the Old Man called the crew to stand to attention, the officers on the bridge saluted while our battle ensign was being dipped in the age-old way in which seafarers showed their respect.

A few miles further on, also on our starboard side, an even larger and more imposing stone column reached for the sky. It was the memorial by which all the sailors of the Imperial navy, who had fallen in WWI, were remembered.

Navy Memorial
Laboe

As before, our ship and her crew showed their respect to our dead comrades. To us rookie-sailors this was almost too much, we felt choked and tears were not far away. Those sailors gave their lives for us and for our country, which raised the question: 'Will we would prove ourselves worthy of them?'

We did not dwell on this very long after we were ordered to stand down. It was back to the old routine.

Once we were out of the Bay of Kiel, ***KARO-AS*** started to get her first taste of the short and choppy seas of the Baltic. Like all landlubbers, I had always imagined the Baltic to be an overgrown sweet-water lake, with numerous sandy beaches and quaint seaside resorts created for the enjoyment of holidaymakers. It did therefore come as a big surprise, when we realised that at storm force 9 or 10 the sea around here could be just as nasty and unpleasant as any other ocean. This was no consolation for those of us who had not yet acquired proper sea legs.

Not that the Baltic was a small backwater either. It reached up 1600 kilometres from Kiel to the Gulf of Bothnia, which was almost up on the Arctic Circle. This sea also afforded direct access to city of Leningrad via the Gulf of Finland. In some places it was more than 250 kilometres wide. Surely that would give us more than enough room to spread our wings. Pity we had to get to know it on a day like this, as both Werner and I were as sick as dogs. We presented the most pitiful sight imaginable, trying to go about our normal work while retching and retching, until there was nothing else to bring up. The wish for a quick and merciful death was not all that far from our minds.

We did not receive a lot of sympathy from the older hands either. Petty Officer Gebler didn't look at all well himself, if you go by the colour of his face, which was as yellow as those of our comrades in arms, the Japanese. Although he must have faced many a storm at sea, it was on large battleships and not on a vessel more suited for life below the waves. He did offer some valuable advice. 'There's no shame in being ill, everybody has to go through this, but while on watch you must be able to carry out you normal duties. We couldn't carry a pail round with us so we just tied an empty tin can round our necks with a piece of string. Whenever we feel the urge, just...'

'OK, OK, that's enough. Please spare us the details.'

Our CPO Schultz had some further advice. It had to do with the fact that it was inadvisable to bring up certain things, organs etc, which might still be needed afterwards. Not going into too fine a detail, it seemed biologically impossible anyway. Anybody, who had ever been seriously sea sick, would understand what he meant.

I, for my part, was just glad that our folks at home couldn't see us in our hour of misery. After swaggering about like Old Salts, whose homes were the oceans of the world, it would have been a very nasty shock for them to see us in our present state - miserable examples of human misfits. However, in the meantime, the trick with the tin cans worked perfectly and we got on with our tasks in between bouts of spewing. (This trick was to become standard procedure in the future, whenever the different oceans sprang surprises on us.)

When it came to the end of our spell, the port-watch presented itself, also looking like death warmed up. After handing over and informing them of the advice we'd received from our superiors, Werner said 'I'll give the usual smoking session a miss today and get my head down.' That was exactly how I felt as well. When we got back to our bunks, everybody else, diesel stokers, electricians, helmsmen and even our torpedo mixer were in similar distress, but just as we had to do, they kept going, in spite of everything the sea threw at them. But unfortunately, one of our pals, the diesel hand August Andreas, who hailed from the mountains of the Bavarian Alps, just couldn't get up from his bunk although it was his turn for watch duty. He might have been shit-hot on a pair of skies up on top of the mountains, since he claimed that he had been his village's downhill champion, but he looked a dreadful sight aboard ***KARO-AS***. We tried everything. We coaxed him, we threatened him and we appealed to his sense of duty.

'How do you think we feel. We're all in the same boat! For all our sakes make a bloody effort.' It was all to no avail; he just wanted to die. 'Let's hope that he'll get over it. Otherwise it'll mean trouble for the poor sod.' Even the MO couldn't help him; it was left to his diesel colleagues to take extra turns on watch to cover for him.

Once Werner and I got our heads down, we felt better, although there was a lot of up and down movement added to the rolling of the boat. When you thought about it and in my state I didn't really want to think too much, the bow and the stern must be the worst places on board in a stormy sea, because it was quite bad enough in the middle of the boat, the control room.

Afterwards, when my stomach has had time to settle down, I looked at the mess-cans hanging from hooks above us, to see what had become of our dinner.

One look was enough to see that our *lieber Smutje* (dear cook) had a kinky streak in him. *Lapskaus* (similar to lobscouse) was a traditional sailor's dish composed of minced salt-herring, cooked meat, pickled gherkins, potatoes, onions and mixed together with lots of beetroot. If the smell or the taste didn't make you throw up, the sight of the reddish mix was sure to do. If you felt brave enough after eating that lot, there was also a pinkish looking pudding, made of what looked like sticky frog's spawn.

Bless you, *Smutje*, we must think of a way to thank you and get our own back on you. Anyway, looking at his offerings I decided that I wasn't hungry after all, but there were those who were cashing in on our discomfort.

The call came through from the Petty Officers mess 'Any *Lapskaus* left?' Those gannets, unaffected by seasickness, liked nothing better than to gorge themselves on the colourful stuff.

The rocking motion and the steady beat of the engines eventually knocked me out. When it was our turn to go back on watch at 0200 hours, the sea had taken pity on us and calmed down. We were still ploughing along at a steady pace and the rumour was that we should reach Stettin by some time in the morning.

Meanwhile we had fallen into a routine at our station in the control room and any spare time we had was taken up with further tuition in preparation for our forthcoming first dive. One of our routine tasks on every watch consisted of collecting a sample of seawater and checking it for its *Sp.G.* (specific gravity), i.e. its salt contents.

Why did we have to do that? When we asked our PO Ebler that question, he told us it was because it said so in the instruction book. However, we learned from other sources that there was more to it than meets the eye.

Many hundred or even thousands of years before submarines were invented, clever mathematicians had studied to see what happens when a body of certain size and weight was immersed, or partially immersed in water. They decided that theoretically a floating body of a known weight displaces an amount of water of equivalent weight. Sounds extremely complicated, but how does it relate to submarines?

It simply means that if the weight of a submarine is heavier than the water it displaces, it will sink and if it is lighter it will float upwards to the surface. To stay at a predetermined depth its weight will have to equal to the weight of water it displaces. Submariners have invented an expression for this very desirable state.

It is called ZERO-TRIM.

To take care of any body weight/volume discrepancies, submarines are fitted with ballast tanks, which can be filled with water to make the boat heavier and which can also be emptied to make it lighter.

This takes care of one side of the equation.

But the other side of the same equation has to be taken into consideration as well. The way we were given to understand this is as follows: A given volume of fresh water, say one litre, weighs one kilogram, but a litre of sea-water can weigh as much as 1.030 kg, i.e. it can vary by as much as 3 % depending on the amount of salt in the water. For instance, here in the Baltic Sea, with its many fresh-water rivers feeding it, the salt content is relatively small. Perhaps only 1 %, but the North Sea and the Atlantic can have as much as 3%. We were demonstrated how this variation can materially affect the behaviour of submarines. If we were to move across from the Baltic to the North Sea without adjusting the weight of the boat, we would find a lovely ZERO TRIM or virtual weightlessness in the first, but experience increased buoyancy in the second. The weight of our boat would have to be increased by as much as 2%, which in our case would mean adding approximately 40 tonnes of water ballast to obtain the same ZERO TRIM.

Of course that would not be done in one fell swoop, but gradually during each watch change. As I have mentioned, it was our duty at the start of every watch, to check the salt content of the water surrounding us, by means of a hydrometer. Floating in a container it would indicate on a scale on the side of the instrument the *Sp. G*, which in turn was noted down in a type of log against the date and time. By comparing each new reading with the last one, ballast was added or subtracted. Of course the whole procedure takes less time, than it took to explain it to us, but it meant that by surface travelling the boat would always be prepared for emergency diving in the best trim condition. There are other occasions when adjustments to the trim have to be done, but those we would learn about later.

Pheeew!!

Well! Well! Doesn't time fly when you are enjoying yourself? At 0800, at the end of our watch, we got permission to come upstairs for fresh air. There was land on either side of us and a pilot was already on the bridge, busily giving instructions to the helmsman.

'Are we in the river already, Wilhelm?' I asked the nearest lookout.

'No, but nearly! Over there on starboard is Swienemünde on the isle of Usedom and that's the isle of Wollin. Ahead is the Bay of Stettin, through which we must pass before entering the river proper.' 'So you've been here before,' I said, to which he replied, 'I was born here.'

A fellow lookout had overheard my inquiry and butted into our conversation with his words of wisdom 'Keep in with Wilhelm if you want to know where to find the best tarts in Stettin.' I ignored him as I had already realised that Wilhelm was easily embarrassed. Of course, he had told me some time ago, when we shared quarters in Bremen, that he came from a farming background. 'Our little village is just inland from the town, on the western banks of the river' he said. 'It isn't a big farm and my mum and my dad work like slaves to make a living from it. But they wouldn't have it any other way; at least they're their own bosses.' He hesitated for a moment and continued, 'Maybe you and I can wangle a day's leave while we're here and you can meet them.'

'I'd love to, particularly to meet that old nag of yours, the one you've been boasting about.'

'Exactly, it'll be your chance to see a real horse.'

When we arrived at the base, home of the 4th Flotilla, ***KARO-AS*** was tied-up to a pack of four other boats. It gave us a chance to say Hello to some old friends. The boat next to us was our sister boat, the '*HERZ-AS',* the Ace of Hearts, which had been build at the same yard and commissioned three weeks before us. They already had their new *Flak* (***F****lieger* ***A****bwehr* ***K****anonen)* or anti-aircraft guns installed, two twin-mounted 20 mm guns on the bridge come wintergarden and one quadruple-mounted 20 mm gun on the lower wintergarden. 'That's quite a bit of fire-power you've got there, but I take it you're waiting to have the usual 10.5 cannon fitted on the mounting in front of the conning tower?' I asked Paul Berger, whom I had first met at U-boat school and who was now serving on the Ace of Hearts.

'We may or we may not get one prior to leaving for our first patrol' he replied. 'The opinion around here seems to be that battles fought on the surface are a thing of the past, as every square centimetre of the oceans can now be patrolled by enemy aircraft from either land bases or aircraft carriers.'

That evening Werner and I met Paul and his friend Peter at a bar ashore and over a few beers we compared notes about our experiences since our commissioning. Being four weeks ahead of us, they had already spent a lot of time off Danzig, practising diving manoeuvres and they were likely to continue with those after re-supplying. 'We still have some work to do to get down to a diving-time of 30 seconds from the alarm-bell to the time of levelling-off at periscope depth.'

At a guess, I would say that we would be following a similar routine.

As the evening went on, and our tongues got a little looser, Paul told us about his CO. In fact we got the impression that he thought the world of the *Kapitainleutnant*, who in the summer of 1942 was in command of a Type

IXC boat, with which he carried out some very successful patrols. As it so happened, or so it was said, he had a brother Erich, a Scientist at a rocket research station somewhere on the Baltic. Collaborating, the two brothers tried out an idea to see whether it would be possible to fire rockets from a submerged submarine. A crude iron-framework, holding six 8 cm diameter rockets at an angle of 45 degrees, was bolted on to the after deck of the Type IXC boat and eventually successfully fired from something like periscope depth. Propelled by solid fuel and ignited electrically from inside the boat, they took off and travelled some kilometres before touching down. The rockets were not sophisticated enough to be guided to a specific target and since nothing more has been heard by any of us about these trials, we guessed that they had been dropped for lack of interest. The idea was probably too radical to be taken seriously by the establishment.

But thinking about it later I was ready to bet my last *Pfennig,* that out there in the big wide world, somewhere, sometime, a boffin or a submarine expert will be racking his brain how to do something similar with bigger and more advanced rockets, such as the Doodle Bug V1.

Next day the rest of the crew went to explore Stettin. Money was burning a hole in their pockets, because there had been very little opportunity to spend it. Before leaving Bremen, all four of us control-room crew had been raised to the rank of Able Seaman (or the equivalent for stokers) which meant a raise in pay. In addition, U-boat crews were better paid than any other branch of the services.

To our dismay, both Werner and I, in accordance with the normal roster, had to stay behind to do guard-duty over our beloved ***KARO-AS***. Although we would have liked to join the communal spending spree, we had to give the festivities a miss. While I was patrolling the quayside, Werner covered me from the bridge of our boat. With our MP 40 machine pistols slung round our necks we watched helplessly as all our mates made tracks for the bright lights.

'Seeing that we're stuck here, please find out for us where we'll get the best beer and the best talent; but do please remember to get your password right when you stagger back drunk out of your tiny minds. Because if you don't, you are liable to get your backside shot off'. This wasn't exactly how I put it, but I think my friends got the message.

Those spells of guarding our ship, while she was moored in either a base or a dockyard, had become a part of our lives; a part, which any normal person would try to avoid, as one would avoid contact with the bubonic plague. Usually it had the effect of grossly interfering with your life ashore, particularly your love life. In addition, there was a certain amount of bull involved. Petty Officer Gebler and six men were involved on this day, and needless to say, he was the only one enjoying himself.

While Werner and I were on duty, he made the other off-duty mates of ours study function of our MP40 machine pistols. At this time we didn't have a weapons mechanic in our crew. He only started when the AK-AK was installed. Hence any servicing and cleaning had to be done without his help. Werner and I were similarly put to the test after we were relieved from our two-hour spell.

'This is just like being back at our basic training,' Werner observed. He went on to tell us about the few weeks as a recruit in North Germany and from what he and all the other fellow guards said, their training time seemed to have been a lot more basic than mine. The difference may have been that they all did theirs in Germany, while I did mine in occupied Holland. We continued to compare notes, but nothing seemed to explain why they did theirs in a few weeks, while I did almost five months of it. It didn't occur to me then, but maybe we were being used to bolster the military presence along the coastline opposite England - in case of invasion? It would have sent a signal to London that the place was crawling with soldiers. My mates couldn't explain it either, after I had told them about the things we got up to in Holland

In May 1943 I found myself among many other 17 or 18 years old chaps on my way to the town of Breda in Holland. I was not alone in thinking that before very many days we would find ourselves on board ship. Since things were not always going our way in the war, it made sense to give new recruits only the most basic training and then get them into action without further delay. Of course, nothing is ever what it seems.

Every sailor fit to serve on a ship had to know how to 'Left Turn', 'Right Turn', 'About Turn', 'Shoulder Arms', 'Stand at Ease', 'Present Arms', as well as 'Eyes Right', 'Eyes Left' and best of all how to 'Fall Out'. All activities were performed at the double or even quicker. Until we were allowed to wear real sailors outfits, we had to do with regulation 'Field Grey' Army uniforms plus steel-helmet. The bell-bottoms etc had to wait until we were fit to be seen to parade in public. Several months of training had to be done by hook or by crook, which we thought a senseless waste of precious time! Even before we did all the "Square Bashing" I've mentioned, we made our very first acquaintance with the Company's barber shop.

In went a normal human being and out came an unrecognisable Recruit No. UN 18898/43.

Another batch of new recruits arriving in BREDA, Holland.

Barrack gates to basic training division BREDA, Holland
-but where is the "Lamp-post"?

Those particular ceremonies were followed another ones, which continued for several days. The immunisation against almost every disease known to mankind such as Smallpox, Typhus or Paratyphus, Cholera and Scarlet fever was administered to either the top of the arm, the chest or the buttocks.

With malice, every place for the inoculation was cleverly chosen to provide the recipient with the maximum of discomfort or even pain when going through the square-bashing routine, which followed almost immediately after.

Oh yes! There was one other important medical matter, which had to be sorted out before we could be called sailors and let loose on the civilian population ashore! We had to be introduced to, and be made aware of, the evils of venereal- disease. A series of lectures were given with the help of some educational films, all cleverly designed to put us off sex for the rest of our natural lives. Or so we concluded after seeing horror films showing male private parts eaten away by primary Syphilis, looking like half-eaten sausages, as well as being shown the effects of other forms of V.D.

This was followed by casually bringing to our notice a list of charges, which would be brought against anybody careless enough to catch even a common complaint such as gonorrhoea, better known as a *Tripper* (the Clap). A Court-martial awaited the careless.

Apart from the welfare of our penises, our superiors seemed to be equally concerned with running noses and unkempt hair.

Why?

Because in future, every time we were inspected prior to going ashore, we had to produce a spotless hankie, a grease-free comb as well as the free-issue condom (reputed to be recycled bicycle tyres).

Soon after this we were kitted out with our blue Naval uniforms, Bell-bottoms and all the rest.

At last!

We've been looking forward to this day when we would finally look like old tars. In spite of all the other reasons for joining the Navy, there was the magic of a Sailor's uniform and the imagined effect it was supposed to have on all the girls everywhere. But nobody could have foreseen how much practice it required to wriggle into a Navy-blue blouse or shirt and how to preserve the sharp creases in your bellbottoms. After this we had to get rid of the 'Rookie' look by first of all getting rid of the wire stiffeners inside our cap in order to pull it over to one ear and arranging for the width of our bellbottom flare to be increased.

At long last - "We are Sailors now."

But before that, a passport-size *Soldbuch* (Pay-book) photo was taken, one that made us look like convicts. By recording our latest hairstyle for posterity, it also made sure that even our loving mothers would not recognise the image as one of their siblings.

To make sure that we wouldn't get lost, we were issued with an oval metal disc, which had our allocated number engraved on it and which became our constant companion dangling from a string round our necks. The *Erkennungsmarke* (Dog-tag) was never to be removed while we were still alive.

Thereafter followed the most important part of our initiation. To officially become members of the German Armed Forces, we were required to swear allegiance to our *Vaterland und Führer.* This is when our initial square-bashing came in handy, as it taught us to march in step to the forecourt of the castle of Breda, where this very important ceremony took place. Here the five companies of some 750 new recruits were drawn up five deep on three sides of a square. The forth side was made-up by a ceremonial 'Guard of honour', the Regimental Band and a party of guests from other units of the Armed Service. Fanfares, an inspection of the Guard of Honour and patriotic Music, all added to the general 'Pomp' of the occasion. Few of us could hear the rousing speech made by the Admiral from the flag-bedecked platform in the middle of the square, followed by the actual swearing of the 'Oath of Allegiance'. One member from each Company was selected to go on to the platform, to hold in their left hand the Regimental Flag and with their right hand raised, swear on behalf of all of us new recruits to defend our *Vaterland.*

One member from each Company is taking the Oath of Allegiance on behalf of all recruits.

I for one found this ceremony to be a very moving experience. Somehow I sensed that the end of playtime had arrived and that now the serious part of soldiering had begun. We had committed ourselves to fight for our country as professional servicemen. The history of the German Navy, always inferior in size to other navies, but never lacking fighting spirit and enterprise, made us proud to be part of that force. We would surely do our duty to our country without hate in our hearts and with respect for our enemies.

Since we now had all the required knowledge to start our actual naval career, not one of us could see what possible purpose was there to prolong our presence here by another 2 to 3 months. Somebody, somewhere, must know something, which had not occurred to any of us poor souls. We knew that things didn't go our way all the time, but surely they were not going to send us to join the men at the Russian front?

On lonely guard duty

Anti-Aircraft watch

To make sure that we could use a rifle like real soldiers, we spend the next few weeks travelling back and forth to a rifle range riding on iron torture instruments. Everybody called them 'Fietje' and they looked just like ordinary bicycles dating back to WWI or earlier and definitely were designed to suit well-upholstered Dutch bottoms much better than ours.

With my usual luck, however, I managed to miss a lot of the boring training, by being admitted to a local Hospital with suspected Diphtheria. I had a very sore and inflamed throat and I must admit to receiving the very best nursing care in this small hospital, which by the way was run by Dutch Nuns. The pink coloured pills I had to swallow by the handful were OK, but until today a can feel the 50cc injection I received and which was administered by the gentlest of Nuns. Apologising profusely and with the loveliest of wrist turns to and fro, she proceeded to take nearly a minute to bore the needle into my left buttock while watching me gradually climbing up the wall. Having been used to the short sharp jab of a Naval Doctors to give you a punch on the selected spot and ramming the needle in simultaneously before shouting: 'Next', I have often wondered, whether this was her way of getting even with a member of the occupying forces. Perhaps afterwards, by way of a prayer, he asked to be forgiven for her sins.

But my mates from our group, also my Company Commander made sure that I lacked nothing in the way of reading materials, cigarettes, food and sweets. My complaint was finally diagnosed as a throat abscess followed by discharge to join my fellow recruits. In fact I was just in time to accompany them on a train to the Dutch west coast. We travelled in first class carriages; even the straw on the floor of the cattle trucks was spotless.

During the next few weeks we had a lovely time on manoeuvres, bringing back childhood memories of playing Cowboys and Indians.

At various times we were also required to stand guard over bridges spanning several canals and that proved to be quite scary. We were trained to work in the dark in emergencies, but that was in the confines of a U-boat and not outside in an occupied country. If ever there was to be an invasion by the Allies, thanks to my usual luck, I seemed to have missed it.

Like cattle - off to manoeuvres in the Dutch dunes.
Are you scared Tommy?

During the time it took to relate my Rookie experiences, we kept busy polishing and cleaning all the hand-weapons carried on board. Werner sat on the opposite side of our table and when he started to tug and tear on the rag he was trying to pull through the barrel of one of the pistol, I asked him to watch what he was doing. It was just one of those manoeuvres which in Breda cost me a black eye and a bloody nose.

How was that?

On manoeuvres in the Dutch dunes.

At the very beginning of our training we were issued with a K98 Carbine, which was the standard rifle used by the Army. Of course after a day of playing soldiers they had to be cleaned. This was our regular after dinner occupation and God help anyone who failed the inspection test that followed. If you failed, you could be sure to do cookhouse fatigues for days on end. It followed that the cleaning was done pretty thoroughly and with great vigour. I was resting the butts of my carbines on the table while pulling a rag through the barrel from the business end.

Blow me!

I must have used too much energy as the butt lifted off the table and caught one of my pals square on the temple. He just had happened to bend down to inspect parts of his carbine. It was a pure accident but unfortunately it happened at a time when our Group's instructors entered our billet. He immediately concluded that we were fighting and ordered us all to the Gymnasium. Here my pal and I had to don boxing gloves and go into the ring. We had half expected this on the way over and agreed to do some shamming. In we went for the first round, but of course our playacting was not brilliant and the instructor kept shouting to get more action. Quite by accident I must have got him on the nose a little harder then I had meant, but that was the end of the shamming. He landed me one peach on the ear and until we both dropped from exhaustion, we went at it hammer and tongues to the delight of everybody else. There wasn't a winner, only two badly bruised and bloodied survivors.

After getting this story off my chest, we still had more than an hour in which to catch twenty winks, before the start of our next stint.

By 23.00 hours we were both back on the beat. This time Werner was patrolling the quay while I kept a watery eye out for uninvited visitors from the seaward side. Standing on the bridge I could feel the warm air drifting up through the open hatch, accompanied by the strains of bright and breezy music, which was transmitted throughout the boat by a radio operator. The Lambeth Walk and the Donkey Serenade were among the crew's favourites and made a change from the eternal marching music and patriotic songs normally prescribed for our consumption.

Then, there was a pause and I could hear a bit of garbled tuning followed by English voices. Well, I assumed it was English. It sounded like English. My only experience of that language was from my days at school.

It was never a subject I studied but there was the paperback book I kept hidden under others, the subjects of which were two London private-eyes called John Kling und Johnas Burthe. Hundreds of those penny novels were doing the rounds in our class. They were in German and were peppered throughout with English phrases such as 'Good morning', 'Thank you' or even 'Stick your hands up or I will pump you full of lead'. Added to those were the sea-shanties we sang in the *Marine HJ*. Many of those were in the English language and although we did sing them with extreme gusto, we didn't really have the faintest idea what the words meant.

But who dared to listen to English broadcasts in wartime?

It was strictly *verboten,* under threat of dire consequences.

As the old saying goes - Mice do play when the cat is away.

Naughty! Naughty!

This time, however, the mice were out of luck as the Old Man and our Medico were the first to return from wherever they had been. Before I could see them, I noticed that Werner was jumping about like a demented rabbit, perhaps trying to attract my attention, but I had already spotted them myself. The two officers were getting quite near to the gangplank as I tried my hardest to alert whoever it was in the radio shack, by banging on the steel-ladder down to the control room. I even tried to drop my old, heavy lighter down on to the steel decking below. But the babble went on and on and on.

The Old Man and the MO seemed to have had a good time ashore. They were laughing and giggling as they climbed up to join me on the bridge. Hell! There was nothing more I could do but to jump to attention and to greet them with an overloud:

'Guten Abend, Herr Kommandant und Herr Doktor.'

Still, down below the broadcast went on. As the Old Man started to descend into the conning tower, he suddenly stopped in his tracks, turned to the MO and exclaimed '*Verdammt, Herr Doktor*, I think I have left my briefcase at the Officer's Club, We'll have to go back right away.' The MO seemed to catch on quickly and together they went back to where they had come from.

Thank God. This was somebody's lucky day.

As soon as dared, I shot down to tell Rudi, who was the nosey listener, to turn the bloody radio off, before hurrying back to my post. I quietly inform him later, that it is not enough to be the tallest member of the crew, when you are also the greatest fool as well.

I was no sooner back on the bridge, when our forgetful officers were on their way back on board. Lili Marlene had taken over the airwaves. As the Old Man went past, he said with a straight face 'I am getting old and forgetful! I didn't take it ashore after all!'

Judge for yourselves, either he was already experiencing problems with his memory at the ripe old age of 31 or he had smelled a king-sized rat. There was no doubt in my mind, which of the two was the more likely alternative.

The remainder of the crew got back in time for the midnight deadline. In spite of a few anxious moments and with Werner's considerable help, all of them negotiated the narrow gangplank leading back on board thus avoiding major mishaps.

Our *Smutje* had also returned, miraculously, however, he seemed to be a lot slimmer than when he left earlier in the evening. 'Did you see all the stuff the bastard took ashore? He had a stack of tins under his reefer jacket. He makes damned sure he gets the best talent.' However, envy didn't get us anywhere and besides, he was one of the most powerful men aboard our ship, the bloody shit. He had access to all the keys to the stores, so that even the officers very nearly called him Sir!

A couple of days of routine work followed. On the trip from Bremen, some mechanical faults had occurred. One or two valves-stems proved to be sticky or were leaking and that was not good enough. One particular valve in need of repair was at the very bottom of the control room bilge.

Because of my 188 cm. in my socks and the narrowness between the shoulders, I was voted to the job of a performing a contortionist's act to repair it. Below the steel deck plates, which were at the widest part of a circular cross section, masses of pipes, ducts, cables, pneumatic and oxygen storage bottles, pumps and a lot of other vital pieces of equipment criss-crossed the length of the boat. To get down to the bilge in order to affect a repair to a valve was a major achievement. The deck-plates were unscrewed and lifted. I was lowered down head first, holding a little torch between my teeth while wriggling my way through this maze of jumble

Once I could reach the valve to be repaired, I hooked one of my knees over a convenient pipe, while spanners and packing were sent down by a piece of string. I had to work fast before the blood rushing to my head made this upside-down lark unbearable. Halfway through the operation I had to take a break, when my crewmates had to haul me up by my feet, complaining about the smell of them.

But after one more attempt I was able to report: 'Success! I'm finished. Get me up quick.'

After this I am renamed *'Spinne',* translated as Spider.

Whenever in the future a job required the services of a contortionist, the call went out, 'Get Spider.'

Since Werner was the main mover of my new name, it seemed the decent thing to do to reward him with one of his own. I had noticed his habit of jumping up and down every time he got excited while talking in a higher than normal voice. 'As a matter of fact, you remind me very much of this cartoon character Mickey Mouse, particularly when you get upset.'

This name caught on with the rest of our messmates and henceforth Werner had a new moniker. Serves him right, but I also knew that he hated it like hell. After all, who would have liked being called 'Mouse'?

While we were having fun below, everybody else was busy as well. Fitters from the base were installing three anti-aircraft guns, identical to the ones fitted on our sister-boat, while just about all of our crew took-on and stowed-away live- and practice-ammunition for those bits of new hardware.

The ammo was in the form of magazines, some of which were stored below deck in any available nook and cranny. The rest went into pressure-proof containers conveniently placed near the guns on the upper and lower wintergardens.

KARO-AS was beginning to look more and more like a real warship.

Having refuelled and taken on further supplies, we were soon on our way out of port. Unfortunately, it meant that for the time being there wasn't going to be a visit to Wilhelm's farm.

On the way out through the deep-water channel, the Old Man drew everybody's attention to a dark looking shape lying moored at one side of the bay. It looked like a half-finished Ocean liner but was in fact the aircraft carrier *Graf Zeppelin,* the only carrier ever built for the German Navy. 23,000 tonnes of mothballed junk, her completion suspended in favour of the U-boat building programme and to release her crews, which were needed elsewhere.

Of what use would she have been anyway? She was probably planned as some sort prestige ship, showing the flag during peacetime. In this war she would have been absolutely useless, as all the action in the skies was taking place inland, over Berlin, Hamburg, Cologne and every other big city. Hermann Göring's lot, the *Luftwaffe*, didn't seem to have the capability to keep Tommy and the US Air Force at bay.

Aircraft Carrier 'Graf Zeppelin'
It was never completed and remained mothballed during the war.

Later, when my duties took me past the chart-table, I was able to see that the course our navigator had plotted terminated at a square north of the Bay of Danzig, where the Baltic was a lot deeper than the parts we had previously visited. Perhaps we will be taking our little lady down to below 100 metres, our supposed maximum, to where she should really feel at home.

'Guess what we are going to do next. Mouse?'

He wasn't quite so familiar with sea-charts, so I explained what to look for. 'Like any atlas, where the height above the sea-level is indicated by contour-lines and a number for that height, so a sea-chart has similar contour-lines and numbers for a given depth of water.' Experienced U-boatmen always insisted that the deep was their friend. In its stillness and darkness, there was safety. It also provided a springboard for sneaky attacks on unsuspecting shipping up above us.

We had already learned a little about life **ON** the Ocean waves, now we were heading at 'Full Ahead' into our first real taste of life **BELOW** the waves.

I wondered what would be in store for us this time.

The first dive went like clockwork, very slow but sure.

The Old Man ordered: *'Klarmachen zum Tauchen'* (Prepare to dive). It was time to remember everything we had learned in the last few months, first at U-boat school, then at the dockyard classrooms and then here on ***KARO-AS.*** The diesel engines were stopped and uncoupled from the propshafts. Electric motors took over at half speed. '*Einsteigen*' (clear the bridge) followed, which was the order for the bridge personnel, usually totalling six men, to make their way down through the top hatch into the control room. One petty officer and one rating went to man the forward and aft hydroplanes; another man took over the helm in the control room. The remainder took up forward stations. The last man down should be the most senior officer; on this day it was the Old Man. He closed the hatch, secured it and then ordered: '*Fluten*!' (Flood the tanks)

This was our cue to open the vents at the top of the saddle tanks. As the air was allowed to rush out through the open vents, the water could now gush into the empty tanks via the always-open slots at the bottom of the tanks. As if by magic, glug - glug - glug, she went down, mostly on an even keel, to keep company with our underwater comrades, the fishes. *'Auf Sehrohrtiefe gehen'* (Go to periscope depth).

It was the Chief Engineering Officer's (*Leitender Ingenieur* or *LI* (pronounced 'el ee')) job to take technical command of the boat, while running submerged. He'd already taken up his station in the control room, standing behind the two hydroplane operators. Here he had a perfect view of all the instruments, dials and gauges displaying the information he needed to make the old girl do his bidding.

Two gauges indicated the speed of the propeller shafts in revolutions per minute, two others showed the angular position of the hydroplanes while another one showed the angle of the boats position. Most important, however, were the various depth-gauges. A large dial indicated the depth of the boat down to 200 metres, but for very accurate depth keeping, i.e. for holding the boat steady at periscope depth, a water-filled vertical glass-tube was used. The scale showed the depth in metres on one side of the glass tube and a picture of the silhouette of the fully extended attack-periscope on the other side. The super-precise '*Papenberg*' was one of the vital tools required to ensure that the boat's periscope only just rose above the water surface, enough to ensure good visibility without undue disturbance of the water surface, which would have been a dead give-away to potential enemies.

To bring her up again meant the whole rigmarole was practised in reverse. Shut the vents and blow compressed air into the top of the tanks to push the water out of the slots at the bottom ... and hey presto and ...abracadabra ... we were back in bright sunshine, with only the noisy and smelly diesels disturbing the peace of the empty sea. The job of getting a U-boat down into her real element and to bring her back to the surface was as simple as the proverbial ABC, always provided of course that the crew knew what they were doing.

We didn't do a lot else during the next few days, staying at sea and cruising back and forth within the squares allocated for our exercises.

`Down and up - again and again.

It was a very gentle introduction to running submerged. We had all along assumed that this training was for the benefit of us rookie sailors. But we came to realise that in spite of having some U-boat experience, none of our superiors had served in their present capacity. They had been promoted since their last commands. Even the Old Man had not commanded a front-boat before now, only a school-boat. All his experience, and he had more than anybody else on board, had been as Chief Petty Officer/navigator on one the most successful boats. He must have been extremely competent at his job, first of all to be given the chance to work for a commission and secondly, which was an even more outstanding proof of his ability, to be given the command of a brand new U-boat. The general attitude that seemed to prevail in the German Officer's Corps and which went back to the Old Prussian days was that 'Officers were born - not made'. But we, the crew of ***KARO-AS*** knew that our *Kommandant* was the exception.

Of his many attributes, his patience had to be admired.

On the other hand, our Chief needed more time than anybody else to find his feet. When the Old Man wanted the boat to run at periscope depth, he had to suffer in silence as one minute she shot up almost the surface and the next minute rendered the periscope useless by running too deep. Our little lady certainly showed that she had a mind of her own. Will he ever get the feel of her?

Well! He'd better, or else we will be here forever. There were some advantages in all this. Meal times for instance could be very agreeable when the tables stayed level instead of pitching and rolling. The very stillness of gliding along below the surface to the faint hum of electric power was something to be savoured after being tossed about in a Storm force 10.

There was another advantage as well; our pay benefited every time the boat submerged. The number of days at sea also had a beneficial effect on our pay! Goody! Goody! Up and down - Up and down - more money in the bank. Roll on next payday!

The Old Man didn't seem too impressed with our efforts up to now, but since time was waiting for no man, he decided to go on to the next step in our working-up routine.

'A L A R R R R R R R M!' He shouted down from the bridge at the top of his voice, this was instantaneously followed by 'Brrrrrrrrrrrrrrr', the shrill sound of the alarm bells, set-off by the helmsman in the conning tower.

There were several bells; one in every room and each one was designed to awaken the 'Dear Departed'. This is where the fun began! If you happened to be standing near the ladder from the bridge, you would be well advised to move to a much safer position. If you didn't, you'd immediately be buried beneath four or five bodies, the bridge watch, all dropping from a great height.

When I said 'drop down', I meant, drop down one ladder into the conning tower, through another hatch and down another ladder to the control room floor, all in free-flight without touching the rungs of the two ladders, just by steadying yourself on a handrail on either side.

The advice to keep out of the way didn't apply to us, as we were busy ripping open the vents to the diving tanks, starting with number 7, the one, which was near the bow. As the bow went under, the E-motors at 'Full Ahead both' drove the boat down at a quite steep angle. The men from the bridge picked themselves up to scramble to their action stations. Meantime, the Old Man, being the last one in, slammed the lid shut, securely locking it. In theory, he only had 9-10 seconds to get the hatch secured before the water started to flow over the bridge. He made it, with time to spare and thus stayed dry.

'Level off at 50 metres' he told the Chief.

There were so many things, which had to be done in a short time; it certainly took a lot longer to describe it. This method of submerging was really only a speeded-up version of the more leisurely one we had practised before and which was only used in dire emergencies.

To disappear from the surface in the fastest time possible was in the majority of cases a matter of life or death. It was therefore the single most important manoeuvre a submarine and her crew were asked to perform.

After a few days of our yo-yo act, up one minute and down the next - up and down - up and down, the result was clear to see. The stopwatches, which were doing overtime, confirmed by showing improved diving-times that there was no substitute for endless training. Not that those improvements were guaranteed on every occasion.

There was one time, when our *1WO* was running the show. The *Alarrrrrrrm* bell rang, the crew was down, the hatch was closed in 10 seconds; the dive had started and was followed by his order to level off at periscope depth. Everything seemed to go like clockwork. 30 degrees nose down she went, like a *Stuka* dive-bomber. At 20 metres deep, the hydroplanes of the boat were set to level off.

But nothing happened!

Still pointing downward and with the motors at 'Full Ahead both', ***KARO-AS*** drove herself deep into the bottom of the deep blue sea.

She shuddered and she shook from being abused in this terrible way.

This is certainly no way to treat a lady!

We, who in answer to the alarm-bell's din, were on our way through the diesel-room to man our *Gefechtsstation* (action-station) picked ourselves off the deck, where we had been tossed like rag-dolls. I was shaking like a leaf; this manoeuvre was not one we were familiar with at all.

'What the god-damned hell is going on here?' The Old Man had been thrown off his bunk as well. Philip told me later: 'He flew into the control-room, cursing and swearing. I have never heard such language in all my life.'

He scanned all the instruments, especially the depth-gauge which indicated 70 metres. He notably calmed down, being reassured by the relative shallow waters. But then reports arrived stating that we had acquired a couple of wounded, which for the first time on ***KARO-AS*** provided some work for our Medico. He couldn't do an awful lot for my friend Wilhelm in the control room, other than to stem the flow of blood from his mouth. He was unable to replace the two front teeth the poor beggar lost in this little escapade.

How was that?

Wilhelm was on the forward hydroplane when we went down. When the electric hand buttons of the hydroplanes appeared to fail, he had switched over to manual, which was a large hand wheel. But unfortunately for him, when the tub hit bottom, the handle was spun back and hit him squarely in the chops. There was blood everywhere - it looked like a battlefield. Much the same thing happened to the bow torpedo room mechanic Peter. It couldn't have happened to a nicer man, pity it wasn't my thorn-in-the-flesh Walter. When the boat hit bottom, Peter was bundled between the four bow-tubes, where he collected a glancing blow on his head from one of the flap-handles. That could have been very nasty, but as it was, a local anaesthetic and a few stitches repaired the damage to the outside. It took a little longer, however, to rearrange his grey cells on the inside of his head.

But in the meantime somebody had to give a bit of thought to our necessity of getting our little lady back on to the surface.

The Chief, who was supposed to be running this show, was as baffled as anybody. 'Both full astern' he managed to order after he overcame his initial shock. The E-motors sprung into reverse, but nothing much happened. 'Blow all tanks.' Compressed air hissed into the top of the ballast tanks, getting rid of the water in them. By now she should have surfaced, but still... not a sausage.

I looked around me to see how everybody was taking all this and noted that my colleague Mouse looked just as white-faced and shitty as I felt. But it didn't seem to impress the older, more experienced hands.

'A giant octopus is holding us down'. Georg Schulz, our CPO was actually enjoying everybody's discomfort and his mood transmitted itself to us youngsters.

The Old Man's experience came into play now. He had a quiet word with the Chief, who ordered 'All hands forward'. All crewmembers, which were free to move around the boat, hurriedly slid downhill toward the bow-torpedo room. As a result there was a slight increase in the angle, at which ***KARO-AS*** was situated.

'All hands abaft.' This time thirty men had to labour uphill through the length of the boat, a climb of some 50 metres. But it was worth it; she dropped her tail by at least 10 degrees.

'All hands forward' and a last 'All hands abaft' did the trick to the relief of all the mountaineers.

Up she popped like a cork.

Proof that she was solidly built was provided by the fact that she didn't break her back. After the Old Man equalised the pressure by slowly opening a valve in the hatch-cover and then threw open the lid, he jumped up on to the bridge.

'Well! Well! Well! Come up and see this' he exclaimed.

After our officers shot up on the bridge, their gasps of astonishment could be heard down below. The Chief came down again and told us 'There is a bloody great mountain of grey slimy mud on our foredeck. It is almost up to the conning tower and just as high.'

A few of us were detailed to get a hold of pails or any other implement we could find, to go on deck and clear up the mess. Arriving there, we found it difficult to keep our feet with our rubber-soled shoes. The slimy mess just stuck everywhere, even to our trousers and shirts. The PO supervising the clearing party first peeled off his shirt, then his trousers and then anything else. We followed suit and before you knew it, there were a dozen sailors, fully dressed in regulation dog-tag (identity disc), busy slinging slime overboard.

It was still a very cold time of the year but because we were so filthy from the stinking gunge, we decided there was only one way to get cleaned-up. We jumped overboard into the icy sea and did a couple of laps round ***KARO-AS***. It turned into a race, but you couldn't call it a contest. There were several chaps quite adept at freestyle, whereas some, which included me, struggled along on breaststroke. Result was that we stayed in the water a lot longer than they did and it meant when we surfaced they could find nothing better to do than to cast aspersions on our rapidly disappeared manhood.

'I think you'd better find out what the devil went wrong, *Herr Oberleutnant* the Old Man said to the Chief*,* 'because if there's any damage at all to the bow, I'll have to report it.'

'On the face of it, it seems that the hydroplanes failed, particularly the forward-ones.' the poor man stuttered, 'but we're checking them out at the moment.' 'You didn't just forget to pull her up in time?' I could only just hear the whispered question, to which he got a frantic shake of the head in reply.

It's best to check the outside for any damage.'

'Who's a good enough swimmer to dive down and have a look at the bow, particularly the condition of the hydroplane and the bow-flaps of the four forward torpedo tubes? The *1WO* suggested 'Bobby' (Josef), one of our three Gyro-copter pilots for this task, as he was a former youth swimming champion.

Bobby asked to get a length of water hose though which he could breathe and also suspended a heavy object on a line at the bow, on which he could pull himself down to do the inspection. Having done his preparation, he got on with the job. When he surfaced after a few minutes he reported that there appeared to be some damage to the shafts of the hydroplanes and possibly also to the bow-flaps of a couple of torpedo tubes. The damage to the latter was not too serious, because we were not yet in a position to use the tubes, but practice diving with dickey hydroplanes was quite another story. Before allowing Bobby to leave the water, the Old Man shouted down to him: 'I'm going to ask for the planes to be moved. Will you report when they move up and when they go down? Bobby replied 'Yes, Sir. They seem to be in the fully up position at the moment.'

Watching the Chiefs face, there was no mistaking the relief he felt at Bobby's words. It proved that he was trying to pull her nose up before hitting the bottom. After some extended to-ing and fro-ing over the air-waves, the Old Man asked the quartermaster/navigator to set the return course for the dry-dock in Stettin. It shouldn't take more than a few days to get back out again.

In the meantime, Georg, our CPO tracked down the real problem. During our march to the base, he made a thorough check of the vent of the diving cell No.1 and there was the culprit. He found a sheared pivot-pin, which meant that nothing happened when the lever was pulled to vent the cell nearest to the stern. It stayed dry as the excess buoyancy at the stern made us plough into the bottom.

We would've been in need of some urgent help from above, if something like this had happened while we were being tracked by an enemy destroyer or similar.

It didn't really bear thinking about!

Everybody agreed that luck was on our side in this instance.

Me? I just made sure that my ***KARO-AS*** playing card was safe and sound in my pay-book.

CHAPTER FOUR

This tree-lined avenue stretched from here to the horizon in a line so straight it might have been drawn with a gigantic ruler. Traces of snow-flakes were drifting down from the otherwise bare branches of the apple trees, providing us with a thin carpet of white on which to travel. It muffled the sound of our horse's hooves on the cobblestones. My companion looked stunning in her riding outfit, a pure picture, from the top of her navy-blue hunting cap to the toes of her black riding boots. It was quite obvious, even to a comparative novice rider like myself, that she was thoroughly at home in the saddle of her beautiful Hanoverian. Everything about her, made me look even more out of place. I was dressed in my best navy-blue sailor's uniform, at home on U-boats... out of my depth on a fiery nag!

But as the old saying goes, 'Don't look a gift-horse in the mouth!'

In any case, what's all this about horses?

After we had made fast in Stettin and heard that we would be here for a while, Wilhelm came to tell me that he had managed to get a couple of days off. 'If you could get away too, you'd be very welcome to come along.'

Our Chief was in a good mood; in fact he was preparing to go off himself to visit his folk, who also lived around here.

So, armed with a two-day pass, we set off early on the next morning. We managed to get a lift into town on one of the many supply lorries. But from the centre of Stettin we had to walk and, if we were lucky, to hitch a lift. After humping along in our winkle-pickers for an hour, a kind farmer came along and offered us a place on his horse-drawn hay wagon. But nothing had prepared me for the warm welcome which awaited us at his home. His Mum was frantic with worry when she saw Wilhelm's face, where he'd collided with the hydroplane hand wheel. 'You should have seen it last week. This is nothing' he told her and I had to swallow the words on my tongue: 'You should have seen the hand-wheel'.

But Mum couldn't hide her tears; she was so concerned for her one-and only boy. But some of her tears were also of joy about the unexpected visit. It didn't stop her from rustling up the most wonderful feast. Talk about the return of the prodigal son. Our plates were stacked high enough to satisfy the whole crew of ***KARO-AS***, never mind just two growing lads like us.

Another guest had joined us as well. Hildegard, a farmer's daughter from the other side of the village, had heard of our arrival by bush telegraph. I got the impression that Hilde and Wilhelm were to be paired-off... the lucky beggar! She might be a couple of years older than my friend, but for all that, she was a real eyeful. There wouldn't be too many men, including myself, who would say NO to any proper or improper suggestions coming from her.

After letting the meal settle, Wilhelm's Dad, who throughout the meal never took his eyes off his son, took me in tow to show off the farm's prize-pigs and the rest of his little domain. The porkers appeared to be their main source of income. Although I had been born and raised in the big city, both my parents came from farming backgrounds. My boyhood visits to my grandparents in the Silesian countryside helped me to understand and discuss work on the land with reasonable intelligence. Horsepower here did all the heavy work, well... one horsepower to be exact. '*Kaiser Willi'* wasn't the biggest horse on earth, but as a retired cavalry horse, he was still fit enough to pull the carts as well as the plough and when not doing that, he doubled-up as a riding horse for Wilhelm and his Dad.

Later, we all sat smoking round their tiled stove in the middle of the room, from which by this time the most delicious smells of baking bread were drifting through the room. We also enjoyed a home-brewed drink or two when Hilde said 'Gerhard, I never knew Berliners could tell the difference of one end of a horse from the other.'

'Spider has been riding ever since he was a baby' Wilhelm told her. That was stretching the truth a little. However, I told them that when my father and his brother, my uncle Franz, happened to come to our neighbourhood in Berlin with their horse-drawn dustcart, they often picked me up and popped me on one of the two Dutch or Belgian draught-horses. As a very special treat, I was allowed to go along to their depot on Sundays. There, in the huge stable blocks, were hundreds of stalls, each one occupied by a lovely big brute. I was in seventh heaven when I was allowed to help feed and brush them. I have never forgotten how I loved the aroma of warm droppings as well as the pungent smell of the smoking hooves as the beasts were being shod.

I also told them 'When I was fifteen I had to transfer from the *Jungvolk* (Baby Hitler Youths) to the actual *Hitler-Jugend.* If there had been a unit of the *Reiter HJ* (Equestrian Hitler Youths) in Berlin, I might have joined them instead of the Naval HJ. By no stretch of imagination does all that make me a competent rider.'

But Hilde couldn't have been listening, because she went on to say, 'I could do with some help to exercise my two big boys tomorrow. How about it?' I couldn't for the life of me think even of one good reason why I shouldn't. Only, there was my shipmate to consider. After all, I was his guest here and surely he was included in this.

'I would love to. How about it, Wilhelm? Give me a chance to see how good you really are on a horse!' 'Can't' he said. I promised my Mum and Dad that I'd drive them to the church in our gig. Our priest is very insistent that I should come and see him. Whilst knowing and respecting his very sincerely held religious beliefs, I couldn't help feeling disappointed. 'Sorry, Hilde, thank you very much for the offer, I really would have loved the chance of a hack in the country.' I said this, but hoped like hell they would try to talk me round and God bless them, they did do just that.

Thank heavens!

'No, you give Hilde a hand, otherwise I'll feel guilty about deserting her.'

So, just after 8 o'clock on this lovely morning she trundled over from her parent's farm, which was not far away on the other side of the village. She rode 'Walt' and led 'Herb'. They were both purebred Hanoverian geldings, as was obvious from the distinctive 'H' marks on their buttocks. She told me their proper names, which were as long as your arm, but which I couldn't remember after five minutes. I really had to pinch myself to see that I wasn't dreaming. 'Are you absolutely sure, Hilde, that I'm up to it?' I said tongue in cheek, desperately hoping that her nags were not as frisky as they looked. 'You'll be quite safe,' she assured me while seeming to use quite a bit of pull on the reins to control them, 'they will quieten down a bit once they get the tickle out of their toes.'

I knew exactly what she meant: If he is going to kill you, it will be in the first few minutes. After that you are OK!

Charming, I thought. To tell you the absolute truth, however, for all my fondness of horses, the thing I had been looking forward to all night was to be near Hilde. Call it pure lust if you have to. But if it meant I had to break my flipping neck on her horse just to be in her company, SO BE IT!

There was no going back now.

And so it happened that I was jogging along on this big brute of an animal. In spite of my inexperience, I had managed to convey to Herby's brain the fact that I was not going to be trifled with. When I clamped my long legs round his belly and squeezed, he didn't argue too much.

Round one to me! Seeing that I had things under some sort of control, my companion confided, 'I suppose you've realised by now, that Wilhelm's Mum and Dad have set their heads on getting the two of us hitched.' she told me. Of course, they and my parents want us to be happy but they're also just a bit concerned about creating a larger and more effi-

cient farming unit.'
'But you're absolutely right for each other' was my reluctant verdict 'there isn't a better or more sincere chap than Wilhelm anywhere in this wide world.' 'Listen, Will and I have grown-up together. Ever since I can remember he has been at my side, playing doctors and nurses and mothers and fathers. Although I couldn't have wished for a better brother, we just do not see each other as husband and wife and believe me, it is quite mutual. The only thing is, we don't want to upset our parents. So for the time being we just keep all options open, nobody else is making any plans either these days'. She went on to say 'Of course, there aren't any other young men in our little village and in a big place like Stettin, unattached young girls are immediately taken for some sort of pick-up. If only this silly war would end and we could get back to normal.'

It was a good job we were on our horses. As she was telling me all this, she looked quite fragile and vulnerable and I would have liked nothing better than to take her into my arms. Come to think of it, I wondered whether all this wasn't a bit of a come-on?

That time when she asked me to tighten her girth and put down her stirrup-leather a couple of notches and when the inside of her leg was pressing against my hand, was that just an accident?

Anyway, I didn't get any more time to think lurid thoughts. She must have felt the tension developing and to break it up she gave her horse an almighty big kick and off they went. At right angles to the avenue, along a dirt track they galloped while shouting and hooping 'Come on, you lazy lot, show a bit of life!'

Well, here goes! I didn't actually have to gee-up my dobbin. Being a herd animal, he took-off after his stable-mate, whether I liked it or not. And I can assure you I didn't like it at all. But in a way, horse riding is quite akin to working on a U-boat in a force 12 gale. After a while you get the hang of the rhythm of the waves and you learn to move with them, rather than against them. Same with the horse; move with him and you're as right as rain. After chasing flat out along this dirt track for a couple of miles, she slowed to a fast canter as we approached a copse. It was not very dense and there was a narrow track snaking it way through the trees.

But trust Hilde, she is always full of surprises. 'Hang on Spider' she shouted as we met the first hurdle. This one was only some 60 cm high and not too solid. The next one looked like 75 cm, the one thereafter 90 and the last one well over one metre. Each one was more solid than the one before. Here I was wrong again, it wasn't the last one at all. Riding round the next bend, we met a massive tree-trunk, as big as the gable-end of a house. I felt desperately like getting my parachute ready. All throughout this episode my self-preservation instinct had looked after me and it did this time as well.

I managed to ride WITH the waves.

But there wasn't any need to tempt fate still further. I decided that enough was enough and that it was time to drop anchor.

'Stop you big bastard.' With all my might I tried to pull the brute up, but all I succeeded in doing was to pull him off the track and through a dense patch of brambles. It was hellish, it was a tangle, it was bloody painful, but it also slowed us down to a walk.

Of course, who would meet us as we emerged from the jungle? Hilde, looking spotless and elegant, like one of the models in the pages of a magazine. I shuddered to think what I looked like.

'I'll help you to clean up. We can tie-up the horses to the rail outside this little shed.' It was only then that I noticed the hut here in the middle of the woods. 'It's been a charcoal kiln in the old days.' I was told. Anyway, it was an ideal place to clean up although it was very dark and gloomy in there, but I could just about make out several bales of straw piled up in one corner.

Hilde was picking some of the prickles out of my back. 'Why don't you take your bell-bottoms off, it will be easier to get the thorns out?'

Sounded OK to me. Being a big boy, I wasn't too shy.

And Hilde was a big girl and had probably seen a man in his underpants before. But what was she up to now... the little minx?

While I was busy taking off my trousers, she was just as quickly getting rid of her breeches. 'I thing there may be some thorns in mine as well...'

Later, after we had returned to the farm, I blushed just a little when Wilhelm pulled a few bits of straw from under my collar and innocently asked 'Did you have a nice time?'

'Absolutely fabulous!' was my reply and it really wasn't a lie!

After we had both safely returned to ***KARO-AS*** and were catching-up on our evening meal, I told my colleague Mouse all about our day at the farm... well, not quite all of it. Walter, who as you know was the bane of my life, asked sarcastically, 'why can't you sit still while you are spinning us this yarn? You are behaving like a demented flea.'

Trust him to notice my obvious discomfort.

'If you want to know, I will let you into a secret,' I spat at him, 'because I wont be able to sit on my bloody arse for at least another fortnight. It's as raw as the steak we were eating earlier.'

During our absence in the last few days, some major changes had taken place in the composition of our crew. One change surprised no one. Our good mate August, the poor devil who went green in the face as soon as we cast off from the jetty, received his transfer to a land-based command. Of course, we were sorry to see him go but we also realised that he should never have joined the Navy. His strength was in his skiing ability in the Bavarian Alps. His leaving was my bad luck (or good luck, as the case may be) because, on one of our boozy nights ashore, he had promised to take me along to his hometown and teach me to ski. His transfer may have saved me a few broken bones, even a broken neck.

The second change affected my immediate superior in the control room, Petty Officer (III) Franz Ebler. His transfer was something we had feverishly hoped for, but never dared to expect. He just went ashore one day and that was the last we ever saw of him. He was not replaced by anyone, but our Chief Petty Officer Georg Schulz, who was in overall charge of the control room personnel, now had the additional job of running our starboard watch. I for one couldn't have been any happier.

CPO Schulz was a hands-on man anyway and for Mouse and me it was a great relief to have somebody in charge that knew his job.

The third man to get his marching orders surprised us even more. In fact, we didn't know he had left, when another Lieutenant (Engineer) came aboard to report to the Old Man. '*Oberleutnant* Klaus-Peter Torsten reporting for duty.'

Was he a replacement for our nervous Chief?

'Welcome aboard' Our Old Man obviously didn't fancy going into battle with an inexperienced man in this important position of Chief Engineering Officer. Who could blame him? It could not have been an 'on the spur of the moment' decision; the change must have been pre-planned. Lets hope, he had made the right choice; only time would tell.

Later on that week we were told to expect some oriental visitors. They were meant to acquaint themselves with U-boats of our type and with our methods of using or abusing them. One PO and one man from each of the three technical departments were detailed to answer questions, which our guest might want to ask. 'You don't have to hold back any information from our Allies, they are due to take over one of our Type IXD2 U-boats at some time in the future.'

A party of ten senior Japanese sailors, probably petty officers and chief petty officers, led by two engineering officers came aboard. As our honoured guests, they were piped aboard in traditional style while we were lined up on deck. Although it was plain to see that they were foreigners with their oriental faces that seemed to look alike, it amazed us to note the similarities of our uniforms.

A lot of bowing and scraping preceded the introductions. The officers disappeared with the Old Man down to his corner. Knowing him, he would extend some old fashioned naval hospitality to them, in the shape of liquid refreshments. It should help to overcome any reticence on either part and make his job easier. I doubt whether his linguistic skills extended to Japanese. My guess was they conversed in English, the natural language of the sea. Our task was a bit more difficult, we had no Japanese or even English and they spoke little German. They had a couple of interpreters from their Consulate with them, but since the pen pushers didn't know a screw from a nut, in fact had no understanding of engineering at all, they found it almost impossible to translate technical information. Most of the time they had to make use of dictionaries, even then they were groping in the dark. So we had to make the best of a bad job and improvise by reverting to the old and proven method of miming. In Hollywood our efforts would have earned us many Oscars. We also managed all right by making pencil sketches on the back of cigarette packets.

But there appeared to be difficulties with the written words, they caused blank faces all round. But it was obvious that those sailors knew their stuff and from the way they moved around the boat and took everything in, they were equally at home on submarines.

When we had finished for that day, we moved up on to the bridge, where we happened to get on to a different subject... the 'Number One Subject' common to all sailors. Now we started to get some real reaction from our inscrutable guests. Quick as flash they pulled out of their pockets the most pornographic pictures I have ever seen. Suffice it to relate that they portrayed nude Japanese men and women in a mixture of poses, positions, which I would have thought to be quite impossible to achieve, if I hadn't actually seen them. Those photos also made liars of our more experienced seafarers with their tales that Oriental woman had their vaginal-split running east to west instead of north to south.

Later on our friends from Nippon, in one way or the other, managed to make us understand what for them was the dearest wish of all. Flashing their money, they wanted us to show them where they could taste the delights of Stettin. Personally, I had no first hand knowledge of where to find the nearest brothel, but we knew a man who was an expert.

Karl-Heinz was called to the rescue.

Why Karl-Heinz?
Not because he was a frequenter of those facilities, but because he was an expert at scouting-out young and fresh talent for his family's business on Hamburg/St.Pauli's *Reeperbahn.* Since his connection with the Red-Light area of Hamburg became known among the crew, he had become everybody's friend.

Anyway, Karl-Heinz took the Japanese crew into town and asked them to form a queue outside one of those places. It was not the last we heard from our oriental allies. At a later occasion, Karl-Heinz told us that he had to listen to complaints from those Ladies. It seemed that the shortcomings of the Nips were not just confined to their lack of their linguistic skills or lack of stature, but to other shortcomings in other vital departments. This should have surprised no one, least of all ladies of ill repute.

But, what the Ladies may have missed in the way of enjoyment, all the lovely wads of money left to them by our guests must have been a reasonable compensation.

Next morning, shortly after breakfast, an order came over the tanoy 'All members of the Second Division, (i.e. all the engineering crew) assemble on the quarter-deck - at the double.' Our chief petty officer, as the most senior of the division, called us to attention and reported to the new Chief Engineering Officer 'All present and correct, Sir.'

Standing there, we had to listen as he introduced himself.
'I am Lieutenant Klaus-Peter Torsten, your new Chief.
You'll find that I know my job and I expect you to be equally effective at yours. I do not suffer fools gladly and I despise slovenly behaviour. Our demanding and highly technical job of running the engineering side of this ship deserves only the very best from everyman. Otherwise, I'm a very easygoing person and it will be entirely up to you how well we will get on with one another. At the end of our working-up period, only perfection in our work will be good enough.'

Hey... hey! What a speech?
And it wasn't the end of it. He next demanded to know every one's rank, name and the position they held on board, while criticising just about every one of us for something or other. We didn't look clean enough, our dress was sloppy and our hair far too long. He had obviously decided to make some sort of impact on his men, before they had a chance to weigh him up. The way it seemed to us, before us stood the most arrogant, high minded and self-opinionated officer of the whole navy.

Only a few years older than any of us, he seemed to be all bluster and not a lot of substance. All his knowledge appeared to have come from books, judging by the amount of those he brought aboard with him. Mouse, who normally kept most of his thoughts to himself, remarked 'Never mind! I don't think he'll be with us all that long. I can't see the Old Man putting up with his style'.

The subject of our new Chief Engineer went out of our minds pretty quickly, as both Mouse and I were opening letters from our folks at home, which had arrived that day.

My mother's letter was dated shortly after we had left Kiel for the Baltic and described what had happened to our house during a night raid by enemy bombers. After hammering the centre of Berlin, one of that lot appeared to just empty his load of incendiaries over our little suburb. 'You have no idea how lucky we have been,' she wrote. 'Twelve of those have come down on our plot. Six of them exploded on the cement path surrounding our house, spattering the stone walls with their red-hot magnesium. I don't know what would have happened if one of them had fallen on our house. Dad thinks that it would have gone straight through the felt roof.'

I must have gone white as I digested the news. Knowing just how narrow the path that encircled our house was, made me shudder when I realised how lucky my parents had been.

However, to end her letter, she had some much better news: 'Last week Trautchen has had her baby, a strapping boy. They call him Joseph, after your dad.' This time I had to let everybody else know as well.

'I'm an uncle' I yelled, because Trautchen was my brother's wife and Joseph my brother's son.

Soon, after the damage to our bow had been repaired, ***KARO-AS*** slipped her moorings again, to continue the work we had to abandon last week. The Old Man steered for the Danzig Deep to a different square, one where the echo sounder measured over 110 metres of water under our keel. It didn't take long to get there. Let's just hope that the Old Man is not going to rely too much on this new clown of a Chief for keeping us alive, instead will keep a weary eye on him.

But the trials must go on.

'Prepare to dive'

'Clear the bridge'

'Dive'

'Go to periscope depth'

We were already quite proficient in all the actions required. The bridge watch got down without fuss and the Old Man closed the lid. The diesels had stopped and the E-motors were humming away at 'Half Ahead'.

The actual diving went like clockwork. The hydroplane operators were in place and ready for the new Chief's orders. In a clear and precise way he started to give his instructions. Less than 30 seconds later he asked for trim adjustments, 'Take on 500 litres.' This translated into making the boat heavier by half a ton.

'Transfer 75 litres fore to aft'.

This had me busy pumping that amount from the trim tank in the bow to the other one at the stern by opening a valve in the connecting pipes and pressurising the forward tank. We were obviously slightly bow-heavy.

'Running at periscope depth, Sir.' he reported to the Old Man in the conning tower.

'Up periscope' the captain requested. For a while silence reigned, but from where I am standing I could see the *Papenberg* depth gauge. There wasn't the slightest flicker to be detected in it.

It hadn't packed-up by any chance?

'Very good Chief, prepare to surface.'

It almost sounded as if the Old Man was pleased with this manoeuvre.

More like beginners luck was our mutual verdict, it can't last. Wait until we go try the *ALARM* routine.

In fact, it wasn't long after this, when we heard the shrill sound of the bell. You could almost touch the tension in everybody. 'We will show the bastard Chief, that we haven't wasted our time in the last few weeks.' 'Level off at 75 metres' has been the Old Man's latest order less than a minute ago. Like a bird the boat had been diving down at 40 degrees forward inclination and started now to respond to the various hydroplane settings ordered by the Chief. Before we knew it, the depth gauge read bang on 75 metres.

'Go to periscope-depth. Slow ahead both' the Old Man shouted down.

This should confirm his beginners luck. We knew it was not easy to hold the boat at a steady depth for the Old Man to use the periscope effectively. But to do so at a slow speed, when the hydroplanes had less effect, should give our new boy something to think about. Maybe he could consult one of his books?

Perhaps it was something the dockyard did to our forward hydroplanes when they were repaired after our mishap, but to our utter amazement, and the *Papenberg* does not tell lies, ***KARO-AS*** acted, as a real lady should, she was utterly submissive.

'Go to 50 metres. Full ahead both'

'Go to 20 metres. Starboard stop, Port slow ahead'
'Go to 80 metres. Full ahead both.' 'Rudder hard to port'
Like a corkscrew the boat almost freefalls down and before you knew it, the Chief reported,

'Levelled-off at 80 metres.'

No matter what the captain requested, in every possible combination of depth or speeds, within a very short time the man confirmed the new depth or speed as having been obtained. Out of the corner of my eye, I caught a glance passing between our CPO and the Old Man as he dropped down from the conning tower into the control room. Both had their eyebrows raised in utter astonishment and bafflement about our new and inexperienced Chief, who had the golden touch of a saint as far as ***KARO-AS*** was concerned. He was, what you we would call a NATURAL and in his hands, the old tub didn't dare to argue... she positively purred with pleasure at his commands!

After witnessing the bucking, kicking and rearing of this very same boat when it had been in the hands of the previous *LI*, this performance on that day was utterly unbelievable. I ventured to tell Mouse, loud enough for others to hear, 'If he's still with us when we leave on our first patrol against Tommy, he's got my permission to be as bloody-minded as he likes.' Our CPO didn't let on that he heard me, but his head seemed to nod agreement. From this moment on, we saw Klaus-Peter in a different light. Even the Old Man, who normally kept his distance from the other officers, except the MO, warmed to him and they were often seen in deep conversation.

Once they were heard to discuss modifications to the forecastle between the conning tower and the bow. Decreasing the width of the deck should improve the handling of the boat. He thought that the large deck area caused it to act like a surfboard. It was fighting the hydroplanes, intending to take the boat to the surface.

It looked as if he was in the ship designing business as well.

Later the Old Man decided to break-up the monotony between dives to give our little observation bird an airing. The weather was holding up, so he wished to be convinced of our ability to get it to fly.

What on earth am I talking about?

It seems several nations were experimenting with placing planes on submarines, but as yet had little or no success. The introduction into our navy of a manned kite was rumoured to be the most successful attempt yet, to overcome the limited range of visibility from the low-slung bridge of a submarine. Until now it had only issued to the IXD2 Type of U-cruiser, the long-range boats of the Monsoon Group. This contraption could be deployed and towed by the boat by a thin wire cable. It could hover at heights of 50-100 metres, from where its pilot, properly equipped with powerful binoculars and in touch with the boat by telephone, claimed to have a range of vision in excess of 30 sea miles.

This novel little number was called the FA330 Focke-Achgelis *'Bachstelze'* (Water-Wagtail), a 'manned tethered auto giro aerial reconnaissance kite'. While towing it, the boat had to steer into the wind and also travel at a certain speed to keep this contraption in the air. Of course, during this manoeuvre the towing boat would be quite vulnerable to enemy attacks. It was only natural therefore that its effectiveness in action was viewed with a certain amount of suspicion. Whether or not our Old Man would ever use it was questionable.

Nevertheless, the bird had to be tested and kept operational at all times. A lot of time and effort had gone into training all pilots, as Teddy once told us, while billeted together ashore in Bremen. It seems that the idea of flying a tethered Auto-Giro and that of training pilots was born at the end of 1942, when under extreme secrecy a group of Gliding instructors and sailors were assembled at a Glider Air field near Frankfurt. To stop awkward questions being asked, why were members of the *Kriegsmarine* instructed to fly, the sailors were issued with *Luftwaffe* uniforms. The Instructors went to try-out flying the newly developed *Bachstelze* in a Wind Tunnel in France, while the sailors, after passing a thorough medical, remained at the airfield to train for their Glider Pilot Licence. They were awarded this licence after a total of 25 flying hours. Teddy was in the 4th Group to pass through this test. He went on to Paris to get the first feel of the real thing. In a large wind tunnel the *Bachstelze* was tethered to a take-off platform 1 m deep and 3 m wide. After some 5 flying hours the kite was released to a height of 1 m and after 5 more hours to the maximum height allowed in the wind tunnel of 10 m. Then he went back to a place in Saxony, where from the back of a lorry, which was travelling on an *Autobahn,* the prospective pilots spent many more hours training, especially since now weather conditions were part of the exercise.

It is a miracle that none of the prospective pilots finished up with a nervous breakdown.

By the way, this particular use of the Autobahns wasn't part of the calculation, when the decision was made to cover our country with super highways. It was always assumed, that the reason was to get rid of the sky-high unemployment, which reigned in the early thirties.

After all this our heroes went to the Zuidersee in Holland to fly those contraptions off an Air Sea Rescue launch, which copied the conditions they would find on a U-boat. I must say, our respect for these people rose to unprecedented heights. If all the *Luftwaffe* pilots get as much training, one can understand why those valuable men must be kept away from the enemy as much as possible.

Back to our trial, the weather was ideal; a northerly wind was blowing at a steady 15 knots. The *Bachstelze* was raised by a freewheeling three-bladed helicopter-like rotor, the initial rotation of which was started by pulling a string, which was wound round the rotor head, not unlike starting an outboard motor. By adjusting the angles of the 4 m long blades with his joystick, the pilot waited until the rotor speed increased to some 150 revs per minute, using the wind-speed and the forward-speed of the boat. Steering into the wind of 15 knots, the towing vessel only had to travel at just 5-8 knots to get the bird off its perch and flying.

The kite was easy enough to assemble. Bolted on top of its very light tubular aluminium construction was a seat for the pilot. Above him, on top of a vertical post was the rotor with its three blades while between the pilot's legs was the joystick. At his feet, he had a pair of foot-pedals for the side-rudder, which he used to keep the kite flying in a straight line. The wires from his telephone were woven into the actual towing cable.

Bobby (real name Joseph Schmidt) was the more senior of our three pilots. It fell to him to do the first flight, while Teddy (Leonard Wegner) started the rotor and operated the winch. Everything went to plan and at a height of 50 metres Bobby reported 'the visibility is excellent. I can see a type VIIC U-boat at 270°, distance 15 km and two small fishing vessels at 170°, distance 10 km.' A little later he asked permission to ascend to 80 metres. 'I can now see the Hela peninsula at O° estimated distance 25 km.'

I watched the exercise spellbound, full of new appreciation and admiration for our two pilots: 'Am I glad I'm not up there, with only a couple of 2 inch aluminium rods between my arse and 80 metres of nothing.'

This was the end of that particular exercise. It took several minutes to winch Bobby down and a further 3 minutes to fold and stow the little beast. He was frozen stiff, but full of the joys of spring about his efforts. He told Teddy: 'this bird can fly all right! It's easier to handle here than from the back of a lorry.' We knew now what he meant by that remark.

The Old Man just looked sceptical and was heard to tell the MO 'It's just a pity that we didn't have them while we could still show our faces on the surface. It's about 2 years too late.'

One got the feeling that he wasn't going to use it, if it could be avoided. In the end it would come down to a straightforward choice. Was it important to have better visibility? Alternatively, was it even more vital to stay invisible to the enemy?

Anyway, this had been a little diversion from the hard work of learning how to make the boat disappear from the surface in the quickest possible time. It will be quite a while yet before the Old Man could be satisfied with our efforts in that respect, certainly not before we manage to get down below in less than 30 seconds - and then not just sometimes, but every time.

CHAPTER FIVE

It wasn't very long after our kite-flying trick, when the Old Man appeared to be satisfied with our crash-diving efforts. More often than not we managed to get off the surface in less than 30 seconds. In his laconic style, he informed us: 'We will get many more opportunities to perfect our act at other trials. Take my word for it, we've a long way to go before our boat will be ready for real action.'

Next stop was the Artillery Training School, where ***KARO-AS*** took on supplies of ammunition for our three anti-aircraft guns. We were being made ready for the second most important exercises on our working-in schedule, the gunnery trials. After practising to crash-dive and show a clean pair of heels, we next had to learn to defend ourselves from the enemy up above. It seems, there were now few places left on this earth where Tommy's or Uncle Sam's aircraft couldn't reach and, day by day, there were more and more of those pests humming around the heavens. Even so, some of our higher-up seemed to think that aircraft are just as unable to eliminate U-boats, as crows are unable to fight moles under ground. But they could also be wrong. For U-boats to stay reasonably effective, they would have to learn to look after themselves against those buzzards, which were based on land or on carriers and were equipped with the most advanced detecting and locating devices. Armed to the teeth with all sorts of nasty things, combined with their high speed and manoeuvrability, they held most of the aces, especially when U-boats were on the surface. To try and counteract this relatively new threat, our first priority had to be the early detection and recognition of those aircraft.

The Old Man, in a class-room at the base, assured us that our scientists were working feverishly to provide us with the means to detect the enemy RADAR signals: 'Let's hope that they'll be available to us by the time we go on our first patrol, when we'll be able to determine when their RADAR signals have locked-on to us and from which direction they're approaching. In the meantime it is up to us to make the best of it by being alert and watchful and by practising our anti-aircraft drill.'

He then introduced a Naval Artillery Officer, who was to brief us on the theoretical aspects of that drill. He explained, that here at the base, reports were gathered from those U-boats, which had been engaged by enemy aircraft and which had survived to make those reports. He went on to sum up those findings: 'Most U-boat captains still favour the safety of the deep when things get sticky up above and downing planes is not what U-boats were designed for. But there'll be occasions when your survival will depend on the eight barrels of 20 mm fully automatic and rapid-firing weapons, with which your boat is equipped.'

He went on to describe the whole procedure in very great detail and followed it by answering questions from the crew. At the end of his lecture we all had a theoretical understanding of what lay ahead when we would start to put everything into practice.

The weekend was here again and there was no good reason for leaving the harbour before Monday as our next bit of training would also involve a lot of the shore-based personnel of the school and, believe it or not, war or no war, they needed their weekends off to be with their families? Although we were itching to get on with our shooting practice, a free weekend was equally welcome. Over breakfast we made our plans for today.

My greatest wish was for some time on my own, to try and catch up with my reading. Some time ago I managed to buy a few interesting looking books at a second-hand shop in one of the ports. My star find was a 1930 Hand-Atlas, which also contained a lot of information, political, economical and geographical about every country in the world. It was so heavy that I laughingly asked my PO whether we would have to adjust the trim of the boat after bringing the thing aboard. It would be handy when we started to travel the world, but it was a reference book, not one to hold you enthralled for very long.

However, the other book I bought was published in 1928 and was written by an officer serving on a World War I U-boat. Its title was *'Höllenmaschine'* (Machine from Hell). As far as I could tell, it contained a lot of information about our comrades of the *Kaiserliche Marine* (Imperial Navy), who like us were up against great odds during that war. Since that war was the first one in which submarines played a significant roll both on the British and the German side, as both combatants heavily relied on the supplies from abroad. Cutting those supply routes meant choking the lifeblood out of the enemy. Being a new and relatively sneaky way of fighting your enemy, submariners in those days were often seen as pirates or even war criminals, who could not look for mercy when caught.

I told Mouse what the story was about and that I wanted to get on with it. 'If you like, you can read it after me.'

Since it was still early in the day, he decided to do a bit of shopping in the town and we agreed to meet in the evening at the *Orchidee* club. 'I've asked Philip and Karl-Heinz to meet us there as well. Perhaps you've forgotten, but you've promised to treat us to a beer or two to celebrate your 19th birthday last week.'

Actually, yes, it had slipped my mind, but there was no harm done. Between now and then there was enough time to really get into this book. It was in two parts, the first part just dealt with general information such as the development of submarines. According to his account, Germany had done some early work in that field; even before internal combustion engines were invented. It meant that everything, including propulsion had to rely on muscle power. Other nation, particularly France, Britain and the USA took the development forward, to a point at the beginning of the 1914/18 war, when those nations could put over 250 submarines to sea. Germany had just about 30, of which 4 were school boats, unfit for front action. Talk about superiority?

Of course, it is questionable how accurate his figures were, but by the end of the war Germany had build an other 350, of which nearly 180 were lost along with 5500 lives.

Following his tale, I realised just how little our so-called modern U-boats had changed from those he described. The engines and electric motors are now more efficient, the optics in periscope more accurate and the general construction now welded instead of riveted and allowing our boats to go to greater depths. But as far as living conditions are concerned, they still are as primitive as ever.

In spite of all that, our predecessors seemed to have caused just as much havoc among our enemies. In fact, they proved so troublesome, that British Admirals had to revert to very extreme measures to deal with them. The author explained in brief details some of the rules, which applied to U-boat, war in those days. In 1915, Germany had notified all seafaring nations that they considered the sea areas around Britain to be a war zone. Ships, with neutral markings or flying Neutral flags could be stopped and asked for a cargo manifest. Ships, carrying cargo for Britain were confiscated. If they could not be taken to a German port, the ship was sunk allowing the crew to take to their lifeboats.

During the boarding and examination of papers aboard a suspect ship, the U-boat is very vulnerable, and to exploit this, Britain deployed some 200 decoy-ships. They were given "Q" numbers and equipped with hidden artillery pieces. Flying a neutral country's flag they waited until a U-boat attempted to come alongside.

Striking the Neutral flag, running up the British flag and simultaneously revealing 10.5 or even 15 cm canons and attempting to blow the U-boats out of the water took only a few seconds, a few seconds too many for a total 14 German U-boats and their crews.

The author went on to claim that early in 1918 the entire British press published a heroic account by British officers, which related to the sinking of a German U-boat by the Q-Ship BARALOG in August 1915. Sailing under a Neutral flag in the English Channel she was stopped and as she declared that she had banned cargo, the BARALOG crew was asked to take to the boats prior to the ship being sunk. After all the crew had left the ship, suddenly, a woman holding a baby was seen to gesticulate frantically to the German boat. As the men on deck of the U-boat held out their arms to catch the child, it was dropped down. Only it wasn't a child at all. It was a bomb wrapped in swaddling clothes. This baby was big enough to destroy the U-boat and the entire crew of 37, 11 of which were helped along by Machine Gun fire.

Of course, TIT causes TAT; in September 1917 Germany declared unrestricted U-boat war. Every ship, British, French, American or even Neutral, which was from then on found in British waters, became a target.

After taking in all this, I had to take some time out. There was some cold coffee in the can hanging from above me, but if I wanted to eat, I had to go to the canteen ashore. I was born lazy; perhaps I can pick up something to eat later at the club. But it was still far to early, so it meant back to my bunk and back to the book.

I now read about a German U-boat, which went missing, presumed lost, in 1915. Again the book's author quotes the British press for reporting the capture of a complete and undamaged German U-boat off the coast of England. Unable to hit it with their shore-batteries, it was decided to investigate. No sign of movement was seen on board, so it was taken in tow and dragged into harbour. The conning tower hatch was opened and the bodies of the entire crew of 31 sailors were found. Two men were found sitting in the control room, with the rest lying in their bunks and on mattresses in their messes.

There were not signs of violence; every man jack seemed to have gone to sleep, not to wake-up again.

How could this have happened?

The favoured explanation went as follows; because of British Destroyer presence, the U-boat was allowed to rest on the bottom of the North Sea, to rest up the crew and put the Destroyers off the scent as well as to preserve air for breathing.

But because they had to stay submerged for such a long time, two men were always posted in the control room to periodically push air through the ventilation duct and through Potash canisters to clean it at the same time allowing a small amount of pure Oxygen to escape from steel bottles to freshen the air up. This should have been done with extreme care, as an overdose of pure Oxygen was known to act like poison gas.

In fact this appeared to have happened. After opening the Oxygen valve, either through tiredness or carelessness the valve was not closed properly, thus inducing sleep, from which there was no awakening. The boat could have stayed on the bottom for weeks until perhaps the still open Oxygen valves were able to push out some of the water ballast. True or not, that was the question. It sounded a little like the Flying Dutchman.

Of course, my description is a lot shorter than the text of the book. By the time I had got to this point in the book, it was almost 8 o'clock in the evening and past the time I should have turned up at the club. And lo and behold, a very irate Mouse appeared through the hatch, foaming at the mouth as if the world had come to an end.

He had done all his shopping, eaten his supper and gone on to the *Orchidee* club, hoping to find me there. Philip and Karl-Heinz had already made a start with the beer and what was more, they already found company. In fact there were enough girls there to go round. Making myself presentable in next to no time, we set sail for the club. After I got used to the din, the dim lights and the thick air, smoke and sweat, he introduced me to two girls. 'This is my friend Marta and her pal Helena. I told them about you and your misfortune.'

What on earth has he been telling them, I asked myself? He was known to spin some awful yarns. Sometimes I really did worry about Mouse and his twisted sense of humour.

But first I must come back to Helena, who was to be my guest. You couldn't say that she had a face to launch a thousand ships, more to sink them without any trace. But to give her the due she deserved, her chassis, which was on full display, more than made up for any facial shortcomings. All eight of us, Helena and I included, found a quiet table in a very dark niche. Through the smoke and fog we could barely make out the stage which was somewhere in the middle of the room.

A very attractive looking accordion player, dressed in a scanty sailors outfit, attempted to make her self heard above the din of drunken voices. One Lord kept advising her to be careful and not to trap her voluptuous bust in the folds of the squeezebox. The rest of the sailors were only interested in paying homage to the local talent.

At this stage I should mentioned that in all ports along the coast, a strict code of segregation operated between the different ranks of the *Kriegsmarine*. Officers had their own clubs, as had the CPOs and the petty officers. This left us, the riff-raff, in serene peace to enjoy ourselves in our own way. It also followed (naturally) that the ladies of those ports had their individually preferred hangouts. Some of the Officers and most of the CPOs were already married and had to behave themselves, but their unmarried comrades had the pick of the classier birds in town.

Next in the pecking order came the Petty Officers. Their companions, apart from being reasonably young and good looking, were the most hard-bitten ones. They had to be tough, to be able to put up with that shower of human dross. Only the influence of four or more years of service in the Navy could possibly turn decent sailors into a bunch of degraded, conceited and thieving wretches.

So, this system left us Lords with the visually flawed, first-timers and most desperate of the female species. I think Helena qualified on the first and last count. Since it was my birthday party, I made sure we had enough beer for us boys and gallons of champagne (coloured water) for Helena and her pals. After an hour or so, in which more than one case of beer had bitten the dust and after we had got down to some serious canoodling, with me just getting to enjoy myself, the heat in the place got to me and without further ado I passed out and slipped under the table.

The alcohol in my veins contained too little blood.

Or was it because I poured the contents of a few bottles down the hatch, on a very empty stomach?

My crewmates wakened me when the time came to get back aboard for the 2 am deadline. 'I am quite capable of standing up by myself, thank you.' was the first sign that I was still alive, 'Where's my friend - what's her name?' was the second. 'Helena left a long time ago and has come back since, with another escort,' I was informed.

'Ah, well. Lets get out of here to get some fresh air.'

Once we were outside, I recovered quickly. I even passed the sentry at the base-entrance on an even keel as we made out way back on board.

'Good night, Wilhelm, see you in the morning' was my greeting to our mate on guard duty on the quayside. He took one look at me and advised 'Watch the gangplank, Spider, you don't look at all well', as my other mates offered to help me across. Brushing them aside I croaked 'I can manage quite well, thank you - stand back please.'

With that I managed to negotiate the very narrow plank, which led on to the forecastle, without undue trouble. Mouse still fussed around me and that really got my goat. 'Can't you give me some bloody space, you fusspot and ... *Verfluchter Scheissdreck'*, and over I went. I picked myself up while spewing slime and dripping from head to toe. Some sticky bits and pieces had slipped down the front of my uniform, which I franticly tried to dislodge by nearly standing on my head. All around me, the horrible creatures I loosely called my friends, stood hooting, shouting and having fun at my expense.

'If you weren't pickled before, you certainly are now.'

Pickled?

That rang a bell in my befuddled brain.

On our way into port a couple of days ago, we had met up with a lone fishing vessel. We passed close enough for the old man to question by megaphone, 'Do you have any nice fish to spare for my crew's supper?' to which the fisherman replied 'If you have a couple of bottles *Schnapps* to spare, we might find some herring'. It was the first time our small dingy got an outing. After hauling it from below deck, our cook was on his way, rowing to do a spot of bartering. He came back with two large boxes of herring and sprats.

Once in port, *Smutje* went on a scrounging mission, to find a suitable container, in which to pickle the catch. The only vessel he could find was a vat, about 3 feet in diameter and 12 inches deep. It was ideal, but far too large to pass down into the boat through any of the hatches. There was nothing for it, he had to bring his vinegar, gherkins, spices and whatnot on deck and do the pickling there. The uncovered vat was left standing in front of the conning tower.

So I dived in, head first. Served me right. Apart from looking utterly ridiculous, I had to fork out hard-earned money to get my uniform cleaned. What a birthday celebration?

But the fish turned out to be absolutely delicious and anybody who liked the taste of pickled herring, as I did, was free to help himself.

It turned out to be one of the best antidotes against hangover I'd ever come across.

By the time we were ready to leave port early on Monday morning, every last little sprat had disappeared. Not more than a few miles outside the harbour, we found a floating target-barge. It was lying at anchor with its target some 10 m long and perhaps 6 m high. In preparation, live rounds had been placed in the ammunition-containers on our bridge.

At noon the port watch had taken over from us. While we were hungrily starting on our meal, the screeching claxon went. This signal meant anti-aircraft-action, at which Mouse and I raced through to our usual places in the control room to take over the stations vacated by our opposite watch, who, at the first sound of the hooter, had sprinted up on to the bridge to make themselves useful. Before long we heard the *FLAK* going hell for leather at some 180 rounds per minute. We could hear the Old Man singing out the estimated distances, 1,000 meters or whatever and "Fire" or "Hold fire". Our mates Philip and Karl-Heinz, who had manned the two twin TypeC/38 20 mm guns, appeared to have a great time - but for heaven's sake - leave some for us!

After standing down the watches changed over and the next time the claxon went, it was our turn to race up to the bridge to take our place behind the C/38s. Mouse and I took our cue from the quadruple, which was pointing to exactly starboard.

The orders came 'Low-flying aircraft at 90 degrees. Distance 800 meters. Port gun hold fire. Starboard and quadruple gun... FIRE!'

Looking through the spiders-web-shaped sight and lining it up with the target right in the middle, I pressed the trigger and held it there. My God, I had no idea how much noise the damned thing would make. I could barely feel the recoil but could very well see the effect of my shooting as shown by the luminous paths of the tracers.

Up a bit and hold it.

The Old Man continually changed the boat's speed and her course.

Great!

'Come on, Tommy, get some of this' I thought aloud.

I was truly amazed by the feeling of power you got behind one of those guns.

New magazines were fed into the breach as required, until we got the 'Stop fire' command. After we had passed the target, the Old Man turned the boat about and this time the port side gun got the all clear to fire, while I put the safety-catch on mine. Why? Because the target is on the same height above the water as our gun position, we would shoot each other to bits with the barrels horizontal.

Talking about this problem, I have just noticed, that somebody had forgotten to take down the flagstaff. The result of this omission stared us in the face... a jagged stump with the top part of the staff hanging by its ropes further down.

Butterfingers!

We made several more passes, thereby giving yet more men an opportunity to get familiar with the guns. After all, in a real fight we would certainly have casualties and the more men could operate the guns, the better the chances of the boat.

Having completed this part of the exercise, we continued our journey to the deeper waters near the Swedish coast, where our training was taken a step further. This time we had a go at a moving target. A cloth contraption was towed by one of our transport planes on a line several hundred metres long. In this way we got a more realistic type of anti aircraft practice.

But to tell the truth, we nearly didn't get the opportunity to do our drill. At the start to this exercise, a radio-operator and our paramedic were at the twin guns.

The plane with the target came in at us from our starboard side. All eight barrels should now be lined-up on the target and as it got within range, the Old Man ordered 'Open Fire.'

With that, the most unholy dim erupted but was almost instantaneously brought to a halt by shouts of 'Hold your fire.'

Somebody threw himself against the gunner on the starboard twin and ripped his right hand off the trigger.

What the hell was all the fuss about?

Our normally unflappable medical orderly Otto was only just stopped in the nick of time from downing not the towed target but the towing aircraft.

The Old Man didn't make a big fuss about the near tragedy, but we noticed that from then on Otto was not allowed near any of the guns but was kept in readiness for prick-parades and in case anybody needed medical attention.

The target was so slow that we just couldn't miss the damned thing. Soon this exercise came to an end as our supplies of live ammunition became exhausted and also because there was very little left of the cloth target.

What next? The answer came on the following day.

A pretty fast seaplane, an ARADO 198, was called in to give us practice in early spotting and identifying.

This time all the Officers including the Old Man were given plenty of work as well. They took it in turns to position the boat in the most advantageous position during a set-to with an aircraft. To understand this, one had to consider that all the *Flak* was located behind the bridge and at the same level or as in the case of the quadruple, at a lower level.

It was virtually impossible to fire at a low-flying plane approaching from directly ahead. Broadside on, on the other hand, provided the plane with too big a target. Ideally we wanted them to come from behind, for them to get a nice taste of all our 8 barrels.

It became a play of cat and mouse from then on.

When he did come in for the first time, he was quite high at 500 feet. One of our lookouts had picked him up easy enough with his powerful binoculars while he was still 7 or 8 miles out.

'Aircraft at 40 degrees' he sang out.

The Arado was coming in from our starboard bow. There would have been enough time to get out of the way by diving. But we were here to practice something else.

"Flieger Alarm"

The claxon blared loud enough to burst our eardrums.

"Full ahead both"

"Rudder hard to port"

The tone of the diesels rose from their normal whisper-like rhythm to a frantic roar. At nearly 20 knots, the boat leant over to starboard until her tail was facing the enemy. The extra speed would also come in useful, if the Old Man decided to show a clean pair of heels in a crash-dive.

We got our first chance to aim and fire at the real thing, even if it was only with blanks. There must have been other U-boats in nearby squares, going through similar trials. After each run at us, he disappeared, only to come back when we least expected it. Sometimes he returned after a few minutes but more often than not it took hours, when he would try and come at us from behind one of the clouds or from the sun. After a while we did get the hang of things.

As soon as the plane was spotted and the Klaxon raised the alarm, the whole crew got involved. The only problem was, that although the blanks made the same noise they didn't of course leave a tracer-path by which to check on your accuracy. It somehow didn't feel right but then, he couldn't shoot back either, except blanks.

'I don't know about you, but I will feel hellish exposed up there on the bridge when the real stuff starts flying.' Mouse, as usual, had hit the nail square on the head. Armour-plated shields probably were too heavy for a tub like ours.

In the meantime, the pilots of our imagined enemy-kites were getting cockier by the hour. It was their job to give us as much experience as possible, because Tommy was certainly not going to stick to any rules and regulations.

Their latest and for us the most unpleasant method, was when they came at us flying low, their floats skimming the top of the waves as if they were on a take-off run. Our lookouts found them extremely difficult to pick up and when they did, the birds were only a few miles out and that didn't give the gun crews more than a handful of minutes to prepare for action. It was all good practice, which kept us on our toes during the next few days. We were getting the impression, that these were the final stages of this part of our exercises.

The next aircraft to stage a simulated attack on ***KARO-AS*** came in low and fast from just off the port bow. 'Aircraft at 350 degrees' one of the portside lookouts sang out.

The reactions were routine by now.

'Flieger Alarm!'

'Full ahead both - hard to starboard.'

The last bellowed words of the *1WO* were drowned out by the Klaxon, but the helmsman knew his onions by now. He reacted to the first shout by crashing both machine-telegraphs to the 'Full Ahead' and at the same time pushing down his right-hand button of the rudder. Again, the diesel crews reacted to the urging of the hooter by pushing the throttles of their 2000 HP chargers right up to their end-stops, before the telegraphs pointers had come to rest.

As Mouse and I were on watch in the control-room at that time, we hared up the ladders to the bridge, only just being beaten to it by the Old Man. Our stations were to be taken over by the off-watch. Two of the bridge lookouts were already manning the quadruple on the lower *Wintergarten,* while the rest of them had opened the pressure-vessels containing the ammunition. When Mouse and I arrived at our respective twins and pushed our shoulder into their rests, the boat had almost completed the 'Arse to the enemy' manoeuvre and all the guns were ready, magazines in place, their sights trained on the *Arado.* He was still some way off when he started to veer first one way then the other, all the time trying to get at us from ahead, which was our blind spot. But at almost 20 knots, ***KARO-AS*** was quite a nimble little lady. The Old Man was able to counteract the Arado's sneaky tricks and when the plane was within range, he gave permission to open fire.

Up to this point everything proceeded in a routine sort of way.

At the end of his first run he pulled to the starboard side at the last second to miss our conning tower, circled and came in again. As before he had to fly right into the business ends of our *FLAK*, but there the similarity ended.

As he approached ***KARO-AS*** at an estimated speed of nearly 200 knots, all the time nearly touching the waves, he left pulling his joystick too late. He managed to gain height, but alas not enough.

There was a hellish crunching and banging above our heads. Picking ourselves off the deck, on which we had thrown ourselves when we realised what was going to happen, we could see the pilot struggling to keep the old kite up in the air. His one remaining float was touching the surface of the water for a time before he was able to get his crate climbing again. There goes one lucky bastard. But how would he get the thing down on only one leg?

Search me.

By then, our Old Man was having kittens. He shouted down to the Chief to try to get the large Metox aerial down into its rest position. But the damned thing wouldn't budge, either up or down. Not that it mattered all that much, it was in tatters anyway and obviously completely useless.

And then, Klaus-Peter noticed that the top of one of the periscopes, namely the much thinner attack one, was not looking too healthy. The Old Man looked sick to the gills. He asked the Chief to lift the scope as he went into the conning tower to look through it. 'I can't see a damned thing...', he said, followed be a string of expressions which were new to my delicate ears.

The Chief climbed up onto the periscope-support on top of the bridge and established that the top of the *Spargel* was bent and that lenses and mirrors were floating around inside. Now this was really serious, for one thing, those optical devices don't come very cheap and this one was of no further use to anyone.

There was going to be hell to pay for this! As it was, there is no way we could have carried on with the exercises. During on enemy-patrol, we would by necessity undertake all but the most serious of repairs. We were even equipped with the latest devices for drying-out the lenses and mirrors on the inside of the periscope to get rid of any condensation But here, while still in our own backyard, it meant an immediate return to port, to let the men of the dockyards do the needful. They were a lot better equipped to deal with *Spargels* and *Matratzen*. The Old Man, after radioing our predicament to the Chief of the Flotilla for further orders, asked the Navigator to set the course for Gotenhaven.

4 hours later we arrived at the dockyard, where we were informed that the repair would take a week at least. Both a replacement periscope and a new aerial would have to be shipped here from further up country.

Since ***KARO-AS*** didn't have to go into dry-dock, she more or less got immediate attention from the dockyard people. Before we knew what was happening, the damaged periscope was dismantled and removed, a job, with which we were able to help. There was no real problem in lifting it out with a crane after the lower part, that is the head-assembly with the eye-pieces and all the hydraulic attachments for raising and lowing were dismantled. Luckily, it had been in its fully retracted position when the Arado took exception to it, hence it was only the very top of the attack *Spargel* that was bent. To save time the whole assembly will be replaced, while the damaged one can probably be repaired again at the factory und that was thought to be the most cost effective way of getting us off the hook. But of course it is going to take a day or two to bring the replacement from the factory and perhaps another day to fit it. The question arises, why is it so important for us to have two serviceable periscopes? The answer is simple: They are the eyes of the captain when his boat is running submerged. Without them, he would be like a blind man.

The two periscopes are quite different from each other in some ways. The forward one is suitable only for searching the skies above for aircraft. In its much fatter top end it houses a mirror, which can be tilted upwards and downwards by the observer in the conning tower to establish whether the air is clear from marauding planes, before giving the order for surfacing.

The much more important one is the attack periscope. It is thinner at the top, so as to cut through the water without disturbing it unduly. It has a fixed field of view, i.e. horizontally. Housed inside an eight meter long sealed, thick-walled tube of some 20 cm diameter are a combination of precision mirrors and lenses, combining to provide the captain with a clear view of ships on the surface. With its help he can establish distances and speeds of targets, in short, it is his main tool for running a successful torpedo attack.

The removal of the aerial however, was a bit more complicated. It stemmed from the fact that during the gunnery practice it was in the fully extended position. Like a periscope it could be raised and lowered hydraulically. In its rest position it disappeared down into the bridge cladding, fully up it rose to the same height as the attack periscope in its down position. That's why it suffered a similar fate. But in addition to almost removing most of the square receiver part, the bit we called the mattress, it had also bent the 10 cm diameter ram, which raised it. It meant that a certain amount of fineness had to be used not to damage the seals where the ram went through the pressure hull. We were most impressed with the fine skills of the men from this dockyard. The team leader was German, but the two men under his wing were Ukrainian guest workers. They completed the task of removing the debris quickly and efficiently.

By the way, it was a matter of absolute national necessity to employ many skilled workers from other countries to make up for the ones called to do service in the forces. As far as I was aware, they were volunteers from occupied areas, mainly from Eastern Europe. At the factory where I did my apprenticeship, at least 25% of the skilled workforce were Ukrainian Nationals, working beside skilled and semi-skilled men, who were too old for military service as well as youngsters like us.

Back on board, all we had to do now was to wait for the replacement parts for both the scope and the aerial.

During the course of the day we took delivery of some mail. How of earth it ever found us was a minor miracle. For reasons of secrecy our nearest and dearest had to use a Feldpostnummer (Field Post Number; Field was perhaps short for battlefield) as our address, which in our case was M00459. The ‘M’ probably stood for ‘Marine’, short for Kriegsmarine. Perhaps there was a central collection point for the whole navy, but here they would have to locate the unit with the number 00459. Because of our various mishaps we never quite knew in which port or base we would be on any given day. But since they did find us in spite of all, they must have been very good at guesswork.

My letter was only a week old, which was quite unusual since mostly we were at least one month behind. But it contained a very welcome update on the progress of my one and only nephew Joseph. It seems, in true Schuler tradition he had aspirations to box in the heavyweight class. The other news was a bit of a surprise for me. My mother had decided that although she had four children of her own, a fact which had won her the rather useless decoration, the ‘Mother’s Cross’, that was no longer enough to keep her busy. Three of the four had flows the nest, so my little brat sister Uschi (Ursula) aged ten, needed company.

While I was still at home she, like all kid-sisters, entertained herself by being a dreadful nuisance. Whenever I wanted some peace and quite to follow my model-making hobby, she would cling to me like a leech. To escape her sticky clutches, I often had to use subterfuge. There were two ways to get up to my little model-making workshop in the loft. The first one was a ladder on the outside of our bungalow leading to a door to the loft space. Using this route I could pull-up the ladder behind me. OK, that was a dirty trick, but it worked. But, like just like the second way up, it resulted in torrents of tears from Uschi, when she couldn't follow me. The second way was used only when Mum wasn't around. In our conservatory there was a loft hatch, but no ladder. I wasn't an acrobat, but by jumping up to get a handhold on the rim of the hatch in the ceiling, then swing-up my legs to get a foothold on the wardrobe, I thus gained entry to my own space.

Anyway, since I was no longer available to annoy, somebody else was to take my place. When things started to go haywire at the eastern front, lots of refugees arrived in Berlin. In the resulting chaos one little girl of Uschi's age had lost contact with her mother. My mother took Helga into the family, while attempts were made to trace her mother. At the bottom of the last page of Mum's letter was a drawing of two little smiling faces and the words: 'Hello, big brother.'

The rest of the letter described how Dad had to clamber up on to the roof every other day with a pot of hot tar, to prise-out the many pieces of FLAK-shrapnel, which had penetrated the roofing felt and then seal the holes with the hot tar. Reading this, I felt thankful that during the actual air raids the family had a safe refuge from all but a direct bomb hit.

While I was still at home, Dad and I had dug a 2 metres deep, 2 m wide and 4 m hole long hole in the back garden, lined the sides and covered the whole lot with old railway sleepers. Another layer of earth went on top of the sleepers to really make it safe. I'd spent many a night in this bunker with my family until I joined the navy. Mum had found an old mattress and placed it in one corner. That bed was for me to sleep on during raids, as I was the only person in the household who had to be at work every morning at 6 am sharp. Little Uschi found an even warmer and cuddlier place to sleep, on mother's lap. I'll never be able to forget the concern Mum and Dad showed for us youngsters and our well being; their anxiety was deeply etched on their faces.

Two days after dealing with my mail, our ladylove had been fitted with a new set of eyes and ears. The *Matratze* and the attack *Spargel* had been replaced and ***KARO-AS*** was once again ready to continue with her trials.

CHAPTER SIX

To take-on provisions for the next chapter of our working-up schedule, we only had to sail one mile, from the dockyard to the base of the 25th U-boat Flotilla. Two of our Type IXD2 sister boats joined us for the next set of exercises.

Most of the seamen were kept busy with paintbrushes, while the diesel crew filled the fuel and lubricating oil tanks. The remainder of our crew had a little time off for a good yarn and watch others do a bit of work for a change.

Moored under camouflage netting beside one of the large storage sheds, sitting around on the wintergarden, we watched as several little rail-carriages were wheeled alongside. On each one rested an ominous looking torpedo, sleek and well greased. A collapsible type of gantry had been erected on our foredeck, with which the *Aale* (eels, our affectionate name for torpedoes) were lifted off the trolleys, swung aboard and deposited on a fixed cradle on deck. This cradle had been assembled to line-up with the open hatch to the bow torpedo room at a downward angle of 30 degrees.

Our Petty Officer Torpedo mixer was one of the most experienced men on board, already sporting the EK1 (Iron Cross 1st Class) alongside his U-boat badge. Working to his instructions, his men handled those heavy and slippery loads with the utmost ease. Without a lot of fuss the eels slipped down into the bowels of the boat, steadied by the block and tackle fastened to the conning tower. The hatch was made to measure and was only just wide enough to allow them through.

'Tight, like a virgin's pussy' was the verdict from the bridge.

Once inside the boat, the torpedoes were held suspended by other blocks, which were sliding on tracks lining up with the torpedo tubes. Ramming the heavy cigars home into their tubes was a job for muscle-power.

KARO-AS was designed to carry 24 torpedoes when in front-line action, but this time we only took aboard four. They looked just like any other torpedo, but we learned that they were specials insofar as their warheads were filled with cement and that after running at the preset distance and depth, they would surface, ready to be recovered and used again. Three were loaded into bow tubes and the last one into one of the two stern tubes.

This was a god-given opportunity for our stern-room's resident torpedo mechanic, Walter, to become overbearing. All our bunks had been dismantled for the loading manoeuvre and no amount of abuse from us, who wanted to get on with either our meals or to get a few minutes kip, could persuade him to hurry-up with his fiddling around. To watch him stroking and caressing this greasy, slippery thing, you would think he was in love with it.

Finally, we were allowed to re-assemble our bunks, while other members of the crew were now engaged on the boring job of taking-on supplies. Under the watchful eye of the boatswain, his men were stowing provisions, fresh or tinned food, which had to last for the next few weeks. The boatswain's job was to ensure that every item was stored in orderly fashion.

Firstly, it was important that it could be found when it was to be used. Secondly, every item must be so securely stored to stop it from clattering-about inside the boat during heavy seas or when diving at a steep angle. Sound travelled much better through water than through the air and we had been warned that a lot of big ears would be listening for even the slightest sounds from a U-boat.

Thirdly and even more important, the stores must be safe from the thieving hands of all and sundry riff-raff. It was only yesterday, that we heard that several petty officers appeared before the Old Man, having been caught purloining a tin of very delectable plums in syrup. Because of the restricted and cramped conditions, in which *Smutje* had to work, the meals were on average plain but wholesome. But what made all the difference and what was very much appreciated by all the crew, was the occasional tin of fruit, which followed the meals. It was therefore only fair that those thieving bastards did get a dressing down. As always, the Old Man was as fair as possible and did not do it in front of the lower classes. But he must have forgotten that directly underneath his own little corner, where he ate, slept and worked when he was not on the bridge, lay one of the two large main batteries. One or other of the electricians were constantly checking those. We got a résumé of what had been said from Paul. While lying on his little trolley, which was running on silent bakelite rails and from which he could check and top-up every one of the 62 two-volt cells, he overheard every word through the thin floor. He was not impressed by the weasel-like excuses put forward by our superiors. But on the other hand, the language employed by the Old Man equally took him aback. It seems he left them in no doubt as to what he would insert into their back passages should anything like this happen again. How he was going to do it, seeing that the tins were about 10 cm in diameter? He left that to the imagination of the hapless shower.

Our resident poet managed to produce a rhyming, but largely sanitised version of the Old Man's 'Sermon' in the weekly W.C. report, which was pinned-up on the inside of the doors of the heads at a level one could read while sitting down.

There was always something going on for us in the control-room. While still in port, we were attempting to calculate the weight and distribution of the newly acquired stores and the torpedoes, to enable us to lighten the boat by an equivalent amount of water from the ballast tanks. The diesel fuel, which a lighter had earlier discharged into our saddle tanks, also had to be compensated for.

The sums, as I saw them, went something like this:
Add four torpedoes at a weight of 1600 kg each = 6.4 tonnes
Add 100 cubic metres fuel at .8 tonne each = 80 "
Add other stores estimated at = 0.5 "
Total gain = 86.9 tonnes.

At first guess Mouse and I decided that we must discharge 86.9 tonnes of water to maintain a constant weight of the boat.

'No. Try again.' suggested CPO Georg. 'We haven't got 86,900 litres in our trimming tanks.'

And then I remembered. I had always been anxious to learn, so much so that I often spent my spare time in chatting with the petty officer of the port-watch. Gerhard Weiss wasn't more then a couple of years older than me, but he already had front experience on a Type IIVC boat. After five lengthy and successful patrols in the North Atlantic, from Murmansk down to the South Atlantic, his Type VIIC boat had been ordered to proceed into the Mediterranean. At the very last minute, before leaving St.Nazair, he was transferred to a Petty Officer's school at Wilhelmshaven. Having been successful there, he had joined our boat as a *Maat* (Mate, as we called all Petty Officers). Unfortunately, a few days ago, he had learned his old boat had run on a mine in the Gulf of Genua, off La Spazia and had been lost with all hands. Understandably he was absolutely devastated, couldn't get the faces of his ex-mates out of his mind. Whenever he thought about it, he kept repeating 'Why only them? I should have been there with them.' What made it even worse, it was thought to have been a 'friendly' Italian mine.

But talking to him, I had learned a few other facts.

I reminded Mouse that oil is lighter than water.

'When you take on 100 cubic metres of oil weighing 80 tonnes, you push out an equivalent volume of water weighing 100 tonnes from the fuel bunkers. Hence the boat becomes lighter, by 20 tonnes - not heavier. Compensating for 6.4 tonnes of torpedoes and half a tonne of supplies still meant adding 13100 litres of water to the trimming tanks, fore and aft.

Before the real shooting exercises were to start, it was going to be essential to go over the procedures that had to be adopted while launching torpedoes. We already knew the difference a few litres of water could make to the trim of the boat. When running submerged and when we got the trim absolutely right; the Chief was able to hold periscope-depth without using the hydroplanes to excess; he could also do it at the slowest possible speed. In spite of having been given a special shape at the point where they broke through the water line, they always produced some sort of bow-wave. The greater the speed of the boat, the greater was the wave. Like all bow-waves, it often showed-up with a phosphorescent luminosity, which was a certain giveaway to an enemy. The maintaining of this most desirable Zero trim at the moment of firing-off one or more torpedoes, should provide us with as many problems as we would like to handle. The weight of each *Aal* was such, that at the moment it was launched, the trim of the boat had to be compensated for, by taking aboard 1,600 litres (or 1.6 tonnes) of water. Compensating tanks were positioned under the torpedo tubes for that purpose. The flooding of those was not something we could simulate; it had to be done during an actual exercise.

The Old Man and his officers, together with all the torpedo personnel, had their own training to think of. It certainly looked as if we were in for a very interesting couple of weeks.

KARO-AS, in convoy with her two sister boats, was heading out toward the deeps off the coast of Gotland, some 10 hours away. Here we could play around in up to 160m of water. The Commander in LI of the 25th Flotilla was on board *KREUZ-AS*, the most senior of the three boats by two weeks. He wished to personally oversee the proceedings.

Before leaving port he had the Old Man and our *1WO* and *2WO* at a meeting, where they and the officers of the other two boats were briefed. They weren't telling us an awful lot about it on their return, one could guess their minds were full of other things. In the next few hours they spent a lot of time inside the conning tower, where the two periscopes were located, one for observing airspace and the other for observing and attacking surface ships.

All sort of weird and wonderful bits of clockwork mechanisms, charts for identifying targets... both ships and aircraft, decorated the walls of this very small room of some 10 feet diameter. Some very technical names had been invented for those gadgets, such as 'firing-interval calculator' and 'deflection calculator'. Those names sounded like double Dutch to me. While servicing the motors and wire-ropes for raising and lowering the periscopes, I had often tried to make sense of all those rotating wheels, discs and flashing lights, which for all the world looked like things from a fair ground. But I was assured they would serve a serious purpose when the action started, to convert distances, speed and direction of travel of a given target-ship into angles of attack. In other words, there was no sense in aiming directly at a ship and fire, because by the time the torpedo arrived at that point, the target would have long gone.

In my own mind, however, I was willing to bet that in spite of all the paraphernalia for calculating and computing, the most successful Commanders did all this off the top of their heads or by the feel in their water, if you know what I mean.

But the theoretical side of training had to run its course.

Through the open hatch, which led from the control room to the conning tower, we could hear the whirring of those hell-machines after one of the officers had entered a sequence of numbers called out by the Old Man on the bridge, which he had read from the markings of the torpedo-director or aiming device. When running submerged the attack-periscope would serve the same purpose. Even then, when only going through the motions, you could cut the tension with a knife. I didn't mind betting there was a fair amount of competition going on between the Commanders of the three boats as to who was going to get the best results at the forthcoming exercises.

'We'd better not let him down,' said the Chief 'or else we are not going to hear the last of it.'

The real trials started one morning.

Since the early hours of that day, the radio operators were kept busy receiving and sending signals. There was also a fair amount of Morse-lamp traffic between the boats of our convoy.

One of the seamen, coming off watch told me that a small, ancient looking coal-fired steamer of some 1,500 tons, called the *Rügen*, had joined our little convoy. It was thought to be the target ship. Even on our off-watch periods we were kept below deck, so we couldn't see anything at all, but only guess what was going on up on top.

One by one, dummy-surface-runs were made by the three boats against the target steamer. When the Old Man made his approach, all the relevant information, such as estimated distance to the target, its speed and course and everything else were relayed by radio to the C in C, who by this time

had transferred aboard the *Rügen*. A flag signal from the target should tell, whether the attack was deemed to be successful or not.
This part of the proceedings went on for a couple of days.
During all this we had little or nothing to do.

Once it all started in earnest, everybody's hands would be full looking after the trim of the boat. A lot had to be done during the launch of a torpedo as it would not do to let the boat's bow rise out of the water.
From the third day on, the same exercises were carried out while running submerged. The crew were now on 'action stations'. We were still not firing anything, so one boat operate on one side of the target, the second was on the other side. The third had to take some time out.

As far as I could make out, the Old Man had to take our boat on the surface to a position just ahead of the target, with diesels at 'Full ahead both'. The trick was, to do this without being observed by their lookouts on the target, which meant keeping at a distance just below the horizon.
Then we dived and the Old Man ran a simulated attack from inside the conning tower. It presented no problem to him, but he had to make sure that everyone else was getting the hang of things.

The Chief stood at the bottom of the ladder, which led from the conning tower, listening to every word from above while keeping his eyes glued to the depth gauges. The periscope was used as sparingly as possible to avoid being spotted.

And so it went on and on.
I got the impression that even after this relatively short time we were getting quite a team together. Everybody was impatient to proceed and go on with the next exercise ... the actual firing.

But that was a few days away yet, rules had to be followed. If the manual states that it should take so many days to complete this exercise, then that is how long it had to take. There are no shortcuts in Prussian Military circles. 'Get your training right and reality will be a cakewalk', or words to that effect.

The time for serious exercising had arrived. At 15.50, just as the 3rd watch was getting ready, the silence was torn by the shrill tone of the alarm-bell. 10 seconds it took to get the five-man watch from the bridge down into the boat and for the *2WO* to close the lid. At 27 seconds we were at periscope depth. Unbeknown to us down below, our boat had already been getting into position ahead of the target. 'Up periscope' came the order from the Old Man, who was now almost living in the conning tower. 'Down periscope' he kept taking the briefest of looks before ducking down again.

The Chief was keeping the boat on a level keel at precisely the right depth. His instructions to the fore and aft hydroplane operators sounded crisp and precise. Fine-adjusting the trim by sending 50 litres from fore to aft, did the trick in this instance.

The Old Man was thoroughly at home now and sounded as if he was going to enjoy every minute of the next few days. Everybody was wide-awake, the whole crew at actions, waiting for action.

'Not bad at all' said the captain and then

'Come and have a look' as he gave up the periscope to the *1WO*.

'Steer 277 degrees, Full ahead both' he was enjoying this.

For a further 10 minutes the killer was stalking his prey. We could hear the rattle of the calculators working overtime upstairs.

'Stand by one'.

'Flood one'

The bow-cap of the torpedo tube was cranked opened.

'Range 3000 - depth 8 metres'.

The torpedoes were set to run 8 metres below the surface.

We heard that the draught of the target was 4.21 metres and the practice-torpedo had to pass under the target to be declared 'a hit'.

'Range 3000, depth 8 are set.' came the confirmation from the men at the tubes.

After a few seconds followed: 'Fire one'.

A very noticeable shudder signalled the firing of our first ever torpedo. Leaving the snout, the eel was pushed out by a compressed air driven piston, from where it was propelled forward toward the target by its own built-in pneumatic motor. At the very instance it left the tube, a vent in one of the forward compensating tank was ripped open to take on 1.6 tonnes of water, during which time the Chief held the bow down using the forward hydroplanes.

I could have sworn that there wasn't a flicker on the depth gauge.

'Fired one' reported the bow-tube mixer.

In real action, ***KARO-AS*** would have shown a clean pair of heels as soon as the deadly cargo had left the boat.

'Periscope down.' 'Hard a port'

'Steer 180.'

Normally he might have ordered to go to 100 metres. This would have been one way to get the hell out of any entanglement with Tommy's defences, with our skins intact. While the boat would have dived down, somebody in the control room would have used a stopwatch to call out the time elapsed from the firing.

At a distance of 3,000 metres and running at a speed of 40 knots the torpedo would take exactly 2 minutes and 24 seconds to blast the target or to miss it.

But this was only make-belief.

The Old Man watched the bubble-path of the torpedo through the periscope and eventually shouted with delight:

'It's a hit amidships, boys!'

We never heard a damned thing, so how on earth did he know what was a hit or a miss?

Because, through the periscope he could see that all along the side railings of the target several observers were stationed. Their job was to watch for the bubble-trail left by an air-driven torpedo. If one passed under the ship, a prearranged flag-signal was run-up on the mast of the steamer, indicating the result.

'Slow ahead both. Prepare to surface'.

The Old Man was absolutely delighted as he dropped down into the control room. There was no doubt about it; it was one up for ***KARO-AS*** and her Old Man.

His white cap was still facing backwards, as its peak tended to get in the way when he was peering through the eyepiece of the periscope. He went on to speak into the tannoy's microphone.

'The position at the moment is as follows: All three boats have had one shot at the target and there has only been one hit.

I am glad to say that it was ours.

Well done, Chief and well done, everybody else.'

He went on to explain that there would be further chances for shots at the target at dusk and during the night. We surfaced and retired to another square to wait for our next turn, using the waiting time to fully re-charge the batteries.

Anyway, as the daylight started to fade, the second of our runs was made. This time it took a lot longer to stalk the quarry. The ruddy target was doing a bit of the old zigzagging to the mild annoyance of the Old Man. As always he was present in the conning tower, but he had given the actual command over to the *1WO*. Nobody on board ***KARO-AS*** had a good word to say about Sub-Lieutenant Schwarz. His bearing and demeanour was that of a typical Prussian officer. Behind his back he was known as the *Hitler Junge* (Hitler Youth). Traditionally, in the cramped and damp surrounding of a U-boat, the dress and general body cleanliness were not in the forefront of anybody's mind. Working clothes were often oil-spattered and greasy, but could be made to look OK when worn with a colourful shirt and/or equally flamboyant scarf.

Anyway, it befitted PIRATES and everybody including the Old Man, joined in this casual dressing, but not *Herr Leutnant* Schwarz.

Nothing was ever good enough for him. He reckoned, his job as second in command, made him responsible for discipline. He even dressed with collar and tie for mealtimes and showed his annoyance when nobody else in the Officers mess did the same.

Disliked he was, but when he got to grips with ***KARO-AS*** at the shooting gallery, he proved himself to be extremely competent. Estimating distances, speed and course of an enemy craft seemed to be second nature to him. Only rarely did the Old Man offer a word or two of advice. He didn't know him well enough to trust him fully and he certainly wasn't going to allow him to screw up the boat's good name.

'Get the *Spargel* up and down as quickly as you can, we don't want the whole world to know where we are,' he offered and followed that by 'You may have to anticipate the target's next move even before he makes it.'

When the *1WO* was running his attack, the *2WO* (Officer of the second watch) was at the calculators. Even the *3WO*, who was a non-commissioned Officer, got involved. In a real situation there was always a chance of having casualties, in which case other trained reserves would be able to take over.

But to everybody's credit, we had another hit. Not quite amidships, like the first, but good enough to blow his bow off, if the torpedo had been real. Our sisters had registered good results as well.

We were still one up on them, but to see who was to finish top of the class still depended on the next two runs.

The first of those runs took place shortly after midnight. An occasional glimpse of moon helped the captain to get the next attack under way.

To keep out of everybody's way, ***KARO-AS*** was running on the surface, way out behind the horizon, making 19 knots, to position herself well ahead of the target. Once there, we held station until we got the C. in C's permission to attack.

From all the traffic over the airwaves we learned that *KREUZ-AS* had just finished her attack and recorded a miserable miss.

We should not have celebrated by shouting Hurray, should we?

'Alarm!'

Down we went like a stone.
We would have to do the rest from down here in the cellar. The Old Man could be heard talking to himself. 'If the target is making 5 knots, we should get close enough by using every last ounce of our battery power'.
'Full Ahead Both - steer 255 degrees'

Once we got close enough to enable the Old Man to use the periscope, he did take the occasional look. Reducing the speed to 'Half Ahead Both', he was calling out numbers to the *1WO* who was feeding them into the calculators. All we could hear is the whirring of countless little wheels inside the clockwork-like machines.
'Stand by tube 3'
'Range 2,000, depth 8.'
'Tube 3 is ready, Range 2,000 and depth 8 set.' came the reply. 'Flood tube 3.' the bow-caps were opened.
The Old Man continued his approach, still impatiently muttering under his breath: 'Come on - come on'
Finally it came:
'Fire three.'
As soon as the torpedo had left the spout, spluttering and hissing on its way, the captain practiced a quick get-away.
'Full ahead both.'
'Hard to starboard.'
'Go to 100 metres.'

This was what ***KARO-AS*** was designed for. Nose down at 40° she dived into her element, on a course, which would take her away from any possible trouble.

We were busy compensating the trim to make up for the loss of 1.6 tonnes, while the PO Torpedo Mixer counted down the 1 3/4 minutes it should have taken the Eel to reach the *Rügen.* When he reached 95 seconds, there was a sharp noise, as if somebody hit the outside of our hull with a hammer.

Before shooting, we had quite clearly heard the steady and monotonous screw noise the old steamer made. Now that noise had been replaced by a chorus of banging, hissing and groaning.
The Chief had reported: 'Boat has levelled-off at 100 metres' Over the tanoy he added 'Report any signs of leaks.'
Every compartment reported that ***KARO-AS***'s hull appeared to be as sound as a bell under the unaccustomed outside pressure.

The Old Man asked the *1WO*: 'What the hell do you think is happening

up there?'
'I've heard similar noises come from sinking ships.'
'So have I' said the Old Man.
'I suppose we'd better go and see what's happening up there' and followed that with
'Go to periscope depth.'
Still at 'Full Ahead Both' she shot up, with the Old Man ready to take a look through the *Spargel.*
'*Gott verdammtes Donnerwetter'.*
What in heavens name is going on?'
We got the impression the Old Man was going to have a seizure or a fit, or both.
'Surface' he yelled.
He threw open the lid as soon as it was clear of the surface and jumped up on to the bridge.
The Diesels sprang into life with their exhaust gases pushing the remaining water out of the ballast tanks. The *1WO* and the lookouts hared up as well.
'Steer 270 degrees' and then, when the tanks had been blown out, he stopped the engines altogether.

Looking up from the control room to the men on the bridge, we could see their faces lit-up by a flickering light. While ***KARO-AS*** was wallowing in a light sea, permission to go up on to the bridge was freely given. Using the opportunity to smoke a cigarette, we witnessed a very odd performance being played-out right in front of our very eyes.

Only a few hundred yards away, on our starboard bow, lay our two sister boats. Their searchlights were fixed on two lifeboats wallowing in the slight swell. Behind the boats we could see the *Rügen*, resembling a floating fireball. While the last of her crew were still scrambling down into the life-boats, bright sparks were flying into the air from her funnel, igniting canvass and ropes lying around on her deck, making the whole steamer look like a Roman Candle.

By the ferocity of the hissing, it was quite obvious, that water was flooding her red-hot boilers and that there was every chance that she would first go up, skyward. All the crew seemed to have got-off safely, so there was no valid reason for us not to enjoy this wonderful spectacle. For a long time she lay in her death-throws, but eventually, still making the most awful racket, she slid down below the waves. Bow first, while a series of muffled explosions could be heard on her way down to John Brown's locker.
Had we sunk the poor old target ship with a cement torpedo?

That question was answered when one of the lifeboats, with several of the steamer's crew in it, made for our port bow.
To help the survivors aboard, the Old Man sent men forward to the forecastle. The very first man aboard was the C. in C. of our Flotilla, who in his leather gear looked like any other sailor.

But there was no mistaking the *Korvetten Kapitain's* (Commodore) mood. He was foaming at the mouth, while his red face glowed in the dark. And his language had its roots in the gutter as he dropped down into the control room and from there to our Old Man's corner.
One got the impression that he was not at all pleased.

The other crewmembers, which had come aboard, went down into engine room to get warm. Once they had thawed-out, they told us their story.
It seemed that the *Rügen* had long been retired as coastal steamer, but at the outbreak of war had taken on a new lease of life as target vessel for U-boats, so that they could practice their torpedo drills. Literally hundreds of boats had them in their sights in the last few years and fired many torpedoes in her direction, for her crew this war had up to now been a real holiday.

Until today, that was.
The first mate of the *Rügen* told us. 'We were all lined up along the railings and watched the bubble path of this last torpedo approaching. It appeared to run below us at exactly amidships.
We were just going to report a 'Hit' to the bridge, when we heard this awful clutter just below us. And lo and behold, less than a metre down, sticking out of the belly of our ship was this bloody great torpedo with its screws still churning away, trying to drive it even further into the boiler room.'

It seemed, when our tin-eel reached the target at a speed of 40 knots, not at the pre-set depth of 8 metres but running just below the surface, it went straight through the thin, rusty hull of the tramp ship.
The poor old dear just wasn't up to such rough treatment any more.
'It took a little while for our captain on the bridge to understand our frantic message. He couldn't see what had happened and by the time he realised the full implication of it and stopped the engines, the surface runner had dislodged itself. This really allowed the water to spurt into the boilers and you all know the rest.'

Glug... glug... glug, down and down she went.
Her proud Ensign, under which she had faithfully served, had still been fluttering from the staff at her stern. Illuminated by the searchlights from

the two watching U-boats, it was the last sign of her as she slid down.
Even now, when she must have reached the bottom of the sea, she could still be heard moaning and groaning.
Apart from the lifeboats, there was only a small amount of debris left on the surface.
'What happened to the torpedo?' asked our Old Man.
'It went shooting off past our ship with its screw still running' he was told by the Flotilla's Chief.

'Right. I think you'd better try and fish it out. That's, if you can manage to get that bit right'. The recovering of the torpedoes was normally the job of the target or her motor-launch. But she was quite unable to do it this time.
At slow speed, with our searchlights blazing, we followed in the general direction indicated by men from the late lamented *Rügen*. The practice eels were designed to rise to the surface when the compressed-air supply ran out. It could then be recovered and returned to the base for resetting and reusing.
Not long after, we approached the errant eel.

'Do not... do you hear me… I say... **DO NOT TOUCH** that *verdammte* torpedo until I've had a chance to examine it's depth-setting!' The Flotilla's Chief was heard to shout from the bridge.
But of course it had to be brought aboard first.
Flooding a forward tank to get our boat's bow down below the water while two of our seamen pulled the offending thing over the forecastle. Blowing the tank again, they lashed the eel to the bollards normally used for mooring-up.

All three boats headed back to base. In accordance with U-boat tradition, from our periscope flew a 20 feet long white pennant, which had the silhouette of a ship and her displacement, i.e. 1 500 Tonnes painted on it.
Our Old Man was hoping, that the Brass Hats at the impending inquiry would see the funny side of the escapade.

He never found out, because when the torpedo was given a post-mortem examination by a senior technical officer at the arsenal, it was established that the depth settings on the eel had been OK, but that a sticky depth-keeping Gyro has been the culprit.

Instead of a Court Marshal hearing, the Old Man got a recommendation for his deadeye shooting.
It would take a few days to find us a new target ship.

Our lovely, tenderly cared-for uniforms stood out sharply against the grey, bedraggled looking kit worn by two infantry men, who were sitting opposite us in this third class compartment of the local train. They had only just been released from their hospital beds, where overstretched doctors had stitched them together after being wounded on their way back from Stalingrad. However, today they were going home to their families for a well-earned fortnight's leave, and where, no doubt, the fatted calf will be there to greet them.

Last night our Old Man decided that we might as well take a few of days off while waiting for the replacement target ship to arrive.

I'd gladly have stayed on board for a few days, just to eat and to rest. I had a few letters to write and apart from that I quite liked the idea of lying in my bunk all of the day, reading or even just to do a bit of thinking. But things are never as simple as that. While I rested, my busybody pal Mouse was busy searching for places nearby, where we could relax for a few days.

Apparently, there were families here in this part of the country, who for a small charge were prepared to put-up service personnel for short stays, men like us, on a few days leave when the time was too short to go home. In the library of the base he found, among the register of suitable places, what he though was an ideal place to rest up for the weekend.

After being briefed about the need for secrecy about the identity of our boat or our mission, we were now en route to Seedorf, a village, not 50 kilometres from here, where we were to lodge with a family by the name of Brauer.

When I looked at the two men in our compartment, I felt really guilty, almost like a draft dodger.

I would've been with them at the Eastern Front, if I hadn't volunteered for the navy and U-boats.

But, bless them; our newfound friends soon made me forget those silly thoughts. When they learned that we were getting ready for the first patrol in our 'Sardine Tins', they assured us that they wouldn't change their lot against ours for all the money in the world. 'At least we could see the whites of the Russian's eyes when they came after us and we could shoot back from our muddy foxholes,' they said. 'Out in the open air you can always run if things get to hot, whereas you're stuck in your iron coffins.'

I began to think that there existed a healthy mutual respect for each other's lot.

During the rest of our journey, while they told us a little more about the condition at the front, we shared our cigarettes with them and even offered

them a nip or two from Mrs.Brauer's bottle. She wouldn't mind!
It seems that things at the Russian front should improve now that the supply lines were getting much shorter. The very vastness of that country was the biggest obstacle to fighting a land war. Often there was no ammunition for the gunners or no fuel for tanks or other motorised units. The troops could manage to miss the odd meal, but without fuel and ammunition they were just sitting ducks.

Funny, isn't it, Mouse, how little we know about the war in the East. Not that you would expect them to tell us everything' I said to him later, after our friends-in-grey had jumped off the coach, amidst shouts of 'Land Ahoy. Have a nice time, Spider and Mouse'.

As the train started to roll again, Mouse nearly had a fit. 'They left their rifles behind' he yelled. But all was well, our soldier friends had already noticed and were frantically running beside the train, trying not to make any more of a fuss than was absolutely necessary. So we managed to slip the carbines out of the window, saying 'Here you are. You might just need them again'. Panic over!

When we arrived at our destination, we could see that Seedorf, which by the way translates as 'the village by the sea or lake', was just a collection of a few farms, some farm workers cottages, a general store, and a little church. As was common practice in Middle-European countries, all the farmers in a particular area, huddled their farmsteads together in villages, which in days gone-by were fortified for protection from gangs of marauding Swedes, Danes, Huns, Cossacks and other assorted riff-raff.

We found *Frau* Brauer's house, it was one of the larger ones in the village; it had started life as two cottages, but had been converted to one larger home. Our knock on the door was answered by a largish elderly woman, who was almost toothless, her hair covered with a headscarf and her eyes obscured by the thick lenses of wire-rimmed glasses. Her face lit up, when she saw two baby-faced sailors on her doormat. Unannounced, as we were, she made us very welcome. Somebody at the base had suggested that we wouldn't be overcharged, as long as we bore a few gifts and I must say, what little we had brought in the way of tins of ham and fruit was most gratefully accepted.

After she showed us to our separate rooms in the attics and told us to make ourselves at home, we were left to settle in. 'Just come down whenever you feel hungry and I will make you a sandwich to put you on to our evening meal at 7 o'clock' she had added. Looking around, my room was quite small, in fact it was almost entirely taken up by the largest and most comfortable featherbed ever invented. We have only been in the Navy for just over one year, sleeping in bunks, hammocks, even on the floor-plates behind one of the diesels and we had almost forgotten that normal people slept in beds.

Hell! I'm going to enjoy this part of our leave to the full. Trying-out the bed for size, I wished it were bedtime already. However, I must see whether Mouse was equally suited. His room was in the other part of what used to be the separate cottages and to get to it I had to go down one set of stairs and up another. He lay stretched out on his equally sumptuous bed, sound asleep with a big grin on his face. God knows what he was dreaming about?

Knowing he had been on watch last night, I left him to it.

I decided to nip down to see whether there was time to clean up before the meal. Of course, during wartime it was difficult to get fuel to heat water, so nobody could afford to be too liberal with it, but the landlady, 'Just call me *Mutti* (Mummy)', assured me that in quarter of an hour I could use their bath and Mouse could have his later.

Blow me down, I couldn't remember the last time I had experienced the luxury of a hot bath. As a little boy, we had a tin bath in front of the fire, with mother scrubbing away on the ingrained dirt on our arms and legs. Later we made do with showers at the local swimming pool or at work. Now, on U-boats, we had learned that a good application of 4711 (eau-de-Cologne) would for a while at least, hide the fact that you hadn't washed behind your ears.

But a hot bath!

Lucky us.

Behind the door in my room, I found a silk dressing gown. Trying it on for size, I found it fitted to perfection and made me feel like a million dollars, straight out of one of Hollywood's films. It didn't only feel good but it looked the part as well, complete with fire-spitting dragon emblazoned on its back. I guessed it was there to be used. So I got ready and made my way down to the second floor and into the bathroom. The water had been run and towels were laid out. Only thing was I couldn't find a key to lock the door. However, whistling and singing to let people know I was here, I dropped the dressing gown on the floor and stepped into the steaming water. The bath was a large cast iron job, certainly more than long enough for my frame and what was more important; the water seemed hot enough to enjoy a really long soak.

It took me a little while to get adjusted to the heat of the water, but when

I did, it was heaven to be able to lay back and admire your own navel, among other things. You don't get too many chances to have a good look at yourself, but then - you don't often have the opportunity to have a bath in a room surrounded by mirrors.

Thinking about this and that I finally became drowsy enough to nearly fall asleep. Peels of laughter from outside the bathroom brought me round at the double. *Mutti* must have company now, female company at that.

Hell! Could they have been watching me from outside?

Quick as lightning I finished and went back to my room to stretch out on the bed.

At 7 o'clock, Mouse woke me up, saying it was time for the evening meal. He looked all clean and shiny. I bet he enjoyed his bath just as much as I did.

Going down we found *Mutti* was now dressed in a long flowing skirt, white frilly blouse and a type of bolero, a bit like a local folk-dress. Gone was the bespectacled and wrinkly old lady. A very attractive lady, who was a picture to behold with her glossy dark hair, horn-rimmed glasses and flashing white teeth, met us.

And yes, indeed, she had company.

Smiling, because both Mouse and I stood there with our mouths open, she introduced the two strangers. 'This is my daughter Lotti and her friend Gretel, who are joining you for the evening meal. And look here, girls, these sailors are called Gerhard and Werner, known as Spider and Mouse to their friends on board their U-boat.'

Well! Well! Well!

Just to feast our eyes on a couple of girls - well not just girls, but very pretty girls, probably of our own age or perhaps a little less.

First lets see what's on the table.

With the usual food rationing in operation, we never expected too much in the way of cuisine, maybe a thick home made vegetable soup made from things grown in the garden. Oh Boy, how wrong can you get? Lit only by two candles, *Mutti* showed us to our chairs. 'Now, boys, you must make yourself at home and if there is anything you want, just let me know.'

We were served with the most fantastic feast we had ever experienced in our young lives. Right enough, the vegetable soup started us off, together with freshly baked rolls and butter. This was followed by masses of roast pork, roast potatoes and vegetables, further followed by fresh peaches and lashings of real fresh cream and as if this was not enough, there were two bottles of wine in an ice-bucket from which *Mutti* kept topping up our crystal glasses.

While enjoying the meal to the full, my eyes wandered round the room and fell on a silver framed photograph on the sideboard. It was of a Chief Petty Officer (Engineer) wearing the black and white ribbon of the Iron Cross 1st Class on his front buttonhole as well as the actual Iron Cross on his chest together with golden U-boat broach. This broach was only presented to those who had seen a lot of enemy action on front-boats.

Noticing my glance, *Mutti* explained that it was of her late husband. He had served on the boat, which had penetrated Scapa Flow in the first days of the war, sunk the British Battleship Royal Oak in Tommy's backyard. But we knew that their boat was lost with all hands later in 1941, after just one patrol too many.

Other photos showed *Mutti*, her husband and a little scrawny little girl, which I guessed was Lotti.

Afterwards, while Mouse and I were lounging in plush easy chairs, drinking Brandy heavily disguised with raw eggs and pretending to be Dutch Advocaat, as well as smoking large Havana cigars, which had appeared from nowhere, Lotti and Gretel helped to clear the table and wash the dishes. Our offer of help was politely declined, allowing us to just sit and enjoy a little bit of the homely comforts normally denied to us.

Maybe I had dropped off in my contentment, but as I looked up next, I was even more flabbergasted than before. Lotti and Gretel had changed from two gawky young schoolgirls with pigtails into two super models, dressed in close-fitting slinky outfits and all the while thoroughly enjoying our admiring, lurid stares.

They proceeded to get their schoolbooks out of their bags to work on their homework for the next day. 'We hope you don't mind, but we must get this done and there is more wine, if you will help yourself.'

We learned that both hoped to go to university, Gretel to study the sciences and Lotti the Arts and Literature for a career in teaching.

Gretel showed me her work, as she knew from Lotti's dad that maths and algebra go hand in hand with engineering on a U-boat. We both worked together through some particularly nasty equations and solved a few geometric figures by dividing them into right-angled and other triangles. But since Gretel had pulled up her chair very close to mine, I must confess that my mind was not entirely occupied with those triangles or geometric figures but with the much simpler and more rounded figure of Gretel herself.

As far as I could tell, she didn't mind being admired by a young sailor. Dream on, big boy, but remember these girls are not the usual harbour side pick-ups.

Mouse and Lotti were also busily engrossed in literature - or were they? It seemed to me that some of the answers to Lotti's homework were located in the kitchen, judging by the number of times they found something to do in there. Mouse's beetroot-red face was a dead give-away - the temperature in the kitchen was too hot for comfort - or maybe it was the effect of too much wine.

Well, well! Boys will be boys.

It was already well after 10 o'clock next morning when I woke up, feeling distinctly peckish. There was a basin and a water jug on the dresser, which helped me to recover some semblance of consciousness. Having dressed in a hurry, but being still in a daze, I went down and opened the door, which I thought was to the sitting room. To my surprise, it was only a large cupboard/larder. Even just getting the barest glimpse of its contents, it seemed to be stuffed to the top with tins of all sorts, corned beef, spam and fruit as well as other farm produce. There was even granite salting trough, full up with salted pork while smoked sausages and hams were hanging from hooks in the ceiling. There was enough here to fully supply a U-boat for a seven-month patrol, including hundreds of packets of cigarettes and cigars, bottles of all description. Dumbstruck I shut the door very quietly as *Mutti* came along the corridor. From the guilty expression on my face, she must have guessed what had happened. As I went into the front room for my breakfast, I heard behind me the sound of a key being turned, shutting the 'stable door after the horse had bolted'. Mouse was already tucking into the freshly baked crispy rolls. Real farm butter, Salami and other types of sausages, smoked ham as well as a selection of jams, marmalade or honey all made the choice of what to put on your rolls an agonising one. Whatever happened to food rationing here in the countryside?

Back home, in the city, we had lived on a few grams of bread, meat and fat per week. Many a time I had gone to work on an empty stomach and could only look forward to a slice of bread with jam for my lunch. This, after Mother and Father were barely eating anything other then the vegetables and fruit grown in the garden.

Rationing here in the country? What rationing?'

The girls had gone back to school long ago, so Mouse and I just whiled away the time by a stroll round the village and spending a few minutes with our thought inside the little church. A final substantial meal, and an invitation, 'Please, come back any time you get the chance, you'll always be welcome here,' from *Mutti*, and off we went to the station.

By the time we got back on board, a rusty old steam tug had arrived to take over the duties of the late *Rügen*. All three boats of our group were allocated another two torpedoes each, to add to the one, which was left over from our last bit of fun. The group had to take up stations once more to complete the exercise with the new 750-ton target ship *Hertha*. The captains of our three boats would have to be even more accurate than before. There just wasn't very much of *Hertha* to aim at.

However, at the end of that week, which went by without any further mishaps, ***KARO-AS*** got a pat on the back for a 'Full House'; every shot had been on target.

CHAPTER SEVEN

Here I was, back in Frau Brauer's house in Seedorf, with Gretel for company. Since I met her a few days ago, she had seldom been out of my mind. With her long blond hair, she played havoc with my emotions every time I dared to think about her. I could quite easily imagine spending the rest of my life with her. Other liaisons had been wiped clean out of my mind. They couldn't hold a candle to Gretel, the beauty with brains.

But smitten as I was with her, she equally seemed to enjoy my attentions and my company. Moreover, on this night I was able to acquaint myself with the many delights of her body. Heavens know, how we managed to meet again so soon, but I couldn't have cared less. Because I was going to thoroughly enjoy this wonderful feeling of being with her and holding her tight. For what seemed to be hours on end, we kissed, explored, probed and tenderly touched... until neither of us could spin-it-out any further. When the climax arrived, it was as if the world had ended; in fact, it seemed to explode with terrifying force. The bed we were lying on shuddered and shook, while the noise tormented my eardrums; it was deafening.

'ACTION STATIONS' yelled this disembodied voice over the tannoy.

The uproar of the explosion and of the tannoy acted like an ice-cold shower; it brought me down to earth with a bump.

Verdammte Scheisse, my latest encounter with the lovely Gretel had only been a dream, a very wonderful dream at that.

However, I had better jump to it and get forward to my battle station. Everything was in darkness, the main lights had failed and my only hope was that the lucky charm of my ***KARO-AS*** card was working overtime to look after the well being of our boat.

Another explosion followed. Again, you could feel the boat shudder and groan, it felt, as if the firecrackers were going off below the boats keel. 'Report any damage or leaks' ordered the Chief over the tannoy ' and be quick about it'. He didn't appear to have too much trouble keeping ***KARO-AS*** on an even keel.

One by one all the department reported that the hull was still watertight and all in one piece.

But, what on earth was going on out there?

The Old Man didn't seem at all worried as he told the Chief 'I suppose you've guessed by now that somebody is dropping *Mülltonnen* (Ash-cans or depth charges) in our wake. It's all part of our drill, because everybody must get used to them before this little war is finally over. Our comrades up on top are supposed to drop their little eggs 100 metres abaft, at a safe distance' to which the Chief replied 'I just hope their tape measures are accurate, Sir'.

My mate Mouse, who has sprinted to his station in my wake, ventured to say: 'Hell! If that was 100 metres behind us, what'll happen if they get any closer?'

'Just pray my boy and hope your prayers are heard, otherwise you can book your passage to heaven or to hell, whatever the case may be,' offered our CPO, who had heard Mouse's remark.

Our training in darkness came in handy now. I was already quite at home in my station, when the order came to trim 100 litres fore to aft. I had the layout of all the valves on my patch imprinted on my brain. It helped that all the valve-hand-wheels had individual shapes and sizes. For instance the valves controlling the pneumatic high-pressure of over 200 kg/sq.cm had a completely different feel from the valve-hand-wheels controlling the low-pressure of 25 kg/sq.cm.

After each further explosion, the Old Man asked the Chief to perform complicated manoeuvres, all carried out blind. The biggest problem for us rookies was to get on with our individual tasks and not to be sidetracked by the infernal noise of those detonations, which sounded like hammer blows on the hull. Nothing could better illustrate the fact that water transmits sound faster and further; and that it adds an almost physical feel to it.

After we had endured the racket of the 10th depth charge and the accompanying emergency procedures, we were declared fit to face the enemy and their deadly rain of explosives.

Finally, the captain nodded to our CPO, who went and tightened up all the fuses in the lighting circuits, which previously and deviously he had unscrewed at the sound of the first bang.

This rude introduction to what may be in store for us should prove invaluable. It certainly frightened the wits out of me, even when we should have known that it wasn't for real.

However, was all this training reason enough to terminate my wonderful dream of Gretel? Maybe so, at least we now knew what our demise would sound like, should we be so unlucky.

We had completed the torpedo shooting trials quite successfully and competently and for once had come through all the exercises without afterwards requiring the services of the dockyard to patch us up.

After all this, ***KARO-AS*** was attached to the 27th U-boat Flotilla. Again, we didn't have to travel very far as it was based at the same port. All we had to do was to replenish our supplies, food and fuel. Diesel fuels had become very short in supply and more often than not, Peter had to be robbed to give some to Paul, to offer him a chance to get some training in. However, enough was taken aboard to see us through to the finish of our working-up period.

So off we went, in company of our sister 'Aces' and a bunch of three smaller type VIIC boats. They made up the convoy as it made its way out to the designated squares, a few sea miles off the Hela peninsular.

The official title for those next trials was 'Tactical exercises'.

Those trials were more or less for the benefit of the Commanders and their officers, designed to brush-up on their tactical skills in tracking and attacking. We were just bit-part players, following their every wish. Officers and the radio-room operators got busy on what could loosely be described as Wolf-pack drill. U-boats were meant to employ those tactics in the Atlantic to get to grips with heavily guarded convoys. If one of our boats happened to come across such a convoy, she would stand off and signal her position to other boats in the vicinity to. This couldn't be done haphazardly, but the communications and tactics had to be practised. When new boats and inexperienced crews were involved, things could get very hairy. As long as every boat kept to her given course and speed, nothing could go wrong.

Or could it?

The exercises had been going on for seven days. Keeping an eye on the course, which the navigator had plotted on his charts, we approached the entrance to the Gulf of Bothnia. It seemed to us, listening to the *3WO* in the conning tower, as he took periodic looks through the periscope that the weather was closing in a bit.

As ordered, ***KARO-AS*** was running at periscope depth, course 25 degrees and engines at half ahead both, in order to meet up with this imaginary convoy.

Mouse and I, because we had little to do in all this, reminisced about Seedorf. 'Hey spider, when do you think we shall be able to take up their invitation to pay a return visit?' Mouse whispered in my ear, to which I replied 'You might as well forget about that little lot, in a few days we'll be in Kiel getting ready for our first *Feindfahrt* (enemy-patrol). It'll be a long time, if ever, before we get back to the Baltic, Gotenhaven or *Mutti*.'

From the radio-room ahead, I heard a quiet word from Rudi to the *3WO* above us in the *Turm* (tower i.e. conning tower). 'Screw noise at 85 degrees, getting louder.' Not very long after this, and this time a bit more urgently, he repeated his report.

In fact, because it was so quiet in the boat, we could hear the churning of propellers without a hearing aid. And it did grow louder and louder and culminated in the most awful crash above us.

'My God! What on earth is going on now.'

Everybody was on the floor, thrown into one corner, as our dear boat almost turned turtle. To rub salt into the wound, we were getting a real soaking from above our heads, where a bloody great hole had appeared.

Now it was really time to panic.

Fortunately for all of us, Klaus-Peter, our Chief, knew his stuff.

'Blow all tanks' he yelled, not waiting for an invitation from anyone else to do something. Which was just as well, as there would have been no way to stop the inflow of water through a 15 cm diameter hole, an opening, where once a retractable *Matraze* (aerial) resided.

Up she came before too much water had been shipped.

At this point, the Old Man made his presence felt with some fruity language. He was still pulling up his trousers having visited the heads. He hared up on to the bridge or, to be quite accurate, where once there had been a bridge.

I thought I knew just about every swearword under the sun. How wrong can you be? The Old Man's vocabulary contained many words, which I had never heard before. His advantage was that he could swear in half a dozen languages, something he must have picked up when he was a boy on the Hamburg to New York run.

We soon realised just why he lost his temper. It appeared that a 500 tonner, type VIIC boat, had run right over us, ramming us where it hurt most, smack in our conning tower.

Whose fault it was would have to be decided later, but a few of us had a very good idea. Someone in the conning tower, who had manned the periscope on that occasion, had been asleep on his feet and with his eyes wide open.

Meanwhile, some of us received attention from our medical staff. The MO busily patched up some of my mates for cuts and bruises they had acquired when they were thrown around. I was crushed against the bank of valves popularly known as the Christmas tree before landing on the floor. A few pain-killing tablets and a kind word 'You'll live', was all I got.

This little how-do-you-do meant the end of tactical exercises for us. We were ordered back to port and the dockyard at Gotenhaven, to have the

damage assessed and repaired. Apart from having lost an aerial in the accident, our bridge was now an open-air stage. Where there had been a shoulder-high bulwark, there was nothing.
No. Actually not quite nothing, a few tattered remnants of thin steel sheeting were still hanging around on the edges. Even the part of the conning tower cladding with our ***KARO-AS*** symbol had disappeared down to the bottom of the Bothnian Sea.
Somebody will have to answer for this carelessness.
Our lookouts were not happy at all, as they were standing up in a void, with breakers coming across every few minutes, soaking them to the skin and we were still 36-40 hours from port.

Mouse and I were detailed to rig-up some temporary awning, to provide shelter for the poor seamen who had to brave the elements. Thanks to our enterprise and resourcefulness, however, they had a relatively dry journey back to base; they were able to shelter behind a high canvass screen made from a few spare hammocks, which had to be sacrificed for their comfort.

Personally, I worried more about the loss of our lucky Ace of Diamond signs; did it mean the end of the boat's good fortune. I made doubly sure that my playing card was still safely tucked away in the back of my paybook. Touching it, before I next went to sleep, did wonders for my moral.
This was the third time we could easily have been wiped-out without ever seeing 'an angry man'. Did we have as many lives as a cat?

Once back in the dockyard at Gotenhaven, there was a slight delay in having the new aerial installed and getting the bridge rebuilt. It wasn't as easy as it looked, inside the bridge parapet were the air-intakes for the diesels and several other ducts for the boats ventilation as well as navigation light and their wiring, auxiliary compass and helmsman's gear. I would have expected the accountants at the 27th Flotilla to have a mild fit at the cost of repairs. All because of utter carelessness. We found out later that the Old Man was hauled over the coals. He insisted that he was meant to be present in the conning tower during this exercise. Well, we knew that he did have to answer a call of nature and in such an emergency the *3WO*'s should have taken responsibility for taking avoiding action when approaching screw noises were repeatedly reported.

But trust the Old Man, he had taken the blame and spent three days behind bars out of loyalty for his *3WO*. We knew it was the Old Man's way of dealing with problems. He had been there himself and learned that it was easy enough to blame your crew for things. Only a fly on the wall would have known what he said to him in private. As it turned out, this was the end of our working-up. Not that it had ended on a very happy note, but perhaps all the mishaps or disasters would help to keep everyone on their toes in future, when it really mattered.

I hoped we would retain our ***KARO-AS*** tactical sign to assure our continued good fortune. To get all the repairs done and have a general mechanical check-over at this yard was estimated to take another two weeks, after which she would be ready for her trip back to Kiel for our final provisioning.

To save time later, we were all given a fourteen-day leave. Great!

Mouse and I thought that considering everything, perhaps one more day in Seedorf wouldn't come amiss before returning to Berlin, to taste the delights of nightly bombardments by Uncle Sam's lot. Why our *Luftwaffe* couldn't put up a better show was something none of us could understand. As far as we knew and we had actually seen a few on training flights, they now had a number of brand new *Messerschmitt ME262* jetfighters ready for action. With their speed of over 800 km/h they should have gobbled up those slow Yankee bombers long before they had come so far inland.

Things were beginning to look decidedly tricky.

But such was life for everyone, worrying about it didn't help.

So lets live a little, it can only improve our morale.

The train took us there by mid-afternoon. As before, we carried a few goodies for *Mutti* and the girls in the hope that they would be equally generous in supplying the things they had to offer. Full of anticipation, we walked the familiar path to their cottage. When the door opened in answer to our knock, we expected the friendly face of *Mutti* to greet us.

We were in for a very big surprise as it was a young man in his dressing gown who came to open the door. Why we should have been so taken aback, I shall never know, but you could have knocked us down with a wet sponge. Looking into the hall, we could see the uniform jackets of naval officers hanging on the hat-stand.

Were we embarrassed? You bet we were.

Stuttering I asked 'Is *Frau* Brauer at home?'

Before I got an answer, a second man who was dressed in the famous dragon-dressing gown, came to see who was calling.

'Oh, Hello chaps, how can we help you?' asked our *2WO* and then turning to his friend went on 'Lieutenant, these men are crew members of ***KARO-AS***'.

Well! We would gladly have disappeared into a deep hole in the ground but at least had the presence of mind to explain that as we were travelling through Seedorf, we though we would hand in a few goodies as a thank you for putting us up the last time. There couldn't have been the slightest doubt in Sub-lieutenant Karl Boden's mind, as to what we had been after. With a smile on his face, he offered to deliver the parcel. 'I'll be delighted to see that *Frau* Brauer gets these and thank you very much. Before you go, perhaps Mutti will offer you a cup of coffee, to sustain you on the rest of your journey'. But Mouse and I could not get away quick enough.

'Thank you very much, *Herr Leutnant,* we must push on.' Like two whipped poodles we departed, to arrange transport back on board. After thinking about it, we realised that we've been a couple of twits, thinking they would be waiting for us to come back unannounced. 'I'm glad they've have bettered themselves and moved up a class' was my jealous reaction, while thinking that Lotti and Gretel may well find out that gold braid on your sleeve doesn't necessarily make you a better companion.

Talking about higher classes, when we got back on board, the Chief, who had stayed back to supervise the repairs, ordered me to see him. 'Schuler, on my recommendation our Commander has put forward your name with a view to train for a commission. Your orders have arrived today, to attend an interview in Wilhelmshaven'.

Blow me down.

This was completely out of the blue and took my breath away. Not that I thought I had the slimmest chance of being accepted. There existed an unseen social barrier, which couldn't easily be overcome. The age-old Prussian attitude still seemed to prevail throughout all our services. The opinion that 'Officers are born ... not made' was still very much in evidence in the *Kriegsmarine* and was, if you could belief rumours, the strongly held opinions of our top Admirals.

Mind you, there must be a good reason why the 'Top Brass' would consider such an extreme move. Losses among U-boat officers might be running too high for normal recruitment and could be the reason for looking for officer material among the lower orders.

However, who would turn down a chance like that, even if it meant foregoing my home leave? I certainly wouldn't.

Armed with my travel-pass I set off on an 800 km round-trip.

Heavens know, how often I had to change trains to get there. More than once a passenger coach was coupled on to a freight train and so shunted around until I finally arrived, dog tired from lack of decent sleep. Here I found myself in the company of twenty other hopefuls. Most of them were 18 to 20 year old youngsters, just like me, but there were also some older men, who appeared to be professionals, such as accountants, solicitors or even clergymen.

First we were given a physical going-over, which gave us younger ones the edge. When it came to doing a few press-ups or basic exercises on the parallel bars or the pommel horse, we were out on our own. By the time we were asked to climb up on the 7 metres high ropes, most of the older applicants had dropped out. So, as far as physical fitness was concerned, it was difficult to see the older ones ever serving on U-boats.

Next came a few theoretical tests in mental arithmetic, knowledge of maths, geography and history. Again I thought that I had done reasonably well. But who knows, we must wait for the interview, which was to follow. I felt really good about the whole thing. Perhaps they were looking for men who showed enterprise, awareness and perhaps they were interested in candidates who had already shown leadership qualities in the Hitler Youths. I started to look forward to the actual interview.

When my turn came, I was ushered into this gigantic room. At the far side, sitting on a long, long table, was the largest selection of high-ranking naval officers I had ever seen in my life. There were more gold braided piston rings on their combined sleeves, than were to be found in all of our four diesel engines. At the centre of the table sat the most senior of them all, a Rear Admiral. Facing him, I came to attention. After confirming my name and rank I waited with bated breath to see what the next question was going to be. 'What is your father's occupation?'

'He is employed by the Corporation of the City of Berlin in the waste-disposal department, Sir' was my reply. 'You mean he is a dust-man' he said, screwing-up his nose. 'Yes Sir'. I looked along the row of other faces behind the table and decided there and then that I had miserably failed to make the grade. Actually there were other questions about my family, their background and about my ambitions for a career in the Navy, but although I answered them faithfully, the panel appeared to think I was wasting their time.

My self-esteem didn't suffer too much, as I wasn't the only one to fall by the wayside. It was only the older men who were considered further. I couldn't see them as U-boat officers; they would never have managed to get through any of the hatches. They could obviously push a pen and man offices and thus release fitter men for duty on board.

The rest of us were excused to return to our units.

Together with another stoker who was also stationed at Gotenhaven, I started on my way back to ***KARO-AS***. If there had been a direct train, we would have been back in a few hours. As it happened, the frequent changing of trains involved a lot of waiting time. In the middle of one night, our carriage, which had been attached to a goods train, was parked in a siding.

By the light of a full moon, we could see gardens and orchards from our train window. The apples looked delicious as the moonlight reflected on their shiny skins and because we felt quite peckish, we decided to pass the waiting time fruitfully. Leaving all our gear behind in the carriage, only armed with only a small sack, we made our way into the orchard to help ourselves. We got quite carried away with our mission, not wanting to stop until the sack was full to the top.

However, this was where we hit a nasty snag.

When we returned to the siding, our carriage had disappeared into thin air. We searched and searched to no avail and that was the time we started to seriously worry.

'There's going to be hell to pay' my companion remarked quite unnecessarily. We didn't have our papers or travel passes, they were in the pockets of our reefer jackets, which in turn were still hanging-up in the compartment. I had visions of being accused of desertion and being shot without further ado.

How stupid can you get?

'We better find our way to the nearest station. With luck we might find a fair-minded military policeman who will accept our explanation about our predicament' I thought. He agreed and since we were going in an easterly direction on the train, we walked along the line that way. Along the way, we chewed some of the still unripe apples. After twenty minutes we came to a platform and as expected we found a guard. We told him of our plight, to which he smiled as much as to say 'Pull the other one.'

Covering us with his machine pistol, he locked us up in one of the side rooms at the station. We were given plenty of time to consider our lot.

After an hour or so, a lieutenant arrived with our reefer jackets in his hand. 'I suppose you will claim that those are yours?' he asked.

'What are your names and prove your identity. In fact produce your ID disks'

Every member of the armed forces had to carry one of those metal tags round his neck. Your identity number was stamped on it and since it tallied with all our documents in our reefer jacket pockets, we could breathe again.

'It was a good job we checked through the train and found your gear, otherwise it would have finished up goodness knows where.'

Panic over!

Not quite, he had reported us to our units. As a result, I spent the remainder of ***KARO-AS****'s* dockyard time behind bars, with only dry bread and water for company.
This was also the time, when a senior CPO replaced our boat's regular 3WO.

We are off to join the Monsoon Group of the 33. U-boat Flotilla, Entry in Visiting book at Stettin

When the day arrived to cast-off for our passage to Kiel, a few people were lined up on the jetty. Among them, we recognised two friends, Lotti and Gretel. The fickle little madams were frantically waving to our officers on the bridge, apparently not noticing us other ranks lined up on the quarter-deck.
'Bye-bye Karl' they shouted to our *2WO.*
But above the noise of all the shouting and hollering from the pier, I imagined I heard a faint
'Bye-bye Mouse', 'Bye-bye Spider'
But perhaps that was just wishful thinking on my part.
It was obvious that my lucky ***KARO-AS*** did not function very well when it came to my love life or my promotion-hopes.

CHAPTER EIGHT

Kiel - the base of the 5th U-boat Flotilla.

There was a real sense of urgency about our final few days in Kiel. As soon as we arrived, ***KARO-AS*** went into dry-dock, where an army of busy bees descended on her. The sides of her keel were opened up, all the steel ballast removed and then replaced by an equivalent weight of lead-ingots.
Somebody, somewhere was desperately short of precious lead.

Our quadruple-mounted 2 cm gun on the lower winter garden was replaced with a fully automatic 3.7 cm *FLAK*. We needed more firepower with a greater range. A 10.5 cm canon had also appeared from nowhere; it was mounted on the forecastle.
In answer to our question: 'Why has ***KARO-AS*** been painted in this unusual light grey, almost white colour, instead of the normal dark grey of the Atlantic Wolves?'

We were told, as we now are a part of the 33rd U-boat Flotilla, the famous *Monsun Gruppe* (Monsoon Group), our first patrol would take us to the Indian Ocean and to German bases in Malaya, on Java or even in Japan. Our task was to get there by hook or by crook in order to deliver the lead-ingots plus other goods and then load up with supplies, such as bales of rubber, supplies of Iodine and suchlike, which were all urgently required here in Germany for the war-effort.
It sounded more like the work of Merchantmen

Once out of dry-dock and moored under camouflage netting on the provisioning-pier, pipes and hoses came aboard to fill-up our fuel bunkers as well as the fresh-water and lubricating-oil tanks. Next to come aboard were the torpedoes - real ones this time. Half of them were stored inside the boat in their tubes ready to be fired or under bunks in either the bow- or the stern torpedo rooms. The remainder went into pressure-proof containers below the decking.

At the same time, pallets with ammunition for our weapons were lifted onto the forecastle. Our 'Number one', the most senior of the petty officers, who was also the armourer, supervised his gang of seamen in stowing the ammo into pressure-proof containers next to the FLAK, the remainder inside the boat by way of the galley-hatch or down through the conning tower into the control-room.
Smutje, as he was trained to do, produced his own storage-plan. With the

help of it he should be able to remember where every single item will be found when it was needed. Where on earth could one store the provisions for 70 men, on a journey, which could take seven months to complete? There was some spare space between pipes and ducts and in bilges. But to tantalise the crew, smoked sides of ham and countless Salami sausages were suspended right in front of everyone's noses, in gangways, heads and between the torpedo tubes. But the most precious things, such as cigarettes, tobacco and other goodies, were kept under lock and key by the *1WO.*

Last of all, in order to fill up any voids, which may still exist, masses of assorted spare machine parts, small electric motors and switches were stowed, mainly in the diesel-room. Those supplies were required to supplement dwindling stores in our bases abroad. Bags of mail, meant for our comrades at those bases in the Far East, were also taken aboard.

During this provisioning period I managed to arrange a job for myself, helping our CPO navigator Rudi Lose*,* whose workplace was at a chart-table in the control room. I accompanied him to the sea-chart stores at the Flotilla's HQ, to collect literally hundreds of charts, navigational books and Almanacs. They covered every inch of the Atlantic (North and South), and all the sea-areas from the Cape Hope to the Pacific and to Japan. Every drawer under his chart-table was filled to the brim. Even then, more than half of them had to be stored elsewhere, mostly under the Old Man's and the officer's bunks.

At the end of the provisioning, the departmental heads double-checked every item, which had come aboard. The delivery notes were then passed to our control room personnel for logging in a manifest, with particular reference to weight.

Our calculations to re-establish Zero-Trim were the same as before, only there were more items to consider. Once we get under way, a trim-dive will confirm how well we had done our calculations.

The final typhus injections had been rammed home.

Outch and three times Outch.

We were issued with tropical kit, lightweight khaki shorts, shirts and cap. But our blue Navy-uniforms (Square rig) as well as our personal belongings, which we'd packed into kit bags, were put in store at the base. If we're lucky enough to return in one piece, we can collect them again.

KARO-AS was just about ready to move.

And in the dark of one night it was *Leinen los* (Cast-off).

There wasn't a brass band in sight, nor did anyone make fancy speeches; there were no flowers and no tears from wives and girlfriends.

Finally, the waiting and anticipation was over.
This was definitely IT.
The time had arrived when we should find out whether the experience gained in training was sufficient to see us safely through the weeks to come.

Quietly we slipped past the U-boat and Navy Memorials on our starboard side and then out of the bay. All our thoughts and hopes were with the ones we had left behind; may they be safe during the time we're at sea.

Before us lay one of the dodgier parts of our trip. The waters around Denmark were hardly deep enough for self-respecting U-boats. Even through the deepest channel, the Store-Belt, which ran between the Danish islands and led to the Kattegat, there was often only 15 m of water under our keel. But with full throttle, and hopefully with some air cover from the *Luftwaffe*, we will soon reached the deep waters south of Norway. At least from there on and through the Atlantic and beyond, we would have more than sufficient water under our keel to try and dodge our enemies, who no doubt will do their best to see that our contribution to this war will be as short as they can possibly make it.
But so far - so good!

By the time ***KARO-AS*** made fast in Bergen, we hadn't really felt any different from our working-up in the Baltic.
I mentioned that fact to one of my U-boat-school friends, who I'd met here. He assured me 'You'll soon change your minds when I tell you how many boats have not been heard of since they left Norway.'

Those losses were never mentioned in any official news bulletins I ever heard. Our troops seemed to be winning battles everywhere, but perhaps a little further back having made tactical adjustments to their positions.
In fact, most of us had stopped listening to the news. Every time somebody put them out over the intercom, we objected and asked for music instead, which was probably normal for 18 year-olds the world over.
A few fresh food supplies, including a small barrel of herrings, came aboard. They would be the last until we arrived at our destination.

But Our Old Man's fear that we would have to ship some passengers as well as supplies proved unfounded. We were given the impression that all Monsoon-boats, which had sailed before us, had transported Japanese official or military personnel back to their homeland. One boat had transported two Indian Freedom fighters to the Far East. An Indian, Subhas Chandra Bose and a compatriot, took a passage to Penang in one U-boat. Described by Mahatma Gandhi as a patriot of patriots, Bose had fought and suffered for his fight for India's independence against the British oppressors. For many years he had languished in the jails of the Empire, right up to the beginning of this war. A determination to fast to death saw him gain his freedom. He used this by escaping to Germany, where he raised a sizeable unit of Indian volunteers to fight against their British masters.

One could be sure that Bose received plenty of encouragement from Hitler while he was in Germany, as well as getting help from the Japs after he got back to the East in this U-boat. When they arrived off Penang Island, he and his compatriot transferred to a Japanese submarine. He then went on to create even more bother for the Imperialists by raising further Armies of regular soldiers and volunteers to fight for the freedom of India from the British Crown.

How did we get to know all those historical facts?

Our Old Man had served on that particular boat as Chief Petty Officer Navigator and had followed up the story as it unfolded.

But he seemed extremely pleased to be able to set out on this particular trip without having to take passengers. A relatively inexperienced crew would keep his hands full.

Once again, without any fuss and under the cover of mist and fog, we departed from Bergen, running as silently as possible on E-motors until we were out of earshot from shore. Sure as anything, soon somebody somewhere would realise that the boat with the Ace of Diamonds painted on her conning tower had disappeared. That information would be passed on to third parties, which were particularly interested in the movement of German U-boats. Hopefully, we would have bought ourselves sufficient time to put as much distance between ourselves and Bergen as was humanly possible before Tommy started searching for ***KARO-AS***.

CPO Rudi had plotted a course, which would take us due north, almost up to the Arctic Circle and then swing to port to pass through the area between Iceland and the Faroe Islands. From there on we should be heading more or less south for something like the next 75 days.

Hell! That's nearly three months? And that is only down to the level of Cape Hope. And we supposed it also meant 'provided that Tommy didn't interfere.' But since it was Rudi, our navigator, who had worked it out, we must believe it.

After a conference with the Old Man, he had worked out a schedule on a day-to-day basis. Only a few U-boats had already been fitted with snorkels and rumour had it that they were proving themselves to be most effective. Those lucky devils were able to run diesel-powered at periscope depth, making 10 knots and replenishing their batteries at the same time. Only the tip of the snorkel, which was rubber coated and about the size of an oil drum, protruded above the waves. It presented only a very tiny target for enemy RADAR. In relative safety they could travel some 200 to 250 sea miles in 24 hours.

However, we'd drawn the short straw. The powers that be had decided that at this point in time our needs were not as great as that of other front-boats in the North Atlantic. Snorkel-less we shall have to manage.

It did not come as a very big surprise to us that the Old Man decided to travel submerged during daylight hours.

Following the Norwegian coast northward, we encountered little in the way of traffic, friendly or otherwise. To be on the safe side we would not surface until perhaps one hour after dark and stay up until one hour from dawn. In distance terms it meant running 10 hours at 10 knots on diesels and 14 hours at 2 knots on electric motors at 50 metres down. Approximate distance covered in a day, not counting any interference from Tommy, would on average be 100 to 128 sea miles or 185 to 237 km.

But you couldn't ever ignore Tommy, not even for the blinking of one's eye. As soon as we left the Norwegian coast and headed over towards the north of the Faroes, near the Arctic Circle, he became active. Next to the control-room and going forward there was the Old Man's den on port and the listening/radio rooms on starboard. While running submerged the radio operators with their powerful acoustic tracking devices only had to listen for screw-noises. They divided their duties between that and by providing us with the pleasure of light-hearted music via the loudspeakers in every department. A sizeable selection of gramophone records was among other supplies taken aboard. Most of those were light and romantic *Schlager* (Pop) music, some classical selection and as regulation demanded, there was a liberal sprinkling of patriotic march-music. You could always turn down the volume control in your mess if you didn't like some of that.

But shortly before surfacing at night, the other listening devices were also manned. Tommy's RADAR was rumoured to have been the downfall of many our comrades, but our designers and scientists had recently come up with some answers. Our sparkies could now detect when we were being targeted by RADAR and from which direction, so no more surprises in the middle of the night.

The Old Man had confirmation that there weren't any screw noises to be

heard from ships in the vicinity, for the moment. He even had all machinery switched off to give the radio boys every chance to listen. All was quiet at the front.
'Prepare to Surface' followed by 'Surface'
Once up, the special aerial was extended and immediately there were bleeps and screeches to be heard from the RADAR traffic in the area. There appeared to be so many ships and aircraft around, perhaps they will confuse themselves. The Old Man asked the Chief to get on with the charging of the batteries. But soon the strength of the signals grew louder and louder.
'Prepare to dive'
'Dive and go to 20 metres.'
The Old Man was not pleased. The batteries had to be full every morning. Screw noises were still absent. Must have been aircraft up above. He was toying with the idea of surfacing and having the *FLAK* manned but that would make crash diving a pretty slow affair. He opted for taking the bull by the horns.

After asking the *2WO* to get his little toys ready for action and after getting confirmation from him that everything was ready, he ordered to 'Surface'.
Again the bleeps are heard from various directions and again some got louder. The lookouts were put on high alert to keep their eyes peeled using their night-glasses, which we knew were pretty good.
Meanwhile the *2WO* got busy with unwrapping his box of tricks. It was merely a balloon, which he connected to a tap on the bridge and filled it with Helium until it reached a diameter of nearly one metre. Then he released it.

From here in the control room we couldn't see any of this, but Wilhelm, my farmer friend told us later that when the balloon went up, it trailed behind a long tail, which was interwoven with silver paper, much like the tails of the kites we played with as children. The whole contraption was of such a weight that it kept hovering just above sea level once it was released.
'Aphrodite' was designed to give a lovely RADAR reflection, much better than a mere U-boat. Mouse, my colleague, much to my surprise, had some knowledge of Greek history, Gods and Goddesses and all that. He let everybody know that this name was absolutely ideal for those little surprise packages. 'Aphrodite was worshipped not only as Goddess of the sea, of seafaring and of war, but most of all and foremost as the Goddess of Love and Beauty.'
I couldn't see his point. 'Why does that make it an apt name for a silver-

paper lure?'
'Well, ladies of the night, prostitutes, both professional and amateur, honour Aphrodite as their patron?
Just as the whores entice sailors into their beds, Aphrodite will lure Tommy up the garden-path.'
This I could understand.

Anyway, whenever the bleeps of our tracking devices got on the Old Man's nerves, he ordered another one to be launched.
The idea was actually pinched from Uncle Sam's bombers.
As their aircraft attacked our cities, they were in the habit of dropping silver-paper confetti, which played havoc with our *FLAK* direction finders.

Whether he had his fingers crossed or not, this time the Old Man brazened it out and lo-and-behold, after initially getting louder, the bleeps diminished. They kept rising and falling in volume. Every unit of the British Fleet and every aircraft of the RAF were after somebody including ***KAROAS***. In that process, Tommy must have had a great time tracking himself and perhaps several Aphrodites.

Even after the batteries were full up, the Old Man pushed on at 'Half Ahead Both', making perhaps 10-12 knots. For four days we ran to this routine and then took the expected turn to the South West to pass between Iceland and the Faroe Island, an area our U-boatmen had christened the *Rosengarten* (rose garden).
We couldn't find out why it was called that. Perhaps it was thought to be a very prickly patch to get through without being scratched to pieces.

On numerous occasions screw-noises were heard while running at 50 metres. Every time they came too near, we changed to silent running at a much greater depth. That meant the absolute minimum revolutions for only one of the E-motors to maintain a little forward speed to help the hydroplanes to keep the boat on a level path or to let it sink a bit further. Every other motor, pump or fan was switched off, while everybody not actively required in the running of the boat, was sent to his bunk. The first man to drop a spanner would be hanged, drawn and quartered. Turning the boat toward or away from the screw-noise helped to present the smallest possible silhouette to their ASDIC. And the deeper you could go, the greater were the chances of staying undetected.

I seem to remember that we had another trump up our sleeve. If things got too hot from ASDIC location, by pinging on the hull until everybody's nerves were in shreds, we had the use of a little plaything called a *Pillerwerfer* (Pill-thrower), a canister-like device, which on contact with seawater dissolved a chemical substance that started to loudly bubble and crackle. After deploying those, we attempted to get as far away as possible from that spot and pray that the racket of the pills would divert the attacker's attention away from our boat.

Some boats were reputed to have used other decoys, which imitated the noises emanating from a sub. They were towed a long way behind the boats, and if things got too hot, they could be jettisoned. If they ever existed, we weren't equipped with any.

But it certainly was a game of cat and mouse.

Most U-boats would have been delighted to find an enemy-vessel in their sights but as we were first and foremost merchantmen, we just wanted to get to the Far East without any hassle. Our task was to slink along as best as we could, keeping our heads down below the parapet. Apart from times of extreme alert, when the crew were at action stations, the routine inside the boat ran along the same lines day-in and day-out. In fact day had become night and vice versa. It was quite impossible for our *Smutje* to do any cooking while we were running submerged. Our 'air-conditioning' was far to primitive to be able to cope with the normal human (or inhuman) smells, which tended to accumulate inside after several hours of running at depth. Ventilating-fans, when we were able to use them, could only re-distribute the pong evenly throughout every compartment. Emerging from the deep at nightfall meant running a higher than normal risk, but it also offered relief in being able to deeply breathe in fresh air. Under the general description of fresh air we also counted diesel fumes and often tantalising smells wafting from the galley. Only the regular number of lookouts, armed with night glasses, were allowed to be on the bridge, to facilitate the quickest possible getaway should the need arise. No one else was allowed up. As the only concession to us poor souls who inhabited the bowels of the boat, permission to indulge in a quick smoke inside the conning tower was given, but only to one of us at one time. Our view of the outside world was therefore restricted to the occasional glimpse of a little piece of circular star-covered sky or the even scarcer little moonbeam.

As the nights were now offering the opportunity to take-on nourishment, it was also the only satisfactory time to see to your regular or irregular body-functions. Running submerged during daylight, the outside water-pressure made it impossible to pump-out the WCs. Then only pails or other receptacles served those in extreme need. Those could be pumped out through the heads by night, which helped to build-up the upper arm pumping-muscles. Alas, there were also times, too gruesome to be reminded of,

when men from the forward torpedo rooms actually transport pails full to the brim, through the boat and then via the conning tower up on to the bridge, to be emptied overboard. The passage of those pails made some stench but thankfully, our sense of smell had dulled.
Lets hope that Tommy hasn't yet developed a smell-tracking device, fine-tuned to U-boat-odours.

Fresh-water was far too precious to be used for washing or shaving. Soap, developed to produce a little lather in seawater was available, but in the beginning it certainly played hell with our baby-like complexions. We got used to it much later, we had to, when the Eau de Collogne ran out. Anyway, why should we bother to shave, all pirates had long black beards, didn't they? Apart from all that, being the second youngest chap aboard, my puny fluff made me the butt of our mess. How I envied to chaps, who without any effort could grow a full jet-black set in a couple of weeks.

For us this has been the longest continuous spell of running our two-watch system. This was how it worked. The starboard-watch for instance was ON for four hours and OFF for four hours during the day and six hours ON and six hours OFF during the night, thus alternating with the port-watch. It represented one of the mysteries of German Naval tradition, that the engineering crew, i.e. the men of the Electro motors, diesel engines and the control-room staff were the only ones to run this two watch regime, while everybody else on board did a three watch stint, only four hours ON and all of eight hours OFF.

Some of us managed to sleep all the time we were OFF, but if I could get a total of seven hours during a twenty-four hour period, I would be quite happy. It meant I had a bit of spare time in which to improve my mind or play cards or Chess. The latter I preferred, because it was a lot quieter and didn't disturb our mates who wanted to kip. But, as luck would have it, there was only one other occupant of the stern room who would show willingness for a battle. It was my sparring partner, torpedo mixer Walter. We never saw eye to eye on anything, but in our liking for Chess we had something in common. If we didn't watch what we were doing, we could even finish up liking each other... God forbid.

Any such feelings for him soon disappeared again as soon as he started to service the batteries in his four slimy charges. I didn't know much about those greasy eels, but one of them gave me an everlasting pain in the back. Two of those eels were in their tubes, always ready to be fired. One of the reserve ones was under the bottom bunks on the starboard side and one under my bunk on port. That would have been OK, if for instance the wire ropes that supported my bunk had been a couple of cm shorter. As it was, the bottom of my canvass bunk, with only a thin mattress in it, rested on top of the 530 mm diameter monster - hence my sore back. But when it became necessary to retract the torpedo in the portside tube, so he could check it over, the bunks on that side had to be dismantled. He only ever seemed to do this when I was absolutely knackered. But then I discovered that you are able to get some decent sleep by taking your mattress and placing it behind one of the diesels. Actually the slow rhythm of those was better than counting sheep, the sheer monotony was made to induce sleep. I grew to look forward to those occasions. Only once did I wake with a hell of a start... when the bloody things stopped in readiness for diving.

There was just one thing I missed, when sleeping behind the diesel. Beside my shared bunk I had a small locker for a few personal belongings. On the back of the small door I had pinned a postcard-sized photo of Gretel in a swimsuit. Even although I knew now that she had other fish to fry, I kept looking at her lovely image, mostly before turning over to get to sleep. The little witch really had got to me good and proper. I had one other photo in the back of my pay-book and which I had pinched one day, when nobody was looking. It was of Hilde sitting on her favourite steed and served to remind me of a wonderful day out on horseback. It wasn't pinned-up in my locker, as I feared that my friend Wilhelm would get the right idea.

And there were my photos from home in a little album. I regularly looked at them while hoping and praying that my folk would stay safe in their shelter at the back of the garden.

There too was my lucky ***KARO-AS*** playing card, tucked in the back of my pay-book. Fingers crossed, up to now it had done the trick and kept us out of mischief.

As I said, during the night the boat was a hive of activity.

Dodging the enemy required the utmost attention from the lookouts. Apart from all the gadgetry such as the various tracking devices, there was no substitute for the human eye reinforced by powerful night-binoculars. I doubt whether the Old Man got any sleep during that time, as he was rooted to the bridge. There was this frequent call from up there 'Coffee for the captain.' One of us down here fetched a type of billycan from the galley and passed it on to the bridge. When it was my turn to fetch it, I tried a few sips. Brrrrrrrr, it was pure poison to all but the strongest of stomachs and explained why the Old Man could keep on his toes for days, nobody could sleep with that stuff inside them.

During those days, most of the activity took place in the engine rooms.

While the two 9-cylinder main engines chugged away, keeping the boat moving along at an economical rate, the two 6-cylinder diesel-generators charged the batteries. The noise and heat generated by those four engines was supplemented by two diesel-powered air-compressors, which kept the compressed-air bottles topped-up. If any of our weaponry had to be serviced, that also had to be done at night. Our one and only weapons-mechanic kept the main canon in front of the conning tower and the *FLAK* on the wintergardens in good order.

However, there was nothing more important, nay vital, to the proper running of this deadly fighting machine than the activity which was taking place in the galley during the night.

Bubble, bubble, toil and trouble - this witches brew was in fact a type of multi-course meal, but all of it mixed together in one large pot. Most of the fresh vegetables had already been used or dumped overboard in a stage of advanced decomposition.

One had to guess what actually went into the *Eintopf* (One-pot) as we called this many-times-a-week main meal, which was simmering away on the stove. On the seventh day, the Sabbath, all the same ingredients were kept separate and were presented in the form of a three-course meal.

Tinned potatoes, peas, corned-beef and *Sauerkraut;* those ingredients were easily identifiable.

But all joking aside, there should have been a very special medal struck for cooks on U-boats. The Commandants got all the glory at a boat's return from patrol, but where would he have been without the bravery and resourcefulness of his *Smutje.*

Once, when I collected the Old Man's coffee from the galley, there came the '*ALARM'*.

One minute his pots and pans were peacefully bubbling away on the stove, the next minute they were hitting the deck as the boat took a dive down at 40 degrees forward inclination. The other half of the meal was saved by the courageous action by our hero. It was just as well that the galley was no more than a few square-feet in area and he could more or less reach those post and pans while he jammed himself between the cooker and the food-cupboard.

Another function, which had to be carried out at night, was our navigator's work. As soon as there was a clear sky, CPO Rudi would rush up on the bridge and start 'shooting stars. It was nothing as war-like as it sounded, it was just a name given to the method he employed to do his job.

For several hundred years, the only reliable way of knowing you actual position at sea, was by measuring the height of a known stars in relation to the horizon. A sextant, a device well known to me since my *HJ* day, was used to measure that height. One measurement was not enough, a second one of another star, preferably at right angles to the first one, was required. Almanacs and other charts helped to interpret those fixings. Your position, at the time of checking, was at the intersection of those two measurements.

However, calculations made from the boats actual speed and her course in relation to the last known position, were influenced by the drift and currents of the sea. There were times when your speed through the water was 10 knots at 180 degrees (due south), the actual way may be 15 knot at 160 degrees when taking into account currents and wind. When the night-sky was overcast it was only the skill of the navigator that could overcome those snags. And here, with CPO Rudi Lose at the charts, we had one very gifted man. As she was cruising along on the surface during the hours of darkness, the feverish activity inside the boat could easily be compared to that of a beehive. In sharp contrast, it was equally true to say ***KARO-AS*** had a tomb-like feel to her, when slinking along with the fish at 50 m below. Then, only a few men were required to run the ship. Usually the Chief would be in attendance in the *Zentrale*, supported by two seamen operating the forward and aft hydroplanes, one more on the helm, two engineers also in the control room and two to run the electric motors. A couple of radio-hams were on duty on the tracking/listening sets. Those few men were able to keep our ship moving along on an even keel. All other crewmembers had retired to their bunks. Most slept, others were reading and the rest just lay there deep in thought, perhaps reminiscing. All of them were conserving precious oxygen. Even the Chief could relax a bit. After the way he had set-up the trim of our tub the hydroplane hands could easily keep the boat at the right depth with one hand tied behind their backs.

Silence reigned; we even talked in whispers during this time. One or the other of the Officers or CPOs had a habit of visiting the control-room when they couldn't sleep. Even our *1WO*, the one we dismissively called the *Hitler Junge*, turned out to be a member of the human race. I learned that like me, he had been in the *Marine HJ* and as it turned out, we were both *Gefolkschaftsführer* (Group leader of ca 150 boys). Every time after this, when passing, he wanted to know all about our set-up in Berlin.

The other thing we had in common was our course on *Gorch Fock*. Funny, how one can change one's mind about a person by just talking to them! I even started to appreciate his attitude toward discipline on board. What to many of us looked like bullshit, he saw as necessity in operating a ship efficiently, whether it was an old four-mast clipper or a super modern U-boat. Having experienced life on a clipper myself and seen how much the running of it depended on discipline, when just a single failure among the crew could cause untold havoc, I could easily appreciate his concern about slackness creeping into the crew, which manifested itself in sloppy attitudes in thought and dress.

And so we went on day in and day out. There had been the odd panic of course, but we must have been sailing under a good star.

About five weeks out and making good headway through relatively calm seas, we passed the Azores while keeping well to the West of those islands. Over on the chart-tables there was more than the normal amount of activity. It was most unusual to see so many very senior crewmembers crowded round Rudi. My casual examination of the vent for ballast-tank No. 5 took me over to within earshot of the group and as far as I could make out, they were only interested in one thing, namely 'When are we due to cross over?'

What did they mean by that? Cross over, where or what?

Surely, they were not thinking about THAT!

I remembered the time my brother Heinz, who served on one of our Big Ships, the *Scharnhorst*, talked about the significance of the *Equätortaufe* (Equator-baptism) and what it used to entail. Going back to the days of sail, men had no right to call themselves real sailors before they had received their official baptism from the good God Neptune on crossing over the line dividing the northern from the southern hemisphere. The proof of having been baptised was the award of a scroll to the successful candidate. Back at home, hanging on our living room wall in a prominent position was my brother's very hard-earned certificate from his days on the Battleships.

But surely those customs didn't apply to U-boats ... and certainly not to U-boats on enemy patrol during wartime, did they?

As it happened, this subject wasn't mentioned again during the course of the following two weeks, when we moved along at periscope depth at just a few knots. Mouse and I had come off watch a few minutes earlier and we looked forward to catching up on our sleep.

Just as my dreams (which in the main were about Gretel, Lotti or even Hilde) were getting interesting, we were almost blasted out of our bunks by the sheer volume of fanfares over the tannoy.

Bloody hell!

Have we won the damned war?

An announcement followed over the address system:

'Admiral Triton with his entourage has come aboard and he is order-

ing all unclean members of the crew to stand by their stations or their bunks to await his inspection!'

None of us in our mess had the slightest idea what all this meant. While running submerged, the trim of the boat was affected by people wandering around in the boat. It stopped us from going to see what was happening.

Later we learned from our mates on the port-watch that this so called Admiral Triton, accompanied by the Old Man, started to interview our officers in their quarters. Our boat's MO, our Chief and the *2WO* were the first to be introduced to the Admiral.

Triton was dressed in this very extravagant uniform, with rows and rows of glittering medals on his chest and a great big beard hiding almost all of his features. He shook hands and was soon in friendly conversation with them. After apparently putting them at ease, he suggested that it was time to give-up their misguided, landlubbering ways. To help them to do so and to prepare them for the actual baptism, he prescribed special pills to be taken and a selection of embrocation to be applied to their midriff. The Admiral's assistants, both with shoulders as wide as a double-wardrobe, were extremely helpful in assuring that the medicine was swallowed and that the balsam was properly applied.

The Triton-party then made their way forward to the CPO's mess, then further to the PO's quarters and the bow torpedo room. Their progress couldn't be followed. But an occasional yell or scream could be heard loud and clear though the ventilation ducts, which ran all the way from bow to stern.

Fed-up with waiting to meet Triton we had gone back to lie on our bunks. Soon however, the peace was shattered by the entry of Triton and his gang into the stern torpedo room. My bunk was nearest to the hatch, so it was to be my turn next. I stood to attention as my name was called out by the Old Man, as the Admiral pushed his face close up to mine

'Oh yes! A Berliner big head, no doubt, who thinks he knows everything there's to know about the sea. I'm afraid Neptune isn't going to like landlubbers who pretend to be sailors. We'll have to make a special effort to show you the errors of your ways and to transform you into a proper seaman.'

There was no answer to that one. By this time I had recognised the face behind the beard. There was nobody else on board with eyes as steely as our CPO G.Schulz. Before he had a chance to tell me how he was going to deal with my misdemeanours, Josef, the helmsman of the first watch sitting on the bunk behind me made the mistake of heckling. He'd been baptised some time ago and being safe from harm, couldn't help laughing at my discomfort.

'Ah! And who are you, my friend?' asked the Admiral sharply.

Having been told by the Old Man, Triton said he was upset by this unwarranted interruption.

'I suppose you think this serious business is a matter for merriment?' he snarled at him.

'Neptune must have been too soft on you when he baptised you. It is my duty to report your attitude to him, so he can take appropriate remedial action.'

Turning to his helpers he prescribed a booster dose of pills.

You would have thought that Jo, with all his previous experience would have known better than to react the way he did.

'I've crossed the line more than once and I can prove it'

Seconds later he recognised his big mistake. As he tried to duck out of the room, something or other made him stumble. Accidentally, no doubt, the Old Man's foot got in the way. Before Jo knew what hit him, he had two pills pushed in his mouth followed by a dose of seawater, by way of a funnel. He was unable to do anything but to swallow the lot and at the same time endure his abdomen being smeared with black rejuvenating ointment. When the two burly helpers stood up after sitting on him, I had to be ever so careful to keep a straight face. If nothing else, this episode taught me a lesson. I decided to accept whatever was in store for me with good grace. I could easily aggravate the situation. It didn't save me from the pills or the sticky rub on my belly, but at least the pills were not forced down my throat. But perhaps it would have been better if they had, because moving the pills round in my mouth made them burn like hell.

Heaven knows, what was in them.

Mustard, salt, pepper, vinegar were easily identified, but there was also the funny aftertaste of castor oil, iodine, sulphur, axle grease or similar substances in evidence.

It was some consolation to me, that the rest of the engineering crew was also going around retching and spewing, trying to get rid of the taste in their mouths. I was convinced it would be weeks before I could get rid of the sticky mess on my stomach, so the stink and the burning sensation lingered on.

For the rest of the day we prudently kept our heads down, running at a respectable depth. It was only at the onset of darkness that we surfaced get a breath of fresh, hot air. The quartermaster managed to 'shoot' a few stars

and soon afterwards announced confidently that by midday tomorrow we shall be crossing from the Northern to the Southern hemisphere at 30 degrees west. This was much nearer Brazil than to Africa.
During our main meal at night, I tried to close my ears to the banter and dire warnings of more grief awaiting us.
What else could they do to us which could be worst than what had gone before?
It couldn't possibly be more unpleasant.
'Ha... Bloody Ha-Ha!'

At noon on the following day, a special watch made up entirely of those who had already been baptised, took over the running of the boat. Running submerged at 50 m at Slow Ahead, only the essential stations were manned. I felt shivers running down my back, which wasn't because of the cold, but had more to do with apprehension.

A fanfare sounded over the tannoy and the God of the Deep Neptune appeared in the control-room, followed by his entourage. He took up his position on the throne; a box perched on top of the chart-table. His wife Amphitrite, to the accompaniment of several wolf-whistles, sat beside him. She looked stunning, her chestnut-wig hiding most of her features but as far as we were concerned she could have put the ladies of Hamburg's St.Pauli red-light district in the shade. Even the odd tuft of hair at the cleavage did little to destroy the illusion. Four other menacing figures made up their entourage, a priest, a barber and two burly helpers. It was obvious; the whole set-up had been carefully planned well in advance of our departure for this patrol. Those costumes, wigs, beards and other paraphernalia could not have been run-up at a moments notice.

The priest, in a high-pitched, monotonous and nasal voice, began by reading out the first name over the address system. Alphabetically we had to present ourselves to Neptune, one after the other, so as not to upset the trim of the boat. Of course, because we were far removed from the scene in the control room, we had to rely on a commentary over the tannoy to keep up with the proceedings. We stayed put in our quarters until our turn arrived. Although I strained to hear what was actually going on in the control-room, other than hearing the occasional commotion we were completely in the dark as to what was happening there. The only clue we had, was the dishevelled appearance of the victims on their way back to their quarters.

When the time arrived, when one of the next names to be called would be mine, I started to get rather worried. In fact, cold sweat started to run down my face.

But just as my name was announced and I made my way to the control room, the radio operator was reporting 'Screw-noises at 105 degrees, getting louder fast'

'Silent running' and 'Go to 150m' ordered the Old Man, he had no intention of allowing third-parties to participate in our fun or possibly spoil it. For over half an hour we kept our head down in line with the view held by all U-boat men, that there are only two types of vessels on the high seas. Who was this intruder? Who knows?

If it was one of our boats, we wished them 'good hunting'.

If it was one of their, lets hope one of our mates will get the buggers, because our own targets were on the other side of the Cape of Good Hope.

But the interruption did have one beneficial effect on the satellite-helpers. When I arrived in the control room, I noticed they looked absolutely shattered. To look at them you would have been forgiven for thinking they had been baptised as well.

Thanks to the interval in the proceedings they managed to get their breath back and by the time the screw-noises had abated, they looked ominously eager to get on with the business in hand. I could have sworn that under his false beard one of them looked suspiciously like a man, with whom I had a recent run-in. It concerned a very young lady he had met in port. I accused him of baby snatching, while he held the distasteful view that if they were big enough, then frankly they were old enough. He had a very nasty grin on his face as he awaited his orders from Neptune.

The priest appeared again. Looking refreshed, he eyed me up and down as he started his litany in his high-pitched voice of his. 'It has been noted that your locker resembles a pigsty. The photos you keep in it are not fit to be seen. They can only be your aid to masturbation. It has also been reported that you have not cleaned your filthy fingernails. In fact, medical opinion fears that you are in imminent danger of getting blood-poisoning the next time you scratch your balls.'

He took a deep breath and continued 'Yesterday Admiral Triton reported to Neptune that although you accepted your preparatory medicine with outward good grace, he suspected that underneath you were resentful. Neptune does not like pretence and is not very pleased.'

A wave of Neptune's hand was enough to get everybody moving. Two more pills of the quality already described were pushed between my teeth, followed by some equally nasty beverage. At the same time the barber, who was hiding behind the largest moustache ever seen, started to soap my hair and face... only it wasn't just soap. It did however cover my whole upper body with lather... very, very sticky lather. To ensure it reached every nook and cranny, he spread the foam around with a monstrous-sized cutthroat razor.

He made sure that the gunge got into my eyes, ears and mouth and before I could draw breath, two of the helper pick me up bodily and pitched me head first into a herring barrel.

What a relief. It will help to wash the muck off, provided that I would be given a chance to come up for breath.

Even thinking about it after all this time makes me want to vomit. The barrel was filled with some rotten old herring slop, thinned down with bilge water. Those lousy bastards made sure that I swallowed plenty before they let go of me. My God! Had everybody, who had been baptized before me, thrown-up in this barrel as well?

Blinded by the stinking, filthy mess, like a drowned rat and to the smirks of my so-called mates, I stumbled through the engine rooms to my bunk.

Please God, let me die here and now!

I felt like throwing the glass of brandy back into the face of the grinning PO, as he offered it to me along with a piece of paper.

To stop myself from being sick and out of self-preservation I tossed it back in one go.

BRRRRRRRRR ... !!!

However, lo and behold, it somehow helped me to cope with the disgust I felt. I even managed to obtain a drop more from the same bottle, while starting to enjoy the discomfort of others coming back from their ordeal.

The bit of paper turned out to be a very handsome and elaborate certificate, which confirmed in lovely scrolled script my baptism by Neptune himself. It will look nice at home, framed and hanging on the wall beside the one of Heini's. It will stop him from looking down at me, me, his little kid brother.

Well... that was that. Tradition had been satisfied and now we could carry on with our objectives.

The celebrations were not quite finished. That night, after we stuck-up our head for air, our 'Master chef' prepared what one could only have described as a banquet.

Where the devil has he hidden all the goodies till now?

He was the only one who knew.

Having thought about it, perhaps banquet was not quite the word for tinned soup, beef, potatoes and vegetables followed by tinned plums and plastic

cream.
However a few bottles of Champagne, which appeared from nowhere, helped with the illusion. Naturally the drink was rationed and was mostly reserved for the baptismal-lambs, who were excused watch for a while.

At the end of it all, everybody was of the opinion, that we would not have liked to miss this experience... not for all the tea in China.
For a little while we had almost forgotten about it, but the war had certainly not gone away, but would shortly show us that it was still very much in evidence.

CHAPTER NINE

It was more-or-less downhill all the way toward the southern parts of the Atlantic. As time went by, the Old Man increased the time of running surfaced; because he was sure that we were well out of reach of all enemy land-based aircraft with their RADAR sets. After we had passed Pernambuco and San Salvator, all the while keeping to within 150 km of the Brazilian coast, we started to run surfaced during daylight hours as well, a move, which was welcomed by everybody, especially by us stokers. Officially, Brazil was at war with us but the Old Man followed a hunch that their war effort was less than enthusiastic and for that reason he kept well over to the eastern side of the South Atlantic.

The ventilation system had more of a chance to draw fresh, clean air from outside and push it into every little corner of the boat, even those furthest away from the only open hatch. Bed covers had been dispensed with some time ago. We didn't have to worry about how we looked, as long as we wore our identity disk. Most of us below deck wore just a pair of lightweight shorts and canvass shoes. I emphasised 'below deck', because, up on the bridge you had a different kettle of fish all together. Although ***KARO-AS*** was uniformly painted a very light colour, almost off-white, the all-metal construction absorbed the heat of the tropics so much, that it was inadvisable to touch any of the rails or bulwark with your bare skin. The few foolish people who dared to expose more than the absolute minimum while upstairs were soon to be found under treatment for sunburn. The MO was not at all pleased, nor was the Old Man. Two seamen, whose skin seemed to hang off their backs in strips, would spend most of their free time behind bars, when next we made fast in a port.

What it really boiled down to was, while travelling under water during the daytime, we were spared the worst of the heat. However, there was a much more important factor to consider. Down below we could only progress at 2 or 3 knots, so as not to kill the electric batteries, whereas surfaced this could be increased to 10 to 12 knots using diesel-power without overtaxing our fuel-stocks. Although we could thus average 450 km per day, there were some drawbacks. The lookouts on the bridge were under constant strain to monitor their allotted quadrants for enemies on, under, or above the sea. Although the biggest concentration of anti U-boat activity was in the North Atlantic, for us there was no place as safe, as staying 50 m

below. The Officers of the watch kept changing the lookouts around the four sectors. Particularly in the mornings and evenings it was pure murder to peer into the very bright sun. Carrier-born aircraft were said to be a damned menace everywhere, even here near the South American coast.
The wireless operators had to be on their toes as well, every little blip on their screen and every peep heard on the airwaves could be a message of doom.

Meanwhile, *Smutje* was overheating his brain, trying to think up new ideas to present old-fashioned tinned stuff in a new and exciting way. He tried frying-up corned-beef in batter and attempted unsuccessfully to do the same with tinned potatoes. It must have been hell to think up variations in the diet, when all the fresh stuff was a far-off memory. The smoked sides of ham and Salamis were gone as well; I doubted whether they would have survived the tropical heat.

Napoleon knew what he was talking about when he observed that 'The army is marching on its stomach', because the same applied to us.
Good tasty food meant a contented crew.
It also kept the Medico happy.
Lousy food... forget it.
There was no shortage of suggestions from the crew, how to solve the age-old problem of keeping sailors happy.

Walter, my sparring partner, chipped in with one of his pearls of wisdom, 'Why can't the Old Man sneak up on the coast of Brazil, at some God-forsaken place, where we could get a landing party to pinch a cow or some other kind of fresh food?'
Why couldn't it be done?
There would be no shortage of volunteers for such an adventurous enterprise.

'I've read in my old atlas,' putting a little bit of my wisdom to the debate, 'in Brazil there are several German settlements south of Sao Paulo, in an area called Santa Catarina. Several places have German names like Blumenau, New Hamburg and New Bremen. Perhaps we could call on them for fresh food supplies?' Why not, indeed?

The Old Man explained to us later, 'Those German settlers have been there for a long time, probably since the last century. They've made their home in a country, which has been at war with Germany since 1942. We couldn't possibly ask them to stick their necks out for us.'
That made a lot of sense; after all, we weren't exactly starving, were we?
In any case, now we were travelling faster during the daytime, we should

be at our destination a bit sooner than we thought.

Since leaving Kiel, the Old Man had kept a strict radio silence. After passing the latitude 15° south, he had sent a brief signal for HQ to advise them that we were OK, but without mentioning of our exact position. He had probably discussed his proposed route with the Chief of Flotilla and asked him not to expect any new before reaching the South Atlantic.

Whether we were safe or not, our sparkies diligently monitored the airways every minute of the day and night. They picked-up some good reports about successes by U-boats, but those were often followed by bad news from all fronts. Recently the bad outweighed the good. I often saw one or other of the radio operators pass messages to the Old Man and usually I was able to judge by his face whether it was good news or bad. Soon we will be heading past Cape Town, where in the past the South African Air Force had managed to make this area a dangerous place for U-boats.

It was probably for that reason that the Old Man and our navigator had long ago decided to give the Cape of Good Hope a wide berth. Anyway, there was plenty of open sea to the South, even though it will be a lot colder and wilder.

In the end we shall have to rely on our usual ***KARO-AS*** luck, it certainly has been with us so far.

But before then, there was some other business to be seen to. When we were almost opposite Rio de Janeiro, we intercepted a U-boat warning, which seemed to have come from a Brazilian steamer. A small convoy, possibly on its way from Rio to Cape Town, had one of their small troop-ships torpedoed by one of our boats. Their one escorting corvette didn't bother about the U-boat, but made picking-up of survivors of the stricken vessel her priority.

Now that was a bit of a change. In the North Atlantic, during some of the bitterest battles, Tommy never appeared to bother about his own ship-wrecked sailors, as all the escorts would immediately go after the U-boat, whose destruction seemed to be their priority.

Meanwhile, the other ships of the convoy had scattered at full speed and attempted to find safety. Except one of them, which had run out of luck.

Just as her captain thought that he had managed to avoid further trouble, she had run straight out in front of ***KARO-AS****'s* loaded tubes. The Old Man wasn't looking for trouble in the Atlantic, but there was no way he was going to turn-up his nose at a chance of bagging a nice fat Ec-2 Liberty-ship. At the sighting of her, we disappeared from the top. For the first time in earnest, two of our bow-torpedo-tubes were readied and with the minimum

of fuss the poor devil was sent to the bottom of the sea, all 10,500 tons of her. It was uncannily like the practice-runs we had made in the Baltic, when the unlucky target-ship *Rügen* was accidentally sunk by us. Even the noise of rupturing bulwarks on the ship's way down to Davis Jones' locker sounded the same. Only this time the noisy drama went on for much longer due to the greater depth of these waters. Shivers ran down my back as I re-called the words of our Old Man after our commissioning: 'Remember men, our war is against enemy ships, not their crews who are only doing their duty - the same as us.'
Lets hope someone got them off in time.
Talk about stirring-up a hornet's nest.

At 'Full ahead both engines' we had beaten a hasty retreat, running at nearly 20 knots for the next two hours. Eventually, RADAR bleeping from all directions persuaded the Old Man, that in company with the fish, we definitely would be safer. Crawling along for the rest of the day while risk-ing the occasional glance through the *Spargel*, the Old Man made ***KARO-AS*** keep a very low profile.

A little while earlier, there was a very instructive conversation going on inside the conning tower between the Old Man and his *1WO*. I am not sure whether we were supposed to be listening, but judging by the Old Man's tone of voice, he didn't care who heard his sermon. The *1WO* may have asked 'should we not see whether we could help the survivors', when the normally placid Old Man nearly exploded. '*Herr Leutnant*, what would you have done if you had been a radio operator on that Liberty ship. You'd have frantically done your best to let all and sundry know your position, before getting off the sinking ship. In minutes we would have the whole world down on top of us. Our orders are clear enough, 'the safety of my boat and my crew is my duty and first priority'.'
We got the impression he would have preferred things to be different though.

`Afterwards it was back to full steam ahead, until we neared 40 degrees south, where we did a smart 90 degrees left turn to head due east, a course which would enable us to miss the bottom end of Africa by some 600 km. The Old Man reckoned this little detour would be well worth it.
Slowly the sun had lost its intensity and our woollen blanket returned to our bunks. The regular denim working gear had replaced the tropical outfits. Even bridge party's Sou-westers had an occasional outing, as the South Atlantic showed its teeth. Albatrosses took up station right above our bridge, barely having to flap their wings. There must be a bit of an up-

draught caused by the boat. Watching those lovely great birds you couldn't help wondering what they would taste like roasted and served in a tasty sauce. Was there any way of catching them, other than to blast them out of the sky with our *FLAK?*

'Forget it' was the Old Man's verdict, but he did hope they would go away as they might give away our position from several miles away.

In spite of our aerial company and not that we minded, the next few thousand kilometres of our journey were quite uneventful, except that it had become even colder, which surprised no one. By the time we were below Cape Agulhas (as my Atlas called Cape Hope) we could feel the cold blast of the Antarctic winds. The Old Man judged that it would be much healthier to be cold than to tangle with the South-African Air Force. There was an awful lot of water around us; so let them pass the time by looking for the needle in a haystack.

Over three months into our patrol and another eight to nine thousand km still ahead of us, before we could unload our cargo in one of the bases made available to us by our allies, the Japanese. Apart from Penang and Singapore on the Malayan peninsula, there was Batavia (Djakarta) and Surabaja on Java. The facilities at the Japanese base of Kobe could also be used for major repairs. Penang, the port we were ordered to call on first, was the nearest, but perhaps not the easiest to get to in safety. Positioned at the wide end of the Straits of Malacca, it will require luck and continuous vigilance from our crew to get ***KARO-AS*** into the base in one piece.

My old Atlas came in handy on occasions like this. Although I had ready access to the sea-charts on our navigator's table, they showed too much detail. To get an overall picture of this part of the world, particularly the oceans between the continents, Mouse and I studied a map of the world. The Indian Ocean certainly was big, possibly the third largest in the world. For U-boats, it was heaven, as mostly it had plenty of depth to it. The Atlas showed the different trade routes, which crossed this ocean from east to west and from north to south. We should have known as much. Britain had colonies scattered all over the world, a great many were in and around the Indian Ocean. Some of the routes from Australia and New Zealand went past the Cape, but the majority of them, including those from India and other Asian possessions, led through the Suez Canal via the Gulf of Aden and the Red Sea. There was no way in which ***KARO-AS*** could get from here in the Antarctic Ocean to the Malay peninsula without crossing some of those supply lines, which surely were vital to Britain.

We had noticed that there had been a lot of discussion between our officers and we guessed it had a lot to do with their plans for ***KARO-AS***. One of their main considerations surely had to be, the safe delivery of our cargo to our Japanese allies. Only if there was excess fuel in our tanks could we afford to linger along the way and perhaps pot the odd steamer or two. Perhaps the Old Man will take us into his confidence as we go along.

At the moment we were steering 315 degrees, due North East, leaving Madagascar 150 km to port. The Old Man was also well aware of the many islands scattered around in this ocean. The shallow banks around Mauritius and the Seychelles he vowed to avoid like the plague, as there was hardly any water under the boat's keel for our safety.

Since leaving Kiel early in Mid-Summer we have been through several changes of climate. We experienced the Equatorial baptism in late summer and the cold of the Antarctic in near winter conditions. Now we are heading for the equator and our tropical kit should get another outing. This time, when crossing the line we need not worry about Neptune and his miserable shower of helpers. The old saying 'Join the Navy and see the world' took on a new meaning. 'Join the Navy and see eight seasons crammed into one year' is our motto.

The rising temperatures made us more tired, but as luck would have it, our lookouts were still on the ball. It happened one sunny afternoon, while the sun was on our port stern. Out of the sun came this nasty little bee. When it was spotted, it was far to late to dive out of the way. The blare of the claxon brought the gun-crews to the bridge. In no time at all the guns were lined-up on the approaching plane, with full magazines in place.

'Come on, you bastard. See how you're going to like our fireworks.' Spoiling for action, with nerves as taught as violin strings, we shall sell our lives as dearly as possible.

The Old Man held his nerve, as the plane, which clearly had South African markings, slowly followed a course, which would take it out of sight in a northerly direction.

Perhaps he hadn't seen us?

But then ...

B-r-r-r-r-r-r-r-r-r-... our starboard 20 mm twin opened up.

'Stop firing you stupid fool!' screeched the Old Man.

His shout came just as my finger started to curl around the trigger of the port gun, which I was manning. To follow the lead of the other gun would have been a natural reflex action.

Thank God I stopped myself in time, because now I could turn round and see the Old Man barely able to control himself from strangling my poor friend. Luckily the plane just kept on flying until it was out of sight. However, Mouse wasn't going to forget this day in a hurry as he was in for the highest of high jumps.

The Old Man had hoped to let sleeping dogs lie and not make ***KARO-AS*** any more conspicuous than she was. Almost foaming at the mouth, he sentenced Mouse to twenty days in the can for firing without authority. The poor old chap was going to miss most of the fun when next we set foot on dry land.

After this little how-do-you-do, it became clear to us that for the first time on this trip the Old Man was actually looking for a bit of action, perhaps he wanted to get rid of some excess baggage in the shape of the many torpedoes we were still carting around with us. I, for my part, would be the happiest man aboard, if Walter would shift the damned torpedo lying under my bottom bunk. It has given me a permanent crease in my back, because the wire ropes, by which my bunk was suspended, were a few centimetres too long. Through the mattress my back was in permanent contact with this wonderful piece of hardware, which applied to the right place would blast everything to kingdom come.

For a whole week, ***KARO-AS*** cruised around in the approaches to the Gulf of Aden without getting a sniff of ship. The radio-boys ceaselessly cast around for any sign of traffic on the airwaves, but to no avail. On several occasions, we submerged to periscope depth in silent running mode. This was to give our very sensitive listening devices a chance to comb-around for screw-noises. We should have a greater chance to hear ships, than to see them. Even that dodge didn't bring any joy.

However, the Old Man's next action came as a bit of a surprise to all of us. Even our Chief's eyebrows seemed to rise by at least half an inch.

'Prepare to launch *Bachstelze.'*

From somewhere in the bow-section there came a very audible 'Yippee! Yippee!'

Bobby and Teddy, our imitation pilots were over the moon and in no time at all they were breaking all previous records to get the little beast ready to fly. Bobby had donned his flying-suit with the helmet and build-in telephone and sat ready with his seatbelts buckled over his life belt. Teddy was standing ready to give the rotor-blades a quick flick to get them started. (By the way, I never found out why they had English nicknames, something to do with being pilots)

Meanwhile the Old Man had ordered a change of course and raised the engine revs to get up the required speed into the prevailing wind.

‘Take off’ he ordered, and ‘try for a height of 25m’
Up she went with only just the slightest wobble. Teddy let the winch out until Bobby, who had an altimeter in front of him, told him to stop. With his very powerful binoculars he would now have almost twice the range of visibility of the men on the bridge. After he spent a good ten minutes searching the horizon, he reported by his telephone ‘Nothing to report, Sir. Permission to go to 50m?’ Teddy paid-out more cable when he got the nod from the Old Man. He had hardly reached that height when he asked to be held steady. He was now using his binoculars again and concentrating his attention in one particular direction.

I should have mentioned at this point, all the guns had been manned, as a precaution. Why? Because it would obviously take a little while to winch Bobby down in an emergency created by aircraft, in which case we would be able to give his some cover.
This also guaranteed that we had a Grand Stand view of the proceedings.
The Old Man was getting a bit impatient, ‘What can you see?’
‘I think I can see mastheads on the horizon at an estimated distance of 15 km at 180 degrees.’
The Old Man and *1WO* got their heads together and weighed-up the situation. We were travelling into the prevailing southeasterly wind, in the opposite direction from the sighted objects. The Old Man didn’t waste a minute and ordered ‘Get that thing down on the double.’

As soon as Bobby had landed on the platform, a change of course and speed had us chasing those shadows. Lets hope, they were not just a few little islands, of which there were quite a few scattered all over this sea-area. For the last few days and nights the weather had been overcast and the navigator wasn’t absolutely sure about our exact position.
We needn’t have worried; it wasn’t an island.

Once the tips of the mastheads were visible from the bridge, the Old Man took the boat down and for once, he didn’t worry about saving the batteries. ‘Full ahead both’ he ordered and set course for the estimated intersection of our course and that of the steamer. When he thought that he was near enough, he raised the *Spargel* and had a look-see.
‘The target isn’t making headway’ he told the *1WO*. ‘Take a look yourself and what do you think of it?’
‘I would say 18 to 20,000 tonnes freighter, distance 5,000m, perhaps stopped with engine trouble’
Since it wasn’t a U-boat, it must be a target.
‘Tubes 1 and 2 ready.’

They were going to shoot this sitting duck. There was no need to calculate deflection or deviation, the Old Man just pointed ***KARO-AS*** at the freighter and ordered

'Eins los - zwei los' (fire one - fire two)

Bang! Bang!

'First one hit the bow-section, the second amidships' he reported. He turned the boat hard to starboard and set course to leave the scene. This was the moment, when he got one of the biggest surprises of his life. The freighter was already listing some 30 degrees to port and dropping deeper and deeper into the water, but the Old Man could now see why the ship had lain still in the water.

On the side away from our boat, a submarine was frantically turning away from the sinking ship, trying hard to get out of sight below the waves. According to our Old Man she had dived before he could properly identify the sub, especially since the light was very poor. Perhaps she was Dutch. A few of those had been reported to infest the waters around Indonesia; their main object in life was to lie in wait for German U-boats of the Monsoon Group.

We were pre-warned to look out for those pests, particularly at the shallow approaches to Penang, Singapore, Batavia and Surabaja. On the other hand it could have been a Yank or a Brit, they took a special interest in us as well.

Anyway, the Old Man was pleased, he was sure we had put a king-sized spanner in their works, right in the middle of a re-fuelling exercise.

The death-throes of the supply-ship were all too apparent; we therefore went down to 150m in silent-running mode and away from the scene. There was no way we wanted to tangle with our Dutch opponents and at a guess, they may have entertained similar ideas. On the other hand, they may come back to pick-up the survivors of their 'Milk cow'.

We, careful as ever, kept submerged until nightfall, before continuing on a general westerly course along the line of the equator, giving a wide berth to the southern tips of mainland India and particularly of Ceylon, where RAF bases were only too ready, to dispatch us to Hades. As it happened, it must have been around here when we got the first news about the Allied troops landings in France. This type of unwelcome news was not designed to improve our morale, as we were worried enough about our folks in the cities being bombed to bits. In spite of this, in our ignorance, we were sure that the invasion forces would soon be defeated and that the invaders would finish back in the drink as they did once before, at Dunkirk. Lets hope that

KARO-AS could still call at St.Nazaire on our return from the Orient, instead of having to run the gauntlet rounding Britain to get home. We were looking forward to the chance of tasting those sexy French Mademoiselles, the ones we have heard about so much. As Mouse and I chewed over this dilemma, I had to dampen his anticipation somewhat. From my initial training time, I remember some very dire warnings of the consequences of meddling with some of the so-called delights of France, and for that matter of all the occupied countries.

I had already told Mouse about those VD facts of life, but I wasn't sure whether I had mentioned that prostitutes, both professional and amateur, were known to deliberately infect 'customers' from the occupying forces.

'Let that be a warning to you, Mouse, you either live like a monk; or, if ever you feel the urge, just nip behind the bicycle shed and do the needful.'

Joking aside, things did not look good at home.

Orders had just reached us from Berlin that the traditional military salute, (fingertip touching the cap) was to be replaced by the 'Heil Hitler' salute, the one our Führer had copied from the Roman Empire's salute 'Hail Ceasar'.

Things must have been getting desperate, to make professional servicemen feel like green-behind-the-ears Hitler Youths. On a small vessel like ours, saluting was quite impractical anyway. Some idiot must have figured that this order would improve the moral of the nation.

Between us ordinary mortals, standing with our arm up in the air like that only meant one thing,

'We're in the shit up to this height!'

However, there was nothing to be gained by becoming too disheartened. Long ago, we were promised that the newly developed V-weapons would be available soon. The type XXI Electro-U-boats and the Hydrogen Peroxide driven 'Walther' submarines, who could stay submerged indefinitely, had started their trials and should soon be ready to take over the U-boat war from our outmoded vessels. The new *Messerschmitt 262* Jet fighters were already in service and will surely help to stop the bombing of our homes.

New guided missiles and other weapons were being developed. The V', in V-weapons (V1, V2 and the promised V3), stood for 'Vergeltung' (retribution). Yes, we actually DID believe in miracles and perhaps that was just as well for our sanity. The secret was not to think too much.

Since earlier in our passage, all the chess-players of the crew had entered a knockout competition. The best of five games went forward to the next round. As we were nearing the end of our outward patrol, our MO and I started to contest the final, which was over the best of seven games. Since we could only play while I was not on watch, it took a whole week to complete. He ran out the winner, beating me four games to three. I was very pleased with myself, at least I gave him a real test and it led to a further challenge, to be played on our homeward run. Competing against the doctor gave me more enjoyment than any other game I had ever played. Here we had a real old-fashioned gentleman. Thank goodness he had very little to do on this trip. Although we lived on tinned or dried food, the health of the crew seemed to be excellent. He often shared the watch keeping on a voluntary basis. But I think in the back of his mind he wondered which nasty tropical diseases we could possibly pick up in Indonesia, other than the ones we had been immunised against, perhaps malaria or beriberi. His medical equipment had lain unused under his bunk, lets hope it will stay there for the remainder of the trip.

Ever since ***KARO-AS*** had joined the East-Asia Monsoon Group, we have been looking forward to see and experience the Orient. When we set out, we mostly talked about our journey's end as being Japan. However, the ports we were scheduled to visit, were in the former British and Dutch East-Indies and were still 5,000 km short of the Japanese Islands. During the final days of our journey, I was a really quite naughty. Whenever I had an audience who was prepared to listen to me, I was telling them all about this part of the world. I told them about the history of Penang and of the Malay peninsular. They didn't know that Penang was once called Georgetown (neither did I until I saw it in my Atlas) and that it was founded about 150 years ago by men of the British East India Company on an isle off the west coast of Malaya. It was a very strategic port on the busy India-China trade route and became a British protectorate along with Burma and the northern part of Borneo. That was until 1942, when the Japanese occupied the whole of Indo-China including Singapore and all the islands of the Netherlands East Indies. For the Empire of the Rising Sun this area yielded rich supplies of much needed oil, minerals and other goods, all required for their war effort.

I also blinded my chums with science about the mixed races and religions we would find in this very densely populated area. The largest group was the Malayans while Indians had come here to work in the rich tin industry and Chinese worked on the rubber plantations. Those last two groups made-up nearly half of the overall total. I also enlightened them

about the climate, the flora and the fauna, from rubber trees and palms to Elephants, Tigers, Crocs and Cobras.
They surely thought that I was one very clever chap.

Thus we spent the last three weeks of our outward journey. Although there had been some radio traffic in the area, we had neither seen nor smelled any sign of shipping. The weather had been kind and the navigator had plenty of opportunities to keep tabs on our exact course. Once we got to the top-end of the Straits of Malacca between the islands of Nicobar and Sumatra, we again disappeared down below. Although the depth of the Strait was not much more than 40m, it was enough to keep out of sight on periscope depth. Like I said before, we were warned of British, Dutch or even American submarines lying in wait for German U-boats as they approached the end of their passages. Every now and then the Old Man ordered the boat to rest at the bottom, with every machine or motor switched off. We would listen for signs of trouble before going on again. At this stage of the proceedings, one couldn't be too careful. Fancy coming all this way to get your arse blown off.

Eventually, still submerged, we arrived off Penang Island and not until then did our radio operators make coded contact with the base. The Old Man was like a cat on hot bricks and we assumed he has had some bad experience in this area when he was here before. He appeared to prefer slipping ***KARO-AS*** into the harbour without announcing his presence to all and sundry. But the possibility of the entrance being mined made that exercise far too risky. A Japanese escort vessel should be with us before long. Taking no chances, we waited below the surface, but in sight of the entrance to the channel dividing the Penang Island from the Malayan mainland. Several hours later, the *2WO* on the periscope spotted a Japanese torpedo boat heading for the spot, which had been agreed for the rendezvous.

Other than the screw noise from the torpedo boat it had been silent on the listening front, so it was decided to show our face. Once we had surfaced, the escort came alongside and a German Lieutenant from the base transferred over, to act as pilot. He brought several boxes of goodies with him. While the patrol boat shepherded ***KARO-AS*** to the safety of the inner harbour, we shared in the oranges, bananas, coconuts and (bless all Monsoon Group bases) the crates of Japanese beer.

The Old Man warned us not to open the latter, not until we were safely tied-up in port. I couldn't remember when I last tasted a real bananas or a real orange and we certainly never tasted real rice-beer before.
Once we got into the inner harbour all hand lined up on deck. The first di-

vision, the seamen paraded on the forecastle and the 2nd division, the engineers or grease monkeys, on the quarter deck. Everybody was dressed in nearly clean tropical kit, khaki shorts and shirts. We not only needed haircuts and a shave, but more than anything we needed lots of hot, steaming water for a bath, we were stinking to high heavens as even the Eau de Colongne (1411) had run-out some time ago. But we were professional sailors and we were determined to present ourselves in a proper military manner. Just because we had been confined to our tin-coffin for several months on end, we were not going to let the Old Man down in front of the Nips.

The Japanese Base-Commander, with the rank of an Admiral, led the reception party, which included the Chief of our German base and his staff. They were lined-up on the wharf.

And the Old Man didn't let us down either.

He ran the most fantastic mooring manoeuvre ever, placing all 2000 tonnes of ***KARO-AS*** alongside the pier with the lightness of a feather, to the admiring applause of the shore party. Within seconds the gangway went across right in front of the Japanese Admiral, who was waiting for our Commandant to report the safe arrival of our U-boat.

In the excitement of making a good impression to our Allies he had forgotten all about the changed saluting orders and greeted him in traditional military style, fingertip to his white cap. The Admiral accepted his report with a broad smile and a similar salute. It was only when the Old Man turned to similarly salute the German Chief, an elderly Lieutenant Commander and when he returned his greeting with '*Heil Hitler*' that the penny dropped with the Old Man.

'I am sorry, Sir' he apologised, but did he really mean it?

Knowing how unpopular the newest salute was with everybody, I had my doubts about that!

CHAPTER TEN

The Old Man turned back to the Japanese Admiral, who continued with his bowing and scraping routine. Using an interpreter, he welcomed ***KARO-AS*** and her crew.

'On behalf of the Imperial Japanese Naval garrison Penang, I extend to you an invitation to join me and my men tomorrow evening, to properly celebrate your heroic passage and your safe arrival in Malaya.'

Of course, we were left guessing what he meant by 'properly celebrating'?

Were we to be pampered and waited-on hand and foot by some of those famous Geisha girls? We'll have to wait and see; but please hurry up.

The Lieutenant Commander in charge of the German base also congratulated the Old Man and thanked him and his crew for the safe delivery of those badly needed supplies from Germany. He explained that his base could only help us in a very limited way. The docking facilities here were fully occupied in servicing the Japanese Naval vessels of this area. We would have to try our luck at Singapore, Batavia or Surabaja to unload the lead in the keel.

But he also pledged that during our stay here, his staff would be at our disposal to help with any repairs or servicing to our ship or see to our personal needs. They would start by taking-over the guard-duties on our boat and see to the unloading of some of the goods we had brought along, while we made ourselves at home in quarters ashore, at the German compound. But before we could look after our needs, we were able to bring a little joy to our lads at the Penang base. The sight of a bag full of mail and parcels from their folk back home resulted in joy and jubilation. Only twenty officers and men were stationed at this far-flung outpost, so each one got a fistful of letters and parcels.

An old bus, a relic from the Imperial British past, was supposed to collect and ferry us to our quarters ashore. Unfortunately it gave-up the ghost on that particular day and had been taken apart by our lads at the base. The only motor vehicle available was a small lorry. Not to worry, the quarters were only a couple of miles away. We chucked our kitbags on this lorry, then fell in and proceeded to march into town.

Mind you, we felt a bit unsteady on our feet.

Terra firma was a distant memory, we were still moving with the non-existing swell. Somehow, we managed to put up a good show as, with a song on our lips, we marched through the town to the barracks.

Barracks? My foot!

Here were some the grandest houses I had ever seen.

They may once have been the homes of the British colonial masters as they lorded over this vital outpost of the East India Company. Perhaps it was poetic justice that we, the archenemies of colonialism, should now be enjoying the fruits of Britannia's ill-gotten gains. I wondered what the rest of the town looked like, surely it wasn't all like this?

But first things first!

At our arrival here, we were allocated rooms in one of those palaces. Our Officers, CPOs and POs were billeted in another part of the base, but I bet their quarters weren't any better than ours.

At least our superiors wouldn't cramp our style every minute of the day, which was the best part of having separate billets.

Four of us from the control room, Wilhelm, one of the helmsmen and Walter, shared a bedroom, which in days gone by could have been a small ballroom. The single beds were made-up with the crispest and purest white linen we had ever seen. Toilets, showers by the dozen - what else does the sailors heart desire?

First stop was the quartermasters store to collect a change of clothes - civvies. Our sense of smell had long ago been blunted, but by the look on the faces of our colleagues at the base we must have been stinking to high heavens. This surprised no one, seeing we were entombed in the stale atmosphere of dear old ***KARO-AS*** during the last few months.

Trust our comrades of the base; they had attended to every little detail. They kitted us out with clean underwear, sock, pyjamas in which I wouldn't be seen dead, slacks, shirts by the dozen and sports-jackets and a raincoat. Every stitch of our own clothes as well as our bed linen and blankets we brought ashore the next day, were rolled up and tied with string.

The bundles were then handed over and taken away by our friends at the base to be laundered. I could just see the Chinese staff at the washhouse holding their noses in disgust while putting the grubby lot into boilers to steam the life out of them.

The next hour or two were dedicated to the cleanliness of our bodies. Thank goodness for real soap, which actually produced lather, scrubbing brushes and a never-ending supply of piping hot water for the showers. Three cheers for the boys of the Penang base, they all deserved medals.

We found out later, that they had the devil's own job trying to arrange proper service and repair facilities for the boats of the Monsoon Group at this far-flung Japanese outpost.

In those early days the Nips seemed to make little or no effort to help our boats. Their own vessels had to get precedence.

But as the CO of the base put it to our Old Man, 'we must appreciate the fact that our Allies are in a very difficult position. There are over 3,000 miles of open and enemy-submarine infested waters between here and the Japanese mainland. In their desperate need for raw-materials they quickly conquered large chunks of mineral rich countries and island around here, but find themselves stretched to breaking point trying to hold-on to them for their vital tin, rubber and oil.'

He went on to say, 'as you may have noticed from the reception given to you, the Japanese have lately realised that co-operation was to their advantage as well as ours. The freight carried by your U-boats of the Monsoon Group was very much appreciated.'

We learned something else from our Old Man: 'On the orders of our High Command, a seaworthy Type IXC U-boat has been handed over to the Nips and was now sailing under the flag of the Rising Sun.'

Mouse gave me a sharp dig in the ribs, he was grinning from ear to ear: ' Can't you just imagine what it must be like if that boat is manned by a sex-starved crew like the one we had aboard in Stettin?'

To top it all, another one of our Monsoon-boats had presented them with a Bachstelze, the same type of autogiro observation kite we carried and which we had recently used in the Gulf of Aden. It had been handed over complete with operating and maintenance manuals and with explicit instructions for their pilots.

If the Japs manage to get one of those contraptions into the air, one could only wish them the best of luck. They would probably need it, unless they were of the Kamikaze variety.

Meanwhile, back at the 'Penang Hilton', we were served with our first meal on 'terra firma'. Most people might have called it an everyday meal, but to us, who after several months at sea, with nothing except tinned THIS and tinned THAT, it was nothing short of a royal banquet. Our plates were piled sky-high with delicious roast pork, backed-up with crisp roast potatoes and an assortment of fresh vegetables as well as a side-salad. They must have got hold of my mother's recipe, as this spread brought back memories from pre-war days. Smutje came in for a bit of FLAK 'why can you not feed us like this', which was probably quite an unkind thing to do to the poor sod.

Local stewards in their snowy-white starched outfits made sure none of our plates or none of our glasses ever got near to being empty. The only thing missing was the fat and the crackling and when I asked one of the waiters, I was told that those were not considered fit to eat and were therefore dumped in the garbage bins. Just as well as we were full to the gills anyway.

To let the meal settle we made our way to one of the luxurious lounges. We had plenty to talk about on this our first day ashore in the Orient as we smoked and with the help of a few beers, whiled away the rest of the evening.

The war seemed to be just a distant memory.

When we turned-in that night, we'd completely forgotten all the pressures and inconveniences of the last few months. Sleep didn't come easy, as we all missed the continual motion of our boat, which acted like the soothing rocking of a cradle. My own thoughts were with the family in Berlin, I wished that just for once they could experience this kind of luxury, being well fed and comfortable, without the need to get up in the middle of the night to seek refuge in the cold air raid shelter.

But, as was to be expected, when the time came to shake a leg, I had fallen sound asleep. Thank goodness, we could stay in bed as long as we wanted, 'I'll just have another five minutes'.

After a very late breakfast, five minutes more had turned into one and a half hour; our colleagues from the base turned up to collected us in a convoy of hired cars. They wanted to treat us to a guided tour round Pulau Pinang, the island of Penang.

The town itself was positioned at the northeastern side of the island and faced the Penang Strait, a three-mile wide stretch of water separating the island from the Malayan mainland. It was a clear day and we could plainly see the mainland and the town of Butterworth on the opposite bank. A few merchant vessels lay at anchor in the strait, perhaps waiting for their turn to either be loaded or to be unloaded in Penang's harbour.

The excursion took us round the island in an anti-clockwise direction with water on our starboard side and a hilly countryside on port. The road ran all the way round the island and was superbly surfaced, all 70 miles of it. Our guides explained that the British had built it after they had acquired the control of the colony to help the rubber trade. The town itself was founded by the East-India Company over 150 years ago and was given the name of Georgetown. In those days the main agricultural product after rice was coffee. But then a newly developed strain of rubber tree, which was suitable for this moist climate, was introduced here in many rubber plantations. The establishment of those made the availability of good roads to and from the port a necessity.

After a very leisurely ride round to the far side of the island, we stopped for a picnic. There were busy rubber plantations behind us on the lower slopes of a small mountain range. In front were arrays of paddy fields in which vast armies of ant-like men or women beavered away. Behind them lay the enormous expanse of the Malacca Strait where it joined the blue Indian Ocean. One of the guides told us that on the top of mountains behind us at a height of nearly 3,000 feet, was the plush Penang-Hill Hotel. It had been host to the crews of various other U-boats, which had called here.

Unlike ***KARO-AS***, U-boats usually remained here for longer periods, mainly for essential maintenance work on the Diesels. During such times their lucky crews were treated to a luxurious ten-day stay. Access to the hotel was by funicular railway, which was a mile long and ran up on the side of the mountain, through original and unspoiled jungle. Even this short trip on the cable car was worth it, our guide told us, because of the teeming animal life, such as apes and monkeys moving through the jungle at speed. Unfortunately, because of our short stay, we were missing-out on this undoubted pleasure, but we weren't doing too badly ourselves.

Beer was the main ingredient of our picnic; the other one was fruit of all description, which thrived in the moist tropical conditions. It was not difficult to understand that in this lovely paradise of an island the temperature stayed at an almost constant 27 degrees C throughout the year. With a very high annual rainfall, this surely was the most fruitful place on earth, our vision of the Garden of Eden.

Once we got all the way round, we saw a bit more of the town. My Atlas had not prepared me for the fact that this Malayan town had a very Chinese look about it. Somewhere along the way was the Snake-Temple, which was reputed to house hundreds of snakes within its walls. Perhaps we will get a chance to see more of it at another time. The Pagoda of the 10000 Buddhas was another attraction we were unable to examine in detail but then, we were not here to improve our minds. In fact, we were much keener to see the seamier down town areas. As soon as we were shown where to reassemble later, we were free to go our own way. Alas, poor Mouse was otherwise engaged, in a solitary place. Here he had all the time to get it into his skull not to blast-away with his port gun until ordered to fire. William, however, agreed to come sightseeing with me. On the way we met Sigfried, who was based here after surviving being torpedoed while serving on an auxiliary cruiser in the Java Sea. He had been collecting a pair of shoes he had made to measure in the town. He also kindly agreed to show us around. Pushing our way through one of the busy main streets, we hitched a ride to a park in comfortably pedal-powered three-seater rickshaw. There was no escaping the mass of humanity; this must be one of the most populated areas of the world. Here everybody seemed to be engaged in gambling of one sort or other. Even Sigfried couldn't explain to me whether they used cards or dice or what else. We didn't feel like pushing our way through the throng to the front of the human circles. One thing seemed clear from the body language of some of the participants, they were not playing for peanuts judging by the bundles of paper money they were clutching as they went on their way. Still sitting in the rickshaw Sigfried explained 'in these part of Malaya there is a lot of unrest among the local population, which is directed against all colonial powers. They certain hope that the British will never come back, as the Japanese had promised self-government after the war and had meanwhile given a lot of good, responsible jobs to the indigenous Malayans.'

He went on to explain that the Japs had also encouraged many of the Indians among the population to join the armies of Subhas Shandra Bose, to fight for India's independence from the British yoke or else to keep working on the plantations to provide the badly needed rubber. In contrast to the way in which the Japs treated those racial groups, they apparently did not get on too well with the Chinese, which made up 30% of the population. They, after all, were Japan's traditional enemies. Many of the Chinese fled after being mistreated. Eventually the Japanese had to learn to tolerate them, so that they would keep producing the valuable Malayan tin, which was urgently required by Japan's war effort. It was those minerals and other resources, which had brought the colonial powers here in the first place. Sigfried reckoned that one day this multi-national country would rise against the foreigners who plundered their resources, whether they were English, Dutch or Japanese. I hoped he would be proved right.

Once back in town we paid-off the rickshaw. The narrow streets were festooned with a mass of colourful shop-signs in large Chinese-looking writing. Underneath there were still a few translations in English. Hundreds of bicycles and tricycles were parked along one side of the street. Behind the facades of the buildings, which themselves looked substantial enough, there was a chaotic jumble of oriental goings-on. Delicious cooking smell mixed with other less pleasant odours. Cats, dogs, goats and chicken vied with humans for a space to live in. The din in those enclosed spaces was deafening.

This was the real Orient, just as we had always imagined it to be. The only way we could tell what a particular shop was selling was to go in and look. All the usual trades were represented, butchers, bakers, tailors, laundries and even a cobbler. There was hardly anything displayed in the window, which was a bit puzzling for a shoe shop. However, Sigfried enlightened me, 'This chap is a bespoke shoemaker. In other words he measures your feet and makes a pair of shoes to your chosen design and, what's more, they'll be guaranteed to fit you like a glove.'

It sounded very good but there was bound to be a catch.

'I suppose they cost the moon and anyway, we're only here for a few more days' I speculated. 'It's a pity, because I certainly could do with a decent pair of black shoes. I've always had two left feet - so to speak. With every ready-made pair I've ever bought, either one foot or the other felt too big or too small, too wide or too narrow.'

'Hang on a second' Sigfried said and disappeared into the shop to have a word with the shoemaker.

Using a mixture of Chinese, English and German plus accompanying hand movements, with an odd word of the local lingo mixed-in, he negotiated on my behalf. 'You can have a pair made in two days at the latest' he translated and the price he mentioned was well within my means. What other chance will I get to spend a few of the crisp Dollars in my pocket?

I was shown a selection of patterns and pictures of different styles and after deciding on a smooth looking pair of dress shoes, I paid for them in advance. I also admired a natty pair of white gumshoes and because they were so cheap, I ordered them as well. The Chink put first one of my feet onto a piece of thick paper and drew round it with a pencil and then did the same with the other. Using a tape with funny looking Chinese or Japanese symbols on it, he measured the height of my insteps.

'Come back in two days' he indicated with two fingers.

I could hardly wait to see the result of this exercise.

My friend Williams, however, was worried in case we would head out to sea before getting a chance to collect them. If that should happen, I told Sigfried to sell them and have a drink on me.

On the same evening, although we were quite tired after our excursion round the island, we took up the invitation of the Japanese Admiral and went to be entertained by our Japanese hosts at their barracks - come five-star hotel. In a hall, which was in fact a ballroom, we were treated like royalty. Our hosts had organised a traditional Japanese band, which played strange-sounding oriental music while a group of girl dancers performed ritualistic Japanese dances. To our western ears this music made little sense but the gracefulness with which the ladies went through their dance routines, particularly the expressive way they moved their hands, drew loud applause from us Lords. But on top of those very petite and elegant girl's bodies were grotesquely painted mask-like faces.

There was no accounting for taste in this eastern culture.

I wished I had been able to ask our hosts about the meaning of those dances and movements. Only a very few of our crew, mostly officers, could talk in English to those Japanese, who also knew that language. There just wasn't enough time to find out a lot about all the strange goings-on around us. Many of my mates, myself included, were left to wonder what it was all about. We watched the performance from a table on one side of the stage. Like all the other tables it was decorated with fresh flower arrangements. But of considerably more interest to us were the glasses and the many bottles of beer, which surrounded the flowers.

We sat on comfortable high-backed chairs, two to each table.

Now here was a bit of a puzzle. We had been led to believe that the Japs always sat on the floor when entertaining or eating. Perhaps they only did that in their own homes.

Each one of us had been paired-off with one of the Japanese sailors. After the ritual bowing to each another, we sat down on a table and my host started to pour out the drinks. All the Japanese seamen were dressed in their best navy-blue outfit, which in a vague sort of way was very much like our own. Our own 'Square Rigs' were in kitbags in a damp store in Kiel and our other gear was being laundered. So we turned up in borrowed slacks and sports jacket.

We had already tasted the Japanese beer in very small doses, but this time we were to feel the full effect of it as well. It was quite impossible to hold any sort of meaningful conversation. It didn't stop my host from trying though. I was sure that he meant well, as he kept topping-up my glass as soon as I had taken just one little sip. And there was this continuous bowing.

What was I expected to do in reply?

Every time he bowed, so did I, although I worried about getting a pain in my back. By then I had started to feel the effect of this very tasty nectar. It wasn't quite to our German taste; Beergardens in Munich would have turned their noses up on this stuff. But since we probably wouldn't get too many chances to absorb eastern culture, we may as well get used to this famous *Saki* or *Sake* rice-beer we had heard so much about. And absorbing it we did, until our heads started to spin out of control. After all, eighteen percent alcohol would knock out an elephant, never mind us poor alcohol-starved Lords. I was ever so grateful to my host for his efforts at being an ideal host, if only I could think of a way to show my gratitude. Keeping my eyes open, I did notice that the Japanese sailors only ever smoked cigarettes. It occurred to me that my partner might enjoy one of my treasured cigars, which I had acquired during my basic training in Breda in Holland. It was one out of a box of Havannas and was of Cuban origin. I had until that day in Penang absolutely refused to share such rarity with even my best pals. But what the hell, here was my chance to show my appreciation to my oriental host.

I had a little etui in my jacket pocket, containing three of the little beauties, and after the usual bowing I offered one to him. I took one myself and with my little penknife cut the ends of both cigars.

My slitty-eyed friend looked a bit embarrassed; perhaps their culture forbade them to refuse a well-meant gift. Anyway, before he had much time to think about it I held out my lighter and accompanied by a bit of coughing he started to puff away.

To my delight he seemed to thoroughly enjoy the lovely flavour.

That was, until the normal yellowish colour of his face had turned to a deep shade of green. He stood up and bowed even deeper than usual and disappeared to the toilets. It gave me the opportunity to tip away the warm beer in my glass. With the continual topping-up of the glass, some of the beer had been in my glass since we had arrived. It tasted as if it was stale, so I helped myself to a fresh bottle.

That's better, I thought.

Little did I know that *Saki* wasn't meant to be fizzy and that it was supposed to be drunk when nearly warm.

Walter sat with his host on the table next to ours. His host tried to ask me in words and mime 'Where is my mate?'

After I mimed back that he had gone to the toilets, he went in search of him. It was a long time later when they both came back. I wasn't sure whether he was annoyed with me or not, his inscrutable face gave nothing away. So we started to bow to each other again.

Later, when everybody felt really good, my mates and I started up a little sing song. We tended to stick to songs of the sea and seafarers, in other words, sea-shanties.

Before very long, we had exhausted our repertoire of German songs and were ready to start on English shanties. To our utter amazement, the Nips knew 'Molly Malone' and 'what do you do with a drunken sailor'.

Whether an English-speaker would have understood our German-English or the Japanese-English version is doubtful but what we lacked in English, we more than made up for in gusto. The evening was unforgettable; I can still see the scene, Japanese and German Lords, walking arm in arm, with a song in our hearts and a tear in our eyes. It was almost time for the rising sun when we stumbled on our way back to our Hotel. But the Imperial Japanese Military Police Officer was not at all amused, as we staggered through the streets of the business quarters of Penang, singing and reciting smutty verses. The knuckles of his fist on the grip of his *tachi*-style sword showed white. One got the feeling that he was itching to disembowel this motley ***KARO-AS*** crew. But he did restrain himself even after some of us were crawling halfway up some leaning palm-trees, making ape-like noises whilst looking for coconuts to throw down at the Hirohito-look-alike. Fortunately for him and us, there were no missiles on those palm trees.

On the next morning, after a leisurely breakfast, which was fit only for royalty, we had all our own clothes returned from the laundry. Spread out on our beds, every item looked as good as new and smelled even better, perhaps of roses or orange blossom? Even our socks appeared to have been ironed. It will be a damned shame to wear them again on a smelly, oily U-boat.

Later this Saturday evening, still slightly light-headed from the festivities of last night, we made our way to the German Club. It was located in the part of the town, bordering the strait, which separated the island Penang from the Malayan peninsular. Housed in a palatial villa with its well-kept gardens, it had at one time been the home of a Chinese Millionaire businessman.

After a wonderful evening meal, washed down with fine wines, we awaited the evening's entertainment with eager anticipation.

We didn't have to wait too long. Soon members of a dance band took their places on the stage. They called themselves the 'Boys *von* Hawai', which was a bit of a laugh, as none of them was under fifty. But what the hell, they turned out to be jolly good musicians. After striking up a Hula Hula type tune, in trooped thirty or more dusky young maidens.

'Ooii... Ooii... Ooii, what do we have here?'

'Dear guests from the ***KARO-AS*** U-boat! You are invited to dance with these lovely ladies...' loud jubilation interrupted his speech, 'but please, gentlemen, behave yourselves. These ladies are dancing hostesses, so please try not to step on their delicate little toes too often. Dancing is their

living and they will be honoured to receive a small fee.'
'Boooooooooooooo.'
'Please understand, that the fee will only entitle you to dance with them.'
'Boooooooo and double boooooooooooooo.'
'Thank you, and have an enjoyable evening.'
Well... well... well!
Perhaps, if the money was right...?
Forget it!

Most of my crewmates didn't feel like swinging the dancing legs and were quite happy to drown their sorrows in *sake*. But I had to admit to thinking 'Well, surely half a loaf is better than no bread at all.' Money wasn't a problem; we had plenty of the local stuff. The first girl I asked to dance was obviously a local Malayan girl. She was only about 1.50 m tall and had a waist so small, I could have circled it with my two hands. Framed by short black shining hair, the skin of her face was as delicate as that of a China doll, almost transparent. I couldn't keep my eyes off her face, especially since her deep brown eyes acted like powerful magnets. In typical oriental fashion they gave nothing away. One minute they might have said 'Come on sailor' and just a moment later they could have meant 'Keep off the grass, Sonny'.

Dressed in a long, tight white silken dress, it had a slit on each side reaching up tantalisingly close to the bottom of the panty-line. It provided boundless stimulation to the imagination of this poor sailor. White silk slippers emphasised the smallness of her feet, not that they seemed to touch the floor at all. She moved to the music with a rhythm, which was surely inborn. Nothing could teach a girl to control every muscle in her body to produce this seductive way of swaying.

I wasn't a slouch at dancing myself and since there was all the space in the world on this dance-floor, we slow-waltzed along in unison. It was extremely difficult to keep one's concentration, especially since she was not shy in coming close. Poor me, because of the heat I was only wearing flannels and a thin shirt.

The points of her breasts seemed to bore straight into my skin so that it almost hurt. But then I realised regretfully that the pain was mainly due to a red metal broach on her dress, which bore the word 'Malayan'.

Once I got my senses under some sort of control and after we had moved round the dance floor a few times, I noticed that all the other girls wore similar discs. To my surprise, the broaches gave an indication of their racial backgrounds. Most of them had the word Chinese on it, but apart from the indigenous Malayan there were also Indian, Burmese and girls of mixed origin, whatever that meant?

Well, I had to admit to feeling some embarrassment for this treatment of young ladies; it must have been the Japanese way to degrade them. It seemed akin to the requirement of Jews to wear the Star of David, something I had not thought about a lot before now.

But if the girls minded, they didn't show it. Perhaps they had been used to this treatment under the colonial powers and were even proud of their origins. In any case, they were all absolutely gorgeous and I wouldn't have minded to smuggle any one of them back home with me. My mum would have approved.

So we danced the evening away. Ninety-five percent of my money was spent on dancing with the little lady in white. Although she must have been able to read my dirty mind, she didn't seem to mind my dominating her time.

In my mind I saw her as an oriental Cinderella.

Probably born in one of the many kampons above the swamps of a river delta, slaving away in the paddy fields during the long day. Only on rare occasions could she don her white outfit and in the evening go to the ball. The money she earned as dancing-hostess would be a valuable contribution to her family's income. She tried to speak a little German or was it Dutch, but it was certainly mixed with Pidgin English.

I tried to tell her 'I am Spider, you are Cinderella.'

She smiled gorgeously but I doubt whether she understood what I was trying to get at, or whether she knew of that fairy-tale.

Anyway, the evening also ended just like the story.

At the stroke of midnight the magic came to an end. Cinders, together with all the other ladies left, not in a pumpkin coach, but by being escorted home by either their mothers or their boyfriends or even their husbands.

'God Bless you, girls. You have given us an evening to remember.'

They have reminded us that amidst all the nastiness and ugliness in this world, there were still many beautiful things left to admire, Europe and Asia in harmony.

On the following day, I went to collect the shoes I had ordered. It took me a long time to find my way back to the shoemaker, as one street looked just like the last one and all the shops looked alike. It would have helped had I understood the Chinese looking writing, but when I finally located him; I was in for a very pleasant surprise. With the broadest of oriental smiles the shoemaker presented me with my purchase. Never in all my life

had I seen a better looking pair of black dress-shoes, nor a sportier white pair with thick rubber soles. But equally pleasing was the way they fitted my un-matching feet like pairs of snug gloves. Moving around the shop in them reminded me of what it must be like to be able to walk on air.
With a broad smile, which must have matched his, I thanked him.
Together both pairs cost less than the normal price for one pair in Germany, that is, if you could have found somebody with equal skills of my shoe-maker friend in Penang.

The order to return on board came on the next morning. Our Old Man, who judging by his body language was in a bit of a temper, met us. While we tasted the oriental high-life, our officers and NCOs had been busy supervising the unloading of the gear we had transported all those this way. Goods for our homeward run had already been taken up by empty spaces thus created. Bales of rubber, a few boxes of wolfram and several jars of Iodine had already come aboard. But there just wasn't any more space available to take more.

The Old Man brought us up to date: '***KARO-AS*** has been ordered back to Germany at all speed, carrying as much rubber, ore and Iodine as was possible to the exclusion of all expendable items such surplus torpedoes, artillery and ammunition. Sixteen torpedoes at 1.5 t each are to be replaced by 24 t of rubber. The 10.5 cm deck-canon will be dismantled and the two pressure-proof containers for carrying the *Bachstelze* will be emptied and filled with jars of Iodine.'
'What the hell is going on?' Why is the Old Man so agitated?

'All this work should have been finished yesterday, but I have been flogging a dead horse with the Japanese and our own base-personnel. All I got is excuses, reasons why things can't be done now instead of later.'
He had to draw breath and then continued, 'It's my intention by hook or by crook to get back home before Christmas. I did tell them that I am going to bring my crew aboard and we shall do the job ourselves, even if we have to chuck all the torpedoes, canon and *Bachstelze* overboard into the harbour.'
He added, 'my intervention had the desired effect and as of this morning, all the work's completed. After taking-on a few more supplies, we are ready to leave.
Magic!

No more time for shopping, that will have to wait. But in future, when I polish my shoes, I will dream of Cinderella and Penang.
The lead-bars in the keel remained there until we could find a dry dock, be it Singapore or even Batavia or Surabaja. If it could be done within the next

two weeks, we would still be on target to get home for *Santa Klaus*.

KARO-AS was designed and built as a fighting ship and she and her crew were finely tuned for her task of attacking and destroying enemy shipping. But for the return trip to Europe she was to be a Merchantman again, a freighter. Just like a submersible windjammer on the East Indies/Germany run. The trip to either one of the three places in question will not be a pleasure cruise either. Nasty things awaited unsuspecting U-boats in the Strait of Malacca. At this end of the Strait, it was nearly 250 km wide. But at some points between here and Singapore it narrowed down to less than 50 km wide, a bit like going through a plughole.

'Unfortunately, there isn't another way to get there' the Old Man told us. Only about 30 m deep in some places, the straight was not an ideal place for U-boats, particularly since this neck of the woods was reputed to be infested with either Dutch, British and American submarines, all queuing-up to stick a 21 inch torpedo up our back-passage. During the last year, the U-boats operating in these waters had many narrow squeaks. 'So this is a very good reason to be careful, we must keep our eyes and ears open. To help us along we have been promised air cover by a Singapore based *Arado 198*. He'll keep a close lookout for stray enemy submarines, which may be lying in wait' he concluded.

As we saw it, blasting through the narrows on the surface at nearly 20 knots, ***KARO-AS*** should get there in less than 35 hours. A Lieutenant from Penang base will travel with us, as a sort of pilot. He knew his way round the minefields in the Strait. The canon and FLAK would be manned and ready to fire at all the times and additional lookouts would be posted behind the bridge. The more eyes were peeled the better. According to our intelligence reports, the Allied submarines were still using the older type of torpedoes, which left an easy-to-see bubble-trail in the water. Spotted early enough, the boat can be turned to face the danger and so reduce the width of the target. Anybody, not actually required below deck running the engines etc., would remain on deck during the whole trip - just in case.

It should be an interesting little do as long as everything went to plan.

Me? I hoped that our ***KARO-AS*** luck would hold as usual.

At exactly midnight, we cast off.

CHAPTER ELEVEN

Mouse and I were deep in dreamland when she left her moorings, as our watch was not due to start until 0200 hours. By the time we had manned our stations, ***KARO-AS*** was well on her way.

She had tiptoed out of port using only one of her electric motors for extreme quietness. By leaving at this time and in this furtive way, the absence from her place on the quay should not be missed until daybreak by those, who were intent on making a little pocket money by broadcasting our departure. Our resident pilot had taken her the long way round Penang Island by the northern route, as he knew the exact positions of the minefields.

Once out of range of big ears, the diesel machine telegraphs had swung to 'Full ahead both'.

KARO-AS' bows rose at 18 knots plus and at 0700 she arrived at the prearranged rendezvous with the aerial guardian angel, the *Arado 198*. 0700 arrived and went; our Old Man was on the bridge to make sure everyone was on his toes. Every one of us knew an *Arado 198* when they saw one, because only a few months ago one of those sea-planes demolished our Metox-aerial as well as our precious attack-periscope by flying too low in one of its mock attacks.

No amount of scanning of the skies by the lookouts could locate the blasted bird.

The Old Man got jumpier by the minute.

As a last straw he ordered 'All engines stop'. The bridge crew strained their ears as well as their eyes - but no dice - silence reigned supreme. It seemed like ***KARO-AS*** has been stood-up, just like Lili Marlene at the Barrack gate.

'So much for that then' (or words to that effect) said the impatient Old Man.

'We can't afford to hang around here one minute more than we have to. Let's push on and rely on our good fortune.'

At exactly 0730 hours he gave the order to disappear from the surface. 'Without the help from our pals above, this little trip is going to take just a little longer.'

Making only a few knots while running silently at periscope depth, a beady eye was kept on things above during the hours of daylight. At frequent intervals the Old Man took time out to bed-down on the bottom of the

straits. Absolute silence inside the boat, our mechanical ears would be able to pick-up even the quietest of screw-noises at a distance of many miles.
Under the cover of darkness the Old Man pushed ***KARO-AS*** along on the surface at breakneck speed, urging the Chief to coax a few more revs out of his diesels. When reminded about the high fuel consumption by an extremely worried Klaus-Peter, he almost snapped at him that 'our safety is a hell of a lot more important than saving a few stupid tonnes of diesel oil. Anyway, I've been promised full tanks for our return trip to Germany.'
He had acted like a stranger during the last few hours and days. Normally unflappable, the Old Man was like a bear with a sore arse.

But thanks to God and the Old Man's skill, our ***KARO-AS*** luck held all throughout the next few days and nights, as we passed through the narrow Strait of Malacca. During those last few kilometres through the very narrow neck of this funnel, the danger from enemy action was at the greatest. There was hardly enough water under our keel to seek shelter below the surface.
Hence we were ordered to spend those last few hours camped out on deck in extremely hot and sticky conditions. As we were nearing the equator for the third time, no place on a U-boat was giving relief from the burning sun. But this sweaty interlude proved to have certain advantages as well, especially after ***KARO-AS*** had reached the southern end of the strait.
Now, utilising the local knowledge of our pilot, it was helm hard to port in order to continue on a northeasterly course into the Singapore Strait. Here we were provided with the most amazing grandstand view of the many island scattered all around us in the approaches to what surely was one of the busiest harbours in the world.

Singapore - the gateway to the Orient?
The harbour, into which ***KARO-AS*** eased herself, was certainly big enough but was at present almost completely empty. Along the miles long quayside, with it's hundreds of berths, docks and warehouses, only a few solitary freighters, a couple of Japanese patrol boats and a medium-sized liner were to be seen. A few junk-like barges were busily shuttling goods from the freighters to other parts of the harbour or town. Our Old Man seemed to know exactly where we were going. He made a beeline for the fairly sizeable liner, which, as we could now make out, was flying the flag of our *Kriegsmarine*. Some of her crew were ready to receive our lines as ***KARO-AS*** moored alongside her.

After a short welcome by the captain of the *Potsdam*, as the liner was called, we were invited to make full use of her excellent bath and shower facilities, her games-rooms, as well as making ourselves at home in her dormitories for the rest of our very short stay in Singapore.

When we boarded her, we took with us the bag of mail we had brought with us for the men at the base from their folks at home. Like our men at Penang, the sailors here hadn't heard from their families for months and of course, this bag of mail was already quite old. But they were no worse off than we were; we were just as concerned about our folk, particularly those of us whose homes were under continuing air attacks.

Meanwhile, our Old Man, accompanied by the captain of the *Potsdam* as well as our *1WO*, reported to the Chief of the base.

After his return we heard the result of that meeting. He had angrily put on record his annoyance about the non-appearance of the promised air cover for the passage from Penang. To his utter astonishment, the pilot of the *Arado* was already present at the meeting.

He had been waiting for our arrival.

When he faced our captain his first question was: 'Why in God's name did you dive out of sight as soon as I arrived at the rendezvous point?'

'What on earth are you talking about, Lieutenant?' Our Old Man replied. 'We stayed surfaced at the rendezvous point until 0730 hours, half an hour after the time you were supposed to meet us. We felt like sitting ducks'.

The doubtful-looking Lieutenant recalled that his vision was somewhat hampered by low cloud: 'I flew low enough to see your boat disappear from the face of the earth at exactly 0640 hours. I didn't hang around much longer, when you didn't reappear I decided to save scarce juice and set course for home.'

'You could at last have waited until the appointed time at 0700' accused the Old Man.

What a conundrum? What could be the explanation?

On the one hand ***KARO-AS*** stayed on the surface until 0730, well after the arranged rendezvous time and didn't see hide or hair of a plane. The *Arado's* pilot, cruising around the same general area, observed a submarine disappearing into the deep at 0640.

'You must have made a mistake in your navigation' the Old Man accused the pilot but he was adamant that he patrolled the area around 4°20'N and 99° 55'S and at the stated time. 'I know the area like the back of my hand, I couldn't get that wrong.'

One thing became crystal clear; the submarine, which dived hell-for-leather when spotting the plane, was not ***KARO-AS***.

But who else was likely to nose around in the Malacca Straits?

Our Old Man looked at the Commanding Officer of the Singapore base:

‘I’m not aware of any other U-boats in this area at the moment’,
They all decided that it must have been one of our competitors, Dutch, American or most probably English, on the prowl and looking for us no doubt, when she was forced to take cover from the *Arado*.
But the mystery sub had something in common with us.
She had shown a healthy respect for visitors from the skies and kept her nose down long enough to cease to be a danger to our little ship.
Phew!! Luckily we didn’t frighten easily.
It was plain to see, the lucky stars were still shining on the boat, which sported a ***KARO-AS*** on her conning tower.

Much later we learned that our Old Man had known all along that less than a month earlier a British Submarine had sunk one of our sister-boats, just as she was ready to enter Penang. She went down with the loss of over forty lives.
Can you blame him for being more than a little jumpy?

But there was at least one piece of good new for him.
The Base commander, who incidentally was the most senior German Naval Officer in the Far East, informed him, that docking facilities should be awaiting our arrival at Surabaja, which was on Java. All we were to do here was to take on enough fuel and provisions for this our next lap of nearly 1,600 km. Once on Java we could off-load our keel-cargo, take on enough fuel and provisions to see us back home to Germany. Though we probably wouldn’t get another chance to experience the delights of the Orient at the taxpayer’s expense, we still hoped to be back home in plenty of time to celebrate Christmas with our families.
Mind you, we, who were trained to repair a severely damaged sub with nothing but a few hand tools, should be able to knock-up something resembling a Christmas tree, should we still be skulking below the waves by then.

It was decided not to advertise the fact that we were to leave at the first possible opportunity. Some scaffolding was put up round the bridge give the impression of a lengthy stay in Singapore, as everywhere else, eyes and ears were all around us.

This short stop-over here gave us, the crew, a golden opportunity to soak-up a bit more of the East and to have a look around an other one of Tommy’s numerous colonies. A ramshackle old bus was made available to us, complete with a young Japanese Officer, who had a smattering of German, to act as our guide on a quick tour through the city.
A selected few members of the crew had to stay behind and mind the shop,

supervising the taking-on of fresh food and enough fuel to see us to our next port of call. There wasn't enough time for us to get more than a fleeting impression of the place. My old Atlas had already prepared me for some of the things we would find here. Not long ago this had been the foremost outpost of the British Empire. It had been developed by Tommy to become his most important military base in the East at this gateway to the China Sea and on into the Pacific. Just like our last port of call Penang, the British East India Company had also founded Singapore

Well! Founded is not really the right description, they pinched it from the natives and declared it to be a British Colony, realising that the locals were sitting on a Gold mine. Any trader who wanted to deal with the Chinese or the Japanese had to come along here at one time or other. After the long journey from Europe their supplies were often exhausted and here they found those kindly traders, all of them ready to make a nice fat profit from re-supplying those passing ships in Singapore's only real natural asset, its excellent deep-water port facilities.

In his broken German and with a disdainful look on his face the Jap Lieutenant told us a bit about the 'Lion City', as Singapore was often called. Although located at the southern tip of the Malay peninsular, Malayans were in the minority. They were outnumbered by more than 4 to 1 by the natural enemies of Japan, the utterly despised Chinese.

As one could expect, he went on to tell us about the glory of the Japanese troops, as they overran the British garrison in 1942. Heavily defended toward the seaward side, Singapore's defenders didn't expect the Japs to attack from the North, through what was thought to be impenetrable jungle.

Our guide proudly related the heroism of the Japanese elite fighting-swimmers, who formed a bridgehead after swimming across the Jahore Strait. 'I will show you later where they first set foot on the island.'

Leaving this almost deserted outer harbour, the actual tour kicked off by driving through the downtown area, through street, which might have been in China itself. Narrow streets were lined by shops, which had living accommodation above them. Behind the shop fronts one could see all types of structures, corrugated iron or palm-leaf covered sheds and shelters. All in all, there was a mass of humanity living on top of each other. I didn't think our European ears would ever get used to almighty oriental din. The same density of humanity existed on the thousands of barges and junks moored all along the busy canals in this part of the city. Those and the shanty-type dwelling of the poor were in sharp contrast to the magnificent white buildings in the banking, commercial and government areas of the former white masters of Singapore. Also standing out against the apparent poverty of the masses were many religious buildings, churches, cathedrals, mosques and temples, a mixture of East and West and any other direction of the compass.

There was little time to dwell here, as promised by our guide the next stop was at the northern end of the island, next to the Jahore Strait. Here, on a small hill, the Japanese had built an imposing memorial to their comrades, which had fallen in the battle for Singapore. All around this high wooden column, which in accordance with their religion was covered in symbols and Japanese writing, ornamental gardens were being created by groups of well-guarded British Prisoners of War.

Yesterday's pukka sahibs, under the bayoneted rifles of their Japanese guards, were sweating under the merciless oriental midday sun. I didn't think that this would have been our way of dealing with a defeated enemy, but others in our ranks reminded us that Tommy had never been too concerned about the finer feelings of coolies, Negroes and others who had been slaving in plantations or mines to produce wealth for the British, whether in Africa, India or in any other of their many colonies

And give the Japs their due, not far from their own memorial, a simple wooden cross had been erected to honour the British soldiers who fell in defence of this very desirable piece of real estate.

We briefly paused to honour the dead at both memorials, while at the same time remembering our own mates who had come a-cropper in this far-flung part of the world.

To get to Surabaja safely would mean taking all sorts of little deviations from a straight course because there were hundreds of islands dotted all over the place. After slinking out of Singapore in the wake of a patrol boat and taking all the tried and proven precautions, running surfaced at night only, with lookouts and all listening posts on full alert, the Old Man took us along through the Java Sea. At the slightest sign of company we disappeared quietly to the bottom, which was only 50 m down and there we rested silently. To the old U-boat hands among us this was quite an alien way of running a war. Wherever there was a screw-noise in the Atlantic, there was sure to be a target to be hunted and attacked. But since our job was that of a freighter, our one and only aim was to get to our next port of call in one whole piece.

There was just one other little job ***KARO-AS*** had to do, which also helped to break the monotony. After leaving Sumatra, Bangka and Belitung behind, the Old Man made a surprise detour due south. Not long after that he seemed to loose all interest in going any further. Down we went to the bottom and there we stayed. The time clicked past on the clocks, one hour, two hours, three hours – and nothing. But then came a word from the radio shack ' screw noise at 180 degrees, getting louder'.

At last the Old Man took notice, 'go to periscope depth, starboard slow ahead, steer 180.' 'Periscope up – surface'.

Once he got up on the bridge he took one look and then yelled

'Both engines full ahead, steer 270' followed by 'Both engines stop.'

And then he shouted down to the control room, 'Bring up the mailbag for Batavia.'

It started to make a lot more sense to all and sundry. It seems that he had been given a rendezvous time and place to wait for a ship from Batavia, which had orders to collect the mail we carried for them and also to give us their return mail to take home with us. What the Old Man didn't expect was that the ship would be a junk-type fishing vessel, which would be intent on running straight up on our fore deck. Hence he made this last minute-manoeuvre to avoid a collision.

Having done that, we were on our way again. The almost incessant rain we had encountered during this trip had eased and eventually stopped as, with the help of a minesweeper, we entered the sheltered harbour of Surabaja. From the sea it didn't look a lot different from Singapore, with the exception that behind the city, in the distant background to the South, the mountains reached up to a height of over 3000 metres. Unlike the almost empty outer harbour of Singapore, this place was brimful with small fishing vessels and lots of other assorted junk-like boats. A few Japanese Escort vessels were ready to take out another convoy of fully laden ships, freighters and tankers, in order to accompany them through all dangers on their way to Japan. The freighters lay deep in the water, proof that they were full to the gunnels. We wished them luck on their way through the hostile waters of the China Sea. Thankfully Surabaja was a much bigger port than Penang and was able to afford us adequate maintenance and docking facilities. To the Old Man's great relief we were able to enter the large dockyard and tie-up in an empty dry dock without delay. He was already fed-up being sent from one place to the other, like a lost child.

KARO-AS' arrival had been eagerly awaited, no least by the sailors of the German base. Since we were the only boat of the Monsoon-group operating in the East at the moment, they were delighted to see us, perhaps for no other reason than to collect the letters and parcels from their loved ones, which we were able to bring them. As happened in other ports, the seamen from the German base took over all the guard duties as well as seeing to the stowing of provisions, fuel and cargo for our journey home. Our Chief wanted to stay back and supervise this work. Before we came off the boat, we overheard our Old Man telling the base commander, 'we'll be here for exactly seven days. On the eighth day we'll leave, whether all the work of repainting, loading and unloading of cargo and the re-provisioning have been completed or not. If you haven't enough men available to do the job, I'll get my crew back to help'

We had already noticed that here in the vicinity of the equator, even the fittest body and the keenest brains seemed to go into a slow gear. It was impossible to work during the mid-day hours. However, our captain was deadly serious in setting time limits, the lost time will have to be compensated for in the evening or at night. Get in touch with me if you have any problems, Chief ' were his instructions.

He told us, 'Take all your washing with you; it will be laundered for you. Having cleaned up, you can spend four days leave holidaying in a hotel up in the mountains.' Now there was something to look forward to.

So off we went to the Hotel Amsterdam in the Wilhelminen Boulevard, which was in the European quarter of the town. Of course, I had almost forgotten that Java was part of the former Netherlands East Indies and that a lot of the place and street names were Dutch ones. Other than those names we found little evidence of a Dutch presence. They, and other Europeans had either fled or were spending time in Japanese internment. Now it was them, the Japs, whose turn it was to do what the Dutch used to do... exploit the local riches, as was apparent from the heavily laden convoys in the harbour.

In the town, away from the European quarter, the Chinese business people and their shops and living quarters were just as prominent as they were in Penang and Singapore. Although here they were in a minority, everyone seemed to be a shopkeeper.

Once we had settled in at the Hotel and exchanged our filthy fatigues for civilian clothes and handed over the rest of our clothes to be laundered, we were free to take a stroll through the town. Most of the European goods were still on sale, but there was a distinct shortage of customers for alcoholic drinks, cigars or even Dutch type food in delicatessen shops. It didn't take us very long to get loaded-up with all sorts of goodies, the like of which we hadn't seen since before the war. Silk scarves, blouses, skirts, shirts, ties and even small bundles of silk cloth were carried back to the hotel. 'We will be back for a lot more before leaving for home', we prom-

ised the Chinese shopkeepers.
But we must exercise caution and leave enough space in the boat for all the essential goods ***KARO-AS*** was scheduled to carry back.

Now followed the highlight of our stay on Java, our four-day holiday in the mountains, where a hotel, originally built for the colonial masters of old, became our temporary home. Set in the middle of what seemed unspoiled and impenetrable rainforest, it commanded a splendid view over the lower lying agricultural areas of eastern Java.
Thank Goodness, the hotel was a far enough away from the nearest one of the many still active volcanoes in this extremely volatile part of the world. The one nearest here was called Kelud had a nasty habit of erupting every 15 years or so. When it blows, it was said to cause mayhem to the villages below it. But oddly enough, the agricultural land around the volcanoes benefited greatly from the volcanic ash and other debris thrown out by those peaks. It made the soil extremely fertile.

At this our mountain retreat, we didn't have to do anything for ourselves other than eat, drink, sunbathe or idle away the time in other ways. At this high altitude the climate was more amenable, not nearly as hot as it was at the coast but at night it got cold enough for us to request extra blankets for our beds. Unlike other shore establishments and more in tune with our normal life on board U-boats, in this hotel officers and other ranks were all treated alike. Royalty, such as kings, princes or even film stars could not have been spoiled more. All crewmembers were billeted together. We ate in communal dining rooms and the leisure facilities such as tennis courts, billiard or table tennis tables and other facilities were open to all.

It was here, high in the mountains of Java, I was introduced to some very intellectual Japanese board games called 'Sho-gi' in addition to the even more interesting one of 'Go' or 'I-go'.
Our MO was mad keen on all types of board games and on our long trip over, him and I had some very close encounters on the chessboard. That evening to my surprise, he asked 'How would you like to try out the game our Japanese brothers in arms call their chess-game.' I jumped at the chance.

Sitting at a table in the plush lounge with drinks by our side, he laid out the board while explaining, 'Our honourable hosts have only be able to supply those games, with the rules in English. I hoped that I'd be able to decipher those, but they don't seem to be very clear. However, I have already learned that Sho-gi possibly had its origin in India or in China, from where it went over to Japan. It is also called the General's game.' He added, 'The Japanese were, or still are, a nation of warriors, hence all their games, including those board games, are based on war.'

The white board was divided into nine by nine squares by black lines, but the tokens or men looked very strange.

They were all the same colour and shape, flat and slightly pointed at one end, almost like little coffins, which were covered with Japanese symbols.

By this time the Doc and I had quite an audience looking over our shoulders. 'There should be a total of forty pieces, twenty on each side' the MO translated. ' They all have names and as in chess they have different values. I think we might have to try and find a Japanese to explain to us which are the pawns or *FU* and which ones are called 'The Honourable Horse', the 'Gold or Silver Generals', the 'Jewelled General' or the '*OSHO*' the King.

'The pieces are set up with the pointed end toward the enemy', the Doc explained further. All in all, after a lot of translation of the rules, it appeared that they were a lot like our own chess game. Like in chess, the various men moved in differing ways toward the opponent's lines, and on the way they could take prisoners. Once they reached the original enemy lines, the individual pieces could be promoted to a higher rank by turning them upside down.

'But where it differed greatly from chess and where this game was uniquely interesting, was that after taking your opponent's men prisoner, they were not dead as in chess, but can be used as your own men by pointing them toward your opponent.

To play the game reasonably well would take a long time, but it seemed to be an absolutely fascinating game and I decided that on our return to Surabaja I would try and procure one of them to take home with me.

During the next few days we had further opportunities to try and learn a bit more about those wild games while keeping out of the midday-sun. To keep the body in some sort of trim, I also tried my hand at tennis on the hotel's grass-courts.

On the penultimate day of our rest cure, our hosts arranged a dance evening for us. As in Penang, we were given the opportunity to dance with the local talent. Far away from the nearest towns, the dancing girls were mainly working girls from some nearby villages. Both the band and the girls arrived by bus to cheers from us. Here was their chance to make a few pence in a relative innocent way and our chance to get rid of some money in return for feasting our eyes on things of beauty.

Here in the mountains they obviously were all indigenous Javanese girls and thus they didn't have to wear a badge.

The one who took my fancy this time must have been one of the youngest and freshest, a dark brown beauty with eyes as black and as deep as the 'Hole of Calcutta'.
The way she was dressed in vivid red silk, from her slippers to her long close-fitting dress, up to her little cap, she was my little Red Riding Hood. She didn't seem to mind the way I dominated her time on the dance-floor, I suppose it didn't matter to her, as long as the money was right. To make sure that my baying mates didn't get too much of a look in with her, I just kept her on the floor between dances, just feeding the meter so to say. What I wished to do to her in the deep forest or in Grandma's bed was nobody's business. The little tease was nearly crawling into me while dancing, where, without doubt, she must have felt the effect she had on me.
Shit! No wonder I sweated like a pig.
Most of my pals worked their way through all the talent.
Me? Like the Wolf, I was quite happy to have *Rotkäppchen* melt into my arms at every given opportunity. I was sure, that in different circumstances we would have hit it off in a big way. But I would long remember her, at least as long as our homeward journey lasted. After that, perhaps some Gretel, Lotti, Hilde or someone else might make me forget the short evening in the jungle-covered mountains of Java; but they would have a hell of a job. Just a pity that this wonderful dream had to end, but such was life on board of U-boats.

Next morning it was back to reality with a vengeance.
We were reminded that there was a war on and that ***KARO-AS'*** small part in helping to win it demanded that she got back to Germany as quickly as possible and preferably with boat, crew and valuable cargo all in one piece. The bars of lead in her keel had been replaced by an equivalent amount of tin, while empty torpedo tubes and containers had been crammed full of raw-rubber, as were all other free spaces inside the boat. Loaded with the gear we had already picked-up at Penang, plus the stuff added here and not forgetting the rations the crew needed on the homeward run, the old tub was again full-up to the gunnels. One couldn't move through the boat without ducking and weaving to avoid all the obstructions created by those supplies. But with our customary resourcefulness we had also managed to find enough spaces to stow away the many private goods we had purchased on that afternoon on our last excursion into town.

In the evening, having collected our now spotless laundry and changed back into our working gear, most of us assembled on the bridge and on the two wintergardens behind the bridge. Radio-operator Hansi was a dab hand at the old squeeze box and to his accompaniment we whiled away the hours until well after darkness by singing sea-shanties.

No doubt, such concerts were seldom heard around the ports of Java. But it must have grabbed the imagination of the locals, judging by the number of people, who assembled just outside the dockyard. Whenever we stopped for breath, there was thunderous applause from them and from all the people watching from little boats and barges in the harbour.

Our performance lasted until nearly midnight and only minutes later, when it was least expected, ***KARO-AS*** was creeping out of port under the cover of darkness.

Farewell to Cinders, farewell to Red and farewell to all the lovely people of Malaya and of Java. If everything goes well, we shall be back to see you again in the not too distant future.

Like thieves in the night we disappeared into the shadowy mist hovering over the almost flat calm sea. Once the echo sounder indicated several fathoms of water under the keel, we carried out a trial dive, when to the delight of our Chief only some minor adjustments were necessary.

'Well done, control-room' he smiled.

'Place her at the bottom, Chief. I think we will spend a couple of days out here' ordered the Old Man.

Soundless and motionless every crewmember, which wasn't needed at his station, was ordered to rest on his bunk to save oxygen and to confuse anybody who might be on the lookout for us.

Would they be foxed by the Old Man's ploy?

We would find out soon enough.

There was steam rising from the huddle round the chart table.

The various options of getting from the shallow Java Sea into the deep Indian Ocean were being weighed up by the Old Man and his officers. The seas around here were good hunting grounds for Yankee and other assorted submarines, all of them aiming to cut the lifeline from oil-rich Java to the Japanese homeland. In their spare time they might even lay in wait for any stray U-boat, trying to plug all the little gaps between the strings of island from Malaya to Australia.

We never found-out whether the Old Man tossed a coin in his little corner behind the curtain, but he opted for one of the narrowest gaps, the five mile wide one, between Java and Bali.

So, on the third night out of Surabaja, during a very dark and wet night, he put ***KARO-AS*** through the eye of a needle.

'Full Ahead Both'

All her 4000 diesel-horses sprang into life.
Flat out at 18 knots she raced along, her bows riding high like a speedboat. It was not very often we stokers got a chance to see her at her speediest, but on this day we were elected to be additional lookouts for metal-fish coming at us from out of the deep.
Our usual luck held OK.

Three hours later we knew that were through the bottleneck, as the echo sounder went berserk. From indicating less than 50 m, it tumbled to over 8,000 m in a matter of minutes. In fact it went off the scale.
The deepness and the vastness of the Indian Ocean shouted 'Welcome!'
It war a fair bet that the rapid increase in depth below our keel as indicated by the echo-sounder, combined with the increase in elbowroom afforded by the now open spaces all around us, had an inverse effect of the rate of our Old Man's heartbeat. It was obvious to all of us that he had been unable to relax for a single minute, not since the day we arrived off Penang.
In the wide, open spaces of this ocean, he was able to run the show as per his rules and to push on regardless, direction South West. It was also a time to catch-up with some gossip over the radio.

There were small bits of good news and a whole lot of bad.
Reading between the lines we gathered that our cities back home were being hammered to hell and back. Both fronts, the East and the West, were sagging under the weight of our enemy's material superiority. But to boost our morale, new and devastating V-weapons were promised again and again, supposedly to restore the balance and to exact (V for) vengeance.
The better news was, that a Japanese destroyer claimed to have sunk a Yankee Sub just off the Lambok Strait.
Were Uncle Sam's boys waiting for us?
If they were, we must thank our Old Man for his foresight, our customary ***KARO-AS*** luck or the chance, which brought down the coin heads instead of tails.
For the next few weeks nothing much happened as we steamed on, covering several thousand miles in a matter of weeks. Only on a few occasions, when the lookouts thoughts that they might have seen something, or when the traffic on the airways seemed to indicate prudence, did the Old Man take her down for a short time. Other than that, the faithful old Diesels, aided and abetted by our busy and dedicated stokers, were hammering out the knots consistently and uncomplainingly.

Rapidly they pushed us from the tropical heat of Java to the chill of latitude 45 degrees South, where by a few hundred miles or so we gave the tip

of Africa a wide berth.
Even then, there was enough traffic around here to make the Old Man take every precaution to avoid trouble. He didn't seem to expect aircraft to hang around here, far from the nearest land, but he made sure that the lookouts were on the ball. In fact they proved to be a little too jumpy, at occasions mistaking gliding albatrosses for enemy aircraft.
But give the South Africans their due; somebody in their navy was going to earn their pay. A hunting party of two Corvettes, presumably South Africans, picked up our scent. Our lookouts were on the ball and registered their mastheads well before they could have seen us. We took time to launch an Aphrodite balloon to take their RADAR's attention before we disappeared deep down into the cellar. It had been a long time since we had occasion to visit our outboard comrades at 180 m down. ***KARO-AS*** gave out a few creaks and groans as every single square centimetre of our hull was subjected to a water pressure of 180 kilograms (more than a ton per square inch).
Running silent, the majority of the crew was banned to their bunks. Any normal depth charge would probably be squashed flat by the time they came anywhere near us and we could only hope they didn't have the latest gadgets, while our Old Man hoped that any SONAR reflections would be confused with those of shoals of fish.

The intermittent pinging against our hull from their SONAR did nothing to calm our nerves, especially when they came from opposing sides. We knew, if they could lock-on from both sides, it wouldn't have taken an Einstein to work out our exact position and so dispatch us into Davy Johns' locker.
But thankfully the pinging was intermittent, our pals up there were obviously still guessing, although they must have got a whiff of us.
They kept going over the area with a fine-tooth comb.
When they got a little bit fed-up with only getting intermittent results, they sought to justify their existence by using their undoubted firepower to plaster the whole area with crackers. This made us think that perhaps those corvettes were of the Stars-and-Stripes variety, as no self-respecting British ship would have been so wasteful. Tommy never fired unless they he could see the whites of the enemy's eyes, so to speak. But the Old Man thought 'they could be South Africans, who were trained by the Yanks. But whoever they are, I am not going up there to try and find out.'

However, apart from scaring the pants off us, their indiscriminate dropping of crackers only damaged a few fuses, light bulbs and our pride.

During the racket made by the exploding depth charges, the Old Man was making a close study of the faces of everybody around him.
Was he was looking for signs of fear?
He needn't have worried about us; the general mood on board was OK. Sure, we were shitty as we had no wish to die young, but we did our best to hide that fact and carried on with our duties as if we were still running trials back in the Baltic.
On the other hand, with more than half of our patrol behind us and mainly thanks to the Old Man's guile, we hadn't seen much of this war. I personally might have felt a bit cheated, if on our return to our folks at home, all we were able to boast about were stories about Neptune's baptism, Cinderella and Red Riding Hood.

Three hours later we seemed to have lost our tail. Nothing was to be heard in the way of screw-noises or explosions. The Old Man ordered the Chief to 'Let her drift up to periscope depth as silently as you can possibly manage. I would just like to take a look around to convince myself that the coast is clear.'
Silently she drifted up under the steady hand of the Klaus Peter. From the conning tower came the Old Man's whisper:
'Up periscope' followed immediately by 'Down periscope.'
Dropping down into the control room he asked the Chief to let the boat drift down steadily to 100 m.
'Those bastards are still there, just wallowing in the slight swell with in complete silence, no doubt having their ears pricked for the slightest sound from us.'
As ***KARO-AS*** drifted down past the 30 m mark, there was renewed activity up above. A new set of SONAR pings hit our hull. This time they appeared to have locked-on.
'Verfluchter Scheissdreck (Shit)!'
The Old Man didn't often show his feelings. But it was quite clear from his manner that this time we had better watch out. 'Launch a *Pillenwerfer*' and as it went on its way he followed with 'Full ahead both, Helm hard to port. Go to 180 m'. Nose down at 40 degrees ***KARO-AS*** was shooting down as deep as she dared.
'Starboard stop, port slow ahead, silent running; and don't' let me hear a needle drop.'
Something I hadn't known before then was that one of the empty torpedo tubes had been filled with some debris and old lubricating oil and that on the way down some of that had been discharged. It would take a little while

before it all arrived on the surface.

Meanwhile, high above us we could hear the frantic thrashing of screws, followed by the splashes of another dose of depth charges.
Bang, Bang, Bang. This time we counted 45 attempts to annihilate us.

They certainly got closer this time and a couple of gauges were blown off their bases, followed by water cascading into the diesel-bilges. Still no obvious panic, valves were shut and leaks sealed in no time at all. Blown bulbs and fuses were replaced. A closer examination of the crew's underwear might have presented a different picture of our outward calm. And anyway, I made sure that my lucky talisman inside my pay-book was still there.

We could only hope that they would run out of ammunition, they would lose our scent or even be fooled by the debris and the oil slick into believing that they did get us.

Sure enough, the pinging of the SONAR seemed to become more erratic the deeper we went into the unknown, i.e. off the scale of the depth gauge in excess of 200 m. Let us hope, that the proud skippers of those Cor-

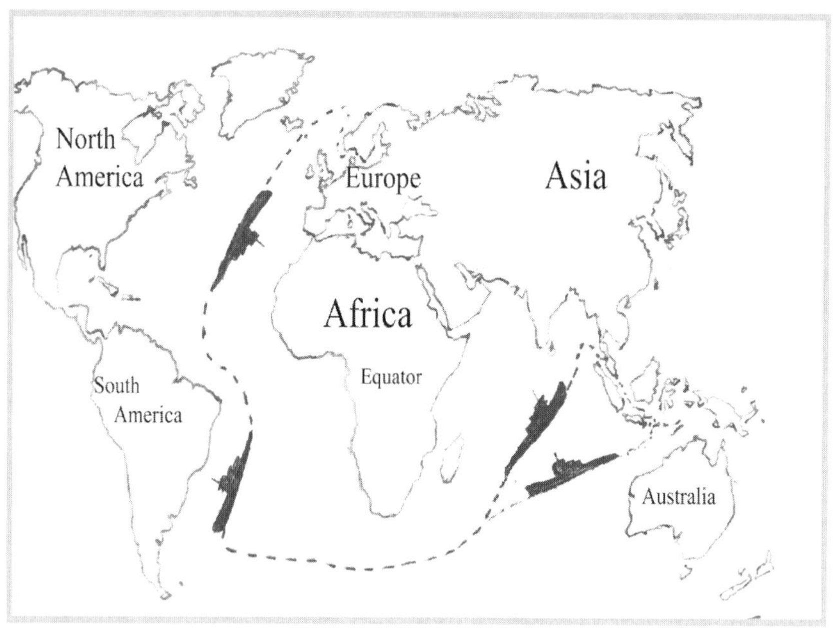

vettes will report the destruction of one more U-boat to their Admiral and rush away home to collect his medals. May they receive them by the bucket full?

If it hadn't been for our orders to get back home with our precious cargo, the Old Man might have been tempted to stick a T5 Gnat homing torpedoes up those bastards above.

Our luck held.

In fact it held for every one of the next 70 days, during which time we were able to made good speed northward through the South Atlantic, crossed over to the northern hemisphere near the Brazilian side, started to tread a bit more gingerly when passing the Azores and finally really got our heads down through the Rosengarten. Luckily for us there was so much traffic in the North Atlantic that a few blips more or less on the old RADAR screen must have gone unnoticed right up to the time we arrived unheralded off Bergen. Until then the Old Man had maintained strict radio silence. Now he called for an escort to take us through the minefields into the base, where we made fast without fuss and with ten days to spare before Christmas.

Our ***KARO-AS*** luck has held.

To say that we were glad to have firm ground under our feet after this long time at sea would be an understatement.

During the last month or two, we had gone from equatorial heat to the cold of the near Antarctic, back through the tropical heat of the Equator to the Mid-Winter conditions in the North Atlantic near the Arctic Circle. The last few days were spent dodging icebergs in addition to evading Tommy's hounds.

Quietly and unobtrusively, our little lady was now moored under camouflage netting, while her crew was looking forward to getting cleaned-up and having a well-earned rest.

Good news was awaiting us. Our orders were to return to Kiel, where at last ***KARO-AS*** will be fitted with a snorkel, have several other modifications made to the forecastle and where her engines will get a thorough overhaul. During the time she was in the dockyard, her crew was to take two week's home leave.

Yippeee!

What's keeping us? Lets get going.

While replenishing our almost depleted diesel fuel stocks, the stone-jars of Iodine had to be unloaded and shipped to the nearest airport to be flown to Germany. Here the overworked hospitals were desperate for supplies.

CHAPTER TWELVE

There was great rejoicing in our control room.

My pal Mouse was over the moon with delight about our orders to make for Kiel. It had nothing to do with our impending refit, nor had it anything to do with a possible chance to visit his parents in Berlin during the time ***KARO-AS*** was being doctored.

No. It wasn't that.

In reality it had everything to do with the fact that before we left on our last trip to the Far East he had met the apple of his eye Erika, even though it was in one of the many low dives in Kiel.

To say that he had been utterly and completely besotted by the not inconsiderable charms of this 18-year-old tease would be an understatement. He went wobbly at the knees, numb in the brain and hot in the groin every time her name was mentioned.

There was nothing unusual about all this; we all had our own individual visions of heaven on earth. Inevitably his vision was in the shape of a female form - just as the good Lord had made her, lumps and bumps and all. For instance, among others, my dreams often included little Red Riding Hood from the mountainous jungle on Java. But then she was definitely unobtainable and I knew it.

Mouse's problem was entirely different as Erika was quite special.

Sure, she had all the basic essentials, perhaps even more than her fair share. But what made Erika special, or so it was said, was her uncanny ability to get at least one fiancé on every U-boat of the *Kriegsmarine.*

While still en-route from Java, this impressionable friend of mine had made plans to ask Erika for her hand in marriage, the bloody fool.

Not that I, or anyone else dared to suggest to Mouse that he intended to become one of a whole battalion of prospective husbands of hers. We must await further developments in that saga.

Things started to move quickly once ***KARO-AS*** had wormed her way through Danish waters to the bay of Kiel and from there into the dockyard's U-boat pen. It was the first time she had experienced the luxury, which one of those pens afforded. At this stage in the war, with the Allied Air Forces now also going after military targets instead of only hitting women and children, sheltering in one those was probably the safest place on earth for a U-boat. Under the cover of a seven metre thick concrete ceiling, we picked up our kitbags, which on arrival we found stacked-up on the quayside. Our best blue uniforms contained in them, showed every signs of having spent a lot of time at the bottom of a dirty great pile of gear. They were out of shape, crumpled and stinking. To restore them to their former glory would entail hard work on our part.

But first we had to empty ***KARO-AS*** of all our personal belongings to assure that everything, which was not securely screwed or even welded down, was safe from the thieving hands of the so-called dockyard workers before we could move to our temporary billets ashore. As was probably true of every dockyard anywhere in the big wide world, workers in those yards had the reputation, probably quite deservedly, for being the biggest thieving bastards under the sun. Anything carelessly left on board, after the yard took over a ship for modification, repair or servicing, was due to be flogged on the black market. If you were unlucky enough to lose some of your prize possessions, there always existed the opportunity to buy them back in one of the town's flea markets.

Having safeguarded our and the *Kriegsmarine's* property to the best of our ability, we went ashore to go to work on our Square Rigs and ourselves. Attacking both with gusto, by shaving and showering, we first transformed ourselves into something our mothers would recognise and then went to work with wet sponges, brushes as well as hot irons in order to transform our sailor's uniforms into outfits, which looked spanking new.

The collars were washed and starched and the bell-bottoms had vertical creases so sharp, you could cut your fingers on them and our skin-tight blue shirts were taken-in at the waist to allow for the fact that we had lost a lot of weight on our trip to and from Indonesia.

Next morning, spick and span and dressed up to the kill, we paraded in front of our temporary quarters at the base.

A very high-ranking Admiral, who turned out to be the Commander in Chief U-boats, took the salute. He formally welcomed ***KARO-AS*** back to Germany, praising her captain and her crew for a job well done. He appeared to be genuinely delighted to see at least one of his flock return to the fold all in one piece.

He didn't offer the fatted calf, nor did he bring along hordes of beautiful young girls to present us with garlands of flowers.

No! Those days were long past.

But he did bring offerings of a kind.

There were gongs for every man, oodles and oodles of them. There were two German Crosses, eleven Iron Crosses 1st class for those previously

decorated and to all of us rookies came Iron Crosses 2nd class. This was one you didn't wear at all, only a distinctive Black, White and Red ribbon on your top-button hole. The Iron Cross itself stayed in a velvet-lined case. In addition we were now entitled to wear the coveted gilded U-boat broach on the left chest of our parade uniform or even our working clothes.
Our chests expanded considerably.
With pride? You bet!
For good or bad - we have had our baptism by fire.

Four days to go until Christmas.
With perseverance and a large slice of luck, we were able to get all our paperwork sorted out, travel documents and train-tickets were in our pockets. We also managed to collect our overdue pay but our fear, that we might need to use a wheelbarrow to cart it away, was unfounded. There was only just enough paper money to fill a brown paper-bag.
So it came about that laden with all our earthly goods, Walter, Mouse and I started on our way to Berlin by the first available train. Among the goodies we carried, not counting the wads of actual money, there were lots of free-issue cigarettes, those we had accumulated during the months on patrol, when we were unable to smoke except on rare occasions. Those cigarettes together with the cigars and tobacco we bought in Surabaja were worth their weight in gold, they were in fact worth more than mere money. Also weighing-down our kitbags were many of the other beautiful presents we had bought in the Far East.

Mouse had thought long and hard whether to go to see his parents for Christmas - perhaps even for the last time - or to take the opportunity to pop the question to Erika and spent the whole time with her. In the end sense prevailed, he decided there would be plenty of time for an engagement after his return from Berlin. The refit of ***KARO-AS*** was scheduled to last at least 5 weeks. And anyway, he meant to sell a lot of his worldly possessions to raise enough for the prize of a real super duper engagement ring.

By the time the train arrived at the outskirts of Berlin, we were caught in an air raid by what appeared to be hundreds of Allied bombers. During the next few hours our train lay stopped in a wooded patch about 5 miles short of Berlin. We were ordered to take cover in the forest just in case some of the bastards were to strafe the train. But they were far to busy flattening the city. Both Walter and Mouse were cursing 'I hope the *FLAK* will get those shits up there, even if our dear *Hermann's* mob are hiding their precious tails.'

Since my home was on the Northern side of the city, I was only a mile and a half from mum and dad. 'So, why are you hanging about here? Get the hell out of it' Mouse suggested. 'I wish my parents lived near here as well.'

From my younger days I knew the *Bucher Wald*, as the woods around here were called, like the back of my hand. I decided to take Mouse's advice to jump ship and to start a little legwork. But before I could leave, I had to get my kit bag with all the swag in it. It was still on the train, where a Military Policeman was looking after everything to make sure nothing was pinched. After being very officious and insisting that I should complete my journey as per travel-pass, I was able to get some co-operation from him. Mind you, it cost me a small bottle of Dutch Gin and packet of twenty-five.

But it was worth it.

'See you in the New Year, Mouse. And behave yourself. Remember to preserve the good name of our ship.'

When the **All Clear** sounded a couple of hours later, I was safely home with my overjoyed mum, dad and sisters Uschi and Helga. The entire bomb-load had on that night been dumped on the city. They had turned the night-sky to the South of us into a sea of red. But the carnage was too far away to hear the cries of the wounded and dying civilians. The whole of Berlin appeared to be on fire.

As we made our way back into the house, I glimpsed some tears in my old dad's eye, something I never expected to experience. One thing I was sure about, it wasn't because he was afraid for himself.

It really was the most awful, stupid war.

Those airmen up there... I wonder how they felt about being asked to fight women, children, old men or babies in arms?

In a way, while cursing them and wishing them to go to hell, I did feel sorry for them and their conscience.

I was so much luckier and thanked God with all my heart that up to then nobody had expected me to fight defenceless civilians. The men who manned our targets knew what to expect when they took to the sea.

Back in the house, Mum wouldn't let go of me. 'This is going to one of the best Christmases ever, at least since the war started.' She was happy, as for the time being, one of her boys was safe and sound at home.

Telling her that 'On balance, I'm much safer on board ship than you're here at home' did little to convince her.

But there was an even bigger surprise in store for her. By 10 o'clock the next morning she needed both arms to hold and cuddle each of her sons.

It had been nothing short of a miracle.

We got the feeling, that Sundays, Birthdays, Easter, Christmas and all other holidays all had arrived simultaneously.

While ***KARO-AS*** was laid-up in Kiel for her refit, Heini's brand new Type IIVC boat with the "1001 Night's Ali Baba" sign, was having her snorkel fitted in a Stettin dockyard. As had happened with our train, he too was held up some way out on the eastern side of Berlin. Since he couldn't walk from there, he had to wait until the morning to finish his journey.

By 12 o'clock midday, two hefty Belgian Blues (tame rabbits) had bitten the dust. Mum and dad always lived in hope for just such an occasion and made sure that some rabbits were always ready for the arrival of the prodigal sons. If nothing else, it showed their optimism.

During times of scanty food-rations the odd hen past her laying-days, along with some tame buck or doe were almost the only meat we had tasted as youngsters. Thankfully, the poor things had no idea of their eventual fate and kept on doing the things rabbits do even better than sailors... they kept on REPRODUCING.

Unfortunately, the job of doing the dirty job of slaughtering befell Dad and I can recall the utter distaste on his face when he was forced to get the knives out. Considering that he was raised on a farm in East Prussia, were the farmers did all their own slaughtering, he was quite squeamish. Mum helped with the skinning and gutting and then went on with the cooking of it. The unpleasant side of this procedure had always been hidden from us as youngsters, all we ever saw was the finished article, when it was presented to us on a huge platter, roasted golden brown in a tasty thick sauce with potatoes and vegetables piled high on the side. We had grown up to imagine that this is what rabbits should look like.

Christmas day was not until the day after tomorrow, but with the help of the delicious smelling roast, the many bottles of homemade wine, as well as the cigars I had shipped from Surabaya, we had to start our festivities right here and now. As I had mentioned before, on U-boats we were well supplied with cigarettes and tobacco, so that on this occasion, rather ungratefully perhaps, Heinz and I turned our noses up at Dad's homegrown tobacco.

I had all of ten days left in which to celebrate being home, but Heini was going to attempt to get to Silesia tomorrow to spend the rest of his leave with his wife Waltraut and their 6 months old son Joseph. The time was near when the proud father could introduce himself to his first-born.

But this day, the 23rd of December 1944 belonged to us in Buchholz.

Heini's little brother had become a big boy and for the first time in his life he had to treat me as an adult. Up until recently I had just been a nuisance, a thorn in his flesh, particularly when he brought a girl friend home and wanted some privacy. In those days I soon realised that it was always worth a Mark or two to be just a little bit nosy.

But now he found it easy enough to talk to me on equal terms, especially after I'd shown him my crossing the Line certificate, which was won in a more unusual way than his. Travelling below the waves, out of sight of any prying eyes, Neptune had nevertheless performed his duty of ascertaining that no unclean landlubbers escaped his attentions when crossing from the northern to the southern hemisphere. Dad, as was his usual way, just sat listening to us spell-bound, every now and then comparing our easy number in the Navy with his hard time in the trenches of Flanders in WW1. The only difference between his Iron Cross II from Heini's and mine, was the date on it, his was dated 1917 and ours 1941 and 1944.

Heini also eyed my U-boat broach with a little bit of envy although he had already earned two other broaches, a Minesweeping one and one from his Battleship days.

Mum just sat there with a tear in her eye, every now and then she just leant over to touch either one of her boys, just to feel that they were real. It had never occurred to me before, but mothers did have the hardest job of the lot. They brought you into the world, scrimped and scraped to make sure you didn't go hungry and then they had to watch helplessly as her brood was taken from her.

I suppose it was the wine, which did it, as we were never very demonstrative and seldom showed our inner feeling. But on this evening we both spent a lot of time hugging her and telling her not to worry.

After we had succeeded in sorting out our little bit of bother with Tommy, we would come and would make sure she never had to worry ever again.

As luck would have it, the same old Tommy and his Uncle Sam were getting ready for Christmas as well. While we celebrated the night away, the Allied Air forces took a day off as well.

Bless you, dear boys.

Next morning Heini wanted to get to the station as early as possible, thinking that he had a better chance to get on one of the earlier trains. Since it would take at least an hour to get there, we had left the house at 4 o'clock in the morning. It had not occurred to us to try and get some sleep before then. I helped him by carrying his kit bag, into which he had stowed a few little presents from mum and dad for their first grandson. I had donated one of the lovely Javanese silk blouses to take to his little wife, who I could imagine looking lovelier than ever while wearing it.

Having helped him to settle in a most uncomfortable coach of the snails-express, I took my leave of him. 'Here's to the next time, *Hals und Beinbruch* (Break a neck or a leg),' I shouted after him as the train steamed out. Befuddled as I was from the home-brew, I couldn't help thinking ... lets pray there will be a next time.

The lucky devil would probably sleep all the way to Silesia, while poor me, tired, as I was, still had to make my way home.

Most of Christmas Eve I spent in bed, but had to surface later in the evening when a few visitors arrived. Several of my aunts and uncles were anxious to hear how we thought the war was going. While I was reassuring them that things would take a turn for the better, SHE walked in.

'You can just close your mouth again. Don't you recognise Irma?' mum asked.

My brain did mental handstands trying to remember which aunt and uncle had a gorgeous, curvaceous, almost Latin-looking daughter called Irma. My face must have been a picture of pure puzzlement.

'The only Irma, I can remember, is the spotty-faced, snotty-nosed little brat from two doors along.' I offered. 'She was then known as Irmchen.'

'That is really very nice of you, to remember me in those terms, considering that both you and Hansi wanted to marry me when we were six or seven years old.' she replied with a smile that nearly sent me wild.

Well, blow me down.

Come to think of it, I must have changed a bit as well from those days, from the gawky, lanky boy with holes in the seat of his short trousers and permanently skinned knees.

here were four of us, all living within shouting-range to one another, Hansi (Hans), his younger sister Uschi (Ursula), Irmchen and I. We were of similar ages, within a year or so and quite inseparable, until we left school and started to work.

When playing fathers and mothers or doctors and nurses, Irmchen teamed-up with Hansi and Uschi with me. But of course, we had lost touch in the intervening years.

I naturally always assumed Irmchen and Hans would pair-up for life.

There was no harm in asking, was there?

'How is Hansi, the old Casanova? I haven't seen him since he joined the Navy.' To which she replied, without moving a muscle, 'According to his mother he is spending Christmas in Hamburg, with his latest fiancée.

Oh dear! Have I put my size forty-fives into it?
But she didn't seem too worried about it at all, as we spent the next hour or so gossiping over old times. After she had gone home, Mum told me that Irmchen had started to take quite an interest in my well being and had become a regular visitor to our house. Now here was something to think about!

On the next day, Christmas Day, when I surfaced at noon from an untroubled night's sleep, the house was already filled with the most delicious smells of the customary roast.
But my mind wasn't on food today. After all, I was only human.
I kept dreaming of the sweet vision living a few doors down our road. By the time our Christmas dinner had settled, I decided that I would have to move the play along a bit. Having rummaged around in my kitbag, I went visiting with a bottle of lovely Java Liqueur for her mum and a Japanese style silk Kimono for Irmchen under my arm.
I got the impression that my calling wasn't entirely unexpected. In fact all the signals seemed to be set at green, for GO. To cut a long story short, Irmchen and I spent a lot of time together in the next ten days. During the daytime we cycled round the old haunts until it started to snow. Then we went frolicking around with our sledges on the nearby hills, while in the evenings we listened to records and the radio. Of course the usual air raids had started up again and during those Irmchen joined us in our dugout. At other times in the evenings, after everybody had discretely left us to our own devices, we whiled away the time re-acquainting ourselves with each other.
And the more time I spent in Irmchen's company, the less I remembered about all the others. What were their names again?
They were merely ships passing in the night, from Stettin to Seedorf, from Penang on to Java.

But with my new love, being the true girl next door, there were limits to how far I was allowed to roam. At the top of her stockings the barriers came down with a bang.
'Watch it, Spider. You'll get squashed in a minute.'
She had curled-up laughing when I told her about my nickname. By this time I had started to fill-out a bit between the shoulders, my skin-tight blue navy shirt was stretched across my expanded chest, there was even a tuft of chest hair visible at the bottom of my sailor's collar; quite plainly, Gerhard was no longer the gangly stick insect she had known in the past.

By day five I had plucked up enough courage to stutter 'If we get through this damned mess with a whole skin will you marry me?' I didn't actually go down on my knees and she didn't exactly say 'Yes', but by the time she let go of me, I took it for granted that she had agreed.

Nobody seemed to be the slightest bit surprised when we told them the next day, it almost seemed they already knew how things were going to develop in that direction.

We took a trip into Berlin's city centre to try and find an engagement ring. I wished we hadn't bothered. I hadn't realised just how little was left of the old place. And yet, there were plenty of people around. From holes in the ground they came up for air, gathering fuel and food. Wandering through those smouldering heaps of rubble we tried to find the shops Irmchen remembered from pre-war days. But we were out of luck; they had all disappeared into thin air.

So we gave up.

I promised to get a nice ring for her when I got back to Kiel.

'If everything else fails, I can always make one. With our lathe on board I could produce a shining example – made of brass. And later, if we get through all this, I can buy you a decent one.'

Until the end of my leave we made plans for our future. I still had at least another nine years to go in the navy, even if the war finished tomorrow. But Irmchen promised that she would be quite happy to move up to the coast to be near me, to wherever my next command would take me.

Fantasies? Perhaps.

Time would tell.

Nearly time to go.

Mum had washed and ironed every stitch she could find in my kitbag, but surprise, surprise, after boiling, scrubbing and drying, everything still stunk of diesel oil.

Well, what should I say?

I couldn't tell Mum that the Chinese in Penang and Surabaja managed to cope with our washing by steaming them. It was better just to forget about the smell, because by the time we got back on board nobody would notice it in the oil-laden atmosphere of ***KARO-AS***.

The last few days of my leave had been sheer murder. There was hardly a minute when we were not engrossed in our newfound love, but engagement or not, exploration of the areas beyond the stocking-tops would have to wait until after the wedding.

Damn blast! I might as well become a monk!

As was to be expected, when saying Good Bye, Mum couldn't hide her

tears and unusually, Dad's were not far behind.
Would we see each other again?

Irmchen insisted to come to the station with me, where she presenting me with a lovely photographs of herself. 'Put this in you locker to help you think of me, instead of all those other girls who've gone before.' She obviously didn't believe me when I swore that she was the first and only love in my life.

On the platform I couldn't find my pal Mouse, but Walter was there. After being introduced to Irmchen, he didn't seem able to keep his eyes off her.

Was I jealous? Not me, mate!

I was sure he was mentally undressing her and what was more; she seemed to enjoy his attention. At the first opportunity, I managed to whisper in his ear: 'eat your hearts out, you stinker. This one is mine and mine alone.'

Irmchen and I had one last clinch, which nearly had me falling out of the open carriage window and off we went - steering due North.

But where on earth was Mouse?

This was certainly the last train, which would get him back to base before his travel papers elapsed.

'Doesn't the stupid ass realise the seriousness of this?'

His absence could be made to look like desertion and men have been put before a court martial for less, usually with a firing squad at the end of it.

Well, there was nothing we could do about it; so Walter and I calmed down and started a game of chess, while the train hugged along.

'Talking about firing-squads' Walter threw in, 'did I tell you about the time I was made to watch the execution of a young sailor?'

It seemed that during provisioning for our last trip, a large smoked Salami had been nicked from between the stern torpedo tubes. Our *1WO* held an inquiry and the suspicion rightly or wrongly fell on Walter. 'I didn't even like the bloody stuff.' In spite of swearing that he was innocent, the officer took him to witness the execution of this sailor by firing squad. Others had to watch as well as a warning to show what happened to men who were convicted of either theft from comrades, cowardice before the enemy or treason.

I didn't particularly want to hear any more of this, especially when Walter started to spell out the details.

'Oh shut up, you're turning my stomach.'

Walter wasn't put off that easily. 'Yes. But did you know that the men ordered to be in the firing squad didn't know whose rifle had been loaded with live rounds and which of them had blanks, so that after the shooting

they didn't know who had fired the fatal shots.'
'Great! The next time I face the firing squad, I will feel much easier knowing that at least some of the shots will be blanks.'
'Now, why don't you tell me about your leave and those dear toffee-nosed girl friends of yours?'

I hit a raw nerve there and I could have bitten off my tongue when he told me the bad news. 'I'm afraid my dearest Lisa has found herself a new boy-friend, which is a laugh really - as he's fat, pen-pushing Lieutenant of the pay-corps and looks at least fifty. Nevertheless, he's an officer.'
'I'm really sorry, mate, I didn't mean stick my big nose into your private grief.'
However, Walter seemed to have got over his loss not too badly as the fact that he checkmated me in double quick time seemed to indicate. But my mind wasn't on playing chess; it wandered back to Walter's story of the execution. I could see the terror on the poor sailor's face before he mercifully copped it. In my mind he did look a bit like my best mate Mouse.
But I needn't have worried; who greeted us on our return to our quarters in Kiel with a loud 'Hello'?

Beaming all over his baby-face, my dear pal Mouse informed me: 'I came back a week early.'
Thank heaven for that. But why?
Well, I could have guessed.
Besotted as he was with his Erika, he had reported back to the base and pretended to the authorities that his home had been flattened by Allied bombs.
Thus he spent the rest of his leave ashore, calling on his sweetheart. For the remainder of that day and into the night, while we were resting on our bunks, the poor sod poured out his heart. 'Everybody is telling me tales about Erika and her past. Surely I would know if she was lying when she told me that she loved only me?' For the next hour or so he told me all about her, about her family and about both their hopes for the future.

'Listen to me, my friend. Don't pay any attention to what people say and don't take everything so serious. God alone knows what the future will hold for Erika and you, or any of us.'
Being two months older than Mouse, I was able to give him the benefit of my superior wisdom concerning life and women.
But in the end I got extremely bored with everybody else's problems. I was dying to tell him and the world in general all about my own newfound love and how Irmchen and I were planning our own future. But that story had to wait until his mind was back with us on board ***KARO-AS***.

There was very little for us to do during the time the dockyard had ***KARO-AS*** in their sticky claws. To stop us from getting bored our Old Man decided that we all needed further education. After breakfast on the next morning, several of us were ordered to report to him. A few petty officers and some stokers, which included Mouse, were sent to attend a three-week introductory course on the latest type of U-boat, the Type XXI. Throughout the whole U-boat service there seemed to be a shortage of manpower, in some cases crews from older outdated types of boat were transferred en block to man the new Electro boats as the Type XXIs were known. In other cases, where men were waiting in dockyards, they were given an introduction ... just in case.

Myself? I was given marching orders to report to the 2nd Radio Operators School near the border with Denmark at Flensburg. Four of us from ***KARO-AS*** spent two weeks operating the newest RADAR detecting devices. (The NAXOS... was capable of receiving the very short centimetre wavelength and was thought to be an answer to the latest enemy RADAR.). I wondered why I, a control room stoker, Walter, a torpedo mixer, Teddy, one of the Kite-pilots and Wilhelm the forward hydroplane operator were chosen for this task? But then I realised that our radio operators had already been trained and we are meant to be the back up, just in case any of them copped it.

KARO-AS must be getting updated, thank God. This tracking of RADAR traffic was going to be one of the most important jobs in the constant effort to stay alive. It was going to be a twenty-four hour job, which meant that more men had to learn how to handle them.

Going back to school was a bit of a culture shock. But because there was a vital purpose to the exercise, the time just flew by. The initial theoretical bit was boring for me. As a trained engineer I had no trouble in following the technical details. This little box of tricks could receive any wavelength down to almost nothing on the short side. After the theory came the practice. After only a few days we were spending hours glued to those sets, tracking signals from over-flying aircraft. A few times we followed friendly ones, on different wavelengths, but more often than not, the ones using RADAR were the decidedly unfriendly. We came to the conclusion that from now on our U-boats would be less like sitting ducks, with no one able to just sneak up on us from out of the dark. If they could locate us with their RADAR, we would be forewarned. That would give us time to show a clean pair of heels. But how long would it be, before Tommy would come along with some other diabolical way of trying to transport us to hell?

After the whole crew had returned from leave and the various courses, we could see that the modifications to our boat had progressed quite well, but there had been snags.
Moored inside the yard's *Howaldbunker*, ***KARO-AS*** was barely recognisable. Two Type IXD2 boats were lying next to one another looking identical. It was only when we got close enough to see the Ace of Diamonds under all the rust, that we were sure it was her. Every single part of her decks, fore and aft, had been ripped apart. Several torpedo storage tubes in front and beside the conning tower had been removed to allow the overall width of the deck of the forecastle to be drastically reduced, to allow for quicker diving and to counteract the tendency of the deck to act like a surfboard, trying to bring the bow up out of the water.

Our new breathing tube

At the starboard side beside the conning tower another chunk of the deck had been removed and a hinged snorkel was being fitted to lay snugly down inside the deck when it was not in use.
From that forward pointing flat position it could be raised hydraulically to

stand upright, so that the head of it was the same height as the raised periscopes.
We had already gone over the operating procedure for snorkels in the classrooms.

The tube forming the mast was oval in cross-section with the forward part forming the inlet, through which the diesel engines drew the air to their cylinders. A division separated it from the back part of the tube, which carried the exhaust gases from the cylinders and which discharged just below the waterline.
The inlet tube was round and was topped by a head, which was the size and shape of a small oil-drum. In it was a ball-cock valve, which closed the inlet tube when water washed over the head of the mast. A small aerial on top of the snorkel head was to aid reception of signals while snorkelling. Friends, from boats with snorkel experience warned us: 'Don't think that it will be all plain sailing, there are several nasty drawbacks.'
I wondered what they meant? We shall see.

Behind the bridge, we came across a whacking great rectangular hole in the top of the pressure-hull. Through the opening, which seemed to measure 1.3 x 1m, we looked straight into the forward part of the diesel room and noticed that our two auxiliary diesel/generators had been removed. The whole thing looked as if ***KARO-AS*** has had a Caesarean operation while giving birth to two generating sets, the poor girl.
But there appeared to be a problem in deciding what to do with the opening. On the orders of our High Command, the yard were to fit a large rectangular hatch, so that the boat could transport bigger cargo items than those which fitted through the normal circular hatches. But while we stood there watching, from below us we heard the very angry voice of our Chief above all the noise around us.

We guessed he was talking to the dockyard people: 'How can you possible stand there and tell us that this bloody botch-up isn't going to collapse round our ears at a depth of less than a few metres?'
As befitted his job as Chief Engineer he objected to any modification, which would affect the structural strength of the pressure-hull in the slightest degree. He obviously wasn't satisfied that the proposed change would in any way be satisfactory.
Thank God, the Old Man was heard to bring the discussion to and end by saying: 'I am not going to take my crew out to sea in a death-trap.'
Later, they all went to see the C in C (U-boats) about this and the result was that the whole shooting match was welded up and checked to be as safe as

before.

While this was going on, all our Anti-aircraft guns had been removed from the upper and lower wintergardens and were replaced with newer and better ones. The 2x2 cm guns now had armour plate shields for the protection of the gun-crews, while the 4x2 cm gun was replace with a 2x3.7 cm quick-fire gun, also with shields for the gunners.
Somebody is really spoiling us!

Other dockyard workers were busily working on the periscopes and their retractable support mechanism. On our larger than normal boats the periscopes tended to be longer and therefore perhaps less stable when fully extended. A hydraulically operated extendible support had been fitted to steady the periscopes. To get the damned thing to line-up and stop jamming between the two scopes, was a very delicate operation and had caused concern ever since we had one of the original periscopes replaced.

Another gang of men pushed us out of the way to get at the newly installed NAXOS aerial, which was made to retract into the cladding of the bridge when it was not in use.
'Give those dockyard men their due, in spite of being thieves, they really got on with the job' Mouse said, and I had to agree with him. Specialists in the different skills were assisted by other craftsmen, which in turn were supported by guest workers, mostly Ukrainians. But they did work very hard to get our boat out as soon as possible. Another week of tidying-up and painting should see the end of our stay in Kiel, or so we thought.

CHAPTER THIRTEEN

Mouse and Erika had decided to go ahead with their engagement. He was completely unable to contain himself after I had let him into my own little secret, Irmchen and me.

The party was to go ahead next Sunday at her house and I was invited to the celebration to give the poor sap some moral support. We had managed to keep back a few little things from our shopping expeditions in Surabaja. A bottle of Champagne, some rotgut gin, one or two cigars and a silk head-scarf would not go amiss on such an occasion.

In spite of my trepidations about Erika's little schemes, I really started to look forward to that day. I had been warned not to call him Mouse in front of her or her friends, but to use his real name. So, while I had better get used to calling him Werner again, I wasn't going to be held responsible for what I might call him after a few drinks.

But hell! My luck had really run out this time. I was required to do guard duties from Saturday until Sunday evening, when, after 10 o'clock in the evening I might be able to join the festivities. With a large slice of luck and by spinning a little hard-luck story, I might even manage to get an all-night pass to make sure that no harm befell my dear pal.

When on watch duty we did two hours on and four hours off. In our "off" time we were also required to do other jobs, maybe help in the galley by peeling potatoes or to pump out the bilges.

Came Sunday afternoon, I had just handed my MP38 to Wilhelm on completion of my latest two-hour stint patrolling the quay-side, when Mouse, sorry - I should say Werner - went on his way ashore looking like a pack-horse. 'I may see you a bit later and remember don't do anything I wouldn't do' I called after him as he went on his way through the dockyard.

Me, I just slipped down the ladders to the control-room to wash-up the officer's mess dishes. While singing along with the music from the loudspeakers, I could hear the distant wailing of air-raid sirens.

Just like Erika and Mouse, the U.S.A.F and the R.A.F. had also made their plans for that day. Unlike other days, when they flew over us on their way to hammer an inland city or other, today, quite unsportingly, they selected us as their target.

Stuck as I was inside ***KARO-AS***, I couldn't see a thing but was able to make-out the distant muffled thuds of the local FLAK. Like everybody else

on board, I was inclined to ignore air-raid sirens, especially while we were safely moored inside a purpose-build pen, such as the *Howaldbunker*.
But this time and not very long after the sound of the sirens, there were other detonations as well and they weren't too far away either.
My first concern was for Mouse. Did he have enough time to get to the safety of a bomb-shelter? Trust him to pick the wrong day and the wrong time for his engagement party.

The infernal din increased by the minute, when the Old Man rushed past me up on to the bridge. Occasionally the explosions were giving the impression that the pen, with its 7 metre thick concrete roof, was shaking. Because I didn't want anybody to think that I was shit-scared, I just went on with my dish washing as if nothing out of the ordinary was happening. From upstairs I heard the seldom-heard raised voice of the Old Man shouting to my mate Wilhelm, who was still at his post - patrolling the quay: 'Kaper - you fool - get away from there and take cover - at the double!'
Why?
The plaster from the ceiling of the pen was raining down in big chunks and this was just like the Old Man - always concerned for the safety of his crew.

But then it got even worst, as all hell broke loose.
From wallowing serenely in the still waters of the pen our dear lady ***KARO-AS*** reared up like a lustful stallion. The loudest crashing and banging on her hull, both fore and aft followed this unusual manoeuvre.

The old girl had gone berserk!
She followed the last trick with another one. She keeled over 30 degrees to starboard and then an equal amount to port. Sitting on my arse, where I had been thrown among the pile of broken dishes, my obvious well-developed self-preservation instinct took over, as it advised me to get the hell out of there while the going was good. I took the quickest route, which was via the ladders leading up to the bridge, preparing to abandon ship as pronto as the proverbial rats. However, there was no need for such drastic action as was clear when other members of the crew quickly joined me. They were just as frightened out of their tiny minds as I was.
It was almost impossible to describe the scene as we could now see the reason for all the thrashing- and banging-about.
The Allied bombers had quite unwittingly found a way of shaking up our boats without actually getting their bombs to penetrate the thick concrete roofs. By accident, one or more of their bombs had fallen into the dockyard basin, a few yards in front of the thick steel shutters. Those huge doors

were closed.
Since they didn't reach all the way down to the bottom of the basin, those exploding eggs pushed the water under the steel doors, thus causing the boats inside to jump around like demented fleas.

To make matters worse, a couple of days ago a squadron of twenty or so Italian Two-man submarines had arrived back from their training grounds in the Baltic. Like sardines they had been packed into the pen as company for our much larger boats.

But look at them now; those midgets lay strewn all over the place. The shock wave had caused some of them to capsize, while other had been lifted clean out of the water and found their new resting place on top of our fore and after decks. They were the cause of all the noise. You couldn't help smiling at their grotesque positions. One was sticking out of our snorkel-recess, as if ***KARO-AS*** had given birth to a Baby-U-boat.

There followed a few more muffled explosions around the dockyard area but as quickly as the action had started it finished. One could have wagered that Tommy and Uncle Sam had a satisfied smile on their lips as they went back to load-up with more of their deadly cargo.
After surveying the mess on our deck, the Old Man decided to wait until a crane could lift those little beauties off our back. In this way the midgets couldn't do any more damage than they had already done, either to us or to themselves.

Not much later after the 'All clear' had sounded, a very bedraggled Mouse dragged himself aboard. He was greeted with a chorus of laughter and the question: 'How did it you get into that filthy mess?'
His reply, after I had decoded and translated it into ordinary language, indicated that he didn't manage to get to Erika's house at all. He was still inside the dockyard gates when the first wave of those bastard insects started to drop things. 'Look at my best uniform. One minute I was going along, minding my own business when, in the next I was diving for cover into a dirty great oily puddle underneath a railway wagon. At first I didn't even notice the mess, because with a full load of coal above me I felt safe enough from the falling FLAK shrapnel and from the stuff Tommy was chucking down.'
From where he lay he could see the sparks flying from the top of our bunker, which he rightly assumed were caused by direct bomb hits. However, his fear, of finding us blown to hell, turned out to be completely unfounded, thanks to the durable concrete above us. Although he was very worried about his ladylove in the town, he couldn't help but smile at the old iron on

KARO-AS's decks. 'We're now going into the scrap collecting business?' On the following morning, a few of us younger and more agile ones were detailed to make our way up ladders to inspect the roof from the outside.

'My - oh - my! What beautiful craters Tommy's eggs have created? Those firecrackers couldn't have been of the old-fashioned type, which detonated at impact. Bombs that were specially designed to penetrate as deep as was possible, before setting off the explosion, could only have produced those 1 1/2 to 2 metres deep holes in the reinforced concrete.

Picking our way through all the cement dust and jagged shrapnel, we came across one hole, which was different from all the others. We could clearly see the fin of an unexploded bomb at the bottom of the hole.

Bloody hell!

Within seconds, we had thrown ourselves flat on the roof and were crawling for our lives to get to the ladders leading down.

The panic was over fairly quickly, as experts dealt with the thing by just blowing it up. It only just added another crater to the existing ones, which were soon filled-in again.

A couple of days later Werner managed to get the old gold ring on Erika's finger. I was there; both of us had been able to get valuable all-night passes. Watching her face light up when the dope was officially asking her to marry him, I could almost believe that all the rumours about her multiple loves were untrue.

With the stuff we had brought ashore there was enough to eat and drink for a whole battalion. Erika's dad was in the Army and her mother had conveniently decided to visit friends. Which left the four of us to celebrate in proper fashion.

Oh, yes! The fourth member of the party was Erika's older sister Katerina. Heavens knows where our engagement couple went, but I do recollect vaguely that Kati and I enjoyed the gin, so much so that the remainder of that particular evening was lost in a haze. When I was woken up early the next morning, lying on the couch with little or no clothes on, Kati told me that I had slept and snored with a dirty big grin on my face. Katerina herself also looked like a cat that had been at the cream... I kept wondering why.

February had arrived and with it, all the alterations and modifications on our new and vastly improved ***KARO-AS*** had been completed. The snorkel installation had gone to plan. The head of it had been coated with a rubber compound, which in turn had been moulded to form a wafer-like pattern. Experiments had shown that this would further reduce the chance of giving a clear RADAR image to our enemies. The running-in trials of our snorkel would have to wait until we get to Norway, where instructors would be waiting to put us through our paces in the deep waters of the Oslo-fjord

The slimming down of the deck in front of the conning tower made the old pot look quite peculiar. You would swear that a giant shark had taken bites out of both sides of the boat. Our seamen had better watch their step when working the lines and fenders during mooring. But on the plus side there was the fact, that with the help of our newly acquired breathing tube or snorkel we would be able to run under water on diesel power all day and every day.

Both the starboard and port diesels had their 60,000 mile service. They would also require a short running-in period at relatively slow revs. And from stem to stern our ***KARO-AS*** was shining like a new penny. Several coats of light-grey paint along with a little bit of camouflage squiggles made her look like the real lady she was. Everybody appeared to be pleased with the changes, even our Chief started to smile again. The exception was our Old Man, who was going around like a bear with a sore behind. It was quite unusual for him to show moodiness.

What had we done to incur his wrath?

Thank goodness it had nothing to do with any of us, because the bush telegraph reported that he had been fighting a running battle with the top brass at the Naval High Command.

Why?

Resulting from the latest reverses on both eastern and western fronts, our Japanese comrades-in-arms in Germany, just like rats, wanted to leave the sinking ship. In addition to shipping urgent supplies to the East, ***KARO-AS*** was to act as Troop-ship for 30 Japanese Officers and Embassy officials. To carry so many passengers in our confined space and for months on end, would inevitably present many problems. But what really floored the Old Man was that he was asked to lose 30 men from our well-trained crew to make room for them.

Could anybody imagine that?

They had picked the wrong man; he told them straight that he was not about to commit suicide or whatever the Japs called it.

We never learned how he got out of that one. Suffice it to say, that he managed it.

The word of a U-boat captain still carried enough weight to convince the politicians who were behind the whole idea that their proposals looked all right from Berlin, but in real life were unworkable.

Relief all round!
Our Captain was smiling again.
All we had to take on this trip were two Jap Embassy Walla's. Lets hope they can play I-GO or SHO-GI to a decent standard and give us some tips.

At long last, the waiting was over.
Final decisions had been taken about our destination, and what cargo we had to take in addition to the passengers. Now it was time to get weaving. The steel ballast in our keel had to be replaced by an equivalent weight of steel bottles filled with mercury. To do this we had to re-visit a dry dock. Luckily there was one inside the bunker.

My apprenticeship gave me a good working knowledge of all metals, but who would have described mercury as a metal instead of a liquid. My only experience with this rare element was in the use of it in thermometers. But there were many other uses in instruments, in switches as well in mercury-vapour lamps. Other uses were in pharmaceutical preparations and fungicides. Our oriental partners were crying-out for supplies of it for their war effort. In pre-war days they apparently got their supplies from the USA.

But Pearl Harbour knocked that on the head good and proper.
Now they had to rely on Germany or Italy, where it could be found in reasonable quantities, to satisfy their needs. It provided our boat and other boats of the monsoon group with a good reason for making this long trip, apart from the fact that in exchange we would bring back iodine, rubber and wolfram, which were needed just as urgently back home.
I was among the lucky chaps who were detailed to supply muscle for the loading of this stuff. Actually, looking at those small steel bottles, only about 13 cm in diameter and perhaps 40 cm long, we could have been excused for thinking that this was going to be a doddle. Those little things couldn't possibly weigh much.
But surprise... surprise...!
There were two good reasons why the handling of those bottles turned out to be extremely difficult. The first reason stemmed from the fact that mercury weighed almost twice as much as solid steel. Our technical training enabled us to work out the weight of those bottles. If they had been solid steel bars of the same size they would have weighed nearly 40 kg, but filled with mercury, they weighed nearer 57 kg. It was little wonder, therefore, that it was almost impossible to get a good enough grip on the bottles to lift them without someone helping.
The second reason was found in the fact that the mercury slopped around inside the bottles.

Why couldn't they fill the damned things up to the top?
The textbooks said? Along with other properties, mercury expanded at a greater rate than steel when subjected to an increase in temperature.
The water-temperature in the North Sea was near freezing point at 0 degrees C, whereas in the Indian Ocean in the equatorial regions it could rise to 27 degrees C. This rise of 27 degrees in mercury would split those thick steel bottles wide open, if they had been filled up to the top - hence the slopping.
Once the exchange had been completed, a lot of empty compartment in the keel bore witness to the fact that mercury was heavier than steel.
To make our work of inserting the mercury bottles a little less heavy, we hit on the idea of rolling them up on thick planks directly into the keel-spaces. It worked like a dream, proving that a little brain could save a lot of brawn.

Once out of dry-dock, we were greeted with lorry-loads of provisions. In addition to taking on 12 torpedoes (six of them directly into their tubes, four stored in the bow- and two in the stern-torpedo rooms), there was the ammo for the newly installed twin barrel 3.7 cm FLAK on the lower wintergarden. On the upper wintergarden behind the bridge, were two new and improved 2 cm twins. There was enough food for a seven-month trip. Very little of it could have been described as fresh. The greens, bread and potatoes wouldn't last very long in the dampish atmosphere, as was known from previous experience. A fuel-barge had scraped together enough diesel oil for our long trip. There was no hiding the fact that fuel was in very short supply.
A lot of Peters were again robbed to get this Paul on his way..
Our kit bags with our uniforms and other private belongings were already put back into store and having shot-off a few short letters to our kin; we were now ready for our next adventure.
We were now in the spring of 1945, when silently, under the cover of darkness, ***KARO-AS*** sneaked out into the Bay of Kiel and on toward Norway. As usual, all the old precautions applied. Once through the shallows around Denmark and as soon as there was enough water under our keel, we were cruising slowly and sedately under water. It would not be long now, before we would be taught the art of snorkelling.

We looked forward to this very short stopover in the Oslo Fjord for familiarisation with our new gadget. Apart from a hasty trim dive just after leaving port, the Old Man said he would wait until we got into the deeper waters around Norway to find out whether the new bow-configuration would live-up to expectation. Together with the snorkel, it would give the

Chief a better chance to hold the old lady on a steady course and at a steady depth while creeping along under water.

Klaus-Peter said he was willing to learn new tricks!

For the first part of the passage to Oslo we had the company of a minesweeper and after it left us to find our own way through the Kattegat, we had to rely on the *Luftwaffe* to look after us. We caught sight of a couple of aircraft in the distance, but were unable to identify whether they were friend or foe. Just to make sure we kept a low profile, we stayed below. They probably were friendly ones, as the boys on the tracking devices didn't pick-up any RADAR signals.

We would rather try-out our new Anti Aircraft defences at a later date and in peace. Our fire power had been enhanced by the new twin 3.7 cm gun, which together with the pair of twin 2 cm guns on the top wintergarden had armour plated shields added to protect the gun crews. Behind those we wouldn't feel quite so naked in the face of machine gun fire from an aircraft. Tracer ammunition would ensure that the effect of our gunfire could be clearly seen. All those new measures, although they were largely untried, should boost our survival chances.

For Mouse and me, being the standby gunners for the 2 cm twins, the time for some real experience with the new gear couldn't come quick enough. In between flapping about aircraft, we had a chance to practice the hydraulic raising and lowering of the new snorkel. In no time at all we got it to work like the clockwork and as far as we were concerned we were now ready for the Training Officer to come aboard and put ***KARO-AS*** through her paces. When the Lieutenant Engineer arrived, his form was plainly demonstrated by the medals on his chest. He didn't win those in a classroom.

Our Chief was to be the star-pupil, as the boat was in his hands during snorkelling. We were only Extras in the drama, which followed. When the trials started our Old Man and his *1WO* were manning the periscopes in the tower, just to make sure we didn't run somebody down when our minds were occupied with snorkelling. The sea conditions at the mouth of the Fjord were practically the same as anywhere in the North Sea. It wasn't too difficult to hold the boat at a nice depth for both the periscopes and the snorkel head. Before actually starting the diesels, we were getting to grips with the handling of the boat with the snorkel erect, as well as with the changed configuration of the quarterdeck. The Chief seemed delighted with her handling and although she still needed a little help from the forward hydroplanes to keep her nose down, she reacted to his deft touch just as she was designed to do. It was still a balancing act, like that of flying a two thousand ton aeroplane. But then crunch time arrived!

The Diesel crews had been on stand-by for some time as the Chief asked for more revs from the E-Motors to gather speed for the switch.

The machine-telegraphs clattered 'E-Motors stop! Both diesels slow ahead'

As soon as the engines fired, it was my job to rip open the snorkel's main inlet-valve, which was now located above my head in the control room and at the same time a diesel-stoker opened the exhaust flaps, to clear the way for the exhaust gases of the engines.

The friction-clutches from the diesels to the prop-shafts had already been engaged and - lo and behold - off we went. We were actually cruising under water, powered by the 4,000 rampant horses of our noisy engines at an unbelievable 10 knots, almost four times our previous underwater speed. Only very small adjustments to the hydroplane settings and trim distribution were required to cope with the extra speed under water. At our stations in the bowels of the boat, we were unable to tell the difference between running on the surface when the sea was flat or skulking down below.

We started to discount the scare-stories, which had made the rounds at the base, of how painfully uncomfortable snorkelling was going to be.

'*Herr Oberleutnant*! Would you please try some changes of course and of speed while holding the boat at an accurate depth at all times' the instructing officer asked the Chief.

This would be easy meat for him. As we all knew, he could make ***KARO-AS*** sit-up and beg with one hand tied behind his back. A quiet word here and a whispered order there, a few litres from stern to bow-trim-tank and at any given speed or change of course there wasn't a flicker to be seen on the *Papenberg* depth-gauge. The instructor tried to hide his amazement at Klaus-Peter's deft handling of 2,000 tonnes of solid steel.

It failed to cause a raised eyebrow among us, who had previous experience of his silken hands on the reins of ***KARO-AS***.

While all this was going on, the radio operators had their first chance to play around with their latest equipment by way of the aerial on top of the snorkel-head. A patrol boat had been given the task to simulate a RADAR search. With ease our chaps were able to locate the source and pinpoint her location. In earnest this would have been an invitation to get the hell out of here rather than wait for the fireworks to start and make it hot for us.

But this wasn't the real thing yet; just be patient, my boys.

From my station behind the periscope housing, I overheard the officers discussing the next step:

'As the sea is far too calm to get a proper test of running in a high sea, we will have to simulate and make the snorkel-head cut-under for short spells.'

We knew that it would be necessary to get the crew used to the variations in pressure inside the boat, which would be caused by the periodic closing and opening of the snorkel's inlet-valve as the sea washed over the head. During the time the valve was closed, the engines would draw the oxygen needed for combustion from the boat's interior and thus cause a partial vacuum. Our Chief requested 'Forward hydroplane down five', to make her bow dip and caused the top of the snorkel to run below the waterline. It lasted only a few seconds before he corrected it by calling for 'Up five degrees'. There was only a slight pressure on our eardrums, nothing which a short swallowing couldn't cure.

'Try it a little longer' suggested the instructor.

This time there was a noticeable difference, but it was still quite bearable. 'And again please and wait with your correction until I ask you to.'

This time Klaus Peter showed a bit more concern as the pressure in our ears were getting worst, causing us to keep swallowing to ease the pain. We started to look like a fish out of water, mouths wide open. The hydroplane operators seemed to suffer similar discomfort as they reported problems in getting the boat up to the proper depth and holding it there.

What is going on?

The Chief opted for a little more forward speed, by increasing the revs of the engines and that did the trick all right. ***KARO-AS*** rose to periscope depth and everybody relaxed again.

'Right then! Lets try it once more, but this time keep her there until your eyes pop out!'

Our Chief agreed, but was it really necessary to prolong the agony, 'I'm sure we've all got the message' he said.

With only very little help from the forward hydroplane the Klaus-Peter got her down until the depth-gauge in front of him indicated 12 meters instead of the usual periscope-depth of 10.55 metres. The normal barometer above his head was off the bottom of the dial already and this time our eardrums started to hurt seriously in partial vacuum inside ***KARO-AS***. Our normally unflappable Chief appeared to suffer more than most of us, judging by the foul mood he got into as our trusted lady got a little tail-heavy.

'What on earth are you both up to?' he shouted to the hydroplane operators. 'Can't you hold the bloody thing steady any more?' and 'Forward up five, aft up ten degrees,' he ordered impatiently to get her back on level keel.

How long is he going to torture us, no wave on earth could be that big and take that long to roll over the snorkel head.

The Chief appeared to lose his head. It must be this bastard pain in our ears ... it was going to drive all of us round the bend.

'Have you gone mad? Can't you see that our stern is dropping lower and lower? Shift 200 litres from aft to forward... and look smart about it' he yelled.

Adjusting the ballast by that amount was not normal; something was amiss in the state of Denmark.

The Old Man had arrived in the control room having been attracted by the Chief's bellowing. 'What the hell are you doing?' (Or words to that effect), he wanted to know from the instructor, whose face was as red as a beetroot. Before the poor man had time to get his excuses ready, the engine room hatch flew open.

'Wassereinbruch im Dieselraum.' (Diesel-bilge is flooding), a frantic diesel-stoker yelled.

By this time all sorts of things started to happen and since we had never trained for an emergency such as this, there was a certain amount of confusion. One thing was very clear; the water has been entering through the snorkel.

I was not aware of any specific orders being given, but instinctively I closed the snorkel inlet valve above my head. Thankfully, by this time the diesels had been stopped, but unfortunately not until they had sucked a lot of air from the inside our iron coffin.

The diesel crew had also closed the exhaust flaps of the engines. That action and the closing of the inlet prevented any more water getting in. Alas, it was all far too late, because our trusty ***KARO-AS*** was on her way down to the bottom, arse first at an angle of 40 degrees. Because the engine room hatch was still open, we were able to see sparks and flashes coming from the switchboards of the E-motor room, thankfully not resulting in a fire.

They were caused by short-circuits, when water entered the electric motors. Things were happening at a rate of knots. With a lot of puffing and hissing our CPO Schulz had already started to blow out all the ballast tanks. It certainly slowed her free-fall, but only slightly.

At the angle she went down we found it difficult to stand up or to get a toehold or fingerhold to keep ourselves from sliding down in a heap. I had managed to wedge myself between the periscope-well and the bulkhead of the engine room. From my position I could still about reach all the valves in my station. Everybody else had also found some valve to hang-on to.

'Is this IT? Is this the moment when our legendary ***KARO-AS*** luck goes out of the window?'
I began to see what it would feel like to be entombed in a tin-coffin.
My eyes, along with everybody else's, were fixed on the needle of the depth-gauge swinging round past the official maximum of 100 metres, past 120 and past 130 and on and on. But before much longer we could feel a shudder throughout the boat as she touched bottom.
The depths gauges in the control room indicated 137 metres.
Fighting desperately for breath, we were taking stock of the situation.
The Chief made a few calculations and reported to the Old Man that at the angle we were resting, the bow would now be at 110 metres and the stern at 165 metres below the surface, certainly deeper than the official maximum ***KARO-AS*** was designed for.

The ensuing silence, interrupted only by an occasional creak or groan from the hull as it was being stressed, was unnerving. Everybody was too shocked to say anything.
We are dead!
Well! If not actually dead, why do we find it so difficult to draw breath? I had always imagined that the act of dying in a submarine would be quick. This fighting to get air into our lungs made it a painful affair. Perhaps it would have been better if we had gone further down, we might then have been squashed flat as pancakes in a mercifully rapid end.

While we were getting ready to panic when the calm voice of the Old Man came over the speakers. 'Right lads! I haven't a clue how this has happened, but as we're still alive – lets just see what we can do to get out of this little bit of trouble. Every man is to remain at his station. Our tail is sitting on something but it may not be the deepest point of the fjord. Rocking the boat might make things even dicier.'
He sounded as if he was short of breath as well, but on the face he didn't show any undue concern. There must be hope!

Perhaps he was just trying to spare us youngsters the ugly truth, as I could have sworn that I had seen a brief exchange of glances passing between him and our CPO, the two most experienced submariners in our midst. When their eyes had met, both imperceptibly shook their heads as if to say 'This is bloody hopeless!'
It did nothing for my confidence but when the Old Man went on to ask the Chief and the other officers to investigate and report the overall position of the boat, I thought 'Well. Perhaps it is not as bad as everybody thought.'

To begin with the Klaus-Peter ordered everybody to sit down, or where possible, to lie down and rest. This should save any remaining oxygen. He certainly had recovered his composure very quickly. Surely it wasn't his fault that ***KARO-AS*** misbehaved the way she did.

It was common practice to use the bottom of the sea as a refuge. During the running-in period, when the sea was rough and the Old Man reckoned we deserved a bit of peace during mealtime, he would drop her down on to the floor, at no more than perhaps 50 m. But in those circumstances, after enjoying the stillness of the deep, we all knew that returning to the surface was just a formality.

Down here in the Oslo fjord it was very still and peaceful too, but then... so was the inside of a grave.

The Chief and our CPO climbed aft to estimate how much water had entered the boat before they could decide what the next move would be, or if in deed anything could be done.

Where Mouse and I were resting on the sloping floor plates, we could still see and hear what was going on in the control room, as our officers discussed ways to get us off this little hook. But I couldn't keep my eyes from wandering to and from our depth-gauge, which still indicated 137 metres. Niggling in the very back of my mind was some information, which I must have heard about somewhere. For whatever reason, it seemed to make me feel very uneasy. Mouse must have had similar thoughts. 'I suppose you know that nobody's ever escaped from a sunken boat below half of our present depth. At my U-boat school (*2-ULD*) at Gotenhaven we were told of only one successful mass escape from a U-boat at a Norwegian Fjord, which was sunk by bombs from a British Carrier-plane at the beginning of the war. All but 8 men of a crew escaped through the diesel hatch from only just over 30 meters.' I had to admit to him that I had similar thoughts on the subject of getting out of here in one piece. 'Lets hope the Old Man and the Chief have some tricks up their sleeves to get the old tub back up to the top, or else we can forget about the all the days of escape training we had at the *ULD*'.

The main object of those U-boat schools was of course to initiate the prospective crews of those 'Sardine Tins' in the crafts required to make all the machinery work in an effective manner, to turn inanimate metal objects into deadly fighting units, fit to do their bit in the struggle for supremacy on the high seas. In my case the school was mainly based on land in an assortment of purpose-built buildings. But our accommodation during the three months course was on a requisitioned 27,000 ton Pleasure Liner called "Robert Ley".

During peacetime, a whole fleet of those almost identical liners, were giving holiday cruises to ordinary working people and their families. Now they served mainly as Hospital ships and as in our case, as additional accommodation for trainee sailors. The buildings ashore all contained replica parts a U-boat's interior, such as the electric installation, diesel motor room, control room, torpedo rooms, conning towers, all designed to give

1st U-boat School on KDF Liner "Rober Ley" at Pillau

hands-on training. Lectures followed lectures. Charts and diagrams by the dozen had to be studied and memorized. One colour for electrical cables running through the boats, one for high and one for low voltage, other colours for compressed air, subdivided into high-pressure and low-pressure, yet another colours for trimming systems, ventilating and venting systems, Oxygen lines, bilge pumping systems, speaking tubes, telephone lines, diesel fuel lines, ect. ect.

For us new sailors it was the first introduction to life on the ocean waves, or what it would be like. Our brains were at that time relatively uncluttered with information about other types of crafts in the Navy. In this way we had an advantage over many of the older sailors. They had probably been trained on Battleships, Cruisers, Destroyers, Mine-hunters and anything else that floats. Here they were to learn, that there would be a vast difference between life on the surface ships and what may be in store for them as a result of their volunteering for this outfit.

It was all theory at this stage. We didn't know yet which type of boat we were to join, so it all had to be in a general sort of way. Apart from that, we were still all together, future seamen, radio operators, engineers and mechanics, in short all the lot. It followed that a lot of useless information had to be assimilated, as well as the parts, which were to be entrusted to us later on board ship.

But the most memorable as well as most enjoyable part of our training was to take place in one of the largest buildings ashore. The enjoyment wasn't diminished by the thought that all this training would be quite useless unless Tommy was considerate enough to sink us in a nice even depth of not more that 50 meters. On the ground floor of this building was a replica control room of a type VIIC U-boat. On top of it that was a huge 10 meter diameter and perhaps 10 meter deep water tank.

The first part of this exercise was to become familiar with the standard submarine emergency escape gear. It was a type of life jacket with an oxygen bottle and valve at the bottom and a flexible hose from a chemical filter cartridge inside the jacket to a mouthpiece. It was designed to give you an independent air supply for a minimum of 30 minutes. With a partly inflated life jacket, the mouthpiece in place a clip on your nose and with the help of a lead-belt to get rid of your buoyancy, you could have a really good time under water, with all sorts of antics in slow motion.

Once we were confident in handling the underwater scene for a lengthy period of time, a group of ten trainees were led through a watertight door into the bottom chamber, i.e. the simulated control room. Step by step we were taken through the procedure which followed. The first step was to equalize the internal pressure of the control room with the pressure of the water above us., to enable us to open the upward opening hatch, which led from the control to the tank above.

To do this we had to flood the room.

As the water rose around us, we fully inflated our lifejacket. Thus we floated up to the top of the room with the rising water. Under and around the escape hatch of a control room was a metal skirt and when the water rose up to it, the air in the room above the level of the rim was trapped. This allowed us to keep breathing with out the breathing apparatus, although now at the prevailing water pressure. By the way, this hatch arrangement with the added skirt, was standard on all hatches on all German submarines.

After the pressure in the room was equal to that in the water above us, the first man to go out had to don his mouthpiece and nose-clip and duck under the skirt and open the escape hatch outwards. He would allow himself to float up through the interior of the conning tower and above it he would fasten a line with a float at the other end. Normally one could have gone straight to the surface and not risk getting the bends, but of course to practice an escape from a much deeper depth would require a more gradual ascent by going up on the line, which had regularly spaced knots, stopping at intervals. Thus the oxygen in your body had time to adjust to the differing pressures around you. Then one after the other would follow the leader up to the surface, all using the line to steady their ascent.

As I said before, it was great fun while it lasted and a diversion from the mental stresses and strains from studying and remembering all the information of the operating manuals.

But back to reality.

Earlier a report had come from the galley, that our *Smutje* needed medical assistance. Normally he would not cook while below the surface, but while snorkelling he would have to do it, because we would hope to stay below much longer. And in any case, fresh air would be circulated through the boat via the snorkel.

Alas, when ***KARO-AS*** turned her nose up, the pots and pans on his stove had tipped over and burned his legs and his feet. During our last stay in dock our old doctor had been found more pressing work; he was now helping to sew people together again at one of the many fronts. It befell our Paramedic Leo to help *Smutje* into one of the chief petty officers bunks, where he started to cut away his socks. He had already been given some painkillers but until they had a chance to act, the poor sod was in absolute agony. He was not far off from screaming out loud as some of the skin came away with his socks.

Another casualty was in the stern torpedo-room. As the boat decided to drop her tail, masses of the unwanted water rushed toward the stern. As Karl-Heinz was climbing through the hatch leading into the engine compartment, he was washed back and smashed against the torpedo tubes. He suffered a bang on the head, a badly sprained shoulder and a profusely bleeding gash on his left forearm. Our other messmates were able to give him first aid, thus he didn't require immediate medical treatment. It was just as well, as the hatch had closed after the first rush of water through it and was now under water and couldn't be opened. Eight men were trapped in the stern, but we could communicate with them on the intercom.

With everything going on around me, I suddenly realised that I was in imminent danger of peeing myself. Crossing my legs, which was not easy in

my position, didn't help. And there was no way I could jump about in here. My CPO noticed the sweat on my face and the way I acted and offered these pearls of wisdom 'Why don't you just piss down into the bilge. It surely does not matter any more.'
Coming from an experienced U-boatman, an old hand at the game, this bucked me up considerably... I don't think.

But I did take his advice and added to the flooding inside the boat. Even the Chief on his way back from the engine room didn't comment when he saw what I was up to. He just said that there was no way we could get to the heads in the stern anyway.
He and our CPO had to sit down in the control room after the effort required to work their way back up from the engines. Breathlessly they reported to the Old Man, who seemed to have aged twenty years in the last few hours, 'We reckon that we've taken on in more than fifty tonnes of water. Part of it went through to the stern-room, but most of it is the main E-Motors. With sea water in the coil-windings they are a write-off.'

The Old Man, speaking to our Chief, said 'Are you absolutely sure the water came in through the snorkel? We should have seen water spouting from the indicator pipe above the periscope in the conning tower. The *1WO* or I should have been drenched if water had entered the snorkel.'
Even the experienced instructor looked lost for a reason.
'Be that as it may, what is the overall position?'
'Apart from the main motors the electrical system is in order, except for repairing a few fuses. All the batteries are full and thankfully none of the sea water had managed to get into the new batteries in the diesel-room.'
Verfluchte Scheisse!
None of us had bothered to worry about those. We all knew, that if the angle of the boat got a bit greater, we must expect acid from the cells to leak into the bilges. And we equally knew what that meant: Deadly Chlorgas... as acids and seawater mixed.

Klaus-Peter went on: 'Since the electrics are in order, all the pumps can be used. But we doubt whether they're capable of operating against the outside water-pressure. The main centrifugal pump located here in the control room will be quite useless and we're sure that the piston pump in the stern can't operate at this depth. But there is a distinct possibility of using the piston pump in the bow, if we can think of a way of getting the excess water there. We have to think about that one.'
Having stopped to get his breath back, the Chief continued his report. 'The High-pressure compressed air cylinders are nearly full at maximum pres-

sure, as are the Low-pressure ones. We could release some air back into the boat, to stabilise the atmosphere in here.'

Listening to the Chief's report and hearing his suggestions for getting ourselves out of the mire, had a rejuvenating effect. After thinking our situation was quite hopeless, we began to look forward to getting our teeth into positive action. Better to fail in the attempt, than to hang around bemoaning our fate. The inquiries will have to wait until much later.

The Officers had their heads together 'How are we going to transfer the fifty tons of water to the bow-room?' the Old Man asked.

'To construct a pipe system to pump the water from the stern to the bow room will take time. Meanwhile, we should try and shift some by forming a human chain and manhandle it up in pails.'

The Old Man agreed and the crew was ordered to form a chain along the full length of ***KARO-AS***. At the angle of fully 40 degrees this was no mean undertaking. But, within minutes the first pails came uphill to us through the open engine-room hatch, from where we heaved them further up towards the bow. There were only a few actual pails, so other containers had been commandeered and adapted for this task such as our huge 10 litre coffeepots and 15 litre mess-tins. After twenty or so the empty ones were on their way down again. After the first fifty I was beginning to feel the strain in my leg and arm muscles. 'Damn - I thought I was pretty fit' I confided in my neighbour in the queue, who happened to our CPO. But when I looked at him there was no doubt about it, he was feeling just as rotten as I was. His chest was heaving from being unable to get enough air into his lungs. And he wasn't the only one.

The Old Man ordered a rest period.

Good new came from the forward pump. My mate Mouse reported that it was coping with the outside water pressure - slowly but surely.

The 3 horsepower motor and its wiring were feeling the strain and were getting warm, but he was ordered to keep pumping regardless. 'Its our only chance, the bloody motor can be replaced.' My brain raced ahead again. How many 10 litres went into 50 tonnes?

We must shift 100 full pails to transport one ton of water.

More actually, because a lot of the water slopped out when the pails were swung from one man to the next.

On we went, pail after pail, until we were ready to drop again. A couple of times I managed to lose my grip on a pail, which didn't please Karl, the diesel stoker was handing them through the open hatch to me. And who could blame him for using foul language after being drowned in filthy oily liquid. I was laughing as he was spluttering like an idiot, until I got a taste of the same medicine when our CPO let one of them go to empty all over me. This went on for some time, with the amount of water being shifted getting less and less. While everybody was gasping for air, those rest-periods became more and more frequent and lasted longer and longer. Everybody, including the Old Man and all the Officers, who had pitched in along with us, were too shattered to go on. After the latest stoppage, the Chief staggered back from the engine room, where he had been working. He told the captain that the men were making progress with changing pipes and so. He suggested that we rest to conserve air, until he's had a chance to try-out his system.

I didn't need a second invitation, as I was more than ready to give up. My short, but relatively eventful life started to flash by in my mind as I sat down on the cold floor plates, utterly exhausted and not caring a damn what was to come next. Pity though, I wouldn't get the chance to marry Irmchen and pity, that I wouldn't see my folk again. It was a good job we never planned too far ahead anyway.

With those thoughts running through my head, wedged into the Christmas tree, the pyramid-like arrangement of thirty-odd high- and low-pressure air valves in my corner, I started to doze. Is this how you slip away in a peaceful, dreamlike fashion, you keep on drifting ... drifting ... drifting ... drif..........?

CHAPTER FOURTEEN

I didn't know how long I spent in dreamland, it may have been a few minutes, or it may have lasted for many long hours.
The truth was, I had completely lost track of time.
But my confusion came an abrupt and painful end.
Oouuch!
The ground under my feet appeared to move, first more or less gently. Then, as the seconds ticked by, it reared and pitched with ever increasing vigour.
I was wide-awake now as I was forced back against the pipes and valves, which were behind me, where the handle of one particular valve tried to split my backside in half.
But to hell, who cares about pain?

Praise the Lord and Hallelujah, as ***KARO-AS*** was succeeding to wriggle herself free from the tight embrace of Oslo Fjord's bottom. As she threw off her shackles, her stern caught up with the rest of her and on a level keel she shot up to the surface like a Champagne cork.
My stomach was left at the bottom during this rocket-propelled ascent to the surface, while my brain laboured to take in this new development. The Old Man just didn't have the heart to call for a slowing down in her quest to reach the top, not that anybody would have heard anything above the shouts of jubilation and relief from every member of our crew.
When ***KARO-AS*** broke the surface, she must have jumped clean out of the water because our feet were whipped from under us, depositing us in heap on the floor, while at the same time knocking any remaining sense out of our heads.
By "us", I meant just about everybody including our Old Man. For a moment I thought I had gone deaf, it was so quiet.

But as we struggled to make sense of our situation, our next impulse was to get the hell out of our prison into the fresh air.
But thank God! Our Old Man kept his head, where others would have lost theirs. He took his time to equalise the pressure inside the boat with that prevailing on the outside, before attempting to throw the 'lid' open.

This long, drawn-out process of equalisation, which was accomplished by slowly opening a small valve in the conning tower hatch, did little for the extreme pain we experienced as our eardrums seemed ready to burst

and our eyes wanted to pop out of their sockets. It also had the effect of turning every last drop of condensation in our boat into a thick, impenetrable vapour. I couldn't see my hand in front of my eyes. I could only hear my mates' breathing, hence I knew they were still here, but their actual bodies had turned into faceless spirits and spectres.
With bated breath we waited and waited and waited.

But eventually, the first smell and the first feel of cool, fresh air reached us through the ventilation system, while from above us came the Old Man's breathless voice:
'Come on up, lads. Believe it or believe it not: Up here this heavenly sun of ours is shining in all its glory.'
No second invitation was needed for every man jack to rush up for fresh air. Young and fit we were, but we had only just enough strength left in our legs to scramble up the ladder leading to the bridge and from there on to the wintergarden. Exhausted we just dropped wherever there was a space. From bow to stern, a solid carpet of bodies was covering the still wet deck.

Philip and Karl Heinz had joined Mouse and me, both of them understandably overjoyed at having been released from their prison in the stern.
Lying flat out and totally exhausted, we were all of a sudden very conscious of our racing hearts, which were pumping so fast, it was impossible to count our pulse-rate. It felt as if my old ticker wanted to pound its way clean out of my chest.

Once I managed think of something other than my own discomfort, I turned to Karl Heinz and asked 'How's the old noddle. Can I assume that the bang on the head helped to get your brain functioning again?' You can't please everybody: He didn't think my remark was desperately funny, especially since his shoulder was also giving him jip.
Taken all together, this little how-do-you-do must have been a very close thing. And it wasn't only us, the youngsters, who thought so. Fear and trepidation were soon replaced by an artificial jollity among us but you could also see that the event had affected our superiors as well and that included the very experienced Old Man.

We should have thanked God on our bended knees for our deliverance. Alas, there was only one man, who did just that. Wilhelm, my friend from Stettin, was sitting below the lower wintergarden, his lips moving in silent prayer. I was convinced that he would end up going into the priesthood, if he survived the war in one piece. I envied him in a funny sort of way, he seemed to come out of his little sessions in which he was talking to Him up there, in a quiet and almost tranquil way. I secretly hoped he was thanking

Him for me as well - just in case...!

In fact, since our resurfacing, there's been non-stop activity in the radio-shack next door. If they had been sending and receiving those red-hot messages by cables, instead of over the airwaves, those wires would have melted by now. A hastily called C in C of the Oslo Base had arrived by launch

He, the Old Man, as well as the instructor and our Chief went down below to take stock of the situation.

What a disaster! Somebody has to answer for this.

Here we were, a valuable U-boat, together with her specially trained crew, fully equipped with all the latest gadgetry such as a snorkel, latest RADAR detection and anti aircraft gunnery gear, loaded to the gunnels with fuel, torpedoes and provisions for its seventy-strong crew to last for at least seven months plus a valuable cargo of material to aid the Japanese in their desperate struggle in the Pacific. Instead of straining to do our bit in the defence of our Fatherland, we were wallowing in utter helplessness in the Oslo Fjord. It would take months to make ***KARO-AS*** seaworthy again, to rectify her electric power plant and repair whatever it was, which caused our new snorkel to malfunction. .

A thorough investigation was sure to follow and at the end of it, somebody, somewhere was going to jump through the hoop. However, this investigation had to wait until ***KARO-AS*** had entered the dockyard in Horten, which was one of our bases in the Oslo fjord.

Thankfully we were spared the indignity of having to be towed there, as our diesel engines were still up to the task.

Once we had made fast, we were relieved of many of the things we were shipping. We had almost forgotten all about our two Japanese passengers, mainly because they had not been seen during our trip to Oslo or during our stint at the bottom of the fjord. They had to leave the bunks, in which they had spent most of the time being seasick, to try and catch a lift on the next Monsoon-boat sailing to the Far East.

A fuel barge took off most of our precious diesel fuel, to allow some other boat to take our place in direction Japan. We got the impression that a few U-boats were marking time in port for lack of fuel. And part of our 7 months rations went the same way, which meant that we would have to get used to the food supplied by the canteens ashore. But it gave us considerably more living space, as countless boxes of tins containing this and that disappeared along with sides of smoked ham and hundreds Salamis, which had been dangling from the ceiling of all departments.

I was going to miss the sight of them, as they always reminded me of childhood days spent at Grandma's and Grandpa's cottage in the country. When visiting, my brother and I usually slept in the loft space on straw mattresses. Above our heads, hanging from the rafters were delicious smoked pork sausages. It was paradise. But the illusion came to an end when one day we returned unexpectedly from mushrooming in the neighbouring woods. A prize porker had bitten the dust and its demise and its transformation into those admired sausages did shatter our illusions. They even turned us into fully-fledged vegetarians, but alas, it lasted only until the next day's mealtime.

Back on board ***KARO-AS*** was put to sleep. Men from the base took over the watch duties for the time being, while we were to seek temporary accommodation at the base. Here we were to await the outcome of the investigation into the accident. But what was more important to us at the moment was the fact that we were starving. Since *Smutje's* accident we hadn't eaten.

As we were making our way over the gangplank to the quay side, carrying bundles of dirty washing, I heard somebody calling; 'Gerhard'. To my mates on board I was just 'Spider' and since all our superiors addressed us by our surnames, I didn't think any more about it. But, when the call came again and this time it was 'Gerhard Schuler', I automatically turned round and nearly fell off the narrow gangplank. There on the quay side, in the uniform of the Naval Coastal Artillery, stood my brother-in-law Willi Hofmeister.

'Willi!

What on earth are you doing here, instead of delivering letters at home?' I shouted across. 'I would have thought you were too old for this caper.'

The last time we met was a few days before I joined the Navy, when we had a going-away party at home. Meeting him here certainly was a surprise and a coincidence. Willi was at least twenty years older than me and seemed happy to be a postman. It was during my last leave at Christmas that I was told about him being drafted into the Services. He was stationed some distance away on the south coast of Norway. On this particular day, he was spending a day's leave here in Horten. And coincidentally he had heard the rumour that a U-boat had sunk out in the middle of the fjord. Curiosity made him join the assembled crowd and wait for hours until the stricken boat had reappeared and finally made fast in the Horten base. He didn't have the slightest idea, however, that he would find his wife's youngest brothers on the unlucky vessel.

After we had made ourselves at home in our quarters on land, I met Willi again. In the canteen and over a beer we talked about old times. As was the custom among most of us, we talked, or even thought very little about our future. We were perhaps secretly hoping and praying that we would actually have one.
But soon he had to take his leave, to catch the transport back to his unit, where he had to report back not later than midnight.

During the course of the next few days, the electricians among our crew dismantled the E-machines, while we were to assist the engineers of the base and the fairly high-ranking engineer from the U-boat High Command, in their effort to find the cause of our accident. You didn't have to be a Sherlock Holmes to realise how the water got in. We knew enough about the snorkel-system to see that there was only one possible reason for that. The ball cock inside the snorkel-head, which should have closed as soon as it hit a wave or went below the water level, remained open during the time the boat ran below periscope-depth. The diesel engines did their bit to accelerate the entry of water by sucking it in.
But why didn't the valve close?

As soon as we'd dismantled the outer cover of the head, we tried to open and close the valve manually.
But it was stuck fast in the open position.
So, there you have it.
One of the engineers busied himself with a camera, taking photos from all angles. Those would be part of the evidence at an official inquiry or a court-martial.
But the question remained: Why on earth had it stuck?

Only after we had started to strip down the guides by loosening the screws, which held the guides in place, did we find the answer. At the first turn of the screws the valve could be closed as intended. Carelessness at the yard in Kiel was the obvious answer.
'Will you take the valve guides off, so we can have a look at them' asked the inspector. After unscrewing a series of five or six screws, I lifted the guides away from their seats.
It was here that we found a tiny piece of wedge-shaped wood, not a lot bigger than a matchstick. It had lodged in a tiny gap between the valve and its guides. This tiny sliver appeared to be the culprit that stopped the valve closing and as a consequence nearly cost us our lives.

The snorkel-head
cause of accident.

I was asked to re-assemble the valve and without the piece of wood it worked perfectly. By this time, word had reached our Old Man about our find and he and our Chief came to have a look. To say that they were furious would have been the understatement of the year. He swore blind that he had personally checked the operation of the valve before the covers were assembled at the dockyard. We all knew that to be true as we had all watched him do it.

But the Old Man couldn't be placated

'Well. If that's so, how do you explain the presence of a piece of wood in the valve? Are you trying to tell me that it got there by accident?'

The inspector, who had watched me dismantle the valve-guides, told him and Klaus-Peter, 'There is no possible way that anything could get in there by accident. I took several photographs during the dismantling of the valve.

When they're developed, you'll see what I mean.'
'You have established the reason why water got down through the snorkel, which raises the next question. Why didn't we get a warning of it at the bleeder-pipe above the periscope?' the Old Man went on to ask. 'Streams of water should have been spouting out of the pipe. Surely it was installed for just such an occurrence, wasn't it?'
'Yes Sir, that was the reason for it being there. I was instructed to make this the next step in my investigations.'
'OK, but please keep me informed of your findings.'
With that, the Old Man and our Chief disappeared again down below.
After consulting his drawings the Inspector asked me to dismantle other parts of the snorkel.
It was here that we found the answer!

It looked like a deliberate act of sabotage?
The small pipe leading from the water-separator in the snorkel-air-intake to above the periscope in the conning tower and to the control room had been blocked with a round wooden peg!
We had never seen a flap like this one!
The Old Man and the Chief were flown back to *Kiel* for a report to the C in C U-boats and for further investigation. It was decided that the most likely time the evil deed would have been done was when a gang of dockyard workers applied the wafer-patterned rubber coating to the head of our new snorkel. That should have made us safe from detection by searching enemies. Instead it had the opposite effect.
No doubt the *Gestapo* would sooner or later find the culprits and deal with them.

But who knows? Perhaps those misguided people have done us a favour? The thought must have occurred to some of us, that perhaps we were a lot safer here, sailing through enemy infested waters on our long journey to Japan.

While the inquiry went on in Kiel, the damaged windings had been dismantled from the main electric motors. The other crewmembers, including us, had little else to do but pass the time freshening-up the boat's paintwork, inside and out. Not that it needed doing again so soon after our last refit, but it may have been designed to keep idle hands out of mischief. Once we had our evening meal however, we had a chance to get ashore and assess the sights... the town, its buildings and its fair *damer (*dames).

In spite of what we had been told of the Norwegians, we had little trouble-making friend with locals. Mind you, there were certain objects, which we carried with us on those trips, objects we had bought way back in Penang. Very unofficially I possessed a light calibre Mauser pistol, along with a few rounds of 2.2 mm ammo, to accompany me while ashore in a strange country... just in case. We never ever had occasion to even think about using them. But they did provide a feeling of security of sorts when on occupied soil.

There weren't any pubs in Norway, not as we knew them.

Norwegians were supposed to be abstainers. But you could have fooled us, When it came to the bit they liked our beer and our spirits every bit as much as we did. Once we got the lie of the land, we finished up in a Norwegian home. The man of the house, I think his name was Nils, was a dockyard fitter while his good lady, called Sonja worked in the dockyard canteen. They were a bit older than us, but like us tried to make the best of the war years. Once the 'old boy' had a bellyful of the fry-ups we had scrounged from our *smutje* and few snifters out of our bottles of *Winebrandt* (Brandy) mixed with raw eggs and sugar, he usually finished up sound asleep in his comfy easy chair, snoring his head off in the process.

I hope that after all this time he won't read this account of what went on during his naps as it would have turned his hair grey. His little Missus had an arrangement with some of her pals from the canteen, who would also come in and take part in the proceedings, which followed. One of them, Greta, kept on talking all the time, while I was busy trying to take her attention away from her work. I thought this was what she was jabbering about, because I could understand only very little of her incessant stream of Norwegian. The only time she stopped in her tirades when during her exploration of the upper regions of my leather trousers she encountered something very hard.

No ... No!

Not what you think, it was only my insurance policy... my 2.2 Mauser.

It did seem to put her off one little bit and after a few more tots of egg-laced brandy... *Skol,* Greta... we found other things to occupy our time. And we didn't need an interpreter for that little lot.

Great, great Greta! *Takk* a million!

I wondered whether all the Norsk girls generated so much heat in this cool climate?

But all good things come to an end.

Along with Mouse, Karl Heinz, Philip and two other diesel stokers, I was chosen to accompany the E-motor parts to Bergen, where *Siemens,* the electrical engineering company had a repair-shop. They had the necessary

know-how and the facilities to repair the damage to the windings of our E-motors.
It provided us with a further chance to see a bit more of this strangely beautiful country, although it looks cold enough to freeze the proverbials off a brass-monkey.

Transportation by road in Norway's most difficult terrain of high mountains, large glaciers and deep fjords was hardly up to German *Autobahn* standards. Late in March the only road between Oslo and Bergen was probably still blocked by snow.
Hence, all the bits and pieces, which had to be sent for repair, were loaded on to a couple of railway freight-wagons. Together with a guards-van those were then hitched to a regular passenger train, as it passed Horten on its way to Oslo.
The guards-van was for us, for one CPO, one PO and for us six stokers. Our officer of the second watch, Sub-Lieutenant Karl Boden, or 'Big Karl' to us, was in overall charge of our mob.

Our job was to be on the alert at all times and to discourage any would-be partisans or so-called freedom fighters from trying anything funny. We were told before we left Horten that Bergen was reputed to be the one place where the partisans had been most active. At no time must we forget that we were the dreaded occupation forces in this nominally neutral country. In a way we hoped that we would get some action, otherwise we look pretty foolish the way we were bristling with machine pistols, revolvers and hand-grenades.

The first part of our journey taking us to Oslo was quite straightforward and didn't take much more than an hour. At every stop on the way, we had to leave the train and make sure that nobody got near our freight wagons. Hopping in and out kept us warm and on the ball.
Once we were in Oslo, our wagons had to be shunted from one station to another, to try and hitch a lift on the train to Bergen.
During the shunting we had left the guard's van and joined the freight wagons to guard their precious cargo.

The super-efficient German sappers, who were organising the train-services and our shunting manoeuvres, managed to lose one of our wagons with ***KARO-AS'*** irreplaceable E-motors aboard. Oh, yes. Two men were also missing.
Blast!
We had arrived hours ago and were ready to join the Bergen train, but we could only wonder where they would be found. It wasn't until early on the

next morning, that it was sighted and brought back to join us. Its guards, Mouse and Karl-Heinz were hungry, angry and frozen stiff. Our Sapper comrades had shunted them to a siding and then completely forgotten all about them. And this was probably one of the more minor mistakes in our war effort.

We had hoped to see a little more of the Norwegian Capital, but because of the lost time, the only view we got of it was from the guard-van windows on the way out. Let's pray that we have more luck on our return journey.

`The next part of our trip turned out to be a bit more eventful than we thought. The one source of energy, which in Norway was in more than plentiful supply, was hydroelectric power. But up to this time in 1945 none of the very few train-routes had been electrified. As in the past, they still depended on steam-power. Since there was little or no coal available in this country, the second largest natural reserve of power had to be used. Soft wood was an almost unlimited source of energy and what was more, it grew conveniently all along the side of the railway track.

It wasn't the most efficient way of raising steam.

The engine gobbled-up an awful lot of it, in order to raise enough steam pressure in the boiler. The tender behind the engine could only hold so much. To provide more wood along the railway line required a lot of planning and organisation and even more muscle-power, as we were to find out. For us guards it meant, that after travelling only a few miles along the track through the fir trees, we had to put down our machine-pistols and other guns and roll-up our sleeves to replenish the tender with pre-cut wood from the heaps at the side of the track. This wood had been cut and stacked by invisible hands. Only at some points did we see those invisible hands, namely Soviet Prisoners of War. They didn't seem too worried about missing all the fun at the eastern front and who could blame them?

Looking about us on those enforced stops, I couldn't help thinking... if ever I become a POW, please let it be in wonderful surroundings like those right here in the centre of the picturesque, rugged Norsk Mountains. The sheer ruggedness of them took this young man's breath away.

'Stop dreaming you fool,' I told myself.

There were other things to look at and to admire.

While we sweated at loading wood, even though the temperature was not much above freezing point, we had shed our jackets and our shirts. But as soon as we did that, we were cheered on by a crowd of young girls, probably students, who were travelling in one of the leading carriages of our train. They weren't allowed to leave their coach, but they certainly looked a bit of all right to our eyes as they pressed against the windows. This was another case of 'look but don't touch'.

After passing the highest point of the long uphill trek, down we went... freewheeling... all the way to our destination in Bergen. Here, having delivered the vital parts of our ***KARO-AS*** to the *Siemens* factory for them to do their bit, we had several days to kill.

We had been allocated sleeping quarters at the base of the 11th U-boat Flotilla. Now came our chance to do a spot of sightseeing.

In a funny sort of way we felt quite at home in Bergen. Not long ago this town was one of the strongholds of German Hanseatic league, whose trade had monopolized Bergen in the last few centuries.

All this was news to us and but it came home to us after we had visited the local museums. But the most noticeable thing about Norway in general, and Bergen in particular, was the fact that fish played a major role in Norway's economy. You didn't have to go very far along any of the harbour-side street to smell them. At the local fish market called the *torget*, we invested quite a few *Kroners* in *gravlaks*, otherwise known as cured and salted salmon.

Needless to say it was as cheap as it was delicious!

And it was a welcome change from our normal fare.

But even far away from the *torget*, the stink of *Fisk* followed us around. In front of all the wooden, high-fronted houses, which lined the streets adjacent to the harbour, fish (*Klippfisk*) had been strung-up to dry, like knickers on a washing-line. Besides salting, this was another method of preserving surplus fish, to be used at times when fishing was impossible because of bad weather. Strung up by their tails, their mouths gaping wide open, this picture of Bergen will stay with me forever.

We didn't have tourist-guides to advise us where to go to find any of the places of note in Bergen. We had to blunder our own way around the town. On the way from the fish-market we happened to pass by the station of a funicular railway, which seemed to go up into the very low clouds.

Oh yes, I forgot, since arriving here it had rained almost incessantly. This was another piece of wisdom we were to acquire - Bergen was the wettest place in the whole of Scandinavia. Babies in Bergen were born with webbed feet, or so the story went.

We were nearly as wet as we could ever be, but our curiosity took us to the ticket-office and here we paid a few *Kroners* to get a lift to the top. The *Floien* hill was one of the seven hills on which Bergen was built. To just over 350 m, we went up in the single carriage. One of the men operating the *Floybanen*, a cable-railway, did tell us that this was the oldest one in the whole of Scandinavia and he also assured us that it had a 100% safety record up to now.

Even now in the depth of war, this trip appeared to be quite a popular excursion for the local people. In spite of the misty conditions and the extremely poor visibility there were quite a number of passengers going up. The whole trip took only some ten minutes and during this time we got a taste of what it must be like to fly blindfolded.

At our arrival at the top, through the mist, we could see a restaurant not far from the terminus. We would call here for some refreshments before attempting the drop back into the town. The rain had stopped and not long after our arrival the mist lifted and was replaced by brilliant sunshine. Sitting on one of the many benches it seemed as if a veil had been lifted from our eyes.

In front of us, literally at our feet, lay what appeared to be a toy-town. One of my colleagues had picked up several postcards and with their help, we were able to identify several of the larger buildings in the town and some of the churches. All were arranged neatly around the inner harbour, the *Vagen,* which dominated the panoramic view in front of us.

It was little wonder that the Bergen folk flocked here to admire the view.

Further out from the centre, at the outer edges of the town, were ranges of hills and mountains, some even higher than the one we were standing on. Beyond the wooden buildings of the town, the sun was now mirrored in the clear waters of the *Puddefjorden* to the left and the *Byfjorden* to the right. Behind those fjords, in the far distance, we could just about see lots of islands scattered along the horizon; a picture postcard view of Norway.

By the time we had finished admiring the panorama from up here, the restaurant had closed for the day. So it only remained for us to make our way back to the town.

Dropping down in the car, I felt like covering my eyes. As we were already halfway down, my stomach appeared to be still at the top. It was reluctant to follow me. The entire downward journey felt like jumping from an aeroplane... without a parachute.

A week went by.

It had mainly been spent sightseeing and playing cards. Right throughout our time in Bergen, the feared resistance movement must have had their holidays. We didn't detect any sign of them, nor did we hear any reports of any mischief caused by their activity. The way the war was going for us,

you would have thought they would have stepped-up their work.
Then came the news that one set of windings was ready and that we were ordered to return to Horten immediately and not wait for the repair of the other set.
WHY?

As soon as we made-fast in Horten with our wagonload of electric's, we learned what had been happening during the last few days
Bad new followed bad news.
The first bombshell dropped when we learned that on this day the Instrument of surrender, whatever that meant, came into force, after which cease-fire orders had gone out to all German armed forces, including all U-boats.
What on earth had gone wrong?

And why were we so blissfully unaware of the seriousness of our position? Allied troops had fought their way over the Rhine and well into Germany.
My hometown Berlin was under siege from the Russians.
Adolph Hitler had asked our *Grossadmiral* Dönitz to take over his position as Head of State.
After this, confirmation had arrived that our Führer Adolph Hitler had died in his bunker.
This was the end.

When I was at home only a few months ago, there had been no indication of how rapidly our forces would cave-in in face of the Allied onslaught.
But cave-in they did.
And this was why we now faced our day of reckoning.
Assembled on the quarterdeck the crew of ***KARO-AS*** was listening to the words of her captain, the Old Man, as he read out the latest signal he had received from the Commander in Chief of our Navy, the Grand-Admiral 'Papa' Karl Dönitz.

'My U-boat men!
Six years of war lie behind us. You have fought like lions. An overwhelming material superiority has driven us into a tight corner, from which it is no longer possible to continue the war. Unbeaten and unblemished, you lay down your arms after a heroic fight without parallel. We proudly remember our fallen comrades who gave their lives for Führer and Vaterland.
Comrades! Preserve the spirit in which you have fought so long and so

gallantly, for the future of the Fatherland.
Long live Germany!
Your Großadmiral.'

Haltingly, our Old Man struggled to read out those words, 'from which it is no longer possible to continue the war.'
To older members of the crew this may not have come as too great surprise. But tears were in my eyes, I, who was still a teenager. This was utter defeat and shame, a result none of us had ever contemplated, not even in our wildest dreams. We were still steadfast in our belief that we had been fighting for a just cause in defence of our country.
Our Commander in Chief had graciously acknowledged that we had done all that could have been expected of us.

During the hours following this announcement the inside of the boat was like a morgue.
It would take time to sink in fully, before we would find the energy to think of what was to happen next.
I wouldn't like to be in the Old Man's shoes at a time like this, I thought. He was the man who had to decide the next step.
But before he could have come to any firm decisions, another signal from the *Großadmiral* arrived, reminding all CO's to strictly follow the terms of the armistice and surrender our U-boats to the Allies. Detailed instructions were also issued for all U-boats at sea to immediately surface and display a black or dark blue flag and thus surrender to any Allied ship or plane or to head for the nearest Allied port.

Together with all other boats, which were not at sea at the time, ***KARO-AS*** was ordered to stay put and await further orders.
Consternation and confusion reigned among our crew.
This condition imposed on us by the Allies was no way to treat men who did their duty to their country in a honourable way, but was designed to humiliate them.

I would have been happy to join a few senior members of crew who were in favour of ignoring this last signal, as obviously it had been sent under duress. We were prepared to run the gauntlet of the British blockade to take the boat to some neutral country or die in the effort.
The majority however, at the sensible advice of the Commandant, agreed that the time for being heroes had long since passed.

Hotheads were reminded that ***KARO-AS***, which had lost both electric motors as well as having a untried snorkel, was unable to run under water and would therefore be a sitting duck to any broken down Allied ship.
And ask yourselves: Of what value would our already outdated boats be to anybody?'

We become extremely attached to the old tub, as she had been our home from home for some considerable time. Between us, we shared lots of adventures, some of them hilarious, others not very funny at all. We had looked after her and cosseted her and up to now she had lived up to her lucky playing-card-sign and not let us down either.
The truth behind the orders of our C in C came out much later.
The order to surrender our boats countermanded the standing orders in operation at the time, which was named 'Operation Rainbow'. In the case of the unthinkable happening, it called for the scuttling of all boats honourably and with all flags flying.

Karl Dönitz, however, had been forced to bargain the surrender of the remaining U-boat fleet intact, in order to gain the Allies' permission to continue for a few days more the evacuation of refugees from the eastern parts of the Baltic. Fleeing from the advancing Russian troops, hundreds of thousand civilians, mostly women and children, were picked-up and shipped to safety to the West by an Armada of small and large ships.

If we had known this at the time, we would have been only too pleased to know that to the end, ***KARO-AS*** had shown her worth by helping our boss to save the lives of many of our countrymen, women and children.

CHAPTER FIFTEEN

Completely and utterly lost!
This is our penalty for loosing the war.

What is going to happen to us?
When would we be allowed to go home?
Our families - are they still alive?
If they fled before the advancing enemies, where are they now?
How much are the Allies going to bleed us this time?
The Old Man didn't know any of those answers, nor did any one else at the base.
We just prayed for more information or even instructions.

It was therefore just as well that we could still get on with our work, if for no other reason than to pass away the waiting time. A few of us busied ourselves on the starboard E-motor, refitting the repaired windings we collected in Bergen. At least ***KARO-AS*** would be a real submarine again, ready to run submerged - if only limping on one leg and at half power. Others were carrying on with their usual daily tasks.

What fate awaits us - May 1945 - Horton.

Every oil reservoir was topped-up, every grease nipple was greased and every bit of brass or copper was polished, as were the lenses of the periscopes and binoculars. In fact, it seemed as if life was just going on, ignoring the happenings of the last few days but with one vital difference; we didn't have a clue why we were doing it.

Habit?

I suppose so.

After all, we are still professionals and we have retained our pride. The words of our C in C rang in my ears, '...unbeaten and unblemished you lay down your arms...'.

So, we were not minded to let him down and allow indiscipline or laziness to creep in.

We had a reputation to keep up.

During this time, our officers had busied themselves with destroying any 'secret' materials, such as codebooks for the *Enigma* machines or other written orders. Even now, when it scarcely mattered, everybody instinctively tended to do things by the book... 'Nothing of use to the enemy must be allowed to fall into his hands.'

On the next day, with this in mind, our Old Man ordered ***KARO-AS*** to cast-off and to sail into one of the neighbouring fjords, I think it was called

Drammen Fjord. All the crewmembers that were not on watch were allowed to sit on deck and admire the picturesque setting. This was everyman's dream of cold but extremely beautiful Norway, with the sun blazing down on the mirror-like water.

As far as the eye could see there was nothing man-made in sight. There was only nature, nothing but stark, barren nature. This idyllic place was to be the setting for our last fling!

The Old Man manoeuvred ***KARO-AS*** into a position, where she was facing the rocks, which towered high above the water on both sides of the fjord. Satisfied with the boat's position, some 1,500 m away from the rocks, he gave the order to start shooting practice – not with dummies this time but with real live torpedoes. The resulting noise reverberated round the steep walls of the fjord; it was truly something to remember for a long time afterwards.

To add to the din made by the exploding *Aale*, we had a homemade fireworks display, made by the tracer ammunition of our three AA-guns. We had imaginary Tommy kites in our sights, while aiming into the side of the rocks.

This exercise had the effect of easing the tension we all felt after the fateful news had hit us a few days ago.

The sight of our 2 cm and 3.7 cm tracer-rounds splashing against the granite walls, made this sunny day seem even brighter. The result was a fireworks display of a magnitude never before seen in these fjords.

Our sea-charts didn't show it, but it seemed that there was a road running along the top of the rocks ahead of us. It became clear to us only, when we noticed an open lorry rumbling along and getting nearer. With the help of our binoculars, we confirmed that it carried a group of Norwegian soldiers. As if by accident, some of tracers seemed to veer-off to just above them. It was only meant to be a bit of a joke, but we didn't expect it to have such an electrifying effect. The soldiers jumped off the truck and ran for cover, leaving the lorry to run on until it stopped nose-down in a ditch.

Oh Dear!

Not long afterwards we ran out of ammo, which was the signal to set sail back to our base. The Old Man hugged the side of the fjord nearest to the road to keep out of sight of any nosy parkers. Here we had a good look at the damage done to the rocks by our bombardment. In fact, there was barely a scratch to be seen anywhere, you would have thought we had peppered it with nothing more than a peashooter. While our luck held, another boat stationed at Horten wasn't quite so fortunate. As part of their attempt to get rid of all things explosive, they tried to ditch a box full of small devices which were to be use only if the normal depth gauges packed-up.

They looked just like a little bomb with fins at the end. They were about 15 to 20 cm in length worked like this. Dropping them into the water while starting a stopwatch they sank at a constant speed until on hitting the seabed they set of a small explosion. Timing the interval from the time they hit the water until you heard the bang, allowed you to establish the depth under the keel of the ship. It seems one of those things, after being dropped into the water, floated instead of sinking to the bottom. One careless chap tried to fish it out again when it went off, with the result of him finishing the war with two or three fingers missing.

Back in Horten we found that the Norwegians we had befriended in the past few weeks were nowhere to be seen. It was a pity, but we could understand their position quiet well. But a couple of days later, men in civilian clothes arrived at the gates to the base. They were wearing armbands to show that they believed themselves to be Norwegian soldiers. They were there to accept the surrender of our base. Would you believe it, their leader was Nils, who until recently was working with us at the dockyard and in whose house and with whose wife we had felt quite at home.

Waiting for the arrival of the Royal Navy - May 1945 - Horton.

We explained that we would only surrender our boats to the British Navy, whenever they would turn up in the Oslo Fjord.

The pseudo Norsk soldiers either didn't want to take NO for an answer, or else they were unable to understand our simple message, which had been a clear invitation to move on from here. But once the A.A.guns on the bridge of our boat were lined-up on them, they accepted the fact that we had no intention of falling into the same trap as some of the German guards at one of the Russian POW camps near Oslo, who allowed themselves to be relieved of their duties by Norwegians. Those Norwegians made the mistake of their lives by releasing the numerous Soviet PoWs. As one could have expected, those men, who had been shut-up for a long, long time, went to town in a big way. Looting some of the German stores they managed to lay their hands on a few bottles of Akevit, which was alcohol was distilled from wood. This terrible, almost undrinkable concoction would make even the quietest of men go berserk. They duly went on a rampage, raping and looting to their hearts content. Nobody had the power to deal with them. The SOS, which went out from the local *Burgomaster* to the disbanded German Command, to re-capture or at least to control the Russians, met with blank faces. 'You will have to do it yourselves or just wait until the Allies get here.
Our war is definitely at an end.'

However it wasn't so very long before the British Navy arrived in force. With their arrival we were able to surrender the boring job of guarding the base. It should have been the end of our stint, but after handing in our handguns and automatic weapons, we were asked to stay at our posts by the gates to the base, in company with armed British seamen.
Unusual circumstances throw-up unusual situations!

I was sure of one thing. I wish to hell that I had been taught English at school. When my next stint on guard duty came, the Tommy pointed at his chest and said 'Me Lofty'. To my surprise, this lad seemed eager to talk. He garbled on a bit, pointing at himself and then at me, in a sort of questioning way. Eventually the penny dropped with me. He wanted to know my name. I said *'Ich bin Spinne'* which of course didn't mean a thing to him. But with the help of a piece of paper and a pencil stub I managed to draw a fair likeness of a Spider.

Having sorted out the introductions, we managed to get some sort of conversation going. Drawings with pencil on paper and by doing a bit of 'Charade' type miming, he seemed to say that he was pleased that the shooting war was over and what we should be doing is to get drunk together to celebrate not having to fight each other any more.

Although the English language was a closed book to me, I was able to follow his story reasonably well. I was helped in this by his repetitive use of the same or similar words, all of which began with the letter F. I gathered that he was more than delighted to be going home to his girl friend Penny. He mimed what he intended to do to her when he got there. Having admired her photo, the one in which she was wearing something which might have vaguely passed for a swimsuit, I couldn't blame him for feeling randy. My Irmchen, if she were still in one piece, would probably have to wait a little longer for similar attention.

Officially, the history dealing with those days in 1945 would undoubtedly fail to mention what really happened then, particularly when British and German sailors first made their acquaintance when there was no further need for shooting each others heads off.

As far as propaganda on both sides was concerned, we were meant to hate each other's guts and on British orders, fraternisation was completely out of the question. This goes to prove that whoever gave those orders, whether they were Admirals or politicians, hadn't a clue about human nature.

I wished I could have asked Lofty, 'what on earth is everybody afraid of? Are they worried that you might find out that in reality we are not so different?' All my colleagues and I were very keen to see what our ex-opponents were made of - to see whether the things we heard about them were true. To judge by their body language, the Royal Navy was just as anxious to discover if we really had horns.

Anyway, after our two-hour stretch, Lofty wanted us to go ashore, to find a pub and have a beer or two. I had the devil's own job to explain to him that Norwegians have funny ideas with regard to strong drink. It was almost impossible to buy any on the open market.

Hence I told him of much better idea.

I invited him to join me in a drink on board ***KARO-AS***.

As far as I was concerned, the time for keeping secrets from the enemy had passed and as far as availability of booze was concerned, we had stowed away a few assorted bottles, in fact enough to drown our sorrows twice over. U-boats had thousands of little places in which to hide things. Behind pipes and valves, in bilges and even inside ventilation ducts, which ran the full length of the vessel, all sorts of forbidden fruits were stowed after we had raided and almost emptied the main stores at the base. We had no intention of letting the Norwegians or anybody else get their filthy mitts on the precious stuff. However, getting to know our ex-enemy was an important enough occasion to unearth a bottle or two.

Lofty obviously needed support, so he had persuaded his mate Mick to tag along. Like Lofty, and for that matter like myself, he was also off-duty for another four hours.
Under the cover of twilight I managed to slip them aboard.
I didn't bother to report our arrival to anybody, least of all to our petty officer of the watch. Instead, I got them to slide quietly down the open hatch to our mess in the stern torpedo department.
I had rightly assumed that all our superiors would be far too busy anaesthetising themselves with strong drink to blot out their own thoughts of misery. Most of my crewmates were lazing on their bunks, some were snoring their heads off, sleeping-off the first few rounds of drink. Others were reading or finishing off the evening meal.
Once installed in our cramped quarters, sitting on the edges of my bunk, my two RN friends were blending in with our surroundings quite beautifully. Their working gear was not unlike ours, and in one respect, it was identical. The smell of diesel oil emanating from them advertised the fact, that they were artificers just like us.

But they, being fully paid-up members of the British Navy, who had proved their mettle at Constantinople, Copenhagen and other theatres of war, were utterly unprepared for the vile taste of the Norwegian lighter-fuel called *Akevit* or *Finsprit.* Made mainly from fermented potatoes, like most other concoctions, it was an acquired taste. But by the time it was diluted with orange-juice or even coffee, it could safely be taken by mouth without any harmful effect on one's stomach lining.
But it did make you glow! After one or two nips the world seemed a much better place.

By the time our guests had to get back for their next stint of guard duty, we had been through a few choruses of 'Lili Marlene' and shanties such as 'Molly Malone' and 'What shall we do with the drunken sailor'.
We got Lofty and Mick back in plenty of time but in spite of keeping our eyes open for them over the next day or two, it was the last time we ever saw either of them - bless them!
Perhaps the authorities had cottoned on to the fact, that in spite of everything, sailors learn to get round the rules. From one of my friends from the 1st division, I learned of a party of mixed ex-enemies, who had gone ashore and where a restaurant owner who refused entry to Germans was asked to change his mind or to witness the Royal Navy in action inside his place.
Some days later, near the end of May, the seemingly eternal waiting ended.
The order had arrived to sail ***KARO-AS*** to England and, as our Old Man

understood it, the same order applied to all the other U-boats still afloat. Well! Well! Well!

Are we going to finish up at the bottom of the sea like our 1914/1918 comrades, after being sold out to the enemies -

Why hadn't we been allowed to scuttle the boats?

When questioned, the Old Man didn't know either.

But since the orders came directly from the U-boat High Command, perhaps even from Dönitz himself, he and all of us had to go along with whatever they decided.

If the boats had to be taken to Britain, it was quite obviously a job for the engineering crewmembers, which were able to cope with the mechanical intricacies of ***KARO-AS***.

It followed that a skeleton crew of approximately half of our original complement would consist of diesel stokers, electricians and us, the control room personnel. Lined up behind the conning tower, our Old Man explained the procedure to us.

This is the last time we are together as a U-boat crew.
Tomorrow, only a few of us take the boat on her trip to Scapa.

'You will have to decide whether you want to disembark here and await further orders about your journey to Germany, or join me in a short trip to Old *Engelland* (Land of the Angels?)'
He couldn't give us a lot of time to make up our minds.
What did I have to lose?
I was more or less homeless, as slit-eyed Tartars had overrun Berlin and I didn't have a wish to meddle with them.
Were my family alive or were they dead?

It therefore seemed a reasonable thing to do, to take a good look at the 'Land of Hope and Glory'. We could also weigh-up the people we had been fighting during the past five years. In any case, our Old Man assured us that we would soon be back home again, certainly in a few weeks or so.
Like a dope, I kept my 100 per cent record of taking a step forward every time volunteers were asked for.
The Old man thus formed a new slim-line crew.
He picked himself and the *2WO* to head it. Our Chief picked himself and persuaded the Diesel, Control-room and the E-room CPOs to come along, as well as several of the engineering POs. They in their turn picked twelve of us stokers from the volunteers, to help man the engine- and control rooms. Even after adding a couple of seamen as lookouts and helmsmen, the new crew was less than half of the original size but there were enough of us to sail this little lady to her next destination. Staying behind, unfortunately, were several of my colleagues who had been my constant companions during the past two years.

We had been together 'In sickness and in health' - so to speak - but not until now had I realised how very close we had become to one another.
Karl Heinz was probably the only engineer who wanted to get back home as quickly as possible. At a guess, his 'ladies' of the red-light district on *St.Pauli's Reeperbahn* would by now be coining it in with the occupation forces, maybe only for pair of nylons, a few fags or a tin or two of bully beef.
Perhaps he thought he was missing out on that deal?

And then, there was my former archenemy, torpedo-mixer Walter. He also had other fish to fry. He could foresee an awful lot of profit to be made from his factory in the western half of Berlin, in helping to rebuild the economy of our country. He and I had many angry brushes in the past, caused probably by the social gulf between the factory-owners son and the son of a dustman. Because we were of roughly equal age, rank and intelligence, we were most of the time competing with each other to be top-dog

in the stern-torpedo room. As time went on, we had come to appreciate each other and although I would never have admitted it - up to then in any case - I had developed a sneaking liking for this bloody toad.
I learned in an oblique sort of way that this was definitely a mutual feeling. When we spent our last evening together, fortified by few drinks, he offered me a job for life in his establishment once I managed to get back. I was sure it wasn't just the drink, which induced him to actually say 'If you come in with me, I'll see that you're all right!'
The bastard nearly had me in tears, and I, for my part, sincerely hoped that he would find his factory still in one whole piece among all the devastation in Berlin.

Wilhelm, on whose farm I had the best ride of my life, was eager to find his parents and his childhood sweetheart Hildegard. He hoped that they had been lucky and had managed to flee from their farm near Stettin before the Russians had overrun their idyllic place in the country.
In a way I felt desperately sorry for him. He never touched alcohol and so, unlike us, was unable to blot out any of his darkest thoughts. He was probably just as sorry for us, as he drew his strength from a different and much deeper source - his religion. The lucky sod found all sorts of reasons for being hopeful and tranquil in spite of whatever he might find on his return. Well, all I could ask him to do when he finally found his family was to give them my regards and thank them for providing me with a few happy moments.

'And should you find your Hilde again, I ask you to give her a great big kiss from me and thank her for a lovely time aboard Walt and Herb, the two most wonderful Hanoverians I ever had the pleasure to have between my legs.
And for heavens sake - marry the poor girl!'
I knew from personal experience that Hilde could be relied upon to make him, or in fact anybody else, very, very, very happy!

Throughout the length of ***KARO-AS*** there were similar farewell drinking sessions taking place. Once, when I had to make my way to the galley to fetch a fresh pot of coffee, I even saw our Chief and the once hated *1WO* talking quite amicably, with Klaus Peter's arm round the Erhard's shoulder. Heaven knows what they had found to have in common all of a sudden - the non-political perfectionist engineer and the fervently believing Hitler Youth leader?
Through the fog of the drink, however, I realised that we could never have gone through all our many adventures together and stayed in one piece,

were it not for being able to rely implicitly on each other, irrespective of rank, age or experience.

But where was the man who had put the original crew together and moulded it into a unit that came up to his extremely high professional standards? Where do think he was?

He was sound asleep on his bunk. He was sleeping soundly in the knowledge that, in reality, his job had been completed in a satisfactory way. He had taken-over a new U-boat together with a mishmash of individuals and successfully kneaded them into a professional fighting machine, to act and to react as one, a unit which had proved its worth in action. The traumatic experience, when finally he had to stand in front of his men to read-out the details of Germany's defeat and convey to us the last orders from the Grand-Admiral, appeared to have turned him into a really old man overnight.

By now, however, he seemed to have recovered and regained his old self-confidence.

There was absolutely nothing of which he had to be ashamed. Sleeping as he was, he was gathering his strength for the last sortie in his proud ***KAROAS***.

The time had come to say farewell to our many comrades who were to stay behind. Would we ever see each other again?

There wasn't a Brass band to see us off and also missing were the beautiful maidens with their bouquets of flowers.

But the cheers of our mates on the quayside made this farewell just as poignant and memorable as any farewell of the past when leaving for an enemy patrol.

There were tears in the eyes of supposedly tough-men.

Lets get going before we break down completely.

We were now in the last days of May.

The grey water of the North Sea was almost flat, with only a few ripples here and there distorting the mirror-like surface. Looking towards the East, we noticed that the early morning sun had risen just high enough above the horizon to take the chill out of the night air.

Calmly and sedately, our convoy could be seen to plough its way westward.

Only the slightest whiff of a breeze moved the otherwise limp ensign on our Flagstaff.

Two days passed and the third day of our passage from Norway started just as quietly. A few minutes ago, after a six-hour stint on duty, the skeleton port-watch had taken over our stations.

'Hell! Am I hungry? I could eat a horse', I thought. In fact, it was difficult to decide what should be done first. Cleaning out the bilges had made me greasy and dirty and it would require a fair amount of scrubbing to get rid of the filth. Apart from that, the warm bunk kept beckoning.

But first things first!

Washing, eating and sleeping, all that had to wait. As usual, I was gasping for a smoke. Even now, smoking below deck was too risky because of the ever-present battery-gases.

It became a race between my colleagues and me to see who could get up upstairs first. I made it by a short head, lit up and had my first drag on a cigarette. As well as the officer and a couple of lookouts going about their normal business, there were now six stokers manning the bridge. Leaning over the lee-side rails, we were able inhale deeply and puff away to our hearts content.

After the customary bout of coughing, which brought tears to our eyes, we were able to appreciate the lovely weather and to take an interest in our surroundings. All around us other vessels provided us with company. A few hundred metres ahead of us, a small escort vessel led the way. Following us, much the same distance abaft, was the next U-boat. Apart from our ship, another eleven made up our convoy. Only nine of us had left Horten. Somewhere along the way we must have been joined by the other three vessels, which were now acting as our escorts. Quietly we steamed in each other's wake, with the exception of two of the escorts. They had a great time rushing around. Darting back and forth, they behaved more like mother hens looking after their playful and naughty chicks.

But yesterday they also showed that they had a very nasty peck!

Just moments after the watches had changed over at midday, when Mouse and I were wondering what we ought to be doing, a frantic shout from the bridge made the Old Man jump from his bunk and race up to the bridge. The Chief was close behind him; he must have smelled trouble too.

The steering gear had jammed and had caused ***KARO-AS*** to sheer off to starboard.

'Both engines stop!'

For us, who were below deck during this panic, our Chief explained afterwards. 'As soon as our boat left the formation, the three escorts came haring along with their guns trained on us. They obviously assumed that we were going to make a break for freedom and were set to blow us, unarmed as we were, out of the water.'

Thank goodness that our Old Man knew English and he also knew how

to operate a signal lamp. He sent this message: 'Steering jammed, have stopped engines.' Give Tommy his due! He kept his head, when others would have lost theirs. If our escorts had been Yanks, one could have expected them to shoot first and ask questions later.
But as soon as we got our steering back on 'manual', we were able to fall back into line and everybody stopped panicking.
Good on you Tommy!

Meanwhile The Old Man and his *2WO* on the bridge in front of us had their binoculars trained on the distant horizon. Not that you needed any visual aids to see that perhaps some 6 to 8 km ahead of us, on both the starboard- and on the port-bow, some shadowy shapes had appeared. They looked like bits of Terra Firma. I puzzled whether this was going to be our destination. In a few hours, our trip might be over and, finally, we will be told what the next move is. I thought that it could be a good idea to get rid of this muck and grease and then try to get some chow. With a bit of luck we might even be able to get some sleep before we get to our goddamned destination. Everybody agreed with this sentiment as we went down below. On the way to our quarters, we had to pass the navigation table with all the charts spread out on it. Always nosy, I couldn't resist having a good look at the plotted course. It might give me a clue to where we were heading, but all I could see on this chart was a group of small islands on one side and a piece of mainland on the other. The names of the places on the port side sound very peculiar... Duncansby Head... John o' Groats... Stroma. I couldn't say, that I had ever heard of them before. Equally odd were the names of the islands on the starboard side...
South-Ronaldsay... Burray... Flotta... Hoy...
Oh yes! Of course! Those are parts of the Orkney Islands.

I don't know why, but a loud bell started to rings in my brain! Where on earth had I heard or read something about those Orkneys?
I had to move a set of compasses, a setsquare and a ruler to read what was printed underneath.
What I saw, took my breath away. There were just two words.
'SCAPA FLOW'

CHAPTER SIXTEEN

'SCAPA FLOW'!

The very mention of this locality sent cold shivers down my back. Mouse, who was going aft on his way from the galley, squeezed past me and asked, full of concern, 'Are you all right, pal?' He had noticed that the colour had drained from my face.

There can't be any doubt about it. This must be the notorious part of the world I have read so much about.

'Look here, have you any idea why we're ordered to this place?' I asked him.

'I don't, but then... what does it matter where we're going. Surely any port in England is as good or as bad as the next?'

'I know, but why does it have to be this damn place? Why Scapa Flow?'

Mouse just shrugged his shoulders. 'No need to get so excited, is there?'

I thought that all German sailors would have known the historic link between this place and the German navy. It struck me as quite remarkable that another small fleet of German ships was set to enter the British navy's home base, after the end of yet another world war.

Nobody else but me seemed the least bit bothered about this goddamned place. As I wandered back to our mess and stretched out on my bunk, my thoughts went back to my schooldays, when I watched newsreels about those events of Scapa Flow at the end of the 1914-18 war.

Then, the entire Imperial German fleet of 70 fighting ships had entered this bay on that fateful occasion - and not a single one had ever left again. Undefeated in action, they had become the pawns in a political game. The politicians in Germany were in disarray and struggling to deal with revolution and mutiny by Bolshevik-inspired soldiers and sailors. The Kaiser had abdicated and fled the country just before the Armistice was signed on the 11th November. Naively perhaps, the Admiral of the German fleet, Ludwig von Reuter, expected his fleet to be sailing into temporary internment in a neutral country during the end of hostilities. He had discharged all ammunition and taken on board enough provisions to last for six months, after which the whole fleet, with all their battle flags still flying, set sail into the North Sea - battleships, battle cruisers, light cruisers, destroyers, as well as other units.

It wasn't long, however, before von Reuter came face to face with treachery on a grand scale.

Off the Firth of Forth an even larger fleet of heavily armed American, English and French warships met his ships. They shepherded the unarmed German fleet into this very anchorage that spread out before us, Scapa Flow.

Instead of laying-up in a neutral port, the fleet and its sailors were left here to rot for many months. From a proudly painted battleship grey, the whole fleet slowly turned red with rust until the armistice ran out in June 1919. And then what?

In the absence of any announcement from his government that a peace treaty had been signed, von Reuter had to assume that hostilities would resume. Defenceless and marooned he gave the order to run-up the 'Flag Eleven' on the highest mast of his flagship. This was the prearranged signal for the scuttling of all 70 ships.

With all Imperial flags flying high from the mastheads, the seacocks were first opened and then damaged by sledgehammer blows, so that they could never be closed again.

Consternation reigned among the many sightseers as they sailed through the fleet. They witnessed the hoisting of the German Imperial battle flags on all ships, not as a salute to people watching, but to accompany the ships down to the bottom of the sea. Before their eyes, one by one the German vessels, large and small, started to sink lower and lower into the water. Some sank straight down until only their mastheads were showing above the water line; others turned on their sides and some even turned turtle with their keels reaching for the sky.

Meanwhile the German sailors had taken to their lifeboats. It was then, as the onlookers watched with astonishment and horror, when a few panic stricken British sailors opened fire from their rifles on the unarmed German sailors.

Ten of them died with their hands raised in surrender and 16 more were seriously wounded. The graves of the unlucky ones should still be around here somewhere.

It was not an episode to be proud of, was it, Tommy?

British newspapers howled about German treachery, but many fairer minded people commented. 'If those sailors had been British, everybody would have said how brave they were!'

The circumstances of our arrival in May 1945 were not so very different. This time our convoy consisted only of nine U-boats, none of them larger than 2000 tonnes. But like the Kaiser's fleet before us, we too entered

Scapa Flow escorted by Allied vessels. Also like our comrades in 1918, our ships were sailing in with their flags flying proudly in the breeze.
It was there that the similarities ended.

Flags, as used on the high seas, have many different purposes.
All seafaring nations use them for signalling from ship to ship. For that purpose internationally recognised signalling flags have been in use throughout the world, a different one for every letter of the alphabet, as well as for every number from 0 to 9. Those flags are mostly flown in groups from the mastheads.
But the most important use for a flag on the seas is to identify the ship, which is flying it from a staff on the stern, as belonging to a particular nation or even a particular branch of the armed forces of that nation.

The flag we were flying on our trip from Norway to England was neither of those. Heaven knows whose brilliant idea it had been; it must have been somebody high up in the Allied Command who had an exceptionally warped sense of humour. The flag flapping lustily on ***KARO-AS'*** flagstaff on our trip from Norway was jet-black in colour, just like the universally feared one flown by pirates in days of old. If we'd had the time, we would have added the skull and cross bones.
In a funny sort of way, we felt almost proud to be honoured in such a fashion by our enemy, who had perhaps been just a tiny bit scared of U-boats in general.
But who knows?
I was so engrossed with my thoughts, I didn't realise I was alone in the mess. My mates had all vanished into thin air, presumably to see what was going on up on the bridge.
It was time I followed.

My assumption was confirmed; the gang was hanging over the railings of the lower wintergarden, watching as ***KARO-AS*** followed closely following in the wake of an escorting corvettes. Obviously her job was to shepherd us past the minefields, which surely were still there as deterrents to nosy interfering U-boats and other assorted riff-raff.
Now there was land all around us, as we were guided through a funnel into what appeared to be a large inland lake.
Our charts on the table in the control room had shown that Scapa Flow was surrounded by many separate islands with names such as Hoy, Flotta, South Ronaldsay, Burray, Glims Holm, Lamb Holm and of course the mainland island of Kirkwall. I borrowed a pair of binoculars from the bridge, but search though I might, couldn't see the slightest trace of the

scuttled German ships from the 1914-18 war, or for that matter of the English battleship that was torpedoed by one of our U-boats in 1939. I dare say they were still rotting away down at the bottom of this hole.
R.I.P.

Shortly before noon, we arrived at the centre of the lion's den, when we got the signal to drop anchor. After this, we were told to assemble on deck all handguns and ammunition, which might still be on board, ready to be collected by launch. This made a lot of sense, but since we had had already had our bit of fun way back in the Drammen Fjord, it didn't really apply to us. The order jogged my own memory. I must get rid of my illegally held insurance policy, a 2.2 mm revolver, with which I had felt more comfortable when going ashore in occupied territories.
Unused thankfully, the Mauser and a few other toys like mine, belonging to others among the crew, came to rest beside the big German naval guns of the First World War, at the bottom of the sea.

However, then we received another request, an unreasonable one we thought. It requested us to hand over all alcoholic beverages still on board.
Now here we had a problem that needed thinking about.
There were many bottles of spirits on board, because of mid-night raids on the semi-abandoned stores at the Horten base which we and other thieving Lords had emptied before setting sail three days ago. Most of the stuff was already well hidden, in bilges, in ventilation shafts, under batteries or in other places only accessible to the initiated, of which there were many on a U-boat. We took those precautions, just in case our own officers would disapprove of dishonesty.

Until we were forced to leave our ***KARO-AS*** we intended to keep on numbing our brains, just to forget the nasty bits about our predicament and to savour the adventures awaiting us in England. We thought, if you really want that stuff, Tommy, just you go and find it - if you can.
However, we did make an effort to put up a show. We lined up a few token bottles of almost undrinkable Finsprit along the side of the quarterdeck. However, there was a bit of a problem. When the Royal Navy launch drew up, our honest but clumsy efforts to catch their lines only resulted in knocking those bottles over the side.
All we were trying to do was to be helpful.
Please forgive us. We're ever so sorry, friends!
The ghosts at the bottom would enjoy the stuff as they kept watch over the rotting hulls.

Following that little ado, we didn't have to wait too long to find out what was to happen next. Another launch drew up alongside and a boarding party embarked`. It was made up of one British naval officer and several ratings, all of them bristling with revolvers and machine pistols.
They officially took over the command of our boat.
After striking our black Pirate's flag, the boarding party hoisted one of their own. We now found ourselves on a German U-boat with the tactical sign of ***KARO-AS*** and still manned by men and officers of the *Kriegsmarine*; however the craft was now commanded by a British Lieutenant RNVR and sailing under the White Ensign of the Royal Navy.

Metamorphosed

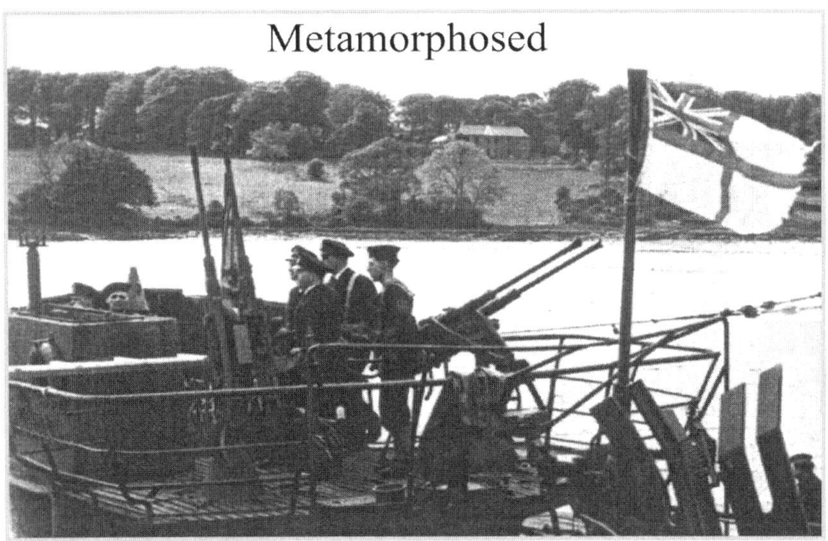

KARO-AS had metamorphosed into the 'Ace of Diamonds'.

And by striking one flag and raising the White Ensign our U-boat became just another submarine. It seems that Mr Churchill had decreed that only German submersibles had to be called U-boats, as they were those dastardly ships, which were sinking all his heroic and brave merchantmen.
Who would have thought that we would get mixed-up in a king-sized farce like this?

Perhaps this was the beginning of a new lease of life for our ship and her crew and perhaps, unthinkable as it might have been, we would sail together into another war against the dreaded Soviet Empire?

For my part, I would have kept up my volunteering-record of stepping forward again if I had been asked politely.
However, more than likely, the whole charade-like enterprise was thought-up and designed to degrade us publicly and to show the world's press, 'Look, what a price we have captured.'
Pictures of our dreaded "Grey Wolves" sailing under the British flag will be flashed around the world and provide a welcome propaganda coup to show how Good has prevailed over Evil.

However, one thing seemed very clear now that our boat and the other ones in our convoy were not yet to be added to the already overcrowded underwater scrap-yard of Scapa Flow!
Up Anchor! Engines at half ahead, we were under way again.
But where will we go next?
Those provisions brought on board by the matelots seemed to indicate a very long trip, perhaps even America?
Surely not!
Moreover, the hilarity was not finished yet.

The British sailors went around the boat looking as jumpy as cats on a hot tin roof.
Heavens knows what they had been told about us?
Whatever it was, they freely waved their weapons around as if, at the slightest provocation, they meant to use them. However, that gave the impression that they were scared of their own shadows.
They even secured a thick chain through the hatch of the conning tower. This ploy was obviously designed by someone sitting comfortably behind a desk, to stop any attempt by us to make a submerged getaway.
But why on earth would we want to do that, after dutifully, and at the behest of our own High Command sailing our boats all the way from Norway.
It failed to make a lot of sense.

For answers to questions regarding our own future and that of our boat, we would have to wait a little while longer, at least until we reach our next port of call. In the meantime we would carry-on with our normal routine of running an orderly ship as if nothing had happened.
Our Old Man stayed on the bridge most of the time, but the IIWO and our Chief seemed to have retired, perhaps even started to do a spot of packing
From the our *Kombüse* wafted the smell of some activity, because whatever there was in store for us, we would be much better equipped to deal with a full stomach. Our newly appointed cook, helmsman Friedrich, had taken the place of our original *Smutje*, who had decided to stay in Norway, to

nurse the injuries he had sustained in our aborted snorkel try-out. Fritz had succeeded in preparing an excellent meal; after all, why hang on to the remaining supplies? In fact, every meal on this present trip had been a semi-feast, followed by strong coffee served in great big 10 litre pots. In normal circumstances alcohol was strictly taboo during patrols on the high seas, except on very rare occasions, when the Old Man issued the occasional bottle of beer. However, since this was not an every-day sort of patrol, it just so happened that behind the back of our officers and away from the prying eyes of our boarding party, our coffee was slightly tampered with and might have been labelled '50% Proof'.

Our guard watched with interest, perhaps even a bit enviously, as we set about our meal. Having finished it, and after enjoying some of the beautiful coffee, we started to feel ever so warm inside. We even felt brave enough to try to make some sort of human contact with the stranger behind the gun, who was standing in front of the chart-table. In fact, he didn't look all that much different from us; perhaps he was a little bit older and more experienced than any of us here in the control room.

In fact he looked very much at home in a submarine.

Since leaving Scapa Flow he has watched with interest the way we operated this mechanical wonder and perhaps realised already that we weren't here to cause problems for him.

We had some previous experience in meeting British sailors while still in Norway and had formed the opinion that there was some indefinable type of affinity between the sailors of all nations. It could be that this stemmed from the days of old, when multi-national crews manned sailing ships. Their main enemy has always been the wily, unpredictable high sea.

We must try and establish whether this imaginary bond also applied to our guards. To start the ball rolling we tempted him to look at certain types of photographs. Pictures, we had acquired from fellow Japanese sailors and which we normally kept hidden from the unappreciative eyes of our superiors.

Still staying at arm's length, he seemed to relax a little when he recognised and even approved of the female forms.

My mate Mouse observed casually 'Well, well, well! At least there is one thing we all seem to have in common. I wonder whether their food also contains bromide to contain their virility?'

Having made a good start to our attempt to break down barriers, and after a he made a half-hearted show of resistance, we even managed to get the Tommy to accept a mug of our steaming coffee.

'Du trink Kaffee, yes? Ist werry gut!
He threw up his arms in a play of horror;
'No-no-no; and continuing with words we didn't understand and miming to indicate that the officer on the bridge had strictly forbidden fraternisation of any kind with Germans and certainly not to touch any of our food or drink. We thought we did understand much of what he indicated, but it didn't stop us from trying again.
'Kaffee ist werry gut.' We followed this with gestures and words, attempting to make him see that his officer was not here and could neither hear nor see us.
'See! We trink, yes?'
'No - No - No! I will go to jail!'
'Vot ist Jale?' I didn't have a clue what he meant.
This mixed-up conversation went on for some time. Watching us drink from the same pot and detecting no visible ill effects in us, he finally showed some interest.
'OK, Fritz, you win, but only a little.'
'Brrrrrrr... bless me!!!'
'What's in this crummy stuff, methylated or potato spirit?'
Mind you, although he spluttered, he didn't offer to spit out one drop if it. After only a few mouthful his mood lightened as I asked him with my newly acquired knowledge of the English language: 'Ist werry gut, No?'
His German had also improved 'It is very good Kaffee, Ja!'

Continuously looking over his shoulder and watching for anybody coming down from the bridge, he indicated that he could do with a little more. He even went as far as to suggest that we would drink a toast in coffee to the end of the hated war. And he also suggested what should be done to every one of the world leaders who got us into this mess.

The fact that every sentence of his was sputtered with words, which meant little or nothing to us at that time, but which we assumed were taboo swear words, inserted to make his speech more real. We had some previous experience of the spicy words used by hardened sailors when we met the British Navy in Norway. Who could blame anybody for calling a spade a spade, after enduring the last few years of a dreadful war, when you didn't know what would happen to you in the next few minutes, hours or days. Our own German vocabulary had also grown considerably since joining up.

In any case, in a funny way we felt quite pleased and honoured, that our newfound friend spoke to us in the same way, and with the same punctuations as he spoke to his mates. We felt he treated us as like equals and he acquired our respect for that.

Mind you, he could also speak a different kind of English when answering his officers. We were to learn much later that this was called the King's English, and sounded as if the speaker had a plum in his mouth. Sailors only used it reluctantly in circumstances when Ladies were present.

Later, when it was time to change over watch, we briefed our opposite numbers on what had taken place since Scapa.

Our guard, who we now knew as Bill, handed his duties over to one of his mates. My pal Mouse and I hoped that they would get along as well as we had done in furthering international relations. As far as we were to gather later, they got on just as well with Jock, Bill's mate.

Later on Bill produced some of his family photos and some of his home and we could only wonder why on earth two nations with so many similarities could fight each other.

Ours is not to wonder why!.

He followed that with a photo of a small warship and in word and mime told us how a U-boat torpedoed him and how afterwards he spent some time in the water.

Talk of embarrassment on our faces!

'It couldn't have been us' we assured him; 'we were in the Indian Ocean at that time.'

He didn't seem to hold it against us anyway. However, he did take a considerable interest in our boat to see what sort it was that caused his discomfort.

Our new CO did come down on one occasion, in order to use our toilet. As mentioned before, the heads, as the toilets on a sea-going sub were called, differed substantially from other ones elsewhere on land or sea.

To begin with, our two heads, which were thought to be sufficient for the entire crew of 70 men, were really only designed for use during surface travel. Even then, like everything else on our ship, they were located some distance below the actual water line. It follows that it was utterly impractical to just pull the chain and walk away.

So it was essential to familiarise yourself with the peculiarities of our "station of need".

The ingenious method adopted to overcome this tricky problem was as follows. After normal use of the facility and after opening a certain valve, the pan was emptied into a holding tank. Next closing that first valve and opening another one, you hand-pumped the contents outboard against the water-pressure; not forgetting to return all the valves to their original positions. In the interest of hygiene and cleanliness and to ensure that everybody left the heads as they found them, every user had then to sign a register.

Then the facility was ready again for use by its next customer.

This tried and proven system was ever so simple!

And what is more, every man jack, from the Captain down to lowliest sailor, was obliged to do the above task without any outside assistance.

It was everybody for himself when it came to eating the same food and to attend to one's other personal needs; after all, it was only fair!

But you try and explain this procedure to someone, who doesn't speak your language.

I drew the short straw and it fell to me to explain this system to the young officer. I just got through the whole performance by miming and sign language and tried to get on my way, when he seemed to get very angry, indicating that I should do the job for him. Now I had a real problem, do as he says or risk being shot down like a dog.

However, it was my lucky day. Just as things got ugly, our Chief happen to come along and quickly defused the situation by explaining to the Lieutenant the facts of life. And like a good man, after asking our Chief to explain the procedure again, he finished his business.

I had made my way back to my station but I wondered whether he managed to get everything in the right order. Many of us had learned the hard way by forgetting that at 2 m below the water line there was enough pressure from outside to throw the content of that pan back at you if you happened to open the outside valve before closing the inner one. As a result we were baptised again, but not with holy water.

After telling my mates all about my little ado, Mouse put his finger on it by stating: 'I should have thought the Royal Navy would have briefed their young officers a little better before sending them out on a man's job of bringing in a German U-boat.

All this took place, while the Ace of Diamonds was quietly moving along the Northwestern coast of Britain.

I don't remember whether we went through the Minches or further out along the western side of the Outer Hebrides.

What we did see, on the very few occasions we were allowed up on to the bridge for a smoke, was a hilly but very bleak heathery type of landscape on our port side. Hundreds of sheep could be seen roaming around and grazing on the hillside, their frisky lambs frolicking beside them. Other than that, there was no sign of other life, human or otherwise. There wasn't a tree in sight, nor a house or other traces of human habitation. In fact, this was exactly the way I imagined the moon's landscape would look like.

'If this is England, the English can bloody well keep it!'

It was much later when my education took a big step forward, aided by an agitated Scotsman, who asked me not to bloody confuse his beautiful homeland and his kind people with England and the hated Sassenachs who lived there.

The sheep we could see on our port side on that day were Scottish Blackfaces, at home in the Scottish Highlands.

Ambling along at about 8 knots, this last journey took perhaps 40 hours, when one morning, just before the break of day, a river-pilot came aboard.

By this time, it was clear, that we were heading into Lough Foyle in Northern Ireland. Herbert, who had recently been promoted to Petty Officer, was on the helm. Apart from our officers, he was one of the few crew-members with a smattering of school-English. He translated for us the conversation, which took place after the pilot took his place on the bridge.

'Good morning, Captain!' the pilot greeted our Old Man. 'Good morning, Pilot!' he replied.

'I would like you to know that I am not English but that I am Irish!

'That's perfectly OK by me' the Old Man assured him, although he seemed unsure of what to expect next. Having been at sea since he was a 16 years old cabin boy and having worked his way up through the ranks to become an officer and captain of a U-boat, the Old Man spoke fluent English and had no problems in understanding the words of the pilot. But what was he getting at?

'I don't like the damned English!'

'Don't you? But that's entirely OK by me as well.'

But then the pilot let the cat out of the bag. Looking over his shoulder to see that the RN Officer was out of earshot, he continued: 'I could do with a nice set of night-binoculars!'

'I bet you can!' The Old Man couldn't keep back a smile as he wondered how many times the pilot had used the same Spiel and how many pairs of glasses he had already acquired in this fashion.

Did the Old Man give him a pair?

They would be of no further use to him or to any of us!

I never learned the answer to this question. But I did hear that not long after our arrival, there was a brisk trade in binoculars and other U-boat memorabilia in Londonderry.

Finally, just before making fast, a tray, with a bottle still half full of Schnapps and with three small glasses, was handed up on to the bridge. Even in times like these, sailors are ruled by long-standing traditions. A pilot, who guides a ship safely into harbour, had to be appreciated.
It obviously was not a tradition approved by the Royal Navy, to judge by the look on the Kiwi's face. The fact that all spirits were supposed to have been handed in at Scapa appeared to bother him. In spite of many offers, he refused to join in but our Irish pilot thought this tradition was a brilliant one and he proceeded to ask for seconds!

Soon after this, we approached the furthest end of a long wooden jetty. The date was the 31st of May 1945.

CHAPTER SEVENTEEN

Of all the docking-manoeuvres the Old Man had ever performed with ***KARO-AS***, this one was by far the most spectacular, or so Herbert our helmsman told us. The wooden jetty looked none too substantial, quite unable to withstand any sort of impact by 2000 tonnes of solid steel. But there was no need to worry. First he put the bow of our boat within a few inches of the wooden structure and then, with starboard engine in reverse and the port diesel in forward, he eased her to within a hand's breadth squarely along side, so that the lines, fore and aft, were only needed to secure her to the jetty.

To us, the crew, this performance of expert seamanship was something we had come to expect. Apparently, there weren't too many people around to witness this, but those that were watching, applauded and although he didn't want anyone to see it, our present Kiwi captain was unable to keep his admiration out of his face, perhaps for once looking at the Old Man as a professional seafarer instead of a dreaded Nazi U-Boat ace.

'Both engines stop'

'Both engines stop.'
This turned out to be the very last order our Old Man was to give on the U-

boat with the playing-card emblem on her conning tower, and which had the stamp of his own personality all over her and her crew.
A deathly hush settled over the boat as the diesel engines were shut down and with a last cough went to sleep. Other pieces of machinery, such as compressors, pumps and ventilation fans had also been switched off. It had fallen so silent; you could hear a pin drop and for once we were able to hear the ticking of the clocks.
Left staring at one another, we were wondering what was going to happen to him and to us?

The boarding party had already gone up on deck while we were ordered to go to our stations below. It gave me the opportunity to consult my old Atlas again. With just about everybody leaning over my shoulder, we enlarged our knowledge of the British Isles. The stretch of water we had entered under the watchful eye of the pilot led all the way to the town of Londonderry. Most of us didn't realise it at that time but my book of wisdom was a little bit out of date. The island of Ireland was shown uniformly pink as being a part of Great Britain.

However, our Chief Engineer came to our rescue. He made his presence known by telling me: 'Get yourself an up-to-date atlas when you get home.' What my atlas didn't show was the fact that only a short distance over the starboard side of the Lough was the neutral Irish republic.
I learned not only that the northern part of Ireland, the Ulster province, was part of the United Kingdom, whereas the remaining part of the island formed the Republic of Eire, a quite independent state. When we sailed into Lough Foyle, County Donegal, part of the republic, was on our starboard side, while Ulster's County Londonderry was on our port side. From our Chief, we learned a little more about the history of the divisions in Ireland, which now made sense of the words the pilot has used to introduce himself.
'I would like you to know that I am an Irishman,' followed by 'I don't like the English!'
Those surely were the words of a dyed-in-the-wool Republican.

Meanwhile, our Old Man was asked to accompany the Kiwi Officer ashore. This must be to sort out our tickets and travel arrangements for our journey back home to Germany. Which meant that the time was rapidly approaching when we would have to say our last fare well to this old girl of ours. She had been our home for a few years and in her we had experienced many good times, and also a fair number of dodgy ones.
We had experienced joy and sorrow, success and failure, frustration and elation, fear and triumph, all mixed up into a cocktail of travel and adven-

ture. Working, eating and sleeping in her, day in and day out, we had come to know all her assets as well as her dislikes, her wrinkles and all of her petulant and temperamental tantrums.
Now, all that was left to do was to remove all our earthly possessions from the tiny lockers, take down any pin-ups or photos of our girl friends and stow them away with all our other belongings in our kit bags.
Not that we possessed a great many things to pack.

Before leaving Kiel at the start of our latest patrol, as was the usual drill, all unnecessary gear, such as our proud 'Square Rig' uniforms were left behind at the stores of the home base of our flotilla. All we were wearing at this time of the year was our usual grey denim-type working kit and when we felt at all chilly, we could fall back on our grey leather trousers and jackets.
Into our kit-bags went a change of working gear, our tropical shorts and shirts, change of underwear, a couple of towels, grooming-kits, other personal belongings such as books and letters from our loved ones, all of that topped by a couple of woollen blankets.
We were ready. All we had to do now is to wait for the Old Man to come back and lead us on our return journey to the *Vaterland* and home.

But it was quite a little while later when he arrived back and held a short discussion with the Chief and the *2WO*, his two remaining Officers.
Finally, he asked them to assemble the crew on deck.
As I made my way up on the ladder, I couldn't help thinking back to the last time we had mustered in this way while still in Horten. At that time, he had nothing but bad news to tell us: The war had ended with our utter defeat.
Anyway! That was all behind us - yesterday's news.
In a way, we felt it was a pity that we wouldn't get a chance to see a lot more of old Engelland!
But then came the bombshell.
'The Allied powers have decided that from this moment on, we are Prisoners of War!'

All of a sudden he looked exhausted and very much older than his 31 years. Tired looking and grey faced he passed on those glad tidings.
Prisoners of War?
More than three weeks AFTER the war has finished?
I can't believe it.
Maybe pawns in a gigantic chess game sounded more like it.
Mouse, standing next me in the line-up, echoed everybody's feelings when

he spat out:
'I always knew that you couldn't trust those English bastards!'
The captain continued:
'I've been informed that I and most other Officers will be transferred to PoW camps in England. A few of you will probably stay here for a time, while others will also be transferred to PoW camps on the mainland. The ones staying behind will be asked to do some maintenance on the boats and will be based in a special compound next to this base which is being prepared now.'

Having got that little bit off his chest, The Old Man came along and shook our hand wishing us all the best, after which he was ordered to go ashore. He took his time, however, as our quartermaster first 'piped' him ashore and then led us in 'three cheers for our Commandant! Hip-hip... Hurrah, hip-hip... Hurrah, hip-hip... Hurrah!'
The Tommies waiting for him on the Jetty did not like this one little bit. Frantically they shouted, 'Come-on. Hurry up. Come on! *Schnell, schnell, schnell!'*
Will we ever meet again?
Heaven only knows!
Now, more than at any time before, we were conscious of how close we had become in the past years.
He was like a father to us.
His own feelings were etched on his face. Only a few years older than us, he certainly had aged far beyond his years. But as he walked across the gangway to the cheers of his men, his shoulders miraculously came back, his head rose and with his chin jutting-out, he threw us the proudest-ever military salute. Maybe he was also as proud of us as we were of him.
'So long, men!' He smiled as Tommy pulled him away.
We needn't worry about him; he had risen over adversity before and surely will do so again. There was nothing on earth, for which he could possible blame himself. Like all of us, he had carried out his duties to the last and to the best of his ability.

Then it was the turn of our *2WO* and of our Chief to be taken to their respective camps. Lieutenant Karl Boden only had his kitbag to carry ashore, but Klaus Peter, our Chief needed help to take his possession ashore. We knew that he owned a lot of books when he arrived on ***KARO-AS***, at the time falsely assuming all his know-how stemmed from them. On the trip over from Norway he was often been found in the engine room, where he occupied himself in some project or other. Now, he tried to negotiate the gangplank, not only carrying his kit bag, but also trying to take ashore a very large chest filled with all his reading material. At one end of the box he had fixed a spindle with two small wheels on either side. Holding it by a handle at the top he wheeled the box behind him. We could also read the beautifully painted address on top of the box, which read: 'Property of Lieutenant Klaus Peter Torban' together with his home address in Bremen.

Everybody present applauded him and his idea of making his box mobile, possibly giving some clever inventor ideas for future use in shopping bags on wheels. After one of the guards had kindly helped him across to the jetty, he also threw us a salute as his farewell to his engineering crew and his baby - ***KARO-AS***.

As for us, we were determined not to let any of our officers down. We shrugged off our disappointment and waited to see what was in store for us. There was just one little job I had to do before it was too late. The little bit of cardboard in the back of my pay book, my 'rabbits foot', was transferred into the lining of my right shoe – just in case.

It was late in the evening when we marched away from the long jetty and out of the immediate base of Lisahally. We were quite determined not to let Tommy's treacherous treatment affect our discipline. We marched in our usual military fashion, left-right... left-right... while singing:

'Das kann doch einen Seemann nicht erschüttern...!'

It roughly translates as, 'You can't upset us sailors...'

No one was going to accuse us of being a bunch of pirates!

We had been informed that some clowns referred to us as the Blue S S.

We didn't deserve that. We were professional sailors and not political fanatics.

Anyway, we marched on with our heads held high, chest out and our backs as straight as a poker.

Our guards, from the "Queens" regiment, seemed to have caught our mood as well as they too fell in step beside us, with some even joining in the singing.

On the 1st June 1945 - bang in the middle of peacetime, as I saw it - I had become Prisoner of War No. B 290074.

The first night ashore as a PoW was spent in a sports hall. Several hundred U-boat men were crammed into this place. Since nearly fifty other U-boats had arrived before us and lay moored on the same wooden pier, it was to be expected that we would meet some familiar faces.

One matter, however, had been occupying my mind since we had put Norway behind us. What had happened to the 'Fairy-tale' boat? Taking the opportunity to speak to others, I combed the hall from one end to the other to find out whether my brother's boat was among those moored here. Unfortunately I was unsuccessful, his boat was definitely not at Lisahally. Maybe she would arrive later. One chap I asked was sure that a boat of that description had left on an enemy mission some months ago, at the end of March. Lets hope she stayed as lucky as our ***KARO-AS***.

The happenings of the last few days churned around in our minds. Late into the night we talked about our fate, but a smuggled bottle of something or other stopped us from getting too morose.

It was true to say that I wasn't particularly anxious to go home, especially not to my home in East Berlin, which was in Russian hands. I wouldn't know what to expect from them, their reputation was not good.

Not that I considered Tommy had treated us entirely fairly. It was quite unexpected of him to keep us behind barbed wire - as if we were some wild animals.

All he had to do was to ask us nicely to stay and look after the boats. We would have volunteered to do it, especially if he had offered to pay us to do the job.

But such was life!

It also showed how naive we were as nineteen year olds, wet behind the ears, as the saying goes.

On the next morning, after a meagre breakfast of a slice of white bread and jam, a panel of officers interviewed us. Among them was at least one German speaker, a middle-aged man, who according to his shoulder tab was an Intelligence Officers.

He was either from the CSDIC (Combined Services Detailed Interrogation Centre) or the PWIS (H) (Prisoner of War Interrogation Service (Home)). But of course, all those units sounded pretty much like double Dutch to us.

We had been briefed in the past, that in the event of becoming Prisoners of War, the only questions we would have to answer according to the terms of the Geneva Convention, were questions about our Names, Rank and Numbers.

'Gerhard Schuler,
Maschinen Obergefreiter,
UW18898/43.'

Those three things should have answered all their questions.

However! It became quite clear to us that Tommy was not going to be satisfied with only that information. Interrogation Centres had long been used by Tommy, if and when it suited him, although he was a signatory to that

Geneva Convention. And did he not staff them with Jewish refugees from Germany who could be relied on to be German-hating by nature? In addition, what is in an agreement you have signed up to, when you have just won the war?

As far as we were concerned, we had already accepted that there was now no further need for heroics. We wouldn't have minded providing more information than was strictly required, had it not been for the utterly disgraceful behaviour of the interrogating Intelligence Officer.

I could see naked hatred in his eyes, which seemed to make it clear to me, that in his eyes the only good German was a dead German. As he spat out his questions, he followed them by a stream of abuse such as: 'Come on and tell the truth, you Nazi pig' and other such insults, all of them delivered in the purest German - with a Berlin accent.

He already knew all of the answers about our boat and our Old Man, but to humiliate us as much as possible and perhaps even to show-off his bravery in front of the other British Officers, he carried on in this silly fashion.

Type and number of your boat?

Name and rank of your Captain?

How many ships with women and children on board did he sink?

What was your job on board?

Where is your home?

Were you a member of the Hitler Youths or the Nazi Party?

What do think about Communism?

And so on - and on - and on.

I didn't know about anybody else, but I was certainly not ashamed to admit to having been a very keen member of the Naval Hitler Youths and that I had been well briefed in navigation, signalling by semaphore or Morse, rowing and sailing in cutters, knotting and splicing and general naval history. I also told them about my time-spent training on the "Gorch Fock", one of the two Tall-Ships used by the German Navy for training Officer Cadets.

Did that make me a Nazi or a War criminal?

I didn't think so; certainly not in the way the interviewer meant it!

As for being a member of the Nazi Party, I had wondered about that very question myself. One had to be over 18 years old to be a member and when I was old enough, I was already serving in the Navy. Whether or not Hitler Youth leaders or officials were automatically affiliated to the party when reaching that age was something I vaguely assumed but could not confirm. I would probably have been officially informed, if it had been the case.

Anyway, I didn't think that this constituted a crime either?
What was wrong in being a member of the **National Socialist German Workers Party**, especially as we were in fact Socialist German workers.

From my colleagues, who went to be interrogated before me, I gathered we were to be classified in one of three groups.
Whites, or class A, were those deemed to be anti-Nazi and ready to work actively for the Allies.
Greys, or class B, were those without any particular political leanings but who would be unlikely to work for the Allies.
Blacks, or class C, were black sheep, those still believing in the National/Socialist cause.
Although most of us were probably Bs, but because of the obnoxious attitude of this interrogator, we kept insisting that we believed in the Nazi cause. We certainly weren't going to crawl or lick his boots.
Which equated us U-boat men with the dreaded Waffen SS.
BLACK AS THE ACE OF SPADES!
What baffled me more than anything about this interrogation were the questions designed to find out our feelings about communism. It had nothing to do with us.
Were the communists not their bedfellows and allies?
One could almost sense their fear of the Reds.
However, here I was able to help the interviewers.
As far as I was concerned, I hadn't the slightest intention of ever going voluntarily near any part of the world controlled by their dear friend Joe Stalin - even if it meant, that I would never see my family or my home again.
Perhaps that made me slightly less than Black?
A little later, while talking to Mouse, I learned that the Interrogator had told him, that he was Jewish and from our hometown but had fled to Britain in 1937.
That explained a whole lot.

Following this interrogations, Tommy supplied us with special Red Cross forms, on which we were allowed to write a short note to our folks in Germany... strictly censored of course.
This could be our one and only chance to find out what has happened to our families during the last stages of the war and it may help to let them know that we were OK.

Before we left Norway, we knew that the Russians, the Americans and the British had completely occupied Germany, but we were still unclear exactly where the dividing line between East and West fell. I was pretty

sure, that Cossacks, Tartars and Mongols had overrun Berlin. So, what does one write in a case like this?
Dear Mum, Dad, Uschi and Helga.
I am well and a Prisoner of War in Britain. (We were not allowed to say exactly where). How are you all? And how is Irmchen? Please write soon, to the address on the form.'
I could only hope that the letter would still find them at the old address. We had heard on the grapevine, that many people from the East had fled from the Russians. We just hoped and prayed that our loved ones were still in one piece.
We shall find out!

Next day, we were ordered to assemble in another hall, a type of gymnasium. Someone had noticed that projection equipment had been taken in there, so we were sure we would be shown a film.
What were they going to show us?
No doubt it would be their usual Hollywood propaganda rubbish.
Or would it be a John Wayne or Gary Cooper Western? Or worst still... Marlene Dietrich or Shirley Temple? Laurel and Hardy we wouldn't mind!
It was none of those, but a film about CONCENTRATION CAMPS, such as Belsen, Auschwitz or Dachau!
I couldn't believe what I saw!
Those films were just cruel fakes!
The bodies of women and children looked the same as the ones pulled out of the cellars and out of the rubble of bombed houses at Dresden, Hamburg or Berlin and deposited on funeral pyres in the streets of those cities.
On the other hand, I didn't think any of us slept well that night!
'After all, it couldn't be true, could it?'
Time will tell!

Following this, the majority of the remaining crewmembers from our boat, and from all other boats were shipped away. I didn't know who did the selecting; perhaps it was as the result of the previous day's interrogations. There was little time to say farewell to them, a fleeting handshake, a hurried *'Hals und Beinbruch'* and off they went in Army lorries – destination unknown. It was the end of our double act; inseparable Mouse and Spider were parted. We knew that it had to happen sometime and had agreed a while ago, that whoever got home first, would look up our folk in Berlin and try to make sure they were all right.

It left 4 or 5 PoWs per boat at the Lisahally base. Their job: to maintain the boats in a reasonable state of seaworthiness. From our 70-man ***KARO-***

AS crew, just four of us were left to keep our ladylove company, weapons mechanic Ernst, electrician Hubert, helmsman Herbert and myself in control room. About 200 of us were living in a temporary barbed-wire compound, from where we marched down to the boats in the morning and back again in the evening, always accompanied by armed guards. I must admit to being quite glad to have stay back, this might turn out more interesting than staying in an ordinary PoW camp, with nothing to do.

Our boat had arrived without any ammunition and my guess was that most of the others had shed theirs as well, before sailing for England. What was left on other boats was taken away and stored in a hangar near our PoW compound.

Having completed that job, we were ordered to strip all boats of provisions and assemble those, mostly tins of all sorts, on the jetty.

As with the ammunition, it was mainly Army chaps who supervised us in this job. Nobody was too keen to clamber down into the claustrophobic surroundings of a U-boat, especially not with a rifle slung over your shoulder. As long as we brought up the stuff, they seemed satisfied with our efforts. They didn't know what was in those rusty tins.

I could have told them that it was mainly rubbish, even hard-up *Lords*, who had been at sea for months, would have to be desperate to eat that stuff; butter made from coal and tinned rye bread. Tins of ham, corned beef, fruit in syrup and other good food, if they weren't hidden away already, were speedily disposed-off down bilges. I'm sure our guards felt sorry for us to have survived a long time at sea with very little to eat.

At this time, I had counted about 50 U-boats at Lisahally. After all the food was assembled, it amounted to quite a lot. It was all taken away and as far as we could tell, it went in to the same hangar as the ammunition. As most of our boats were moored five-abreast, along the full length of the long jetty, in nine groups, they presented quite an imposing sight to any passing ship on their way in to Londonderry. Our working party, with 20 men in it, was supposed to look after the Ace of Diamonds and four other boats moored alongside, at the furthest end of the pier.

A favourite pastime in those early days was to spend part of the time checking the hydraulic raising-and-lowering mechanism of the periscopes.

Some of the 50 U-boats assembled at Lisahally

None of us stokers ever had a chance to look through the thing, as our job required us only to maintain it and raise or lower it, as and when the Old Man needed it. It was a novel experience for us to be able to take time out to look through those intricate and delicate instruments, taking in the base, the stunning views up-river toward Londonderry, as well as studying the lie of the land at the opposite bank of the Foyle.

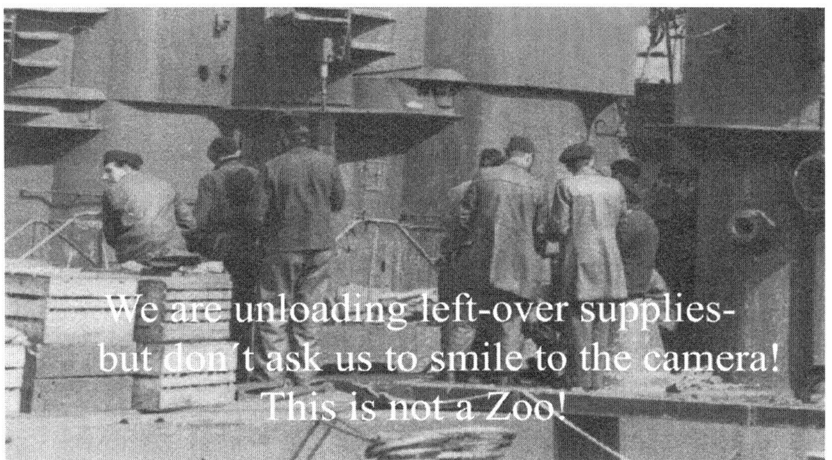
We are unloading left-over supplies-
but don't ask us to smile to the camera!
This is not a Zoo!

Here we had an almost uninterrupted view of green pastures or parkland surrounding a large white mansion in the far distance.

One day the buzz went round all the boats that one of us, on examining the other side of the river, had watched a group of young colleens sunbathing - TOPLESS.

Of course, nobody believed a word of it. 'Why don't you have a look yourself. Just turn the scope to point at 97 degrees and you'll see what I think is a school for young ladies.'

So it came to pass that on this day many periscopes were pointing Northwest-by-West. Those *Spargels* were powerful indeed in their magnification, but all the searching turned out to be in vain. There, in the distance - probably in County Donegal, was this big white house... but no scantily clad young girls.

They called us all the names under the sun, but it wasn't our fault that the sun had gone in. However, many *Lords* in their eagerness to take a sly look, failed to notice that the eyepieces of the scope had been smeared with black shoe polish or 'engineers blue'.

The poor fools were a sight for sore eyes. Serves them right for being so nosy.

As time went on, we even got bored with looking through those things and we tried to figure out other ways of amusing ourselves. It was actually Hubert's idea to see whether the periscopes would make a good fair ground ride.

'What on earth do you mean?'

'We can make up a clamp-bracket to fit over the top of the attack-periscope. On the opposing sides of the bracket we fix ropes, which are tied to two boatswains chairs. Two of us can sit on them, while somebody else will raise the scope and then he can run round on inside the conning tower while turning it as fast as he possibly could.'

In theory this seemed a reasonable proposition. We went ahead and got all the gear together and fixed it. But unfortunately the person turning it just could not run round fast enough to make the chairs fly out as we had anticipated they would.

And there was this Royal Navy bloke, who stood shouting obscenities at us from the jetty, who mustn't have had a sense of humour and so spoiled our fun.

Not that this kind of treatment would have done the very expensive *Zeiss* lenses and mirrors any good.

Anyway, who cared?
I was again proved right in my assumption that being here was more interesting than being shut-up in a normal PoW camp.

Early on in June, Tommy decided that one of the Monsoon-boats, the Type IXC *Herz Dame* (Queen of Hearts), had to be taken to Pembroke to go into dry-dock.
Having arrived back in Norway from a lengthy patrol to the Far East a few days before the end of hostilities, she was thought to have a valuable cargo aboard in containers below the deck but mainly in the keel.
A mixed crew was formed, made up of an English officer/captain, a dozen English seamen, and a dozen Germans PoWs, to tend the engines. When not on watch, we stayed in the stern, while the RN personnel lived in the bow torpedo room.

And off we went in her, running mainly due south through a very rough Irish Sea. We were familiar with the longish swell of the North Sea and the even longer one of the Atlantic, but it had not prepared us for the choppy and short wave-pattern of the Irish Sea. Needless to say, as soon as we set out I was as sick as a parrot.
Fortunately it didn't take long to find my sea legs again and as a result my colleagues required me to cook-up some brew from the stuff brought aboard for us by the Tommies. Talk about blind trust!
It was loosely called soup and consisted of the regulation potatoes, dried mixed vegetables and a very large helping of cooked tinned and diced ham. I had no idea whether the amount I used was meant to last one day or for the whole journey. Time would tell.
The concoction was nothing to look at, but everybody thought it was to be preferred to the stuff they had been feeding us at Lisahally. 'Well done, *smutje,* lets hope there will be more of this for the rest of the trip.'

On watch in the control room I was joined by an English matelot, who obviously was a submariner like us. He had a good look around and soon we got on like a house on fire.
We communicated in word and action about this and that and found that we were on similar wavelengths. And before I had a chance to say anything, I found myself being challenged to a game of chess.
Since I had no immediate plans to go anywhere else that day, I accepted.

Now here was an opportunity to foster good relations between the Royal Navy and the *Kriegsmarine*. The rules of the game were international ones, which made the understanding of each other's language superfluous.
AB Ralph Haigh gabbled away in English to which I would nod my head

vigorously and probably call him a cheating *Englischer Schweinehund* under my breath.

I had a distinct advantage over him in the language department, having had contact with English sailors before this day, first of all in Norway and then on the way from Scapa Flow. I already knew a lot of the choicier English expressions, which he was calling me, especially when I checkmated him.

However, I learned to flatter him as well, indicating that I thought he was a superb player. Whether that was the reason or not, but every time he won, he offered me his tin of beautiful blond Navy-Cut shag to roll myself a few beautiful cigarettes. Those I would enjoy later up on deck. Talk about birthdays and Christmas arriving together, what a change from the rubbish we could buy at the camp. Mind you, the bastard didn't mind my tongue hanging out whenever I won too many times. We played on a home and away basis. One game was played in the stern-torpedo room, i.e. our quarters and the next we played in his quarters, the bow-torpedo room. I didn't think this fraternisation met with the full approval of the English Commandant.

But he didn't stop us.

A couple of days after leaving Northern Ireland we arrived at the mouth of the waters leading to Milford and Pembroke Docks. Since a couple of guys could easily look after the 4,000 odd horses under our bonnet, the rest of us gathered up on the upper wintergarden to take in the view. And a rather spectacular view it was. Sunderland Flying boats by the dozen were chasing in and out of the estuary. Ever so ungainly while sitting on the water, they looked just like lazy, fat ducks and appeared to labour strenuously to get airborne. Were they ever going to make it? But once they were in the air, it became apparent why the name of 'Sunderlands' had struck fear in the hearts of U-boat men. In flight they were sleek and menacing... and we knew that they could carry a very effective load of depth charges. They were no longer looking for us, although you could have fooled us when they kept flying low toward us and over us. But it gave us a good chance to give them a cheerful wave, as if in appreciation of the good scrap they had given us.

Our entry into the Pembroke dock area was quite spectacular. Crowds had gathered on the quay side by the hundred to see this once dreaded type of ship approach and finally make fast in a dry-dock. But most of all, they wanted to see what sort of monsters had manned them. They must have felt let down when all they could see were some young chaps in oil-stained working kit, most of them barely old enough to shave.

As far as we were concerned, it gave us a chance to study form. Many of the young ladies among the crowd on the dockside were well worth studying!

Our unanimous verdict? Those Welsh girls are a bit all right too.

And their body language seemed to indicate that they didn't believe all the things they had heard about us either.

Unfortunately, we were denied the chance to further our knowledge of the Welsh, as we were informed that during the next day or two, the dockyard's men were going to take charge of the boat and unload it.

Great! We didn't feel like humping a lot of stuff either. Our rations were not designed to be sufficient for heavy manual work.

The English sailors were given a few days leave and as far as we were concerned; we were surplus to requirement until the start of the return journey.

Hence, in the late afternoon an Army lorry arrived to take us somewhere. A Sergeant from the Intelligence Corps accompanied us. During the journey the Sergeant gave us a few hints on how to avoid getting into trouble when arriving at our destination.

'You'll be strip-searched and if they find anything which Prisoners of War shouldn't have, you might find yourself in a lot of trouble.'

'We've never been told what we could have and what not.'

'Well! You are not allowed to possess any jewellery, such as rings, charms, bracelets, or necklaces, nor should you have any watches, cameras, binoculars, or Nazi propaganda books. Before we get there, you'd be well advised to hand those over to me.'

I doubt whether he managed to collect a great deal.

In my kit bag there was in fact a very nice camera and also a gold wristwatch, which I had bought in the Far East and become very attached to.

To keep possession of those I would have to become a smuggler.

How?

Well, on top of all my personal belongings such as underwear, socks, pyjamas, I had packed a couple of woollen blankets.

We had noticed already that when searching through belongings English guards were in the habit of taking out each item and shaking it to be sure that nothing was concealed in it. In one blanket I had carefully sewn in my wristwatch and in the other my small camera.

If I thought that somebody was going to make a profit from my misfortune, I would rather have smashed both against a wall. So I decided, rather then handing them over now, I would take my chance with the searches.

Unfortunately, we saw very little of the Welsh countryside from the back of the covered-in Army lorry and we had no idea at all where this bumpy trip was taking us. After a drive lasting nearly two hours we arrived at a large PoW camp, a village made up of several dozen Nissen huts.
Our helpful Sergeant handed us over to the Camp Commandant. There had been only a very superficial frisk of our kit bags when entering the camp after which we were allocated a dormitory hut at the centre of the camp right next to a football pitch.

We didn't expect to be here very long, unlike many of the inmates who had probably been here for several years. I didn't know whether we should be sorry for them or not. They seemed to have drawn the long straw, as here they were of lot safer than their comrades at the front.

After we had settled in and claimed our bunks, we had time to sit in front of the hut and to look around. The camp was situated in the most beautiful part of the country. From our vantage point, we looked down on several valleys, where smoke could be seen to rise from the chimneys of rows and rows of cottages.
On the hillside above the villages we saw acres and acres of deep green fields, which seemed to be covered with hundreds of sheep. The early summer sun was doing its level best to illuminate this panorama, but the beauty didn't end there.

Right here in the camp, we were able to admire the hard work put in by the resident prisoners. The flower-borders in front of the huts competed with each other to be the most colourful. Most of them depicted the emblem of a city or town. Not far from the hut we were allocated, were three huts with the hanseatic emblems of Hamburg, Bremen and Danzig, all depicted in the glorious colours of flowers in bloom.
Further on was the one, which was of most interest to me. This one showed the white shield of my hometown Berlin, with the upright figure of the Berliner Bear, wearing a large golden Crown. If that wasn't enough, a glorious Brandenburg Gate adorned the plot next to it. I went to see the hut's elder and told him that he would have me crying in a minute. 'But all joking aside, those emblems are a work of art, they must keep you busy throughout the summer.'

During the week we spent at this camp, we were not required to take part in any of the camp's activities, nor did we have to go out to work as most of the others did. We used this opportunity to first of all fatten ourselves up on all the excellent food and then either sleep or play cards or table tennis in the lovely camp-canteen.

It was only in the evenings that we could make contact with our fellow prisoners. They were most anxious to hear what had happened to their homelands in the last days of the war. They were very suspicious of the English papers or of the radio, as propaganda was the norm of the day.
There was little we were able to tell them, as we were just as much in the dark as they were. Everybody wanted to know 'How far did the Russians come into Germany?
'We only knew that they had overrun Berlin.'
Like us, they still awaited answers to their latest Red Cross letters, which would perhaps tell them the answers to their questions in one-way or the other.

But we did benefit from the information they were able to give us. Some of them had fought in the *Afrika Korps* under Fieldmarshall Rommel and others were taken prisoner at the American invasion of Italy. While we were busy in the Baltic and later in the Indian Ocean, we learned little of what was going on at the various fronts. All of those boys were extremely fed up and felt letdown by our comrades-in-arms... the 'Spaghetti eaters'.
But just like us, they were looking forward to the day, when they could get back to their own folk and start with the rebuilding of their homes and their careers.
Our holiday only lasted one week.

Then, after we had said farewell and good luck to our new friends in Wales, we were driven back to Pembroke to rejoin the Queen of Hearts.
She didn't look any different from when we left her; she was just as bedraggled and rusty as before. But the dockyard men had almost completed the task of replacing the keel-cargo with an equal weight of steel-ingots.
It was late afternoon when we got back, but for some reason or other we were unable to leave the dock until the next day.
Why?
Well, for one thing, the English matelotes were not due back from their leave until then!
So we made the best of it. After we had our evening meal, we got together on the bridge of the old tub.
Many sightseers, among them the dockyard canteen ladies, were sitting and standing around in the area beside the dock, as we struck-up a sea-shanty and in which we were accompanied by a couple of mouth organs. The more we sang, the more applause we got from our audience. But it was not always for the quality and melodiousness of our musical talents, but perhaps more for our effort.

Shanty Choir in Dry-Dock

When 'Lilly Marlene' was on the Menu, we had audience participation and for 'Molly Malone in Dublin's fair city' we had the massed Choirs of the Pembroke Docks to accompanying us.
It was nice to be appreciated.

We finished in style. Our *pièce de résistance* was a song we had learned only recently from a record one of the British matelots had brought on board.
Our harmonised version of 'It's a long way to Tipperary....' had the audience in raptures. It was a great pity that we didn't have any Welsh songs in our repertoire; there would have been a riot in Pembroke Docks. But all in all, there was one fact that stared us in the face during our stay in Wales.

Those Welsh folk really did appreciate a good singsong!

CHAPTER EIGHTEEN

At the end of our Welsh experience, it was time to get back to our temporary base at Lisahally. During this return-trip, I teased Ralph, not only because he had just been promoted from AB to Leading Seaman Haigh, but I also wanted to know all about his girl friend Susan. Had she been nice to him during his one-week leave?

In my question I didn't use exactly those words, but he got my message all right... he just smiled in silly sly way, the dirty old pig.

I had hit on the one sure way to trounce Ralph at chess... make him think of Susan and thereafter he became putty in my hands.

ut, he did show that he was a proper gentleman at heart by presenting me with the one thing I most longed for in those dark days, a whole tin of golden yellow Virginian cigarette tobacco. By this time, I had more than enough of the taste and stink of the old Turkish rubbish, enough to last me a lifetime. Furthermore, Ralph had also presented me with my first German-English pocket dictionary, one that would serve me well during the rest of my PoW days. This action of Ralph's was just one more reason for thinking that there was very little wrong with the average member of the Royal Navy.

At the end of this trip, the Queen of Hearts looked more than ever in need of a lick of paint. She also had travelled many miles in action, with only minimal maintenance - and it showed.

After we had moored her on the outside of a pack and when the Royal Nave crews had gone on their way, I returned to the familiar surroundings of our Ace of Diamonds. Here it was back to the endless routine of avoiding work, if it was at all possible. My skills at playing *SKAT* improved beyond recognition. While we were stuck on the boats, it was impractical to play board games.

Why ever not?

Because every time we heard footsteps above us on deck, we scrambled to various stations in the ship, to give the appearance of doing something in the way of maintenance.

It was therefore much easier to run a card-school. We could just drop our "hand" in our pockets and continue with our game when the all clear came.

When you haven't any money, there was little point in playing Pontoon. We therefore resorted to *SKAT,* which was one of the most popular card games in Germany and had the added advantage of keeping the brain in reasonable working order. To hold a good hand was obviously the most important thing, but afterwards it came down to doing mental handstands in arithmetic.

Our one purpose in life had been the dispatching of ships to the bottom of the sea. When that requirement no longer existed, there was the danger of getting into a rut, to get out of the habit of using your brain. So it was natural that we would try and think up new ways of passing the time. If we could only think of ways of turning our spare time into hard cash, it would be a welcome boost to our dreams of obtaining edible food, decent cigarettes or even smokable tobacco.

Some members of our gang stationed on this pack of five boats took to making silhouettes of sailing ships or other ships, even U-boats. Those were cut out of any available bits of thin copper, brass or aluminium sheets, polished and mounted on rectangular pieces of stained wood.

There was nothing new about this little scheme. This hobby had been a regular source of extra income long before we got here. It had always been a legal way to lay our hands on some sorely needed extra cash.

Other budding entrepreneurs had set up a foundry in the engine rooms of one of the boats. A makeshift furnace, heated by an oxy-acetylene gas torch was constructed, while the toolmakers among us made-up little wooden moulds. It was amazing what could be achieved with a minimum of gear, but with a lot of imagination.

What did we aim to make?

Apart from all the aluminium, steels, lead, brass and bronze used in a submarine, the high-powered electrical motors and switches contained pure silver contacts. Expensive as it was, it was the only material suitable for use in heavy switches.

We knew that at this stage of the proceedings, a few of those would never be missed, as those vessels of ours are not going need them again. While our electrical geniuses were dismantling all the contacts, which in their opinion would not be missed, we worked on the moulds for casting ornate silver signet rings. Because the moulds were made of hardwood, they could only be used once, when they were burned out.

Silver melts at 960° C, so that even the stainless steel-ladles, in which we heated the silver, glowed dark-red. During the months of July and August, we must have cast more than twenty rings, one for each one of our gang.

U-boat's silversmiths at work

After casting them, there was still a lot of work to be done. They had to be finished by filing and polishing, until our handiwork could not be differentiated from professionally manufactured signet rings. Some of them had initials engraved in them, in reverse letters of course. My ring had a precious black stone set in it.
Precious? Yes. But only to somebody doing a spot of welding.
A lens from one of our welding goggles had been ground to the required shape and set into the ring.
It looked beautiful and only needed a hallmark, but that was something we had to do without.
To be safe, we kept all our craftwork in hiding places known only to us. The opportunity to sell them would surely present itself in good time.
Later in August, there was another flap.

We were informed that both our Ace of Diamonds and her sister-ship, the one with the Cherry-blossom on her conning tower, had to go into dry-dock to unload the mercury in their keels.
Blast!
The shortage of silver contacts in the switchgear was now going to be noticed. Since it was impossible to unmelt them, we had to find other ways to

make the switches operate normally again. This we managed to do, by going on a scrounging expedition through the other boats. Most of them were of a smaller type (VIIC), but all switchgear was of standard design and fitted perfectly. Alas, there were now a couple of partially disabled Type VIIC boats in our midst.

A few days later the mixed Pembroke crew was re-united on board of the Cherry Blossom and after taking on extra fuel and provisions, we set sail for Birkenhead. A few hours later Ralph and I were found to be re-engaged in mortal combat on the chess-board, while this floating home of ours slid ever so sedately through the sea, which on that day was as smooth as a baby's bottom.

Apart from the odd 'check mate' nothing much happened until, thirty hours after leaving the Foyle behind us, the entrance to the Mersey came into sight. A pilot was already waiting to take us in. The poor pilots here were out of luck- not a sniff of a tot of something or other.

Hasn't the RN any manners at all?

With the lights of Liverpool on port, it was straight across to the other side of the river into Birkenhead dry-dock. By the time the lines had gone across to secure the boat to the sides of the dock, it was far too late for us to go anywhere on that day.

At 10 on the next morning another one of those awful Army lorry arrived to take us away for a few days holiday in some god-forsaken camp or other. As before, there was very little one could see from under the canvas top of those lorries. Sitting on a hard bench on either side, getting thoroughly shook-up, all we ever could see through the open back was where we had come from. Herbert, who knew a bit more about England than any of us ignorant dunces, was of the opinion that we had travelled through the outskirts of Manchester and must now be in the vicinity of Oldham. Thankfully, the whole journey took not much more than an hour. At last, the lorry rumbled to a halt in front of a very large, four-storey high factory building, which was surrounded by a 3-metre high barbed wire entanglement, with heavily armed soldiers patrolling the perimeter.

If ever in this big, wide world there existed a less inviting place than this one, I would try my best to avoid it at all cost.

Even with the sun on it, the grey building looked bleak and desolate. Whether daylight could ever penetrate the grime and dust on the window-panes was debatable. This place looked empty and deserted.

But why guard it so heavily? Was that just for our benefit?

Of course not!

When we were frog-marched through the heavy inner and outer gates and into the ground floor of the building, we found that we were anything but alone.
A German officer bad us welcome to Camp II in what appeared to be some type of reception area.
I wasn't very familiar with the ranks in the other services, but I assumed him to be an Army Major by his interwoven shoulder straps.
One of my new crewmates Kurt enlightened me later, 'This Camp-leader is in fact an *SS-Obersturmbannführer*. He had noticed the four silver pips on the collar-patches of his tunic, which meant the equivalent rank of a Major in the army.
It was the first time I had met somebody from the *Waffen SS* and by the look of this one I hoped he would be the last.
With him was a group of other ranks, some men from the SS, some *Luftwaffe* personnel, some from the *Panzer* Regiments and even some of our own U-boat service. Over a cup of tea, they were most anxious to find out how we got there
We told them our tale of woe, of being taken prisoners after the war was finished, of our subsequent adventures at Northern Ireland and how we brought our boat to Birkenhead to be dry-docked.
All the members of our reception committee from Camp II sat and listened, all-the-while looking at us as if we had grown horns.
What we were to find out was beyond our understanding!

Like everybody else on board ***KARO-AS*** or any other U-boat, we had tried to carry out our duties according to the oath we had all taken, to defend our *Vaterland* of Germany. However, there came the day when we had to accept our cause was lost. There was nothing left but to carry out the last orders of our *Großadmiral,* who after Hitler's death also took over the responsibility as our Führer, which required us to surrender our boats and ourselves to the enemy.

We were now in September 1945, over four months later.
Here in the centre of England we find ourselves in the middle of a group of our compatriots who would not believe us when we told them 'the war is over'.
'Our Führer is still Adolf Hitler', the poor devils claimed.
We went on to tell them that we had sailed our boat to Birkenhead while it was flying the 'White Duster' of the Royal Navy.
It was utterly unbelievable, the instrument of surrender had been signed on the 8th May, and not one of the men we spoke to was prepared to accept the

inevitable.
However, later we learned the reasons behind their disbelief.

We found out that this camp was in fact a special one, where all the hard-cases and political fanatics had been brought together, probably because the building was thought to be more secure than most others.
The camp committee, led by the *Obersturmbannführer,* had prohibited the presence of English (propaganda) newspapers and the possession of radios.
They still believed that the promised V-weapons would eventually turn the war in Germany's favour.
However, they did believe that we had just come from a U-boat, as they could not miss the smell of diesel-oil on our clothes.
'What are you really up to?' they asked.
'Were you sent in here to spy on us and to destroy our belief in our Führer *und Vaterland?*'
We tried very hard to make them believe us, but had to give-up after a while.
After this initial reception, we were allocated bunks at the top storey of the building. Our bunks had been moved into one of the corners, some distance from the other PoWs.
At a guess, there were some 250 men bunked on the top floor. During the meals that followed and throughout the rest of the day, we were strictly left to our own devices.
Everybody had clearly been warned to give us a wide berth.
As we were quite used to our own company on a U-boat, being shunned by the rest of the camp during the next ten days wouldn't be a major problem to us.
At lights-out we did start to feel a little uneasy - the tension in the air began to get to us.

Whether it was a foreboding or not, unknown to all our own mates, we had all gone to bed with some sort of weapon in our hands.
Hidden under my bedcovers I tightly clutched my dinner knife and my fork as I tried unsuccessfully to get to sleep.
From all directions in this big hall one imagined hearing whispered plotting, which did little for our peace of minds.
Tossing and turning in their bunks, my friends next to me, obviously found the tense atmosphere equally disquieting.
But then, just before midnight, a group of Tommies arrived beside us, urging us to get dressed and packed.
'Schnell - schnell' they were whispering.

As a result, we were whisked out of the camp and on to the regulation Army lorry. This time, there were absolutely no complaints from us about this horrible mode of transport.
We were just glad to turn our backs on this - the spookiest place we had ever had the misfortune to experience in all our lives.

Our accompanying guard enlightened us about this sudden decision to break camp. A resident mole among the fanatics had reported to the British Camp Commandant that an attempt was to be made to dispatch us from the 4th story-windows at some time during the night, as it had been decided that we were traitors to the cause of the *Dritte Reich.* Phew!
We could only wonder how the hot-heads would eventually be persuaded to accept the inevitable truth and learn to live with the defeat of their cause, as we all had to do.
To our surprise, we were taken back on board of our Cherry-Blossom, instead of to another PoW camp, of which there must have been a few in the vicinity.

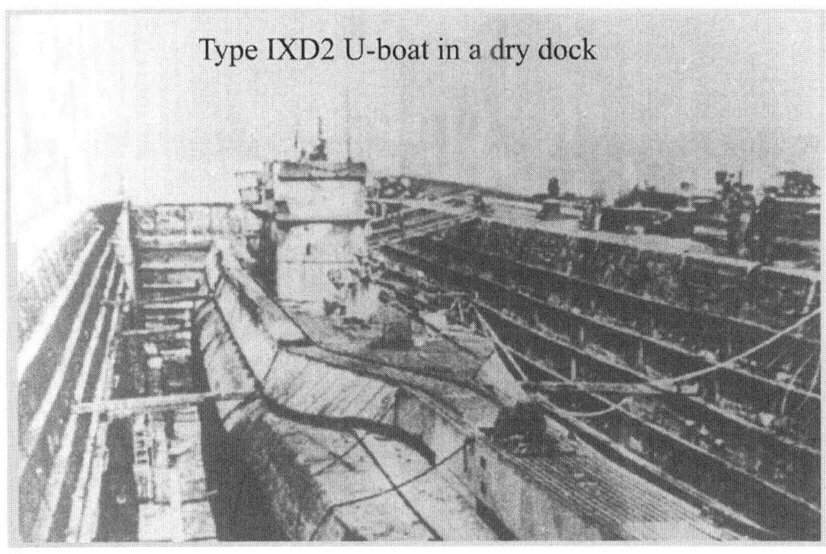
Type IXD2 U-boat in a dry dock

I had absolutely no problem in getting to sleep in the stinking old bunks of ours, among the reek of humanity and diesel oil and there wasn't anybody to wake us next morning. Once I did get up, having decided that I needed a smoke more than anything else, I saw that the dry-dock had been drained of

all the water and our boat was lying high and dry, with only a narrow gang-plank connecting us to the sides or the dock.
An armed Tommy patrolled the dockside, while on deck waited an interpreter, to inform us of the latest decision by our captors.
'For your own safety you'll be allowed to live on board of your vessel during her time in dry-dock, but you're asked to promise not to leave her on your own.'
Well! That sounded fair enough.
Most of the English matelots had gone on leave, with the exception of a few, who also supervised the unloading of the Mercury bottles from the keel of 'Cherry Blossom' and also to ensure that an equal weight of iron ballast was replaced.

By the second and third day, the news of the presence of a Nazi U-boat in Birkenhead had got around and masses of sightseers were watching us from all sides.
Now we were beginning to see, how goldfish in a bowl or monkeys in a Zoo might feel, with all and sundry gawking.
At one time, both a radio reporter from the BBC and a newspaper reporter from one of the national rags came to the gangplank and with the permission of the Tommy on guard, asked for any English speaking Lords to come to chat to them.
Herbert was the only one to fit that description, so he went for a talk with the hacks. When he returned later, he gave us an ides of what they wanted to know.

He told us that the reporters would have liked to spice-up their stories a bit by getting him to say that we were all dyed-in-the-wool fanatical Nazis. They were not so keen to hear him say that we were professional sailors doing a professional job for our home country; in much the same way as their sailors in the Royal Navy did their duty by their lot.
He told them that we respected the men of the Royal Navy. That we did so without hate - as fair opponents rather than as enemies and that we hoped that they felt the same about us.
At the same time, we were as pleased as anyone else that the mass-slaughter had come to an end and that we looked forward to hearing from our loved ones to see how they fared in the last days of the war. They also interviewed some the Royal Navy guys who had sailed up on board the U-boat from Lisahally with us.
We wondered afterwards, just how the reporter did write his report

Somebody brought a newspaper on board the next day and Herbert

proudly read his own name in print and how he, as the only English speaker among the U-boat crew, had stated his point of view. It seems that the report was a reasonable and fair reflection of what Herbert had told them.
The rest of our ten days stay at Birkenhead turned out to be just another holiday for us.

Ralph was one of those chaps kept back on board to do a bit of supervising the dockyard work. When he was off duty, he wanted nothing more than an interesting, closely fought game of chess. I had come to the conclusion, that he was a glutton for punishment and was getting used to being taken to the cleaners.
But maybe I had underestimated the bastard's sense of humour. He came up with a brilliant idea. He would give me his spare Square Rig uniform to wear so that we could both go ashore to enjoy a cool beer or two.
I had promised not to go ashore by myself, so there was no problem with my conscience.
Even so, I took a bit of persuading. But in the end I accepted - 'what the hell' - even though I was under strict instructions not to open my 'effing mouth'. I had great faith in his judgement and relied entirely on him to see that we would be all right.
Thus, on that evening well after 8 PM, we set sail for a public house, which was not far from the docks.
From his gabble with the chaps in the bar and after he had ordered a couple of glasses of beer, I gathered that he had introduced me as a Polish sailor, who had been doing his bit for his country and for old England. But unfortunately the poor chap couldn't speak a word of English.

As far as I was concerned that was OK.
I just nodded and smiled from ear to ear every time someone tried to tell me something, while I enjoyed my first taste of English bitter. I had heard that the Bavarians drank their beer out of large *Steins*, but myself, I had never seen a glass as big as this pint-glass, and it came complete with a proper handle. The German beer, which I knew, had normally been dispensed in .2 or .3 litre measures, which was less than half that size and looked like a thimble compared to this.
I kept smiling at the barmaid, not because she was particularly lovely, or very desirable, or even very young.
I was smiling, because after tasting just a little of the beautiful liquid, I could feel myself beginning to take-off - to float away into the wide blue yonder. In fact I couldn't remember having even the smallest care in the world.

When I was at my most relaxed and most contented, it happened. I was rudely stirred into action. One minute I was getting deeper and deeper in love with my beer, in the next I found myself staring at a wall in the Gents toilets while Ralph was busily prying-open the tiny window on to the yard behind the pub. Small as it was, it had to double as an exit for both of us on our speedy way back to the docks.

Once we had regained our breath, poor Ralph tried to explain himself.

He indicated that he felt a stupid idiot. He wished that he had known that a small warship, manned entirely by Polish Navy personnel, was being refitted in one of the other yards. The barman in the pub had just told him that the Red-cap MPs were patrolling the harbour area together with one of the Polish seamen, to keep their crew in order, when through the open door Ralph could see the patrol approach. Knowing that I was equally ignorant of the Polish language as I was of English, he thought that reticence was the order of the day.

Hence the ignominious exit.

A thought, which went through my mind at that stage, was, that here we were in Birkenhead - which was in jolly old England - but nothing had really changed for us. As had happened many times before in the ports of the Baltic or the North Sea, even the Japanese ones at Penang, we were playing cat-and- mouse with the Military Police. Pitting our wits against those in authority was the spice of life.

But all too soon our holiday came to an end.

The short trip through the dreaded Irish Sea, which this time was still benign, brought us back to our friends at Lisahally.

In comparison to our adventures, they had quite a boring time.

They were trying to look busy while actually doing as little as possible. On our return from Birkenhead, we had a job re-orientating ourselves. Many changes had taken place; for one thing the U-boat fleet seemed to have shrunk. Where at the beginning in June I had counted more than fifty boats, moored in bunches of five abreast, there were now gaps everywhere.

My fellow inmates informed me, that during our absence in Birkenhead, some ten or more boats had been transferred to one of the Scottish bases. Since two of the boats from our original pack had gone, I was not in the least surprised to hear that even on the short hop over the little pond called the Irish Sea, several boats gave up the ghost. In Germany, the chronic lack of non-ferrous metals such as brass and bronze frequently meant that less suitable materials had to be used in the manufacture of U-boats. It had often resulted in valves seizing or bearings running hot. Only the most meticu-

lous maintenance and lubrication of those parts of machinery made them perform as efficiently as they had done in action. Alas, and this was certainly the only reason, they had not been getting this 100% attention since the end of the war. Why anyone should have expected anything else, having made us prisoners after the end of hostilities, was beyond my understanding. So it turned out to be a good precaution, when the transferred boats had an escort of British war-ships, which could double as tugs - as one by one - the U-boats packed up.
And there was no way that we were going to explain the absence of silver from many of the electrical switches!

When were whiling away the time during our jaunt to Birkenhead, a surprise was sprung on our comrades at the base. Unknown to us, in preparation for the impending winter, a totally new camp had been prepared for us at the edge of the base. By the time we rejoined, our happy band, the rotters had already booked all the best and most comfortable bunks. All we were left with were the ones near the doors to the ablution block, where an unending stream of traffic to and from the toilets threatened to keep us awake all night.

The very thought of it made me feel sick inside, but I should have had more faith in my fellow men. One good pal, Paul, with whom I had earlier struck up a chess-friendship, had reserved me a top-bunk next to his own right in the middle of the hall. He had made sure we could continue to play while resting in our warm beds. But several men from our returning trip to Birkenhead were out of luck. They played merry hell about having to take the bunks that were left. Good old Paul had saved my life and I promised to dance at his wedding.
Our new address was
PoW Camp No.172 - Lisahally/ Northern Ireland.
But had you addressed your correspondence to the Lisahally Hilton, it surely would have found us as well.

A very posh hut, the size of an aircraft hangar, formed the main part of this camp. The compulsory barbed-wire entanglements of course surrounded it. Illuminated during the periods of darkness by searchlights and guarded by our own guard of honour from the Queen's Regiment.
Inside the huge building, hundreds two-tier bunk beds were lined-up in three or four long rows along one side, taking up about half of the hall. In the other half there was plenty of room for chairs and tables, on which we could eat or engage in all kinds of card- or board games. A couple of table tennis tables were normally stacked away at the side, but were used to the

full at every opportunity. The first class wash and toilet facilities were located just off the main hall, on the side next to the bunks.

Now that we were all living under one roof, so to speak, it was possible to recruit enough chess players to run a few competitions. It helped to pass the time at times when we were not needed on board ship.
Furthermore, I was able to introduce the more interested ones among our mob to the war-game of "I-go", or sometimes called just 'Go', a game which we had found to be extremely popular with the Japanese.

But it wasn't all play; during weekdays we had to make our way back on board. Marching in orderly fashion from the new camp to the long wooden jetty took only about twenty minutes along a narrow country road. Halfway along we passed a few industrial buildings, which somebody identified as lime-burning plant. As we go near them, we felt obliged to strike-up a lusty marching song. It brought all the office staff and other employees to the windows. We started to look forward to the smiles of the twenty or so young and beautiful Irish colleens, among them - and we thought this to be a bit of a paradox as the area around here was almost pure white from the lime dust- two coal-black girls with the largest flashing eyes I had ever seen in my life. Their smiles were a real tonic for us to start the day with. But it had its dark side as well, as to us it brought home the awful truth that it had been a long time since we were able to actually touch and hold somebody soft, warm and female.
These lovelies reminded us of home, civvy-street and in my case Irmchen, Lotti, Gretel, Hilde, etc., as they represented the future and our impending freedom.

And so the days passed by with nothing much happening except one time, when our dear captors decided to make our little lot a bit more unpleasant. Some said it was done as a reprisal for alleged mistreatment by German guards of Canadian soldiers at a PoW camp in Germany.
They decided to put us on hunger rations for a while.
Today I can't recall the menu for a whole day, but slices of chewing-gum-like bread and jam seemed to form our breakfast and lunch, while the main meal of the day consisted of a bowl of steaming hot, green water, which smelled if not actually tasted of cabbage. A few drops of fat swimming on top provided the clue that at one time this concoction had at least seen some actual meat. Prizes were offered to anyone finding an actual piece of a cabbage leaf in their ration.

To us, who were barely twenty years old and still developing physically, this could have been a most serious matter. We had all been hungry in the

past. For instance, before joining the forces, we had all lived on the very meagre portions of food available on our ration card.
But here in Britain we were supposed to be Prisoners of War and protected by the Geneva Convention which was signed by all nations, including the Allies.
Reprisals against PoWs were explicitly banned under its provisions.
But then, Tommy had won the war and assumed the right to do whatever he liked.

Our Officers, who must have been in quarters nearby, complained to the Commander of the base about those breaches of agreements. Since they got no satisfaction, they threatened to go on strike. Of course this gesture turned out to be futile, the CO just picked out two of the spokesmen among the officers, labelled them the blackest of Nazis and had them transferred to a penal camp. He probably earned himself a pat on the back for this brave deed. We did appreciate the gesture of our own officers, but we were not particularly impressed with Tommy's treachery.

While we still had to maintain our boats at the jetty, we had access to the tins of food we had hidden on board during the trip over from Norway and which we had forgotten to declare on our arrival here.

Once they were the proud 'Wolves of the Atlantic'.
Now the boats are rusting away at Lisahally.

However, the action by the CO Lisahally removed even the slightest inclination on our part to do any real work. We got better and better at acting busy.

There was one little snag with our food-supply situation. At weekends, we were now confined to our quarters at the Hilton and we had to rely entirely on the rubbish Tommy was feeding us.
The guards, who supervised our marching to and fro and who also ran the guarding of the camp, had all been handpicked from the "Queens" regiment and all of them had been PoWs in Germany. We assumed that they were selected to make life a little more difficult for us.
If that had been the idea, then it certainly backfired.
Most of them, so they told us, had been working on farms in Southern Germany and had been treated very fairly by the local farmers.
None of them held a grudge against us. In fact they often closed one or both eyes when we had to resort to the odd bit of smuggling in and out of the camp.

We used our imagination to smuggle tins of food from the boats into camp, to be use at weekends. We draped our leather-jackets over both shoulders without putting our arms into the sleeves. Those sleeves had five or six tins of various foods in each of them, prevented from falling-out by the elasticated cuffs at the end of each sleeve.
Thus we marched along, singing loudly so as to drown out the clatter of the tins of bully beef, sausage-meat, jam, ham or fruit in syrup hidden in our jackets. Our guards often joined in our singing but I refused to believe that they didn't smell a king-sized rat or two.

But finally the supplies from the boats ran out.
Other sources had to be found.
The camp-committee, which had been formed a few days ago, held a secret meeting, at which certain decisions were taken.
Lots were drawn to decide who of the camp's inmates were to become heroes.
A devilish clever plan had been developed and was almost ready to be implemented.
It would involve every man jack in our camp, as each and every member would be given a specific task to perform.
If the scheme worked, then everybody was guaranteed to benefit from its success.
How?
As soon as it was dark enough that evening, every member of compound assembled in one of the huts at the northern side of the camp where one of our Officers, who had previous musical training, held a massed-choir practice.

There was no shortage of singing-talent in our ranks, but for this particular exercise the quality of our singing was of considerably less importance than its volume.

And can anyone guess why in the cool of an evening, all the windows in that particular hut were gradually opened?

If I had been a guard on the outside of the barbed wire, I too, would have enjoyed the harmonious rendering of old sea-shanties and other well-known folk songs as a welcome diversion from the monotonous pounding of the beat.

When I said that everybody had assembled in this hut, I had forgotten about the five specially selected chaps, who, equipped with kit bags, had crawled on their bellies through or under the barbed wire barriers into the large hangar adjacent to our prison camp, while our guards were listening and soaking up some culture.

Herbert, the ex Petty Officer helmsman from ***KARO-AS***, had been one of the five lucky ones selected to become celebrities. A few weeks ago we still had to address him as *Herr Bootsmaat* and salute him at every turn, but now that we were stuck in the same old hellhole and because there was only one year between our ages, we had become more like old buddies. He told us afterwards how he fared on that particular evening, when everything had been planned down to the last detail. A time-schedule had been set up, according to which each phase of the operation had to run.

At the prearranged time, a particularly vigorous and noisy piece of the choir's repertoire had been struck-up, which was the cover for the first phase of the exercise - the exit.

Once the five-man raiding party was safely inside the hangar, which incidentally was the store of the food removed from our U-boats at the time of their arrival in Lisahally, the mood of the singing changed with the renditions of quieter and more sentimental numbers.

He went on to say, 'this first phase went like a dream. We knew exactly what we wanted to take and where we would find it. In fact we had to wait nearly 15 minutes before it was 21.45 hours, the time prearranged for our return dash.'

All this information helped to explain why the choirmaster kept consulting a watch at every opportunity and why at that time we had to put our heart and soul into one of the many marching songs in our repertoire. What he didn't explain was, why we had to practice this section for so long. But again, this became clear when Herbert went on to relate the next stage of the adventure.

‘The first, second and third men had sneaked back and it was my turn to go next. The kit bag was quite heavy and the corners of the tins stuck into my back. Making sure that I didn’t make any sudden moves, which would cause the tins to rattle and give the game away, I started out and covered the distance to the fence in no time at all. The loud singing drowned out any small sliding noises I made.’

Up to this point everything had apparently gone to plan.

But trouble lay ahead.

‘I still don’t know how on earth I managed to get stuck right under the bloody barbed wire. My kit bag must have snagged on one of the barbs and the more I struggled to get free, the more I seemed to get entangled. Even the seat of my pants got ripped to hell.’

I could sense how foolish Herbert felt. A lookout inside the wire kept the choirmaster informed of how things were going. He kept urging Herbert to get a move on and there was the fifth member of the raiding party, desperately trying to get past him as well. But he was truly stuck when behind him, he heard this English voice, ‘Now I’ve seen every-bloody-thing! I’ve been trained at great expense to prevent prisoners from escaping, but here we have a smart-arsed PoW trying to get INTO the camp? What am I supposed to do now?’

Herbert drew a big breath to compose himself before continuing ‘this big Lance corporal stood there towering above me. I nearly shit myself, but thank heavens I could speak enough school-English to tell him about the desperate food situation inside the camp.’ Herbert also assured him that those tins only contained some synthetic butter and black bread, whereupon, unbelievably, the Tommy untangled him from the barbed wire. He also held up the wires to allow him and the fifth person to crawl through, urging them to get the hell out of it and not to give him any further trouble.

That night, we all took part in a beautiful midnight-snack.

Not long after, thank goodness, the food-situation eased again.

A few days later, it became the turn of our Ace of Diamonds as she was now, while sailing under the British flag, to have her Mercury-containers removed from her keel. I wondered why I was always one of those chosen to accompany the boats on their docking trips. But here I was again, *en route* to Birkenhead. The Tommies, who accompanied us this time, were a different lot from the last trip. There wasn’t a chance of getting a game of chess during this short journey. In fact, this lot of Brits was not in the least like the last lot. They were a lot younger and perhaps more inclined to believe all the stupid tripe they were told about us. Whichever, they were apt

to keep their distance.
Well, well. Not to worry.

As this was our own little tub, we knew just a little bit more about her than anybody else on this earth. Both Hubert and I knew that down in the bilge, below the No.1 and No.2 batteries, there used to be stores of beer. Surely it was our duty to service the electrics. After all - they were the source of all power on this ship. Lets hope, that nosey-parkers of all descriptions, had left our treasures alone. Who would look for booze under tons of battery-lead and acids? There was just one snag. The trap-door down to No.1 battery was right beside the Captains corner and although he would not think it strange for one of us to disappear down there, he would certainly be aware of any bottles of beer finding their way up and back to our quarters.

There was nothing else for it - should we be so lucky and find any goodies down there, we would have to enjoy them while lying flat out on the battery-service trolley, me in No.1 and Hubert in No.2.

We were lucky!

Having tasted the English bitter on our last trip to Birkenhead, this beer here, which we had purloined in Norway, was relatively tame.

However, it was cool and it went down a treat.

I didn't dare to have more than just two bottles, for fear of giving the game away to our Capitano. While we were down there, we did check the battery cells as well and found that a few of them needed topping-up with distilled water. There should have been a supply of it down here, but the container in its keeper was empty. It gave me an excuse to surface and replenish the special can from a large carboy in the E-room. Hubert was already there, doing the same thing.

'Guess what I found down there?' he asked me.

'I don't know about you, but I located about twenty bottles of beer in No.1. How on earth can we get the stuff out of there without Tommy getting wind of it?'

'I can go one better' he smugly announced ' I found three bottles of Akevit as well as some beer.'

Listening to his boasts I had a flash of inspiration. 'I tell you what to do. After you've topped-up the battery, empty the rest of the water down in to the bilge and then fill up your container with Norse hooch. Nobody will take any notice of you when you bring distilled water up with you.'

Lovely!

The remainder of the trip to the Mersey went like a dream.

I was off-watch and sleeping-off the terrible Akevit when the pilot took the ACE into Birkenhead and into the same dry-dock, which we had recently vacated. There was no call to get us out of the way into a PoW camp. After the last debacle at Oldham, we were just as pleased to be staying on board. We would find things to do, to while away a few days.

There was one thing though, which on the crossing-over had caused us a bit of concern. The old diesels had stood the test of time fabulously and never missed so much as a beat, but in the E-room, which happened to be next to our mess, there had been a few fireworks.

Well - fireworks perhaps was an exaggeration. From the switch boxes over the one serviceable E- motor, which was used to recharge our main batteries, there were a few sparks and spitting noises. While we were in dock we looked for the trouble. I had a fair idea what the cause of that problem was, and so had everybody else. When we opened the switch-box, we could see the frazzled, coal-black and burned-out remains of the contacts therein. Some thieving bastard or other had found a use for the silver and during the trip here it was the steel-parts, which normally should carry the silver inserts, which made a very bad contact. It was just a miracle that the two parts of each switch-section had not welded themselves together, with the 110 Volts passing through them.

What could we do to get the tub back to Lisahally without Tommy getting to know about this state of affairs?

One electrical wizard came up with the answer. As the other Main-E-motor was still lying in bits in the Siemen's Works in Bergen, the switch-gear for it would not be required again. With a little bit of fiddling he managed to repair the damaged switches in a kind of a way, cannibalising others in doing it. This botch-up should see us back to Ireland safely.

Having done our good deed, we carried on having a nice holiday at Tommy's expense. Leaning over the rails of the deck beside the conning tower we could see the eager beavers of the dockyard labour force humping the small but extremely heavy mercury containers. We had helped to put them there, so we knew exactly how much of a job it was.

Since our boat was not the first U-boat to enter Birkenhead, there didn't seem to be such a great demand for the general populace to come and stare; at least not during the daytime.

Some of my chums played endless games of cards; others still had some books, which they probably had already read so often that they could recite the individual pages from memory. We also still had a collection of records on board, only the very contentious propaganda ones had been tipped overboard a long time ago. But there were also a few new English ones, which had been added by somebody. The 'Lambeth Walk', the 'Donkey Serenade' and 'Tipperary' had already been in our collection along with our original 'Lili Marlene'. But now we could relax, with the tanoy blaring out 'Put an other Nickel in' and 'The stars at night are big and bright, deep in the heart of Texas'.

But then, as the evening drew near, the number of people on the edge of the docks got bigger. We once more decided not to disappoint our public as we assembled to sit around on the bridge and the wintergarden behind it. Some of the ladies of the dock-canteen recognised us from our previous visit and waving they encouraged us to give them a song or two.

As on previous occasions in Pembroke and here in Birkenhead, we obliged. And this became a regular nightly command performance and was thoroughly appreciated by all and sundry. In addition, as before, there was nice audience participation when we rendered our party-pieces 'Tipperary' and our latest 'Roll out the barrel.' It must be said however that this fraternal activity was not altogether appreciated by some of the Brass hats. They were probably quite happy to see the end of us, when finally the work in dry-docks had been completed and we had set sail for our return to Ireland. The sea was still reasonable calm, but it could change any day now. Now, in the first part of October, one could expect a few storms chasing up from the West. They would severely test our sea legs, which with lack of use had become rusty.

All was well until after we had picked-up the old familiar pilot at the entrance to the Foyle. Just as we began to look forward to our next meal and a good nights rest, it happened.

From my station just below the ladders to the bridge I could hear all sorts of commotion, yelling and shouting taking place among the bridge-party. I could also hear the helmsman pounding the buttons of his switches with both fists. But before you could say 'Jack Robinson', there was the sickly slithering and sliding noise below us under the keel as our pride and joy ran onto a sand bank and got thoroughly stuck fast.

As far as one could tell from the language on the bridge, we had experienced a slight steering problem. Our Royal Navy Lieutenant CO had apoplexy, which must have affected his speech. He could hardly get his words out, as his face took on a deep purple colour. But when he finally found words, we couldn't find any of them in Herbert's or my ordinary standard dictionary.

But the diesel crew got a German translation of his speech, which went:

‘Both effing engines full a--stern.’ The old girl shuddered and shook as engines ground to a stop, went into reverse and then had the revs built-up to the maximum. But there was no chance of getting free from this slimy grip on her keel.

As the tide was on its way out, there wasn’t a snowball’s chance in hell to get into Lisahally that day. The next high tide would do the trick, but what exactly went wrong.

We were ordered to examine the steering gear, which was stuck at ‘Full to starboard’. Having disengaged the electric motor drive, by using the manual hand wheel we were able to move the twin-rudders in any direction. So there were no mechanical reasons for the malfunction, but how about the electrics?

Indeed, here we found the reason for the trouble. One of the homemade silver contacts had come adrift inside the switchgear and jammed itself into an awkward position to make permanent contact, resulting in the rudders jamming ‘Full to starboard’.

The official accident report spoke of the poor quality material used in the construction of the switchgear, an excuse, which was all too often, used to cover-up other failings in the maintenance system.

If Tommy had only known the truth!

We decided that it would be extremely prudent to keep our silver rings well out of sight. Anyway, the switch was easily repaired and when the Ace of Diamonds was re-floated at the next high tide, it was all systems go again until we were safely moored at the head of the wooden jetty.

Since now all three Type IXD2 boats of the Monsoon Group had their keel cargoes removed, this trip was probably our last one to a dry-dock.

So! What next?

CHAPTER NINETEEN

My pocket-book calendar showed that we were in November. The weather had taken a turn for the worst. Even when tied up on the long wooden pier in the sheltered river Foyle, our boats were being tossed around a bit. Not having been to sea recently, some or our chaps started to feel queasy again, or perhaps it was just their imagination. I was given a nice surprise on one afternoon. An interpreter informed me that on the next day I would be required to go to one of the other jetties, where the Type XXI boats were moored. There I was to assist the U.S.Navy in their effort to familiarise themselves with the two boats allocated to the USA.

After returning from the Far East at the end of last year, we were surprised to see so many boats of this type in every dockyard. Many had already been commissioned and were being put through their working-up trials by their new crews. Along with the promise of other miracle-weapons, the arrival of those technically advanced boats had acted like a tonic on the flagging morale of all and sundry. The propaganda had made them out to be wonder-weapons, indestructible because of their ability to remain undetected.

I had first learned about them while still at submarine school.
And on that evening back in the PoW camp, I refused all offers of a game, but wanted to lie down on my bunk and try to remember exactly what it was I had been told about them. As a trained engineer I knew all about the propulsion systems, their diesels, main- and silent-running- motors and their large, super-powerful batteries. A snorkel-tube, similar to the one we had now on ***KARO-AS***, allowed them to stay submerged indefinitely, making the Type XXI boats, or Electro-boats as they were now known, the very first true submarine vessel. Combined with a completely new streamlined shape of boat, which made no provision to running on the surface, it was those powerful batteries and electric motors, which gave the new boats hitherto unheard-of underwater speeds. Of the many other improvements built into the new boats, as for instance their stronger hull which allowed them to go to far greater depths, their new tracking and torpedo systems, which allowed them to track and fire from way down in the cellar, without actually having to see the target, I knew only very little.

They could also dive quicker (20 sec) and deeper (270 m) than any of the older types. Hundreds had been completed by the time the war finished, but to the best of my knowledge, because the crews had to learn all about those new innovations, none of the boats had actually been in action. As a last desperate step to speed-up their manufacture they had been built by revolutionary new methods. Manufactured in eight or nine pre-fabricated sections somewhere inland, preferably beside a navigable river or canal, they were shipped on barges to the major shipyards for final assembly. We had seen hundreds of those sections lying all over the place. If the entire forward planning worked-out and the right sections were available at the right time, it took only six months to complete a new boat. To man all the new ships, entire experienced crews were transferred en-block from the older and largely outdated type of boats. Although they were already confident with each other, they still had to learn a completely new ball game of running this U-boat.

It was only because ***KARO-AS*** was of the Monsoon-group and intended to take cargo to the Far East, that we had stayed with our lucky old lady. She could carry a lot more fuel than the Electo boats and was therefore able to operate over far greater distances, even though in all other ways she had become outdated 'Old Iron'.

Fewer and fewer German crewmembers were now left at the Lisahally base and none of them had served on Type XXI boats. Hence the Yanks would have to make do with me.

At 10 am on the following day, we had already been working on board for an hour, when a guard called me up on the jetty and accompanied me on my walk to the Yankee-boats.

On the way over, my guard, while walking beside me with his rifle slung across his back and with his hands in his pockets, told me that apart from the two boats allocated to the USA, there were other Electro boats getting ready to sail to Russia.

He kept up a constant chatter, of which I understood less than half. I thought to myself, I really must make an effort to learn this damned lingo.

I think he was trying to tell me that he wished that he and I would get home to our folk soon, instead of wasting our valuable youth here.

He was a man after my own heart!

Once we arrived at our destination, he handed me over to a Yankee Naval Lieutenant, who took me down below into the control room.

Here I was met by a group of half a dozen US Officers. And would you believe it, judging by the heaped ashtrays, which certainly had never been part of the equipment of a German U-boat, they had been chain-smoking here for hours.

It must be that our regulations of absolutely no smoking below deck because of possible chlorine battery-gases, were on the over-cautious side, but this was ridiculous. But before I could make any comment about their carelessness, one of them offered me one of his Lucky Strikes.
Well! Well!
Do I warn them about the dangers of their action?

Not on your Nelly- I accepted the weed with thanks like a drowning man accepts a lifebelt. If the bloody caboodle goes-up - so be it.
Meanwhile I was going to enjoy my decent, if heavily perfumed, cigarette. Unlike, the stinking Turkish Pasha rubbish Tommy sometimes gave us, it didn't even make me cough.
During the next few hours the American Naval Officers grilled me about the function of various instruments and other gear. One of them acted as an interpreter.

It seemed a decision had been taken recently by the Allied powers, which had allocated those two Type XXI boats as well as two of the equally advanced but much smaller Type XXIII boats for transfer to the US Navy for evaluation. Britain also decided to keep some and re-commission them into the Royal Navy for trials. Since the Allies had seen the type XXI and XXIII boats, they lost all interest in the older types.

Russia, when conquering the East German provinces, had plenty of Type XXIII boats, but wanted 2 Type VIICs, one Type IXC and four Type XXIs. Those had also been assembled on the other end of this jetty.
According to the interpreter, IVAN had been very cross with everybody, including the Royal Navy, if only the slightest bit of gear disappeared from those boat. The REDS had come armed with accurate detailed inventories for each boat and caused a major international incident if a pair of binoculars or even a simple manual - say for the *Junkers* compressors - was not in its proper location.
When my Yanks complained about them, I could only point out sarcastically:
'They're YOUR friends and comrades in arms, aren't they?'

After further lessons about the trimming system and other matters, they confided that they were very highly impressed with the technical advances incorporated in this new type of U-boat.
'Its a damned good job you didn't get them into action against us in time.'
By this time I must have smoked at least ten further cigarettes, Lucky Strikes as well as Camels and all with a bad conscience, while in the back of my mind I had been racking my brains how I could get a hold of some

more to take away with me. One Lieutenant had already slipped me a packet, which was more than half-full. He had noticed my all-too-apparent delight in having a decent drag.

When it was time for my return to my own boat, I plucked-up courage to ask him whether he thought that among his fellow Officers there was a demand for a nice camera in exchange for cigarettes. He said 'If it is a *Leika* you can name your own prize, otherwise ...

But I wouldn't mind one for myself, if it is a decent make and has a good lens. Bring it with you when you come back tomorrow.' This was news to me; nobody had told me that they needed me again.

With that in mind, I went up on deck and across the gangplank on to the jetty. I expected the same guard from the Queen's Regiment to escort me back.

But No!

There was this young American G.I. waiting for me.

Ah, well. I gave him a cheerful 'Hello' and fell in beside him with my hands in my pockets to keep them warm in the slightly chilly evening air.

But before I knew it, I had the business end of his rifle poking hard in my back, while he was screaming at me:

'Take you effing hands out of your effing pocket you effing Nazi bastard and get an effing move on.'

There was nothing in our naval manual to give us any suggestions as to how we should behave under those circumstances.

In the absence of divine guidance and while he had his finger on the trigger, this didn't seem to be the best time to argue. So I just followed my instinct and fell-in with his wishes in extra quick time.

The poor bastard had been shaking, either with passion or with fear. But then, he was barely out of nappies and had probably been subjected to all sorts of daft fairy tales.

At the double, we jogged all the way back to where I could rejoin my mates and because the brat was dressed in a very heavy winter coat, 'Billy the Kid' was puffing and panting a hell of lot more than I was.

On our arrival we were met by the regular Tommy guard. When he saw the way the Yank had escorted me back, he went purple in his face and sent the little boy on his way home, accompanied by some very choice words.

The second visit to Uncle Sam's boats went more or less like the first one. This time I carried my leather jacket draped over my shoulders, on account of having a camera sewn into my left sleeve. It had to be the left one, as my Tommy guard always wanted to walk to the right of me, because then his rifle was on the side furthest away from me.

Clever?

No. Just careful!

When I produced the camera and showed it to the Yanks, they turned their noses up in disdain. Not knowing too much about photography, I had accepted the word of the Chinese Gent in Surabaja, when he extolled the virtues of this gadget. According to the price tag, it should have been a really good one.

When the Yanks had recovered from their laughter, the interpreter Lieutenant put me wise to the fact that it was a bad Japanese copy of a good camera.

'But we will take it as a souvenir, but at best we can only give you 200 Camels for it, mostly for "good will and as a thank-you for your help with the systems."

Can you imagine this?

Two hundred American cigarettes in exchange for something I was forbidden to possess anyway.

I was absolutely delirious with delight!

Those Yankees can't be all bad, can they?

As a thank-you, I for my part helped them a bit more with their understanding of the new and improved toilet facilities on those new Electro-boats. Being able to stay submerged indefinitely necessitated new methods of waste disposal, such as could be operated against the considerable outside water pressure. On our older boats, the system of using elbow grease to pump-out the contents of the WC pan in order to feed the fishes, was of no use here. On the new XXI boats were a total of three heads, from which you flushed the waste into a holding tank. Those, when full, were emptied by means of compressed air. Sounds a lot more civilised, but one supposed that care would still have to be taken to make sure that any potential submarine-hunters were up-wind when the tanks were emptied. Knowing submariners, you wouldn't have needed sniffer-dogs to locate the source of the pong.

At the end of that day I was escorted back by a Tommy guard.

Thank God.

As I said before, since dear Tommy had managed to get his filthy mitts on a few of our latest types XXI and XXIII boats he appeared to have lost all interest in our older ones. But it wasn't the new ones, but those heaps of old iron, of a design which stemmed from the Ark, which had given him more trouble and bother than he could have wished for. At one point, near the beginning of the war, those Grey Wolves had given him a real fright.

It must have dawned on him by now that his trouble was not all to do with our hardware, but the dedication and discipline of their young crews. They and they alone had made those bits of old-iron work like Swiss-clockwork.

But the future was to be found in faster and newer designs of submersibles. Boats which were able to stay down below for indefinite lengths of time and which were to be equipped with better and deadlier homing torpedoes and other weapons.

For us Lords here at Lisahally it meant our almost daily excursions from the POW compound to our boats became less frequent with the resulting deterioration in their maintenance.
Our once proud Ace of Diamonds had left Germany over eight months ago, with coats of sparkling light-grey paintwork covering every inch of her hull.

Her appearance had stood out from all the other U-boats, which normally hunted in the North Atlantic in their dark, almost black paint, which was meant to match the dark waters of that pond.
As she was scheduled to again try her luck in the lighter and brighter oceans of the East, she had sported an almost off-white camouflage. Against that background the red diamonds on both sides of the conning tower, which had given our tub her name, stood out like a shining beacons.
Lying idle for months on end, exposed to the summer sun, the autumn rain and the biting wind, which came with it, had transformed her and the rest of the fleet to a uniform reddish-brown rust colour. The worst affected ones were the boats which had been in action as the war ended, just like the boat with another still very bright looking playing card on her conning tower.

The Queen of Hearts, the boat we had sailed to Pembroke during June, had not seen any paint since leaving Surabaja at the end of last year.
Apart from their outward appearance, which was bad enough, some boats were beginning to list to either port or starboard at funny angles. This was probably caused by the lack of attention to their trim.
It really broke our hearts to see those pathetic rust-buckets. They were lying there like a herd of useless old nags, waiting for the Coup de grâce from the knackersman.
Whatever your plans are Tommy, get a *verdammtes* move on!

His annoying indecision meant that all PoWs had a lot more time on our hands. Many of us passed the time playing cards; others preferred board games or table tennis. We would have appreciated some outdoor sport to keep our fitness up to scratch, but because of chronic lack of open-air facilities, that would have to wait.

In the meantime, we had managed to persuade one of our English-speaking Officers to organise lessons in Tommy's lingo. A few of us were particularly keen to learn the rudiments of elementary English grammar.
From our contacts with men from the Royal Navy we had already started to learn a lot of English words. Whether we would succeed in finding some, or most of those words in any standard dictionary, would be another question. Even the Camp's CO got interested in our efforts and promised to ob-

tain some German-English-German dictionaries for sale in our canteen. Heavens knows what we would use for money, after we had bought a few cigarettes and matches.

Shortly after the opening in October of the Lisahally Hilton, Tommy decided there should be a daily head-count of all its inmates. Presumably, the British Army or Navy manuals demanded stricter treatment of Prisoners of War and how to stop them from wanting to escape.

It might have occurred to those Brass hats that we had nowhere to go anyway and the way things were in our homeland, occupied as it was, we were much better off right here.

But the little book said that we must have daily Roll Calls. They were useless and a bloody nuisance.

At the most inconvenient times of day or, more often than not in the middle of the night, an NCO, accompanied by couple of guards, would roll up, bawling and shouting the odds.

'Fall in for a Roll Call and look smart about it.'

It took me a little while to figure out what all the noise was about. They wanted us to get out of bed and line-up in three ranks.

U-boat men never undress to go to sleep; in any case it was getting too cold for that at this time of year. Little wonder that we were anything but keen or in too great a hurry to comply.

When order was established in the ranks, the NCO reported to his Officer and together they walked along our lines to take the count. On several occasions the count had to be repeated, sometimes even for a third time, as the former military precision with which we would have followed the orders of our own Officers had deserted us.

The semi-chaotic assembly was indeed difficult to count and we didn't consider it to be our job to make it any easier for dear old Tommy. The whole procedure turned out to be a bit of a laugh, as many of us were quietly barracking or banging things to try and break the concentration of the counting Officer. We did get the distinct impression, that he was not enjoying his work at all.

As with all good things, there was always a snag. Try as we may, it proved impossible to shut-up some of the more noisy specimen at the back of our ranks. The trouble was, those voices behind us were swearing at the top of their voices ... in English!

It must be difficult to believe, but this was really happening at the Lisahally Hilton.

Imagine the scene:

Some hundred or so Prisoners of War lined-up to be counted, when from somewhere at the back came this:
'What the effing hell is going on here?'
Those couldn't have been the words of men who were only just now starting to learn this language.
So, who was behind those blasphemous outbursts?
History stories will never tell you about this.
The victor writes the History books, but only the parts, which fit in with his saintly image.
They ignore anything that doesn't fit into the pattern of heroism and patriotism of their victorious Army, Navy and Air forces.

But there was another side to the coin. In spite of all the propaganda and all the orders of 'strictly no fraternisation', there were ordinary Brit matlows prepared to stick out their necks to show that they understood the real situation much better than their 'so-called' superiors.
They appreciated the fact that we were human and had human needs and that we were a long way from our loved ones, our wives and girl friends.
And their solutions to that problem were quite simple.

A few *Lords* had received invitation to go ashore, in order to spend a few precious hours in female company. Any Naval base could pride itself of having hangers-on, the original groupies of the nineteen-forties and Londonderry proved to be no exception.
But there remained the problem of the head-count.
Simple!
For every PoW who was given the chance to go ashore, a matelot would stand in, after first swapping clothes. When we were marched back to camp in the evening, after a day's work on the boats, a phantom PoW would march with us.

Once inside the barbed wire, every one of them invariably complained that our quarter were better than their own, lighter, airier and infinitely less cramped.
On the other hand there was the food! We were told it was the same as served at the British base. But was it?
Since on this particular day it was my friend Hubert, who had the day off in Londonderry, it fell to me to look after Able Seaman Peter White.
Chalky White had been part of the crew that took the Ace of Diamonds to Birkenhead and was well known to all of us. But I had the devil's own job to keep the beggar quiet. He had strong opinions on just about everything.

'Somebody is on the make with your grub.' was his opinion, and 'I am not very hungry, you might as well have my share.'

During the evening we had a good chinwag, lying on our bunks, which were next to one-an-other. He had photos of his family in his pocket and to tell you the truth, his Mum and Dad looked every bit as proud of him as my parents were of me. Long into the night we talked, or because of the language difference, we mimed about our thoughts and hopes for the future.

But then, shortly after we had felt inclined to turn in for a night's sleep, the quiet of the early hours was shattered by the arrival of the roll-call party. And this was the time when I had to work overtime to keep Pete out of trouble.

I had never heard him swear before.

But on that night he went through his whole vocabulary of obscenities, half of which I didn't understand.

But that half of his speech was enough to give me the idea that he was not very pleased. Me? I was just satisfied when the count was over without Pete being carted-off in handcuffs.

Next morning the return swap took place.

'Your damned love life is giving folk heart-attacks' was my greeting to Hubert on that particular morning. 'I just hope it was worth it for you.'

A very tired smile was his answer.

All those little happenings helped to ensure that there were very few dull moments in our lives at the Lisahally Hilton.

There was one particular aspect about our home here at Lisahally, which brought wonderful images to my mind's eye.

They concerned a very plush Rococo-style Palace located in Potsdam, not far from Berlin. I remembered that every single room and every corner of each room in the palace had been in pursuit of the arts, painting, literature or music. The library, a room as big as your normal common and garden cathedral, its long walls covered with books from floor to ceiling had been occupied by funnily dressed men, who were either writing or reading while studying subjects from mathematics to astronomy. Among them was a French guy called Voltaire, who went in for philosophising. He had a permanent key to this place, as he was well in with the man of the house who could speak French better than the language of his own kingdom.

In the ballroom, the lady of the house held a knees-up attended by all the young things of the neighbourhood. Dressed in all their finery, their faces masked by powder and make-up, their body odours hidden by perfume, they were engaging in daring dances such as Gavottes and Quadrilles while string quartets gave renditions of the latest pop-tunes by Wolfgang Amadeus Mozart and others.

In another room, which was as large as any average concert hall and which was playfully called the Music-room, the master of house was practising his flute playing while being accompanied by an equally ancient musician on the spinet. The date was in the latter part of the eighteenth century, or thereabouts.

The man of the house was King Frederick the Great of Prussia.

This magnificent pleasure-palace at Potsdam, which I kept dreaming about, had only one thing in common with our dump at the Lisahally Hilton and that was the name displayed in large letters above our makeshift stage located in the corner of our hangar.

Sanssoucci.

Which in French stood for 'Without care' or 'Without worry'.

Nobody knew where the material and trimmings for this enterprise had sprung from, but it appeared out of nowhere. A few artistically minded sailors had organised themselves into a theatre-type company, to try and entertain the multitude. Led by a few Officers of Bohemian background, they organised short plays, musical or vocal recitals and other variety shows.

Having a captive audience was an advantage, but even so, many of us would have paid to see the fun.

Every Sunday evening they had something else up their sleeve.

Prior to one of the very last performances ever to be held at our own stage, our ***KARO-AS*** helmsman PO Herbert had produced several programs for that night's performance. It promised to be quite a night.

A budding academic, Herbert's copperplate hand-written programs were pure perfection and a joy to behold. He had spent hours on producing a couple of dozen copies. Only a few special friends managed to get a hold of one but as far as I could establish, only a single original ever survived the PoW time. Herbert managed to hide his original design between the inner soles of his shoes, when overzealous guards in later camps relieved him of any diaries or notes, even those scribbled on toilet paper.

The date on the programs was the 8th of November 1945 and that day remained in my mind as one of the most enjoyable in all the time spent as PoW in Northern Ireland.

We were becoming more and more convinced that the time was fast approaching when we would say a final Good-Bye to our boats. No wonder we were thoroughly fed-up and in urgent need of a tonic.

The show on that Sunday evening at our camp's Sanssoucci provided just that. After fully seven months behind barbed wire, we were ready to be entertained. There weren't enough seats available, so we just squatted on the floor in front of the stage.

The musical purists would have been able to pick fault with several of the singers' voices. Number 4 on the program, the medley of Folk-songs, provided us with an opportunity to join-in and the volume of our singing immediately helped to compensate for any shortcomings in the ability of the soloists. The next item on the menu gave the soloists their real chance to shine. By the time the camp-choir gave their rendering of the Soldiers- and Spinner Choruses from the Flying Dutchman, there wasn't a dry eye in the house. We had always thought ourselves to be tough and hardened individuals, but being reminded of the time when we were sitting on our Mother's knee while she crooned those lovely old tunes was just too much.

By the time we arrived at Mozart's 'Cradle song' and a little later at Brahms' "Good evening, good night", we had worn ourselves out applauding every soloist, the choir and the 'Ensemble' of harmonicas, combs and home-made percussion instruments, which was light-heartedly called the 'Camp Orchestra'.

A copy of Herbert's handwritten program looked like this.

Sonntag den 8 Nov. 1945

SANSSOUCi

in

Ton und

1. Deutscher Sängergruß "Nichts kann uns rauben." H.Splitta.
2. "Abend auf See...." G.Wolters
3. "Wind weh'n.... " Alt Finnisches Volkslied.
4. Volkslieder-potpourri
5. "Ännchen von Tharau..." F. Silcher

"Rosemarie..."

"Am Brunnen vor dem Tore..." Franz Schubert

"Kein schöner Land..."

6. "Matrosenchor

"Spinnerchor v "Der Fliegende Holländer R. Wagner

7. "Geliebter mein..." Altdeutsches Liebeslied
8. "Wir segeln in die Ewigkeit..." Altenglisches Seemannslied

"Als Büblein klein an der Mutterbrust..." aus Die lustigen Weiber von Windsor.

9. "Ständchen Heike's.
10. "Allein, wieder allein..." auks "Der Zarewitch" von Lehar.

"Von Apfelblüten einen Strauß..." Land des Lächeln v. Lehar.

11. Menuett Boccherini.
12. "Santa Lucia..." Italienisches Lied.
13. Wiegenlied W.A.Mozart.
14. Pilgerchor Tannhäuser, R.Wagner
15. "Deutschland die Ferne..." ?
16. "Guten Abend, gute Nacht ..." Brahm

Verbindene Worte: Klaus Webel

Es wirken mit:

Das Lagerchor unter Werner Zacharias

Das Lagerorchester unter Hans Jürgen Mussel

CHAPTER TWENTY

On the morning after the *Sanssouci* concert I woke up with a splitting headache. Served me right, I supposed. But what could you expect, when after an abstinence of some time you engage in a bout of drinking. Only five of us shared the secret of finding a rare and long forgotten bottle of *Schnapps* from deep down in the bowels of ***KARO-AS***. It had lain there since we had entered Scapa Flow at the end of May and it couldn't have come to light at a more opportune moment. It was still quite easy to smuggle bits and pieces into the camp, as Tommy probably thought nothing worth smuggling could be left on the rusting hulls.

Almost ready for the "coup de grace"

We were utterly fed-up, with life in general and with the continual hanging-around, so a little tipple would ease the gloom.

While everybody else sat in front of the stage, giving the performance the undivided attention it deserved, one by one we had made our way to the ablutions, where we partook of the delicious liquid. It helped us to appreciate the performance even better, so much so, that at the end of it our hands were numb from our enthusiastic clapping.

However, let us return to the subject of U-boats.

Way back in the summer and unknown to us, the Allied Big Nobs had been bickering about the future of the surrendered U- boats and in apparent frustration decided to get rid of the lot, with the exception of a few of the Types XXI and XXIII, which were to be kept for research purposes by the four powers, USA, USSR, France and Britain.

The politicians had made the decision. Since they didn't have a clue about the technicalities of such an undertaking, it was then left to the Royal Navy's hierarchy to settle on the details.

We got to know about it in a roundabout way late in December. We were heading for our first Christmas behind barbed wire, in this strange country. It was hard to believe, but just one short year ago I was sitting at home with my childhood sweetheart Irmchen. Her photo was still among my few personal possessions, a bit creased but still good enough to make me dream vividly of our future together. Heaven knows where and when I shall be able to get a suitable gold ring instead of the brassy one I gave her last year.

But that problem soon resolved itself.

A Red-Cross letter arrived.

To the envy of all my fellow PoWs, who were still waiting to hear about the fate of their loved ones, I learned to my utter relief that both my Mum and Dad, as well as my two sisters and my fiancée Irmchen had survived the terrible battles around Berlin. They obviously couldn't say a lot about what had actually happened to them, as all letters were censored by first the Russians and then the Brits. 'We were so relieved to hear that you are alive and well, but are worried about your brother Heinz. All we have learned so far is, that his boat has been reported missing.

Until now we have been unable to hear what has become of his wife Trautchen and son Joseph. We pray that they and our other relation in Silesia are well. '

The further news about my dear sweetheart Irmchen was not what I had expected.

'We have seen very little of Irmchen lately. She appears to have found some new and influential friends among the leadership of the local KPD (Communist Party of Germany)' wrote Mum.
Reading between the lines, and then using my imagination, I concluded that our engagement had not stopped her from using her obvious physical attractions to ease her and her family's hardship. 'They don't appear to suffer from any shortages of food or other things' the letter continued.
Of course this hurt the old pride and after calming down I decided, that for the time being, there was little to be gained by losing sleep about a wedding-ring.

It was therefore a bit of a blessing in disguise when we were called upon to do a bit more sailing in the old crates. Without any prior warning, instead of engaging in the usual maintenance routine, a few of us engineers were detailed on board of one of the Type VIIC boats. We found ourselves in the company of some familiar matelots from the Royal Navy and after painting a broad white stripe right across the boat's forecastle, we proceeded to sail her out of the Foyle.

The flagstaff was bare this time. The destination: Unknown.
Well, we didn't take her right out to the open sea, only to the mouth of the Lough where a Royal Navy Destroyer hooked up a towline.
We were baffled: 'What the hell is Tommy up to this time?' Our POs or Chief POs didn't know either, but Herbert, with his smattering of school-English, had ascertained from one of the matelotes, that all the remaining U-boats were to be towed to an area 100 miles offshore to 600 meters of water and then used for target practice by all and sundry, particularly Beaufighters, Mosquitos, Sunderlands, Liberators, Warwicks and Catalinas. The scuttling was called 'Operation Deadlight'.

We had time to think about all this as a high-speed launch came alongside and whisked us off back to the base at Lisahally.
Well... Well... Well...!
What a stupid waste of scarce and valuable metals.
Copper wire and piping by the mile, brass valves and other trimmings by the tons, two - and in some cases four huge batteries weighed down with tons of precious lead. Diesel engines with could have powered many a new ship, silver and hundreds of tons of the highest grade steel making-up a U-boat's pressure-hulls.

A U-boat, just like any other submarine, was a gold mine for somebody taking the trouble to break her up carefully.
However, it was none of our business. Politics was not a subject that fol-

lowed reasoned lines. Furthermore, to try and take U-boats out into the open sea towed by a Destroyer instead of a tug, in near winter wind-and-sea conditions, reeked of lunacy.

Anybody with a grain of reasoning would have realised that up to 90% of the U-boat's mass is below the waterline, it would be like towing a sheet anchor. Destroyers are built for speed, like a racing car. At a towing speed of a few knots they would be as useless as a car without any low gears. To get the boat anywhere near the target area would require a large slice of luck!

But the politicians knew best ...or did they?

On the way back to base we passed another Type VIIC boat on her way out, possibly to the same destination.

During the next few days we took out two or three boats per day until after Christmas. Then, on the last day of the year it was the turn of our ***KARO-AS***.

By far one of the largest U-boats at Lisahally, she was one of the last ones to start on her final journey. During the two-hours it took to reach her rendezvous with the towing craft, the past years flashed through my mind like a speeded-up film.

In my minds eye I followed her from the days she entered the water for the first time to her commissioning into the *Kriegsmarine* by our Grand Admiral, on the day when she also acquired her lucky tactical sign, the Ace of Diamonds.

From my station on the starboard side of the control-room I smiled across to the ghosts of the two hydroplane operators. My good friend Wilhelm seemed to smile back at me with two of his front teeth missing from the day his mouth collided with handle of the large hand wheel of the forward hydroplane. The other hydroplane seemed to be operated by my archenemy Walter, the chap who treated his greasy Eels better than his fellow men.

Klaus Peter, our Chief Engineer was standing over them while he was studying the depth-gauges and other instruments while giving his almost inaudible depth-keeping instructions to the men in front of him and the man on the machine telegraph. I saw Mouse again in my mind's eye, jumping around as usual, just like the little rodent, which he was named he bore grudgingly.

From inside the conning tower I appeared to hear the Old Man's voice with his orders to keep the boat steady during his attack-run on the enemy, while the IWO's monotonous voice read out the readings of his calculating wizardry. I also remembered the accidents and the near misses both in the

Baltic and in the Oslo Fjord as well as the good times of meeting Mutti, Lotti and Gretchen as well as Hilde with her two fiery steeds. And then I saw the East Indies again with the slinky silk-clad “Snow-White” and “Red Riding Hood”, as well as the stark natural beauty of Norway and its inhabitants.

I close my eyes and reached out to the familiar valves beside me. I was still able to identify every single one of them only by touch. The many trimming valves, the venting levers, the main snorkel inlet valve right above my head, all had become important parts of my life, as important as breathing itself.

By touching them all for the last time I said my

'*Auf Wiedersehen'* to the old girl!

This was it!

My dream was ended when the 2,000 HP Diesels stopped for the last time and we were told to assemble on deck.

As we were taken off by launch, I noticed that her 'Ace of Diamonds' had all but disappeared under the rust.

Never mind!

It had done the trick and kept us safe while the world around us had collapsed.

Was it too much to hope that on her way out to the designated area she would just quietly slip under into her natural element? Perhaps a carelessly left-open valve or vent combined with the high seas and an open conning tower hatch would spare her the last indignity of being used for target practice like a sitting duck merely to amuse a few trigger-happy Tommies.

Perhaps the faded mascot, the ***KARO-AS***, would grant the old girl this last favour.

A high-ranking British Naval Officer later commented on Operation Deadlight, after only half of the boats managed to get to the designated area.

‘The U-boats were towed-out at the wrong time of the year, in the wrong weather, by the wrong ships and using the wrong towropes.

Apart from that, it was a great success!’

The U-boats are resting at the bottom of the sea.
We are off to a PoW Camp in Belfast,
and are in no mood to “smile” at the camera.

For the crews life went on. As Prisoners of War we spent another two years behind barbed wire in various parts of the United Kingdom. It escapes me how I found out about it, but to my enormous relief I learned later that my U-boat, the one with the lucky Ace of Diamonds on the conning tower, didn’t make it to the target-area either.

'Rest in Peace' old girl!